The Ethical Life

The Ethical Life

*Fundamental Readings
in Ethics and Moral Problems*

Third Edition

RUSS SHAFER-LANDAU
The University of Wisconsin-Madison

New York   Oxford
OXFORD UNIVERSITY PRESS

Oxford University Press is a department of the University of Oxford.
It furthers the University's objective of excellence in research, scholarship, and education by
publishing worldwide.

Oxford   New York

Auckland   Cape Town   Dar es Salaam   Hong Kong   Karachi
Kuala Lumpur   Madrid   Melbourne   Mexico City   Nairobi
New Delhi   Shanghai   Taipei   Toronto

With offices in
Argentina   Austria   Brazil   Chile   Czech Republic   France   Greece
Guatemala   Hungary   Italy   Japan Poland   Portugal   Singapore
South Korea   Switzerland   Thailand   Turkey   Ukraine   Vietnam

For titles covered by Section 112 of the US Higher Education
Opportunity Act, please visit www.oup.com/us/he for the
latest information about pricing and alternate formats.

Published by Oxford University Press
198 Madison Avenue, New York, New York 10016
http://www.oup.com

Oxford is a registered trademark of Oxford University Press

Library of Congress Cataloging-in-Publication Data
  The ethical life : fundamental readings in ethics and moral problems / [edited by]
Russ Shafer-Landau, The University of Wisconsin-Madison. — Third Edition.
    pages cm
  ISBN 978-0-19-999727-5
1. Ethics—Textbooks. I. Shafer-Landau, Russ, editor of compilation.
BJ1012.E882 2014
170—dc23

                                                                          2013046665

9 8 7 6 5 4 3 2

Printed in the United States of America
on acid-free paper

CONTENTS

PREFACE

B rief yet thorough, *The Ethical Life: Fundamental Readings in Ethics and Moral Problems* is a collection of original writings in ethics. Its four parts—The Good Life, Right Conduct, The Status of Morality, and Moral Problems—serve to introduce readers to each of the major branches of moral philosophy, with readings that have been carefully selected for their engaging style and their accessibility. This book can be usefully read on its own, and is an ideal way to acquaint students with the major themes of moral philosophy through a large selection of primary source material.

Changes to the Third Edition

This edition of *The Ethical Life* contains eight new selections. Perhaps the most significant is the addition of three pieces that have been specially commissioned for this book. I asked three outstanding philosophers, expert in their fields (Chris Heathwood—value theory; David Enoch—metaethics; Daniel Hausman—political philosophy), to offer their thoughts on central topics in their areas of specialization. As a result, there are new pieces that develop and defend the desire satisfaction theory of well-being (Heathwood) in Part I, defend the objectivity of ethics (Enoch) in Part III, and assess the merits of affirmative action (Hausman) in Part IV.

In addition, there are three new sections of readings on offer in Part IV: Poverty and Hunger, Enhancing Human Beings, and Affirmative Action. New readings in those sections include papers by Jan Narveson (defending limited duties to those in need of life-sustaining assistance), Michael Sandel (who opposes the genetic enhancement of human beings), and Julian Savulescu (who argues on behalf of such enhancement). Louis Pojman's critique of affirmative action accompanies Hausman's qualified defense of it in the new section devoted to that topic. A new piece by Raymond Frey, defending the use of animals in medical experimentation, has been added to the section on the moral status of animals.

The following articles have been deleted for the third edition: Aldous Huxley, "Brave New World," and Richard Taylor, "The Meaning of Life"

(Part I); Ayn Rand, "The Ethics of Emergencies" (Part II); Michael Smith, "Realism" and Renford Bambrough, "Proof" (Part III); Jonathan Bennett, "The Conscience of Huckleberry Finn," Hugh LaFollette, "Licensing Parents," and Jane English, "What Grown Children Owe Their Parents" (Part IV).

Instructor's Manual and Companion Website

There is a great deal of supplementary material designed to help students and instructors who are using this book. All of this is available at the book's website, www.oup.com/us/shafer-landau. The Instructor's Manual and Test Bank are also available on the Oxford University Press Ancillary Resource Center (ARC) at http://oup-arc.com/shafer-ethical-life. I encourage you to visit these sites, which provide all of the following resources:

The Instructor's Manual and Computerized Test Bank on the ARC (http://oup-arc.com/shafer-ethical-life) includes:

- An Instructor's Guide on how to use the Manual and Test Bank
- Short abstracts of every reading with accompanying essay questions
- A randomizable computerized Test Bank includes essay and multiple-choice questions on every reading
- Further Reading for each of the four main sections
- Lecture outlines on PowerPoint slides for every reading
- Weblinks to interesting sites for each of the four main sections

The Companion Website (www.oup.com/us/shafer-landau) includes:

For instructors:

- All of the material from the Instructor's Manual and Test Bank, under password protection

For students:

- Introductions to each of the four main sections of the book
- Self-quiz questions with answers for each reading
- Further Reading for each of the four main sections
- Lecture outlines on PowerPoint slides for every reading
- Weblinks to interesting sites for each of the four main sections

I want to thank my expert research assistants Justin Horn and Ben Schwan for their terrific work and initiative in putting these materials together.

Learning Management System (LMS) cartridges are available in formats compatible with any LMS in use at your college or university and include the following:

- The Instructor's Manual and Computerized Test Bank
- Student resources from the companion website

Acknowledgments

It has been a lot of fun putting this book together, but it hasn't always been an easy thing to do. By far the most difficult aspect of the project was the winnowing. Ethics is so large a field, with so much that is provocative and interesting within it, yet books must have their page limits, and those limits often forced me to leave a prized piece behind. It has been a real challenge to offer a representative sampling of subject matter and viewpoints within a book of this size. To the extent that I have met with any success, it is owing in large part to the helpful suggestions and kind critical advice I have received from the following philosophers: my colleague Jim Anderson at the University at Wisconsin-Madison, Kristofer Arca at Miami Dade College, Ben Almassi at College of Lake County, Fidel Arnecillo at CSU-San Bernardino, Ralph Baergen at Idaho State University, Jeffrey Brand-Ballard at George Washington University, Patrick Martin Breen at the College of Staten Island, Adam Briggle at University of North Texas, Claudia Card at Wisconsin-Madison, Tom Carson at Loyola University Chicago, Charles Comer at Harrisburg Area Community College, Christian Coons at Bowling Green State University, Richard DeGeorge at the University of Kansas, Neil Delaney at the University of Notre Dame, David Detmer at Purdue University Calumet, Tyler Doggett at the University of Vermont, Andrew Fitz-Gibbon at SUNY Cortland, Amber George at Le Moyne College, Deke Gould at Syracuse University, Christopher Grau at Clemson University, Craig Hanks at Texas State University, Richard Haynes at the University of Florida, Darren Hibbs at Nova Southeastern University, Kelly Heuer at Georgetown University, Richard Hine at the University of Connecticut, John Huss at the University of Akron, Carla Johnson at St. Cloud State

University, Keith Korcz at the University of Louisiana at Lafayette, Jacob Krch at University of Wisconsin-Madison, Mark LeBar at Ohio University, Richard Lee at the University of Arkansas, Hilde Lindeman at Michigan State University, Patrick Linden at NYU Polytechnic, Jessica Logue at the University of Portland, Eugene Marshall at Wellesley College, Michael McKenna at Florida State University, Brian Merrill at Brigham Young University-Idaho, John Messerly at Shoreline Community College, Christian Miller at Wake Forest University, Richard Momeyer at Miami University of Ohio, Nathan Nobis at Morehouse College, David Pereplyotchik at Baruch College, Philip Robbins at the University of Missouri, David Sobel at Syracuse University, Stephen Sullivan at Edinboro University, Mark van Roojen at the University of Nebraska, Lincoln, Dave Schmidtz at the University of Arizona, Paul Wagner at the University of Houston Clear Lake, Kit Wellman at Washington University in St. Louis, Jason Zinser at the University of Florida, and Christopher Zurn at the University of Kentucky. I am very grateful for their assistance.

I would also like to acknowledge the terrific support of my editor at Oxford, Robert Miller, and his crack assistant Emily Krupin, who helped shepherd this book through its various stages. I feel very fortunate to have had a chance to work with Robert on this and other projects over the years, and am, as always, grateful for his advice, constant encouragement, open-mindedness, and inspired good sense.

R. S. L.
Madison, Wisconsin

A NOTE ON THE
COMPANION VOLUME

This collection can be used as a self-standing introduction to ethics. It includes readings from each of the major divisions within moral philosophy. Together with the General Introduction, an Introduction to each reading, study questions, and all of the supplementary materials available at the book's website, I hope that readers are able to get a very good feel for just how interesting moral philosophy can be.

This collection is designed to serve as a natural partner to *Fundamentals of Ethics* (Oxford University Press), an introduction to moral philosophy that I have written. *Fundamentals* is a textbook, though I hope that it is a bit more lively than such a label implies. Both books offer coverage of the good life, the nature of duty and virtue, and the status of morality. The book you have in your hands also offers extensive coverage of many practical ethical problems, such as abortion, the death penalty, famine relief, etc. My hope, of course, is that the two books work neatly in tandem. The theories and positions I present and analyze in *Fundamentals* are here represented by some of their finest defenders. For those who are content to get the view directly from the source, this book should do. But if you would like a moral theory or an ethical position placed in a broader context, its main lines of argument laid out clearly and then critically assessed, then a dip into the companion volume might not be a bad idea.

I am very interested in hearing from readers who are willing to offer me their feedback, both positive and negative. Perhaps you have found some pieces dull or uninspired, or some that were especially exciting and challenging. For teachers who are familiar with this terrain, perhaps you've been disappointed at seeing a beloved piece gone missing, or would like to pass along the success of a given selection in sparking conversation. The easiest way to reach me is by email: *shaferlandau@wisc. edu*. I'd be very pleased to receive your thoughts on how this book might be improved.

R. S. L.

The Ethical Life

INTRODUCTION
===== ❧ =====

M oral philosophy, or ethics—I use the terms interchangeably—is, in its widest application, the study of what we should aspire to in our lives, and of how we should live.

There is no agreed-upon definition of morality, or even of philosophy. We can offer vague (very vague) platitudes, on the order of: philosophy is the love of wisdom; morality is the code that we should live by. It isn't clear to me that we can do *much* better than that. More instructive, I think, is to describe the specific fields within ethics. Through an understanding of these areas, we can better appreciate what moral philosophy is all about.

Nowadays, it is standard to distinguish four different areas of moral philosophy. And (surprise!) the four parts of this book correspond to each of these areas.

The first is known as *Value Theory*. This is the part of ethics that tries to determine what is valuable in and of itself, what is worth pursuing for its own sake. Is happiness, for instance, the ultimate good? Our first two authors, the Greek philosopher Epicurus and the Englishman John Stuart Mill, certainly think so. But others are skeptical. These include the late Harvard philosopher Robert Nozick. Perhaps what is most important is simply that we get what we want out of life—no matter what we want? That's what Chris Heathwood argues, in an article that he has written especially for this book. Yet others (represented here by Jean Kazez) reject this idea, and offer a variety of things (self-determination, moral

1

virtue, happiness, loving relationships, etc.) that are said to be good in their own right.

In Part II we turn to that area of moral philosophy known as *Normative Ethics*. This large branch of philosophy is devoted to identifying the supreme principle(s) of right action. Many philosophers have sought just a single, fundamental principle that will unify the entire field, that will explain, for instance, why keeping your word, telling the truth, and helping the poor, are each morally right.

There are many important contenders that seek to fill this role. Consider, for instance, the Divine Command Theory, which tells us that acts are right just because God commands them. The first extended discussion of this view appears in Plato's dialogue *Euthyphro*, a large portion of which is presented here. Socrates, Plato's teacher and mouthpiece in this work, doesn't look too kindly on this view. Though Socrates assumes that there are many gods rather than one, and focuses on what makes actions pious rather than right, the central philosophical concerns about the Divine Command Theory that worry philosophers today are just the ones that Socrates advanced 2,400 years ago.

If God is not the ultimate source of morality, what is? Many have looked to nature—and human nature, in particular—to answer this question. *Natural law theory* takes this idea most seriously, and in one form or another (there are many varieties), it tries to show that moral action is a matter of acting in a way that respects our nature. Thomas Aquinas is the greatest of the natural lawyers, but owing to the difficulty of his work, I have decided here to provide a contemporary offering by British philosopher Philippa Foot, whose elegant writing may make her distinctive natural law view a bit easier to understand.

We next turn to *utilitarianism* (defended here by Australian philosopher J. J. C. Smart), which instructs us always to produce the greatest happiness for the greatest number. Utilitarianism focuses on an action's results—did it yield the greatest happiness of all available actions?—to determine its morality. The German philosopher Immanuel Kant, by contrast, tells us that results are morally irrelevant. Acts are right, he says, just because we can use their guiding principles consistently, without involving ourselves in contradiction. This isn't an easy thought to understand, but the basic idea is pretty simple. The essence of morality, Kant thinks, is fairness and justice. Immorality is a matter of making an exception of yourself, of living by rules that, in some sense, cannot possibly serve as the basis of everyone's actions.

Kant's view shares some features with another important normative ethic, the *social contract theory*. Though this theory was briefly discussed as far back as the ancient Greeks, it was not fully developed until well into the 16th century. It was brilliantly set forth in the work of Thomas Hobbes, whose book *Leviathan* is excerpted here. The social contract theory tells us that morality is essentially a cooperative enterprise, and that the moral rules are those that self-interested people would obey on the condition that all others do so as well. Both Kantianism and the social contract theory take the natural ethical question—What if everyone did that?—quite seriously, and both use an answer to this question as a foundation of their normative ethical theory.

One thing that each of the theories canvassed so far has in common is that it tries to identify just a single, supreme moral rule that serves as the ultimate basis of all of our moral duties. But what if there is no such thing? British philosopher W. D. Ross took this question very seriously, and argued against the existence of any such moral rule in developing his ethic of *prima facie duties*. Prima facie duties are those that can be outweighed by competing duties. If Ross is right, *every* general duty is like this. We have a standing duty to keep our word, to do justice, to prevent harm, etc. But sometimes these duties conflict with one another. When they do, only one can be our "all-things-considered" duty, the thing we really must do on that particular occasion. The problem, though, is that there is no fixed ranking of the moral principles, and so it can be very difficult to know what to do when they conflict. Sometimes it is more important to prevent harm than to keep our word, but sometimes the reverse is true. The same is true of all conflicts of duty. While Ross thinks that we can know each prima facie moral duty just through careful reflection, things get much more complicated when it comes to knowing what our final, all-things-considered duty is in specific situations.

Aristotle is next. By many accounts, he is the greatest philosopher who ever lived. He developed the first elaborate version of *virtue ethics*, the view that places the virtues at center stage in ethical inquiry. Virtue theorists reject the idea of a single formula that can provide ethical advice for every occasion. They instead tell us to look to virtuous role models and imagine what they would do if they were in our shoes. It is tempting to begin ethical thinking by selecting a standard (such as the utilitarian standard), and saying that a virtue is a steady commitment that tends to produce right action, as measured by that standard. Virtue ethicists turn this on its head, and argue that we can understand the nature of right action only by first understanding the virtues.

Some of the most exciting recent work in normative ethics has been done by those who consider morality from the perspective of *feminist ethics*. This is best understood as an approach to ethics, rather than as a single view that is a direct competitor with the normative ethical theories we have briefly looked at thus far. In her selection here, philosopher Hilde Lindemann sketches the distinctive features of a feminist outlook on morality. These include an emphasis on taking the experience of women seriously when developing one's ethical ideas and ideals, and eliminating the many ways in which sexist assumptions creep into traditional philosophizing. Lindemann offers a variety of examples and interesting points as a way of introducing us to the large family of feminist approaches to ethics.

We have thus far canvassed those areas of ethics that deal with the good and the right, value theory, and normative ethics. But there is another part of ethics that takes a step back from these debates, and asks, more generally, about the *status* of moral views in both areas. Philosophers call this branch of moral theory *metaethics*, and it is the focus of Part III.

Metaethics studies such questions as these: Is morality just a convenient fiction? If not, can moral standards be true? Suppose they are: Does their truth depend on personal opinion, social consensus, God's commands, or something else? If there are genuine moral truths, how can we know them? And do they have any authority over us—is it always rational to be moral, or is it sometimes reasonable to take the immoral path?

I have divided the authors in this section into two camps—those who are skeptical of objective morality, and those who defend it. As I understand it, morality is objective just in case there are some moral standards that apply to us regardless of what any human being believes.

Opponents of moral objectivity get the first hearing. The Scottish Enlightenment thinker David Hume starts us off. His criticisms of reason's place in ethics have been extremely influential across the past two and a half centuries, and rightly so. Most of today's important critiques of moral objectivity have their ancestors in one or more of the arguments that Hume provided. Hume thought that if moral claims were objectively true, then we should be able to discover our moral duty just by thinking hard about it. But Hume argues that no amount of careful reasoning could do that. And therefore morality cannot be objective.

Hume did not seek to undermine ethics, but rather to offer a diagnosis of its true nature. A. J. Ayer seeks to go further, and to show that there are no moral truths. Ayer thinks that moral judgments do nothing but express our emotions, and, as such, can be neither true nor false. When we say, for instance, that "genocide is immoral," we aren't saying anything that could be true. (Nor could it be false.) What we are doing, in effect, is venting our hatred of genocide, and saying "genocide—boo!!" That sort of claim can't be true (or false). According to Ayer, meaningful claims must be either tautologies (e.g., all red things are red), which are true by definition, or claims that are scientifically verifiable. Since moral claims aren't tautologies, and cannot be confirmed by science, he thinks that moral claims are meaningless. Meaningless claims cannot be true. Therefore moral claims cannot be true.

John Mackie agrees with this conclusion, but arrives at it in a different way. He argues that all of our moral thinking is based on an error. Mackie believes that moral thought starts from the view that morality is objective. He offers some important arguments to try to show that it isn't. He sees morality as a product of human insecurity and imagination, with no real authority over us. If we all do assume that morality is objective, and if Mackie is right about its being (at best) a useful fiction, then morality really is bankrupt.

We then turn the tables and allow the ethical objectivists to have their say. Harry Gensler starts us off by arguing against cultural relativism, which is the idea that a society's guiding ideals are the ultimate moral standards. Since different societies have different ideals, relativists believe that there is no universal or objective morality. Gensler offers four reasons to oppose relativism. First, it cannot allow for consistent disagreement with one's social code. Second, relativism is a very poor basis for defending tolerance. Third, relativism is a counsel of unthinking conformity. And, finally, relativism is unable to offer any advice about how to act when one is a member of different cultures.

In an article written especially for this book, David Enoch argues that almost all of us, whether we realize it or not, are committed to some form of objectivity about morality. He devises a number of tests to help us see the extent of this commitment. That we are committed to morality's objectivity does not prove that our commitments are correct. But we should assume that they are until such time as we have excellent reason to reject them. Enoch considers a number of arguments designed to show that morality is not in fact objective, and then offers his reasons for rejecting those critiques.

This concludes the section on metaethics, and with it, the first half of this collection.

No philosopher sees his field in just the same way that others do. My take on what really matters in ethics is bound to be personal and, to some degree, not shared by my fellow practitioners. Still, I have aimed in this volume to respect standard divisions within this large field, and have tried to balance selections from classic works with some relatively unfamiliar material that strikes me as important and provocative.

Whether beginners or old pros, each of us improves our moral thinking by being exposed to a variety of viewpoints on the deep questions that interest us. The ideal philosophical introduction, therefore, would present at least the main competitors within the various subfields that make up ethics, thereby giving newcomers a taste of the different perspectives that have shaped debates within this rich area of philosophy. I hope that I have managed some success on this front, but in at least one case, it would have been clearly impossible to achieve this within a reasonable amount of space.

I am thinking here of the last and largest section of the book, Part IV, the one devoted to a variety of *moral problems*. There are far too many interesting moral conundrums to fit them all into a collection of this size. I hope that the topics on offer are compelling, but I recognize that many exciting subjects and insightful articles have been left behind. Short of greatly increasing the size of this collection, I see no way to avoid this, and must hope that the nineteen offerings available here are of sufficient interest and importance to do what they are meant to do— inspire you to grapple with their puzzles, thought experiments, and arguments, and to appreciate a bit of the complexity of the moral issues that take center stage in this part of the book. What you have in this section (and all the others) is just a small sampling of possible positions and supporting arguments. The readings throughout this book are designed to whet your appetite, not to sate it.

There is no theoretical unity to this half of the volume. The authors here represent a variety of different theoretical approaches, and some, as you will see, do not argue directly from any normative theory at all.

This might be surprising, because a time-honored picture of how to argue about moral problems is to claim that you must first identify the correct normative theory, take note of the relevant nonmoral facts, and presto!—out comes your moral verdict. This way of arguing actually happens less often than you may think, which is why the more common term for this sort of moral philosophy—"Applied Ethics"—is a bit misleading. That label implies that all practical moral problems can all be solved in a top-down way, by first selecting the proper normative ethic, and then just "applying" it—as if that were a straightforward matter of cranking out its implications.

One reason that philosophers don't always proceed this way is because there is still huge disagreement about which normative ethic is the correct one. And so any philosopher who restricted her arguments to applying a single normative theory would be losing a good deal of her audience—specifically, the large segment of it that disagreed with her normative ethic. As a result, most philosophers who grapple with real-life moral problems begin not with the grand normative theories but rather with more concrete principles (keep your word, don't violate patient confidentiality, avoid imposing unnecessary pain, etc.) or examples that we are already expected to accept. Armed with these, the author then tries to show that a commitment to them implies some specific view about the problem at hand.

The topics covered in this last section are of the first importance: famine relief, same-sex marriage, euthanasia, terrorism, torture, animal rights, environmental ethics, abortion, the death penalty, civil disobedience, drug laws, the morality of genetic enhancements, and affirmative action. Are there other topics that deserve a place at the table? Absolutely. But these strike me as being worthy of our attention, and the pieces I have selected all present interesting sets of arguments that deserve careful scrutiny. Some of these pieces do represent pretty direct applications of the normative theories discussed in the second part of this book. In these cases, you can use the arguments contained here as a way of testing those normative theories. In other cases, as I mentioned above, the arguments will be theoretically more free-standing. In any event, I hope that there will be plenty to inspire your interest, curiosity, and, occasionally, youroutrage. I have found that each of these reactions can be an excellent catalyst to serious philosophical thinking.

PART I

The Good Life

1

Letter to Menoeceus

Epicurus

Epicurus (341–270 BCE) was the first of the great hedonists. He argued that pleasure is the fundamental human good, and that the best life is one that is as pleasant as it can be. But his sort of hedonism would be unrecognizable by many nowadays, as Epicurus encouraged moderation and prudence in all things, and counseled us to minimize our indulgence in sensual pleasures. He thought that the most pleasant state was one of emotional tranquility. Here he explains how to gain such peace of mind: through a moderate lifestyle, coupled with the curative powers of philosophy, which can dispel the false beliefs that lead to so much emotional turmoil. Foremost among these false beliefs is the view that death can harm us.

Epicurus to Menoeceus, greetings:

Let no one be slow to seek wisdom when he is young nor weary in the search of it when he has grown old. For no age is too early or too late for the health of the soul. And to say that the season for studying philosophy has not yet come, or that it is past and gone, is like saying that the season for happiness is not yet or that it is now no more. Therefore, both old and young alike ought to seek wisdom, the former in order that, as age comes over him, he may be young in good things because of the grace of what has been, and the latter in order that, while he is young, he may at the same time be old, because he has no fear of the things which are to come. So we must exercise ourselves in the things which bring happiness, since, if that be present, we have everything, and, if that be absent, all our actions are directed towards attaining it.

Those things which without ceasing I have declared unto you, do them, and exercise yourself in them, holding them to be the elements of right life. First believe that God is a living being immortal and blessed, according to the notion of a god indicated by the common sense of mankind; and so believing, you shall not affirm of him anything that is foreign to his immortality or that is repugnant to his blessedness. Believe about him whatever may uphold both his blessedness and his immortality. For there are gods, and the knowledge of them is manifest; but they are not such as the multitude believe, seeing that men do not steadfastly maintain the notions they form respecting them. Not the man who denies the gods worshipped by the multitude, but he who affirms of the gods what the multitude believes about them is truly impious. For the utterances of the multitude about the gods are not true preconceptions but false assumptions; hence it is that the greatest evils happen to the wicked and the greatest blessings happen to the good from the hand of the gods, seeing that they are always favorable to their own good qualities and take pleasure in men like themselves, but reject as alien whatever is not of their kind.

Accustom yourself to believing that death is nothing to us, for good and evil imply the capacity for sensation, and death is the privation of all sentience; therefore a correct understanding that death is nothing to us makes the mortality of life enjoyable, not by adding to life a limitless time, but by taking away the yearning after immortality. For life has no terrors for him who has thoroughly understood that there are no terrors for him in ceasing to live. Foolish, therefore, is the man who says that he fears death, not because it will pain when it comes, but because it pains in the prospect. Whatever causes no annoyance when it is present, causes only a groundless pain in the expectation. Death, therefore, the most awful of evils, is nothing to us, seeing that, when we are, death is not come, and, when death is come, we are not. It is nothing, then, either to the living or to the dead, for with the living it is not and the dead exist no longer.

But in the world, at one time men shun death as the greatest of all evils, and at another time choose it as a respite from the evils in life. The wise man does not deprecate life nor does he fear the cessation of life. The thought of life is no offense to him, nor is the cessation of life regarded as an evil. And even as men choose of food not merely and simply the larger portion, but the more pleasant, so the wise seek to enjoy the time which is most pleasant and not merely that which is longest. And he who admonishes the young to live well and the old to make a good end speaks foolishly, not merely because of the desirability of life, but because the same exercise at once teaches to live well and to die well. Much worse is he who says that it were good not to be born, but when once one is born to pass quickly through the gates of Hades. For if he truly believes this, why does he not depart from life? It would be easy for him to do so once he were firmly convinced. If he speaks only in jest, his words are foolishness as those who hear him do not believe.

We must remember that the future is neither wholly ours nor wholly not ours, so that neither must we count upon it as quite certain to come nor despair of it as quite certain not to come.

We must also reflect that of desires some are natural, others are groundless; and that of the natural some are necessary as well as natural, and some natural only. And of the necessary desires some are necessary if we are to be happy, some if the body is to be rid of uneasiness, some if we are even to live. He who has a clear and certain understanding of these things will direct every preference and aversion toward securing health of body and tranquility of mind, seeing that this is the sum and end of a blessed life. For the end of all our actions is to be free from pain and fear, and, when once we have attained all this, the tempest of the soul is laid; seeing that the living creature has no need to go in search of something that is lacking, nor to look for anything else by which the good of the soul and of the body will be fulfilled. When we are pained because of the absence of pleasure, then, and then only, do we feel the need of pleasure. Wherefore we call pleasure the alpha and omega of a blessed life. Pleasure is our first and kindred good. It is the starting-point of every choice and of every aversion, and to it we come back, inasmuch as we make feeling the rule by which to judge of every good thing.

And since pleasure is our first and native good, for that reason we do not choose every pleasure whatsoever, but will often pass over many pleasures when a greater annoyance ensues from them. And often we consider pains superior to pleasures when submission to the pains for a long time brings us as a consequence a greater pleasure. While therefore all pleasure because it is naturally akin to us is good, not all pleasure should be chosen, just as all pain is an evil and yet not all pain is to be shunned. It is, however, by measuring one against another, and by looking at the conveniences and inconveniences, that all these matters must be judged. Sometimes we treat the good as an evil, and the evil, on the contrary, as a good.

Again, we regard independence of outward things as a great good, not so as in all cases to use little, but so as to be contented with little if we have not much, being honestly persuaded that they have the sweetest enjoyment of luxury who stand least in need of it, and that whatever is natural is easily procured and only the vain and worthless hard to win. Plain fare gives as much pleasure as a costly diet, when once the pain of want has been removed, while bread and water confer the highest possible pleasure when they are brought to hungry lips. To habituate one's self, therefore, to simple and inexpensive diet supplies all that is needful for health, and enables a man to meet the necessary requirements of life without shrinking, and it places us in a better condition when we approach at intervals a costly fare and renders us fearless of fortune.

When we say, then, that pleasure is the end and aim, we do not mean the pleasures of the prodigal or the pleasures of sensuality, as we are understood to do by some through ignorance, prejudice, or willful misrepresentation. By pleasure we mean the absence of pain in the body and of trouble in the soul. It is not an unbroken succession of drinking-bouts and of revelry, not sexual lust, not the enjoyment of the fish and other delicacies of a luxurious table, which produce a pleasant life; it is sober reasoning, searching out the grounds of every choice and avoidance, and banishing those beliefs through which the greatest tumults take possession of the soul. Of all this the beginning and the greatest good is wisdom. Therefore wisdom is a more precious thing even than philosophy; from it spring all the other virtues, for it teaches that we cannot live pleasantly without living wisely, honorably, and justly; nor live wisely, honorably, and justly without living pleasantly. For the virtues have grown into one with a pleasant life, and a pleasant life is inseparable from them.

Who, then, is superior in your judgment to such a man? He holds a holy belief concerning the gods, and is altogether free from the fear of death. He has diligently considered the end fixed by nature, and understands how easily the limit of good things can be reached and attained, and how either the duration or the intensity of evils is but slight. Fate, which some introduce as sovereign over all things, he scorns, affirming rather that some things happen of necessity, others by chance, others through our own agency. For he sees that necessity destroys responsibility and that chance is inconstant; whereas our own actions are autonomous, and it is to them that praise and blame naturally attach. It were better, indeed, to accept the legends of the gods than to bow beneath that yoke of destiny which the natural philosophers have imposed. The one holds out some faint hope that we may escape if we honor the gods, while the necessity of the naturalists is deaf to all entreaties. Nor does he hold chance to be a god, as the world in general does, for in the acts of a god there is no disorder; nor to be a cause, though an uncertain one, for he believes that no good or evil is dispensed by chance to men so as to make life blessed, though it supplies the starting-point of great good and great evil. He believes that the misfortune of the wise is better than the prosperity of the fool. It is better, in short, that what is well judged in action should not owe its successful issue to the aid of chance.

Exercise yourself in these and related precepts day and night, both by yourself and with one who is like-minded; then never, either in waking or in dream, will you be disturbed, but will live as a god among men. For man loses all semblance of mortality by living in the midst of immortal blessings.

Epicurus: Letter to Menoeceus

1. Epicurus claims that "Death is nothing to us." What does he mean by this, and how does he argue for it? Do you find his argument convincing?

2. According to Epicurus, pleasure is "the starting-point of every choice." Is it possible to make decisions based on considerations besides pleasure? Is there ever good reason to do so?

3. Epicurus thinks that pleasure is "our first and kindred good," but he does not recommend indulgence in the pleasures of drinking, fine food, and sex. Why not?

4. What does Epicurus think is the most pleasant sort of life? Do you find the type of life he describes appealing?

5. Epicurus says that a pleasant life is inseparable from the virtues, and that "we cannot live pleasantly without living wisely, honorably, and justly." Do you think he is right about this?

2

Hedonism
John Stuart Mill

John Stuart Mill (1806–1873) was one of the great hedonistic
thinkers. In this excerpt from his long pamphlet *Utilitarianism* (1863),
Mill defends his complex version of hedonism. Sensitive to criticisms
that it counsels us to pursue a life of brutish pleasure, Mill distinguishes between higher and lower pleasures", and claims, famously, that
it is "better to be Socrates dissatisfied, than a fool satisfied." He also
offers here his much-discussed "proof" of hedonism, by drawing a parallel between the evidence we have for something's being visible (that all
of us see it) and something's being desirable (that all of us desire it). He
also argues for the claim that we do and can desire nothing but pleasure,
and uses this conjecture as a way of defending the view that pleasure is
the only thing that is always worth pursuing for its own sake.

The creed which accepts, as the foundation of morals, Utility, or the
Greatest-happiness Principle, holds that actions are right in proportion as they tend to promote happiness, wrong as they tend to
produce the reverse of happiness. By happiness is intended pleasure and
the absence of pain; by unhappiness, pain and the privation of pleasure. To
give a clear view of the moral standard set up by the theory, much more
requires to be said; in particular, what things it includes in the ideas of pain
and pleasure, and to what extent this is left an open question. But these
supplementary explanations do not affect the theory of life on which this

theory of morality is grounded,—namely, that pleasure, and freedom from pain, are the only things desirable as ends; and that all desirable things (which are as numerous in the utilitarian as in any other scheme) are desirable either for the pleasure inherent in themselves, or as means to the promotion of pleasure and the prevention of pain.

Now, such a theory of life excites in many minds, and among them in some of the most estimable in feeling and purpose, inveterate dislike. To suppose that life has (as they express it) no higher end than pleasure,—no better and nobler object of desire and pursuit,—they designate as utterly mean and groveling; as a doctrine worthy only of swine, to whom the followers of Epicurus were, at a very early period, contemptuously likened: and modern holders of the doctrine are occasionally made the subject of equally polite comparisons by its German, French, and English assailants.

When thus attacked, the Epicureans have always answered, that it is not they, but their accusers, who represent human nature in a degrading light, since the accusation supposes human beings to be capable of no pleasures except those of which swine are capable. If this supposition were true, the charge could not be gainsaid, but would then be no longer an imputation; for, if the sources of pleasure were precisely the same to human beings and to swine, the rule of life which is good enough for the one would be good enough for the other. The comparison of the Epicurean life to that of beasts is felt as degrading, precisely because a beast's pleasures do not satisfy a human being's conceptions of happiness. Human beings have faculties more elevated than the animal appetites; and, when once made conscious of them, do not regard any thing as happiness which does not include their gratification. I do not, indeed, consider the Epicureans to have been by any means faultless in drawing out their scheme of consequences from the utilitarian principle. To do this in any sufficient manner, many Stoic as well as Christian elements require to be included. But there is no known Epicurean theory of life which does not assign to the pleasures of the intellect, of the feeling and imagination, and of the moral sentiments, a much higher value as pleasures than to those of mere sensation. It must be admitted, however, that utilitarian writers in general have placed the superiority of mental over bodily pleasures chiefly in the greater permanency, safety, uncostliness, &c., of the former,—that is, in their circumstantial advantages rather than in their intrinsic nature. And, on all these points, utilitarians have fully proved their case; but they might have taken the other, and, as it may be called, higher ground, with entire consistency. It is quite compatible with the principle of utility to recognize the fact, that some *kinds* of pleasure are more desirable and more valuable than others. It would be absurd, that while, in estimating all other things, quality is considered as well as quantity, the estimation of pleasures should be supposed to depend on quantity alone.

If I am asked what I mean by difference of quality in pleasures, or what makes one pleasure more valuable than another, merely as a pleasure, except its being greater in amount, there is but one possible answer. Of two pleasures, if there be one to which all or almost all who have experience of both give a decided preference, irrespective of any feeling of moral obligation to prefer it, that is the more desirable pleasure. If one of the two is, by those who are competently acquainted with both, placed so far above the other that they prefer it, even though knowing it to be attended with a greater amount of discontent, and would not resign it for any quantity of the other pleasure which their nature is capable of, we are justified in ascribing to the preferred enjoyment a superiority in quality, so far outweighing quantity, as to render it, in comparison, of small account.

Now, it is an unquestionable fact, that those who are equally acquainted with and equally capable of appreciating and enjoying both do give a most marked preference to the manner of existence which employs their higher faculties. Few human creatures would consent to be changed into any of the lower animals, for a promise of the fullest allowance of a beast's pleasures: no intelligent human being would consent to be a fool, no instructed person would be an ignoramus, no person of feeling and conscience would be selfish and base, even though they should be persuaded that the fool, the dunce, or the rascal is better satisfied with his lot than they are with theirs. They would not resign what they possess more than he for the most complete satisfaction of all the desires which they have in common with him. If they ever fancy they would, it is only in cases of unhappiness so extreme, that, to escape from it, they would exchange their lot for almost any other, however undesirable in their own eyes. A being of higher faculties requires more to make him happy, is capable probably of more acute suffering, and certainly accessible to it at more points, than one of an inferior type; but, in spite of these liabilities, he can never really wish to sink into what he feels to be a lower grade of existence. We may give what explanation we please of this unwillingness; we may attribute it to pride, a name which is given indiscriminately to some of the most and to some of the least estimable feelings of which mankind are capable; we may refer it to the love of liberty and personal independence,—an appeal to which was with the Stoics one of the most effective means for the inculcation of it; to

the love of power, or to the love of excitement, both of which do really
enter into and contribute to it: but its most appropriate appellation is a
sense of dignity, which all human beings possess in one form or other, and
in some, though by no means in exact, proportion to their higher faculties,
and which is so essential a part of the happiness of those in whom it is
strong, that nothing which conflicts with it could be, otherwise than
momentarily, an object of desire to them. Whoever supposes that this
preference takes place at a sacrifice of happiness; that the superior being,
in any thing like equal circumstances, is not happier than the inferior—
confounds the two very different ideas of happiness and content. It is
indisputable, that the being whose capacities of enjoyment are low has the
greatest chance of having them fully satisfied; and a highly endowed being
will always feel that any happiness which he can look for, as the world is
constituted, is imperfect. But he can learn to bear its imperfections, if they
are at all bearable; and they will not make him envy the being who is
indeed unconscious of the imperfections, but only because he feels not at
all the good which those imperfections qualify. It is better to be a human
being dissatisfied, than a pig satisfied; better to be Socrates dissatisfied,
than a fool satisfied. And if the fool or the pig are of a different opinion, it
is because they only know their own side of the question. The other party
to the comparison knows both sides.

It may be objected, that many who are capable of the higher pleasures,
occasionally, under the influence of temptation, postpone them to the
lower. But this is quite compatible with a full appreciation of the intrinsic
superiority of the higher. Men often, from infirmity of character, make
their election for the nearer good, though they know it to be the less valuable, and this no less when the choice is between two bodily pleasures than
when it is between bodily and mental. They pursue sensual indulgences to
the injury of health, though perfectly aware that health is the greater good.
It may be further objected, that many who begin with youthful enthusiasm
for everything noble, as they advance in years sink into indolence and selfishness. But I do not believe that those who undergo this very common
change voluntarily choose the lower description of pleasures in preference
to the higher. I believe, that, before they devote themselves exclusively to
the one, they have already become incapable of the other. Capacity for the
nobler feelings is in most natures a very tender plant, easily killed, not only
by hostile influences, but by mere want of sustenance; and, in the majority
of young persons, it speedily dies away if the occupations to which their
position in life has devoted them, and the society into which it has thrown

them, are not favorable to keeping that higher capacity in exercise. Men lose their high aspirations as they lose their intellectual tastes, because they have not time or opportunity for indulging them; and they addict themselves to inferior pleasures, not because they deliberately prefer them, but because they are either the only ones to which they have access, or the only ones which they are any longer capable of enjoying. It may be questioned whether any one, who has remained equally susceptible to both classes of pleasures, ever knowingly and calmly preferred the lower; though many in all ages have broken down in an ineffectual attempt to combine both.

From this verdict of the only competent judges, I apprehend there can be no appeal. On a question, which is the best worth having of two pleasures, or which of two modes of existence is the most grateful to the feelings, apart from its moral attributes and from its consequences, the judgment of those who are qualified by knowledge of both, or, if they differ, that of the majority among them, must be admitted as final. And there needs be the less hesitation to accept this judgment respecting the quality of pleasures, since there is no other tribunal to be referred to even on the question of quantity. What means are there of determining which is the acutest of two pains, or the intensest of two pleasurable sensations, except the general suffrage of those who are familiar with both? Neither pains nor pleasures are homogeneous, and pain is always heterogeneous with pleasure. What is there to decide whether a particular pleasure is worth purchasing at the cost of particular pain, except the feelings and judgment of the experienced? When, therefore, those feelings and judgment declare the pleasures derived from the higher faculties to be preferable *in kind*, apart from the question of intensity, to those of which the animal nature, disjoined from the higher faculties, is susceptible, they are entitled on this subject to the same regard. . . .

It has already been remarked, that questions of ultimate ends do not admit of proof, in the ordinary acceptation of the term. To be incapable of proof by reasoning is common to all first principles; to the first premises of our knowledge, as well as to those of our conduct. But the former, being matters of fact, may be the subject of a direct appeal to the faculties which judge of fact—namely, our senses, and our internal consciousness. Can an appeal be made to the same faculties on questions of practical ends? Or by what other faculty is cognisance taken of them?

Questions about ends are, in other words, questions of what things are desirable. The utilitarian doctrine is, that happiness is desirable, and the only thing desirable, as an end; all other things being only desirable as means to that end. What ought to be required of this doctrine—what conditions is it requisite that the doctrine should fulfil—to make good its claim to be believed?

The only proof capable of being given that an object is visible, is that people actually see it. The only proof that a sound is audible, is that people hear it: and so of the other sources of our experience. In like manner, I apprehend, the sole evidence it is possible to produce that anything is desirable, is that people do actually desire it. If the end which the utilitarian doctrine proposes to itself were not, in theory and in practice, acknowledged to be an end, nothing could ever convince any person that it was so. No reason can be given why the general happiness is desirable, except that each person, so far as he believes it to be attainable, desires his own happiness. This, however, being a fact, we have not only all the proof which the case admits of, but all which it is possible to require, that happiness is a good: that each person's happiness is a good to that person, and the general happiness, therefore, a good to the aggregate of all persons. Happiness has made out its title as one of the ends of conduct, and consequently one of the criteria of morality.

But it has not, by this alone, proved itself to be the sole criterion. To do that, it would seem, by the same rule, necessary to show, not only that people desire happiness, but that they never desire anything else. Now it is palpable that they do desire things which, in common language, are decidedly distinguished from happiness. They desire, for example, virtue, and the absence of vice, no less really than pleasure and the absence of pain. The desire of virtue is not as universal, but it is as authentic a fact, as the desire of happiness. And hence the opponents of the utilitarian standard deem that they have a right to infer that there are other ends of human action besides happiness, and that happiness is not the standard of approbation and disapprobation.

But does the utilitarian doctrine deny that people desire virtue, or maintain that virtue is not a thing to be desired? The very reverse. It maintains not only that virtue is to be desired, but that it is to be desired disinterestedly, for itself. Whatever may be the opinion of utilitarian moralists as to the original conditions by which virtue is made virtue; however they may believe (as they do) that actions and dispositions are only virtuous because they promote another end than virtue; yet this being granted, and it having been decided, from considerations of this description, what is virtuous, they not only place virtue at the very head of the things which are good as means to the ultimate end, but they also recognise as a psychological fact the possibility of its being, to the individual, a good in itself, without looking to any end beyond it; and hold, that the mind is not in a right state, not in a state conformable to Utility, not in the state most conducive to the general happiness, unless it does love virtue in this manner—as a thing desirable in itself, even although, in the individual instance, it should not produce those other desirable consequences which it tends to produce, and on account of which it is held to be virtue. This opinion is not, in the smallest degree, a departure from the Happiness principle. The ingredients of happiness are very various, and each of them is desirable in itself, and not merely when considered as swelling an aggregate. The principle of utility does not mean that any given pleasure, as music, for instance, or any given exemption from pain, as for example health, is to be looked upon as means to a collective something termed happiness, and to be desired on that account. They are desired and desirable in and for themselves; besides being means, they are a part of the end. Virtue, according to the utilitarian doctrine, is not naturally and originally part of the end, but it is capable of becoming so; and in those who love it disinterestedly it has become so, and is desired and cherished, not as a means to happiness, but as a part of their happiness.

To illustrate this farther, we may remember that virtue is not the only thing, originally a means, and which if it were not a means to anything else, would be and remain indifferent, but which by association with what it is a means to, comes to be desired for itself, and that too with the utmost intensity. What, for example, shall we say of the love of money? There is nothing originally more desirable about money than about any heap of glittering pebbles. Its worth is solely that of the things which it will buy; the desires for other things than itself, which it is a means of gratifying. Yet the love of money is not only one of the strongest moving forces of human life, but money is, in many cases, desired in and for itself; the desire to possess it is often stronger than the desire to use it, and goes on increasing when all the desires which point to ends beyond it, to be compassed by it, are falling off. It may, then, be said truly, that money is desired not for the sake of an end, but as part of the end. From being a means to happiness, it has come to be itself a principal ingredient of the individual's conception of happiness. The same may be said of the majority of the great objects of human life—power, for example, or fame; except that to each of these there is a certain amount of immediate pleasure annexed, which has at least the semblance of being naturally inherent in them; a thing which cannot be said of money. Still, however, the strongest natural attraction, both of power and of fame, is the immense aid they give to the attainment of our other wishes; and it is the strong association thus generated between them and all our objects of desire, which gives to the direct desire of them the intensity it often assumes, so as in some characters to surpass in strength all other desires. In these cases the means have become a part of the end, and a more important part of it than any of the things which they are means to. What was once desired as an instrument for the attainment of happiness, has come to be desired for its own sake. In being desired for its own sake it is, however, desired as part of happiness. The person is made, or thinks he would be made, happy by its mere possession; and is made unhappy by failure to obtain it. The desire of it is not a different thing from the desire of happiness, any more than the love of music, or the desire of health. They are included in happiness. They are some of the elements of which the desire of happiness is made up. Happiness is not an abstract idea, but a concrete whole; and these are some of its parts. And the utilitarian standard sanctions and approves their being so. Life would be a poor thing, very ill provided with sources of happiness, if there were not this provision of nature, by which things originally indifferent, but conducive to, or otherwise associated with, the satisfaction of our primitive desires, become in themselves sources of pleasure more valuable than the primitive pleasures, both in permanency, in the space of human existence that they are capable of covering, and even in intensity.

Virtue, according to the utilitarian conception, is a good of this description. There was no original desire of it, or motive to it, save its conduciveness to pleasure, and especially to protection from pain. But through the association thus formed, it may be felt a good in itself, and desired as such with as great intensity as any other good; and with this difference between it and the love of money, of power, or of fame, that all of these may, and often do, render the individual noxious to the other members of the society to which he belongs, whereas there is nothing which makes him so much a blessing to them as the cultivation of the disinterested love of virtue. And consequently, the utilitarian standard, while it tolerates and approves those other acquired desires, up to the point beyond which they would be more injurious to the general happiness than promotive of it, enjoins and requires the cultivation of the love of virtue up to the greatest strength possible, as being above all things important to the general happiness.

It results from the preceding considerations, that there is in reality nothing desired except happiness. Whatever is desired otherwise than as a means to some end beyond itself, and ultimately to happiness, is desired as itself a part of happiness, and is not desired for itself until it has become so. Those who desire virtue for its own sake, desire it either because the consciousness of it is a pleasure, or because the consciousness of being without it is a pain, or for both reasons united; as in truth the pleasure and pain seldom exist separately, but almost always together, the same person feeling pleasure in the degree of virtue attained, and pain in not having attained more. If one of these gave him no pleasure, and the other no pain, he would not love or desire virtue, or would desire it only for the other benefits which it might produce to himself or to persons whom he cared for. We have now, then, an answer to the question, of what sort of proof the principle of utility is susceptible. If the opinion which I have now stated is psychologically true—if human nature is so constituted as to desire nothing which is not either a part of happiness or a means of happiness, we can have no other proof, and we require no other, that these are the only things desirable. If so, happiness is the sole end of human action, and the promotion of it the test by which to judge of all human conduct; from whence it necessarily follows that it must be the criterion of morality, since a part is included in the whole. . . .

John Stuart Mill: Hedonism

1. Mill claims that "Pleasure, and freedom from pain, are the only things desirable as ends." Are there any examples that can challenge this claim?
2. What does Mill propose as a standard to determine which kinds of pleasure are more valuable than others? Is this a plausible standard?
3. Mill states that it is "Better to be Socrates dissatisfied, than a fool satisfied." What reasons does he give for thinking this?
4. In order to show that an object is visible, it is enough to show that people actually see it. Mill claims, similarly, "The sole evidence it is possible to produce that anything is desirable, is that people do actually desire it." Are visibility and desirability similar in this way?
5. Mill claims that "Each person's happiness is a good to that person." He then concludes from this that "the general happiness" is therefore "a good to the aggregate of all persons." Is this a good argument?

6. According to Mill, "The ingredients of happiness are very various, and each of them is desirable in itself." Does this contradict his earlier claim, given in question 1?

7. At the beginning of this selection, Mill says that pleasure and the absence of pain are the only things desirable as ends. Toward the end he claims that "Happiness is the sole end of human action." Are happiness and pleasure the same thing?

3

The Experience Machine
Robert Nozick

In this brief selection from his book *Anarchy, State, and Utopia* (1974), the late Harvard philosopher Robert Nozick (1938–2002) invites us to contemplate a life in which we are placed within a very sophisticated machine that is capable of simulating whatever experiences we find most valuable. Such a life, Nozick argues, cannot be the best life for us, because it fails to make contact with reality. This is meant to show that the good life is not entirely a function of the quality of our inner experiences. Since hedonism measures our well-being in precisely this way, hedonism, says Nozick, must be mistaken.

. . . Suppose there were an experience machine that would give you any experience you desired. Superduper neuropsychologists could stimulate your brain so that you would think and feel you were writing a great novel, or making a friend, or reading an interesting book. All the time you would be floating in a tank, with electrodes attached to your brain. Should you plug into this machine for life, preprogramming your life's experiences? If you are worried about missing out on desirable experiences, we can suppose that business enterprises have researched thoroughly the lives of many others. You can pick and choose from their large library or smorgasbord of such experiences, selecting your life's experiences for, say, the next two years. After two years have passed, you will have ten minutes or ten hours out of the tank, to select the experiences of your *next* two years. Of course, while in the tank you won't know that you're there; you'll think it's all actually happening. Others can also plug in to have the experiences they want, so there's no need to stay unplugged to serve them. (Ignore problems such as who will service the machines if everybody plugs in.) Would you plug in? *What else can matter to us, other than how our lives feel from the inside?* Nor should you refrain because of the few moments of distress between the moment you've decided and the moment you're plugged. What's a few moments of distress compared to a lifetime of bliss (if that's what you choose), and why feel any distress at all if your decision *is* the best one?

What does matter to us in addition to our experiences? First, we want to *do* certain things, and not just have the experience of doing them. In the case of certain experiences, it is only because first we want to do the actions that we want the experiences of doing them or thinking we've done them. (But *why* do we want to do the activities rather than merely to experience them?) A second reason for not plugging in is that we want to *be* a certain way, to be a certain sort of person. Someone floating in a tank is an indeterminate blob. There is no answer to the question of what a person is like who has long been in the tank. Is he courageous, kind, intelligent, witty, loving? It's not merely that it's difficult to tell; there's no way he is. Plugging into the machine is a kind of suicide. It will seem to some, trapped by a picture, that nothing about what we are like can matter except as it gets reflected in our experiences. But should it be surprising that what *we are* is important to us? Why should we be concerned only with how our time is filled, but not with what we are?

Thirdly, plugging into an experience machine limits us to a man-made reality, to a world no deeper or more important than that which people can construct. There is no *actual* contact with any deeper reality, though the experience of it can be simulated. Many persons desire to leave themselves open to such contact and to a plumbing of deeper significance.[1] This clarifies

---

1 Traditional religious views differ on the *point* of contact with a transcendent reality. Some say that contact yields eternal bliss or Nirvana, but they have not distinguished this sufficiently from merely a *very* long run on the experience machine. Others think it is intrinsically desirable to do the will of a higher being which created us all, though presumably no one would think this if we discovered we had been created as an object of amusement by some superpowerful child from another galaxy or dimension. Still others imagine an eventual merging with a higher reality, leaving unclear its desirability, or where that merging leaves *us*.

the intensity of the conflict over psychoactive drugs, which some view as mere local experience machines, and others view as avenues to a deeper reality; what some view as equivalent to surrender to the experience machine, others view as following one of the reasons *not* to surrender!

We learn that something matters to us in addition to experience by imagining an experience machine and then realizing that we would not use it. We can continue to imagine a sequence of machines each designed to fill lacks suggested for the earlier machines. For example, since the experience machine doesn't meet our desire to *be* a certain way, imagine a transformation machine which transforms us into whatever sort of person we'd like to be (compatible with our staying us). Surely one would not use the transformation machine to become as one would wish, and thereupon plug into the experience machine![2] So something matters in addition to one's experiences *and* what one is like. Nor is the reason merely that one's experiences are unconnected with what one is like. For the experience machine might be limited to provide only experiences possible to the sort of person plugged in. Is it that we want to make a difference in the world? Consider then the result machine, which produces in the world any result you would produce and injects your vector input into any joint activity. We shall not pursue here the fascinating details of these or other machines. What is most disturbing about them is their living of our lives for us. Is it misguided to search for *particular* additional functions beyond the competence of machines to do for us? Perhaps what we desire is to live (an active verb) ourselves, in contact with reality. (And this, machines cannot do *for* us.) Without elaborating on the implications of this, which I believe connect surprisingly with issues about free will and causal accounts of knowledge, we need merely note the intricacy of the question of what matters *for people* other than their experiences. Until one finds a satisfactory answer, and determines that this answer does not *also* apply to animals, one cannot reasonably claim that only the felt experiences of animals limit what we may do to them.

---

2 Some wouldn't use the transformation machine at all; it seems like *cheating*. But the one-time use of the transformation machine would not remove all challenges; there would still be obstacles for the new us to overcome, a new plateau from which to strive even higher. And is this plateau any the less earned or deserved than that provided by genetic endowment and early childhood environment? But if the transformation machine could be used indefinitely often, so that we could accomplish anything by pushing a button to transform ourselves into someone who could do it easily, there would remain no limits we *need* to strain against or try to transcend. Would there be anything left *to do*? Do some theological views place God outside of time because an omniscient omnipotent being couldn't fill up his days?

Robert Nozick: The Experience Machine

1. Nozick suggests that most people would choose not to plug in to an "experience machine" if given the opportunity. Would you plug in? Why or why not?
2. Hedonists such as Epicurus and Mill claim that pleasure is the only thing worth pursuing for its own sake. If some people would choose not to plug in to the experience machine, does this show that hedonism is false?
3. One reason Nozick gives for not getting into the experience machine is that "We want to *do* certain things, and not just have the experience of doing them." Do some activities have value independently of the experiences they produce? If so, what is an example of such an activity?
4. Nozick claims that "Plugging into the machine is a kind of suicide." What does he mean by this? Do you think he is right?

= ❧ =

4

Faring Well and Getting What You Want

Chris Heathwood

....

Chris Heathwood opens his contribution with a very helpful discussion that distinguishes a number of different concerns we may have when talking about the good life. When we speak of a good life, we may be referring to what it is that makes for a *morally* good life. Or we may be asking about how a person can manifest various nonmoral excellences, such as being a great athlete or musician. In asking about the good life, we might also be wondering about life's meaning, and how we can live a meaningful life (if we can). While these are all interesting topics for reflection, Heathwood focuses elsewhere: he wants to know what it is that, in and of itself, makes our lives go better. What, in other words, is intrinsically good for us?

Objectivists answer this question by presenting a list of things whose possession, all by themselves, is supposed to make us better off. Familiar candidates include pleasure, friendship, knowledge, freedom, and virtue. The idea is that no matter our attitude toward such things, our lives go better to the extent that we have more of these items on the list.

Heathwood rejects all objective views about what is intrinsically good for us. He endorses *subjectivism about welfare*: the view "that something we get in life benefits us when and only when we have an interest in it, or want it, or have some other positive attitude towards it (or it causes us to get something else that we have, or will have, a positive attitude towards)." Heathwood asks us to imagine a scenario in which, for any supposedly objective good, a person feels no attraction to it at all. If a person doesn't like, care about, or want (say) freedom, then how could freedom, in itself, improve her lot in life? If Heathwood is right, the answer is: it can't.

....

The Question of Welfare

One of the greatest and oldest questions we can ask ourselves is, What is the good life? What is the best kind of life for a person to live? What are the things in a life that make it worth choosing over other possible lives one could lead? It's hard to imagine a more important question. However, I want to focus on what I take to be a narrower question, namely, What things in life are ultimately to our *benefit*? Or to put it a few other ways, What things make us *better off*?, What makes a life a good life *for us*?, What is it to *fare well*? Taking our cue from this last expression, let's call this *the question of welfare*. In what follows, I'm going to offer my answer to the question of welfare. But first, let's clarify the question further.

I think that the question of welfare is a narrower question than the question of the good life because there are things that make a life a better kind of life to live without necessarily being of any benefit to the person living it. That it would be beneficial to you is one reason for you to choose a life, but not the only reason. Another reason is that the life would be beneficial to others, or, more generally, would exhibit *moral virtue*. Although it is often in a person's self-interest to do the right thing, sometimes doing good is of no benefit to the do-gooder. Imagine a bystander who saves a child in a flash flood, but loses her life in the process. This praiseworthy deed was of great benefit to the child, but, sadly, not to the hero who did it.

Another way a life can be good without being good *for* the person living it is by manifesting *excellence*. People manifest excellence when they excel at certain worthwhile activities, such as playing the cello, proving interesting mathematical theorems, or mastering Szechuan cooking. As with moral virtue, a life that manifests excellence seems to be in that way better, but an activity's being excellent isn't the same thing as its benefitting the person doing it. Someone might have an amazing talent for basketball, but find the sport boring and repetitive, and claim to "get nothing out of it."

This is likely a case in which manifesting excellence in a certain aspect of life would be of no benefit to the person.

A third value that we should distinguish from welfare is *meaning*. When I ask what things are of ultimate benefit or harm to us, I don't intend to be asking about the meaning of life. Whatever having a meaningful life consists in, I take it that it can vary independently from how well off one is.

There is another important clarification of the question of welfare. If someone asks what things improve the quality of a person's life, he is likely to have in mind the question of what things *tend to cause* a person's life to be improved. He might be wondering, for example, whether all the new technology in our lives really makes us better off; or he might be wondering whether he would have been better off now had he gone to graduate school years ago. These causal questions, while immensely important, are not our question. Our question is rather the question of what things make us better off *in themselves*, independent of any other changes that these things might cause in our lives. In terms philosophers use, we are asking what things are *intrinsically good* for us rather than what things are merely *instrumentally good* for us (i.e., good for us because of what they lead to). The question of intrinsic value has a kind of priority over the question of instrumental value, in that any answer to the question of instrumental value will presuppose, if only implicitly, an answer to the question about intrinsic value.

Preliminary Steps in Answering the Question of Welfare

Now that we have a clearer understanding of the question of welfare, how do we go about answering it? One natural way to begin is to devise a list of things whose presence in our lives seems intuitively to make our lives better. In developing such a list, we should keep in mind the distinction just introduced between intrinsic and instrumental value. Since the question of welfare is the question of intrinsic welfare value, we want to include on the list intuitive *intrinsic* goods only. Consider an example: while medicine can certainly make our lives better, there is no plausibility to the claim that possessing or taking medicine is good *in itself* for us. If medicine benefits us, this is due to the effects that it has on our health. We can also ask, in turn, whether being healthy is an intrinsic or merely an instrumental good. My own view is that bodily health, like medicine, is of merely instrumental value; we'll get to that view shortly.

So what might such a list include? Here are some natural candidates: happiness, knowledge, love, freedom, friendship, the appreciation of beauty, creative activity, being respected. Why think that the presence of such things in themselves makes our lives better? One reason is that these are things that we tend to want or value in our lives, and, moreover, to want or value *for their own sakes*—not merely for their effects. Next, note that such desires *seem reasonable*. These aren't crazy things to want in your life; it makes sense to want them. If it does, what explains this? The view that these things are intrinsically good for us would explain it.

Subjective vs. Objective Theories of Welfare

But now I want to ask a question, consideration of which, I believe, pulls us in the opposite direction—that is, away from the view that all of the items above are intrinsically good for us. It's true that many of us, much of the time, want the above things in our lives, and that we are glad to have them when we get them. But do we want them because it is good to have them, or is it good to have them because we want them? To put the question slightly differently, Do the items on our list above make our lives better only because they are things that we want and are glad to have in our lives, or do these things make our lives better even if we have no interest in them? This question—one of the deepest and most central questions in the philosophy of welfare—is the question of whether welfare is objective or subjective.

Subjectivists hold that something we get in life benefits us when and only when we have an interest in it, or want it, or have some other positive attitude towards it (or it causes us to get something else that we have, or will have, a positive attitude towards). *Objectivists* about welfare deny this, and maintain that at least some of the intrinsically beneficial things in our lives are good for us even if we don't want them, don't like them, don't care about them, and even if they fail to get us anything else that we want or care about. They are good for us "whether we like it or not."

The debate over whether welfare is objective or subjective should not be confused with the debate over whether *morality* is objective or subjective. In my view, morality is pretty clearly objective. It is wrong to light a cat on fire for one's amusement. And the fact that this is wrong does not—as subjectivists about morality would have it—depend upon my or anyone else's negative attitudes towards this kind of act. It's not wrong to light cats on fire because we disapprove of this; rather, we disapprove of it because it's wrong. I feel pretty confident about that. Much less obvious is the notion that a person can be *benefitted*, can have her own interests advanced, when she gets things that she herself in no way wants, things that leave her cold. Indeed, it seems to me that this cannot happen. It seems to me to be a truth about welfare that if something is truly a benefit to someone, it must be something she wants, likes, or cares about, or something that helps her get something she wants, likes, or cares about.

If I am right that this is a truth about welfare, I think that it is probably a foundational truth. That means that there are no deeper truths about welfare from which we can derive it, and hence argue for it. But there are still considerations that can help us to see it. Concrete examples can help do this. Consider the following case:

> Charlie wants to improve his quality of life. He has heard that it is philosophers who claim to be experts on this topic, so he looks through some philosophy journals at his library. He finds an article claiming to have discovered the correct account of welfare. It is an objective theory that includes the items on our list above. The paper is in a pretty good journal, so Charlie decides to go about trying to increase his share of some of the items on the list. For example, to increase his freedom, he moves to a state with higher speed limits. Charlie is careful to make sure that the move won't have any detrimental side effects—that it won't cause him to fail to get less of any of the other goods on the list.
>
> After succeeding in increasing his freedom, Charlie finds that he doesn't care about it, that he is completely indifferent to it. Although he is free to drive faster, he never does (he never wants to). Nor does the freedom to drive faster get him anything else that he is interested in. Charlie considers whether he is any better off as a result of the increase in his freedom. He concludes that he is no better off.

Do you agree with Charlie's own assessment of his situation? I do. I feel confident that Charlie is right that his gains in freedom turned out to be of no benefit to him. Note that the objective theory in question implies otherwise. For according to that theory, *freedom itself*—not freedom that you happen to want, but freedom itself—makes your life better. Since (i) this objective theory implies that Charlie's life is going better as a result of this increase in freedom, but (ii) in fact Charlie's life is not going any better as a result of this increase in freedom, the theory must be mistaken.

Importantly, the point here generalizes. For any of the alleged goods on the list, so long as it is an objective putative good—i.e., a putative good that bears no necessary connection to any positive attitudes on the part of the person for whom it is supposed to be good—we could construct a case similar in all relevant respects to Charlie's case. This would be a case in which someone gets the supposed good, but is in no way glad to have it, and is in no way glad to have anything else that it gets her. I believe that we would again feel confident that this person receives no benefit. And the reason we can always construct such a case, I submit, is the idea mentioned earlier: that if something is truly a benefit to someone, it must be something she wants, likes, or cares about, or something that helps her get such a thing. This is why I'm inclined to believe that whereas objectivism is the correct view of morality, subjectivism is the correct view of welfare.

If there are such good reasons to be a subjectivist, why would anyone reject the view? One of the main reasons that some are driven to reject subjectivism about welfare is that, intuitively, it's possible for a person to want, like, or care about getting *the wrong things*. Some pursuits, for example, strike us as pointless or meaningless. What if someone wants never to step on a crack when he walks on the sidewalk? Would his life really be going better for him each time he satisfies this desire?

But the objection may be most forceful when it appeals to pursuits that are positively bad. Consider, to take a real life example, the serial rapist and murderer Ted Bundy. What Bundy wanted most in his life was to inflict pain on innocent strangers, to wield power over them, and to watch them beg, suffer, and die at his own hand. For quite a number of years, Bundy got just what he wanted. According to subjectivism, when it comes to welfare, anything you take an interest in is as good as any other; that is, it doesn't matter what you want, so long as you get it, and so long as your getting it doesn't conflict with your getting other things that you want. Thus, assuming that Bundy wasn't plagued with guilt or regret during his reign of terror, and that he avoided other unwanted side-effects of his lifestyle, subjectivists must say that Bundy benefitted greatly in doing what he did, that he was quite well off, at least before he got caught. Objectivists, by contrast, have the resources to condemn Bundy's behavior, not just morally, but from the point of view of his own self-interest. They can say that Bundy would himself have been better off if he had had, and had achieved, more admirable goals.

Thus we need to ask ourselves a question. Consider the years before Bundy was caught, the years in which he lived just the sort of life he most wanted to live. Were these years good years for Bundy? Did he live a life that was in his interest to live? Was he just as well off as he would have been during these years had he had morally acceptable interests, and success-fully pursued those? Note that our question is not, Did Bundy's lifestyle *make him happy*? Objectivists can agree that it did. Our question is not, Did Bundy *get just what he wanted*? Objectivists agree that he did. Nor should we be distracted by the fact that Bundy's lifestyle led to his eventual ruin. Subjectivists agree that his choices harmed him later on, after he got caught. (Bundy was eventually executed for his crimes.) Rather, our ques-tion is, Were the years before he got caught good years for Bundy?

I agree that Bundy was a monster. I condemn what he did in the stron-gest terms. But it strikes me as a false hope to think that Bundy could not have benefitted from doing what he did. Thus, I "bite the bullet" and main-tain that Bundy in fact was quite well off before he got caught. To be honest, I don't even think of this as biting a bullet. It strikes me as the genuinely correct verdict. Remember that all we are saying is that Bundy *benefitted*, for a time, from his lifestyle. We are not saying that his lifestyle was mor-ally acceptable or that it was worth emulating. Indeed, the claim that Bundy benefitted from his monstrous lifestyle helps explain something. It helps explain why we find the whole situation so sickening: here is this monster, doing the most unspeakable things, and all the while living large because of it.

The Desire Theory of Welfare

Subjectivists maintain that being well off has to do with the attitudes we have towards what we get in life rather than the nature of the things them-selves. Being benefitted is a matter of having a positive attitude towards things, whatever these things are. Subjectivists often hold that *desire* or *wanting* is the special positive attitude here. Desire may even be an ele-ment in all positive attitudes, attitudes such as liking, preferring, caring about something, or having something as a goal.

According to the desire theory of welfare, human welfare consists in the satisfaction of desire. Whenever what a person wants to be the case is in fact the case, this constitutes a benefit for the person. Whenever a person's desires are frustrated, this constitutes a basic harm. The theory recognizes no other fundamental sources of benefit and harm. Many other kinds of event—making money, becoming sick, gaining freedom, appreciating beauty—can cause our lives to go better or worse, but only by being things that we want or don't want, or by causing us to get, or fail to get, other things that we want or don't want. *How* good or bad a desire satisfaction or frustration is for its subject, according to the theory, is a function of the strength of the desire; the more deeply we want something to be the case, the better it is for us if it is the case, and the worse it is if it's not. How well things go for us overall in life is determined by the extent to which we get what we want throughout our lives, both on a day-to-day basis and with respect to larger life goals.

We can distinguish two different things we might mean by the term "want." One sense of the term is merely behavioral. If we voluntarily do something, it follows, on the behavioral sense of the term, that it is something we wanted to do. According to a second sense of the term, we count as wanting something only if we are genuinely attracted to it, only if it genuinely appeals to us. Sometimes a person voluntarily does something that holds no appeal for him. On the behavioral sense of the term, it follows that he wanted to do it. But this kind of desire satisfaction does not seem to be of any benefit to the person faced with doing the unappealing thing. Thus I believe that the best version of the desire theory of welfare is one that understands "desire" or "want"—I use these terms interchangeably—in the "genuine attraction" sense mentioned above. Only when we get, or get to do, those things that we are genuinely attracted to or that genuinely appeal to us—the things we "really want"—are we made better off.

What about Pleasure and Happiness?

One of the simplest and oldest theories of human welfare is hedonism, the view that pleasure is the only thing that is intrinsically good for us. Almost everyone accepts that pleasure is an intrinsic welfare good. Hedonism is controversial mainly because it claims that there are no other such goods. How does the desire satisfaction theory of welfare accommodate the value of pleasure?

Whether it can make such an accommodation, and whether it should, depends upon what pleasure is. On one view of the nature of pleasure, pleasure is an indefinable feeling or sensation, in the same general category as the indefinable sensations of seeing red, of the taste of chocolate, or of nausea. If this is what pleasure is, I don't think that pleasure is good in itself for anyone. For imagine a creature who is completely indifferent to this feeling, or even finds it unbearable. It is not plausible to suggest that such a creature would be having a good experience—an experience that is good for it, and makes its life better—when it experiences this indifferent, or even reviled, sensation. Rather, if this view of the nature of pleasure is right, then pleasure's value depends entirely on the creature's wanting it, liking it, or taking an interest in it. It would be just like the taste of chocolate, which (ignoring side effects) is good for a creature to taste when, but only when, the creature wants to be tasting it.

On a competing account of the nature of pleasure, pleasure is a positive attitude, an attitude that one can take up towards things like the chocolate taste one is currently experiencing, the music one is hearing, or the fact that one has gotten a raise. The attitude of being pleased that something is the case certainly a good state to be in, but it is one that, in my view, ultimately involves desire. Taking pleasure in a chocolate taste sensation just is to be wanting to be experiencing it as you are experiencing it. To be pleased that you have gotten a raise is to want the raise while seeing that you have gotten it. Thus, if pleasure turns out to be a kind of state that is indeed intrinsically valuable, it is a kind of state whose value the desire theory of welfare can recognize, and even explain.

The desire theory can also accommodate the irresistible idea that it's good to be happy. Consider being happy that one has gotten a raise, or that the sun is shining, or that one is living in Barcelona. These are good states to be in. But, just as above, I believe that they are states that essentially involve desire. They involve, respectively, the desire for a raise, the desire that the sun be shining, and the desire to be living in Barcelona. If one gets a raise, and is happy about this, one will necessarily be receiving a desire satisfaction. In this way the value of happiness can be accommodated by the desire theory of welfare.

Refining the Desire Theory

Sometimes our desires are based on ignorance or confused thinking. When they are, it can seem doubtful that satisfying them benefits us. Thus we have a potential problem for the desire theory of welfare, and probably for any subjective theory. To take a simple example, suppose that I have a strong craving for cherry pie, not knowing that I have recently developed a serious allergy to cherries. If I satisfy my desire, I'll need a shot of adrenaline to avoid suffocating to death. Still, in my ignorant state, cherry pie is what I want most. The desire theory of welfare seems to imply, absurdly, that it is most in my interest to have cherry pie.

For this reason, many subjectivists revise the theory so that what determines our welfare is not our actual desires but our *idealized* desires. These are the desires we would have if we knew all the facts, were vividly appreciating them, and were thinking rationally. If I knew, and vividly appreciated, what eating cherry pie would do to me, I would prefer not to have it; the informed desire theory thus does not imply that it would be most in my interest to satisfy my desire for cherry pie.

Subjectivists who are troubled by the problems caused by pointless or immoral desires may hope that the move to idealized desires will help here as well. Perhaps if Ted Bundy had appreciated the effects that his actions would have on his victims, and had been thinking rationally about it, he would not have desired to do the horrible things he did. Perhaps he would have instead wanted the things on the objectivist's list. This is a nice thought, but for it to be true, it would have to be that no one who was fully informed, vividly appreciating the facts, and thinking clearly could have pointless or immoral desires. But surely it's just wishful thinking to believe that.

In any case, the move to ideal desires faces a problem: it begins to abandon the core idea of subjectivism. That idea is simple: what is good for you must be connected to what *you yourself* want, like, or care about—not what someone else wants for you, even if that someone else is an improved version of yourself. If you had full knowledge and appreciation of all of what was possible for you, perhaps you would prefer caviar and experimental music. As it happens, you prefer peanuts and baseball. Surely you benefit when you receive the things you actually want (peanuts and baseball) rather than the things (caviar and experimental music) that you merely would want if you were fully informed and rational. For this reason, I believe that we should regard our actual desires as the ones whose satisfaction directly benefits us.

Fortunately, the problem that motivated the move to idealization— the problem to do with desires based on ignorance—can be solved within the original theory, the theory that appeals to one's actual desires. Recall the case of the allergenic cherry pie. The actual desire theory can say that it is in fact not in my interest to eat the pie. The theory does imply that I'll receive *some* benefit from doing so, but that is plausible—I crave the pie, after all, and I will be very glad to be eating it. But the theory doesn't imply that I'll receive a *net* benefit. For I also have strong desires not to be sent to an emergency room and not to be suffocating. Eating the pie will frustrate these very strong desires. The theory thus delivers the desired result: that overall I'm better off not eating the cherry pie. The move to idealization, which violates the spirit of subjectivism, is not necessary in the first place.

Other objections pose more serious problems for the desire theory and may require that we refine it. Here is one such objection. Suppose that my uncle must go into exile, and I know that I will never see him again. Whenever I think of him, I think of him fondly, hoping very much that he is happy and healthy. As a matter of fact, though I couldn't know this, my uncle *is* happy and healthy. According to the desire theory of welfare, a person benefits whenever a desire of his is satisfied. For a desire to be satisfied, all that is required is that the desired event actually occur; the person need not know this and need derive no satisfaction from it for it to be true that his desire was satisfied. The desire theory thus implies that I am made better off when my uncle achieves happiness and health.

Many (though not all) desire theorists regard this as an unacceptably counterintuitive implication of the theory. They think that I have not been benefitted in the example. I agree, though there is little agreement on how best to handle such a case. One popular solution is to revise the theory so that it counts only desires that are *about one's own life*. My uncle's being happy and healthy is an event in his life, not mine, and thus when it occurs, this revised theory denies that I am benefitted even though I wanted the event to occur. But I believe this restriction excludes too much; it excludes, for example, the desires of fans for their team to win. In my view, the lesson of the exiled uncle is rather that in order to be benefitted, we must *be aware* that the desired event has occurred, or is occurring.

This raises all sorts of issues that we cannot explore here. But I hope I have made a decent case for the ideas that subjectivism is the better approach to welfare, that the desire theory is the way for the subjectivist to go, that the desire theory should appeal to desires in the "genuine attraction" sense of the term, and that your actual rather than ideal desires are plausibly regarded as what determines how well you fare in life.

Chris Heathwood: Faring Well and Getting What You Want

1. Heathwood claims that the meaningfulness of a life can vary independently from how well off the person living it is. To see whether you agree, try to describe an example of (a) a life that you think is meaningful that is not beneficial to the person living it, and (b) a life that is beneficial to the person living it without being a meaningful life.

2. Suppose someone claims that being healthy is intrinsically good for us. Can you think of a way to test whether this is true? Here is one idea: describe a pair of cases that are exactly alike except that in one of the cases, the person involved has greater health than in the other case. It's crucial that there be no other differences between the cases. Describe such a pair of cases. What do you think it tells us about the intrinsic value of being healthy?

3. Do you agree that Charlie's gains in freedom turned out to be of no benefit to him? If they are of no benefit to him, is that enough to show that objectivism about well-being is mistaken? If not, what more is required?

4. What is an ideal desire as opposed to an actual desire? Which kind of desire does Heathwood think is connected to welfare? Why does he think this?

5. Do you believe that Heathwood benefits when, unbeknownst to him, his exiled uncle achieves happiness and health? Why or why not?

6. According to one version of the desire theory of welfare, a person is benefitted just when a desire that is about her own life is satisfied. Is this theory plausible? Explain.

7. Heathwood thinks that our life is a good life for us to the extent that we get what we want, so long as we are aware of it, and so long as this is a want in the "genuine attraction" sense of "want." Are there any cases in which your life goes better for you even though no such want is satisfied? Are there any cases in which such wants are satisfied, but one fails to be benefited as a result?

5

Necessities

Jean Kazez

....

In this excerpt from her wonderful book on the good life, *The Weight of Things* (2007), Jean Kazez argues for the view that there are a number of basic goods that add value to a life. She thus adopts an objective view of human well-being, according to which certain things make an essential contribution to a good life—even if we don't believe this, or don't value these goods. Here she defends her favored roster of such goods.

One of these is autonomy—the ability to decide for yourself which principles will govern your life, and the ability to follow through on those decisions. She also thinks it essential that a good life improve over time. A life that contains a great amount of good things, but all within one's first decade, followed by a steady decline till death, is not a good life. Also on the list: self-expression, a commitment to morality, and happiness taken in worthwhile activities. Kazez defends each of these claims with interesting examples taken from memoirs and literature.

....

What kind of evidence would show that something is a fundamental good that's not just relevant to living well, but necessary? There certainly isn't anything like a sure-fire test.

We can only aspire to say what seems most reasonable. We certainly should not expect to be able to recognize which are the critical goods in one intuitive flash, without spending time looking at any sort of evidence. It may take you some time before you come to think that happiness or morality, or any other candidate, is fundamentally good. A person could come to think so only after reading a searing biography, or watching a movie, or reflecting on a life experience. At the very least, you would have to sift through examples. We're all familiar with lots of lives and we deem some better than others. If the lives we deem good consistently are lives of—say—eating lots of popcorn, then eating lots of popcorn looks to be a fundamental good with relevance to human well-being. If we deem lives bad when they're lacking popcorn consumption, then that's a reason to view popcorn consumption as a necessity.

Beyond this sort of sifting of cases and discovery of patterns, we learn something from looking at human motivation. Since I'm no more astute a judge of value than anyone else, it pays to think about what people value and how they value it. If many people will stop at nothing to procure popcorn, that's some support for regarding eating popcorn as a necessity. That's not to say that we need to do surveys to show that everyone wants popcorn. The occasional popcorn hater doesn't refute the theory that it's necessary, because . . . desires are manipulable; they're not definitive. But they're certainly a piece of relevant evidence. . . .

HAPPINESS IS A REASONABLE place to begin. Some philosophers have questioned whether feelings of happiness are good at all, let alone fundamentally good. The Stoics, for example, argue that plain physical pleasure adds nothing positive at all to a life that is good because of virtue:

> It is like the light of a lamp eclipsed and obliterated by the rays of the sun; like a drop of honey lost in the vastness of the Aegean sea; a penny added to the riches of Croesus, or a single step on the road from here to India. Such is the value of bodily goods that it is unavoidably eclipsed, overwhelmed and destroyed by the splendour and grandeur of virtue. . .

Kant takes a kindred stand when he says that the only thing that's good without qualification is the morally good will. If feeling happy is sometimes good, and perhaps even for itself, it's not good at those times when it's enticing us in the wrong direction or rewarding evil deeds.

My intuitions side with the Hedonistic Utilitarians. . . . Happiness is a good thing, always. We don't like to see bad people experience happiness precisely because we do think it's something good, and we want them to have no share of what's good. There's something disturbing about ill-gotten happiness. It's especially creepy to contemplate sadistic pleasure, pleasure that's actually derived from causing others to suffer. But I don't think we can assess whether five minutes of happiness is good or not based on its pedigree. Happiness is good, period.

And it's relevant to how well a life is going. In *Darkness Visible*, William Styron tells the story of a depression that overwhelmed him and nearly drove him to suicide; as the depression lifts, and he has his first moments of non-misery, and then moments of happiness, there's no doubt that his life is going better. You could insist that greater happiness was life-enhancing for him because it paid off in greater creativity or healthier relationships, or some other coin, but that's not what seems to be the case. Think of a time when your own life was not going well. Gradually, you started to be happier. You found your days more pleasant. You enjoyed the company of your friends more. Your boss didn't annoy you as much. You weren't dwelling on worries about the future any more. This change of mood probably improved your life—directly, and because of itself. Happiness, whether it comes about in mysterious ways, in good ways, or in bad ways, is a fundamental good that can directly affect how our lives are going.

If happiness is relevant to the way a life is going, is it also necessary? Without at least some happiness, it does not seem like we can reach the level of even minimally good lives. A person without any happiness at all is unconscious, or continually miserable, or at best in a neutral frame of mind. Of these possibilities, neutrality certainly seems the most appealing, but it's hard to imagine a person constantly in such a state whose life could be judged positively, overall.

HAPPINESS IS CRITICAL, BUT it's not the only critical thing. David Shipler portrays the lives of people struggling to make ends meet in his recent book, *The Working Poor: Invisible in America*. His stories have a recurrent theme: the lack of control that's the cost of poverty. The low-income workers he portrays are deprived of independence, autonomy, self-determination. They have no chance to be the authors of their own lives.

One of his portraits is particularly touching. Caroline works in the women's department at Wal-Mart. She needs to be home with her teenaged daughter in the evenings, because of her mental retardation and epilepsy, but she's forced to work night shifts. She'd have better hours and make better money as a manager, but—perhaps because she's missing all her teeth—she's repeatedly passed over for promotion. She finally quits the Wal-Mart job, and then one business after another gives her irregular night shifts, until her daughter's teachers become concerned that she's being neglected. Caroline finally loses both her home and her daughter, who goes to live with a relative.

Nobody has perfect control. But there is a level of autonomy beneath which we do not want to fall. Barbara Ehrenreich, in *Nickel and Dimed*, describes the way control is lost even before a person is hired. The job applicant has to take drug tests and fill out phony psychological question-naires. If hired, the blue-collar worker finds herself being told exactly how every aspect of the job must be performed. In the worst cases, the worker becomes little more than a cog in a machine. Shipler describes a woman in Los Angeles sewing flies into blue jeans at a rate of 767 per hour, on pain of being docked a portion of her hourly wage of $5.75. In the very worst cases, the worker is physically prevented from escaping her thing-like sta-tus; she is nearly a slave.

Having more control is one thing, it seems, that would have made Caroline's life better. It would have been a major improvement if she could have controlled her work schedule to accommodate her daughter's needs. Advancing to a managerial position would have increased her control over her daily activities. It would have been some improvement if she had been given the chance to initiate and innovate on the job, instead of having to follow rigidly prescribed routines.

Is autonomy really something we should value in itself? . . .

What I'll say about foolish exercises of autonomy is just what I said about ill-gotten happiness. Autonomy is always, as such, good. What would be *too* counterintuitive would be to say that every increase in auton-omy automatically makes a person's life overall better. But we needn't say that. There are other things a life needs besides autonomy, and foolish exercises of autonomy will typically get in the way of the fulfillment of those other needs.

Lack of autonomy tends to be accompanied by unhappiness and greater autonomy by greater happiness. It's difficult, therefore, to disen-tangle the desire to be more autonomous from the desire to be happier. Still, unless we are utterly determined to construe happiness as the sole motivator in life, the pursuit of autonomy is everywhere to see: it's evident when slaves demand freedom from masters, when teenagers demand more independence from parents, when workers wrestle some control over their hours from managers, when women demand the right to vote. In contemporary Western culture, there's no doubt that we place a huge premium on personal autonomy. Autonomy is regarded in quite a different way in other settings. Certainly we should avoid drawing a picture of the necessary kinds and amounts of autonomy based on what's in our own backyards. Arranged marriage is alien to us, but does it cut into autonomy excessively? An Indian couple I know tell me how their marriage was arranged in their twenties by thoughtful parents looking out for their best interests; their marriage seems as good as most. On the other hand, in traditional Hindu villages, it's not unusual for parents to arrange the marriage of a girl as young as eight, who is then kept behind the walls of her home until she's old enough to join her husband's household. In this case, unlike the first, there's a disturbing loss of control. In saying so, we're not necessarily holding an alien idea about individual lives over the local one. The local assumption seems really to be that the girl is just a girl, and not entitled to the best life—an idea we are compelled to reject. Her individual interests are regarded as subordinate to the interests of men, or families, or the village as a whole.

Insisting that a good life includes "enough" autonomy seems to particularly conflict with the most traditional Islamic ideas about the good life for women, but again, the contradiction can be read in another way. In Saudi Arabia, women live out their lives in *purdah* hidden in their fathers' or husbands' homes, and behind veils. They depend on male relatives to take them places and are denied the right to vote. As Martha Nussbaum points out in *Women and Human Development*, it's not necessarily true that social arrangements reveal a vision of the best life for a woman; arrangements are often defended because they're thought to be best for society as a whole. The good for individual women doesn't count, or counts for less. By contrast, she supports—persuasively—"a principle of each person as an end."

Surely, though, there are cultures quite unlike our own that really do conceive of what it is for an individual to live well in ways that give less emphasis to autonomy. In Thomas à Kempis's fifteenth-century classic, *The Imitation of Christ*, the advice to the devout is to find someone to obey. Letting someone else run your life is regarded as good, not bad (as long as you attach yourself to the right superior). The ideal of limiting oneself is taken about as far as possible in some of the medieval religious orders.

In *Galileo's Daughter*, Dava Sobel describes the religious order where Galileo—that highly disobedient Catholic—sent his own daughters. In the order of Saint Clare, life was spent within the confines of a convent. The confinement was supposed to facilitate a virtuous life. So Saint Colette explains:

> He Himself deigned and willed to be placed in a sepulchre of stone. And it pleased Him to be so entombed for forty hours. So, my dear Sisters, you follow Him. For after obedience, poverty, and pure chastity, you have holy enclosure to hold on to, enclosure in which you can live for forty years either more or less, and in which you will die.

Imprisonment in the convent was taken to be a good life for the individual sisters, not just a means to some greater collective good.

Stretch our preconceptions as we may, we have to be prepared to say that some views are just wrong. The idea that loss of autonomy is conducive to living the best life is a view that has been superseded by other ideas, even within the monastic tradition, and rightly so.

HAPPINESS, AUTONOMY. Could those be all the necessities there are? "Nowhere Man" must give us pause. He is well endowed with both, but his name is based on the fact that one week he's working at a slaughter-house, but the next week he quits and works at the local animal shelter. Now he's actively involved in Republican politics. Next he's earnestly supporting the Democratic Party. He gets excited about Buddhism and then he's moved on to Jewish Mysticism. "Doesn't have a point of view, knows not where he's going to," as the Beatles song so aptly puts it.

Nowhere Man's problem, on the surface, is that there is no unity or continuity in his life. That sounds like a merely aesthetic criticism (this novel is choppy; it doesn't hang together; the midsection doesn't belong). It seems too abstract to really be relevant to evaluating a life; until, that is, we reframe the problem as a lack of self. We want to be amply endowed with the ingredients covered so far (happiness and autonomy), but we want our way of pursuing them to spring from our "selves."

If we really have a grip on Nowhere Man's problem, we ought to be able to identify instances of it in the real world, and that is harder than one might expect. People's lives can exhibit considerable contrast and variety without anyone suspecting a missing "self." There's no problem with Arnold Schwarzenegger's life, just because he went from action hero in the movies to California governor, or because he's a Republican married into the famously Democratic Kennedy family. It's not the sheer disunity of a life that's bad, but an underlying weak self, a self without any strong preferences. A weak self is indifferent to what, for the rest of us, are big differences. No steady convictions and personal traits control perceptions of what's appealing and what's not. Beyond that, it's hard to say what a strong self is, exactly. But it seems critical to our lives going well. If being autonomous and self-determining are as important as they seem to be, it must be equally important for a person to have a self that does the determining.

A sense of identity tends to make us happy, like the other fundamental goods do. But self and happiness don't always go hand in hand. There's probably some situation in which each of us would choose self over happiness. Some people face that choice as the result of a mental illness. For a person who is profoundly depressed, a treatment of last resort is electroconvulsive therapy, which can result in memory loss. With whole swaths of one's life erased—who your friends were, what you read or wrote, where you traveled, what happened in the world at large—you can become virtually another person. Jonathan Cott reports just this in his memoir *On the Sea of Memory*; he seems to lament having chosen ECT to treat severe depression, longing for a return of self, even a self that was depressed. In *Listening to Prozac*, Peter Kramer worries that the alteration of identity is a quite standard effect of anti-depressants, and wonders whether mood improvement is worth the cost.

Injury to self can be done by medications and memory loss, but the causes are innumerable. Shipler's book sheds light on one of the many ways that people stuck in poverty sometimes come to have problems of "self." Many are victims of sexual abuse who suffer dissociative disorders. In other words, they split off a part of themselves and become mere observers of the abuse. This spares them some of the pain of their victimization, but later they continue to observe as things "happen" to them. They watch themselves neglecting their own children instead of choosing to neglect them or choosing to stop neglecting them.

But problems of self are not just outcomes of poverty. To cite just one literary example, in Zora Neale Hurston's *Their Eyes Were Watching God*, Janie's first two marriages are to well-off men who define the social role she is supposed to play. The way they use her to adorn themselves stops her from finding her own voice. Descending to a lower socio-economic stratum, ironically, she discovers a sense of self. Shipler describes how rich parents neglect children and bestow on them an insidious hunger for attention. They become anxious "people pleasers." A child like this reaches adulthood with a set of traits, interests, and abilities that win Mom and Dad's approval. The adult child winds up with no deep-rooted self at the helm. She casts about, now doing this, now doing that. Even if the thises and thats are good things and produce some happiness, there seems to be something amiss with such a life.

Like autonomy, self-expression is especially prized in contemporary Western societies. But is self merely a Western preoccupation? On the face of it, Buddhist thinking involves a diametrically opposed sense of value. Buddhist sages urge us to lose ourselves, not find ourselves; the very highest thing we can achieve is "no self." . . .

Though Buddhism encourages the realization of no-self, it doesn't encourage us to be like Nowhere Man. I'm inclined to think a Buddhist *doesn't* reject self as I am using the term. What no-self really means is not being rigidly identified with some narrow set of characteristics (I am a female liberal intellectual), not being focused on acquisition, not being egocentric. It is being open, receptive, compassionate. . . .

My intuitions about the critical role of morality agree with the ancients— Plato, Aristotle, and the Stoics—who all regard moral virtue as central to living our lives well. For some of the ancients, the benefit of morality is so significant that morality is the only thing that determines how my life is going. I can't swallow that whole, but morality can, intuitively, make me a better person and my life a better life. It's not always a matter of morality making me happy—though frequently it does. Morality seems to make a direct difference to how well my life is going.

Certainly, there are stories of life getting better because of moral improvement. In Dostoevsky's *Crime and Punishment*, Raskolnikov kills an old woman, struggles to justify himself to himself and his friends, but eventually feels compelled to take responsibility. At the end of the book, he walks up the steps of the police station and confesses, with no particular sensation of pleasure or pain. We know his life is now going better, even before we read the epilogue and find out what happens to him. It's true that his confession has rewards: he's given a lenient sentence because he's admitted to his crime; he's now able to enjoy and reciprocate the love of the devoted and saintly Sonya; and he winds up turning tentatively in the direction of her religious faith. Moments of "infinite happiness" arrive while Raskolnikov serves his term in a Siberian prison camp, and more are assured in the future. But the moment when his life has become better precedes the happiness payoff. The sheer moral improvement at the moment of his confession establishes some life improvement before greater happiness comes along and yields more. . . .

Depending on how morality is understood, it can be easier or harder to see the connection between being moral and living well. The ancient conceptions, with their focus on virtue, are most conducive to seeing the connection. . . . The Aristotelian virtues are sustainers of stability and balance. Being angry at the right time, at the right person, to the right degree, would save a person from being a doormat or a volcano. It's harder to say why a person can make his life go better by sending money to help flood victims on the other side of the world, or by telling the truth in an awkward situation, or by apportioning grades or pay increases fairly. What's the relevance of doing these things for other people to making your own life go well?

Perhaps it comes down to a connection between living well and living among others. If you concern yourself not at all with what you owe to others or with what they need from you, you live in profound isolation. Yes, there are people out there, but in your scheme of things, they're just things—like the rocks in a quarry or the cornstalks in a field. Without morality, you would enjoy, protect, exploit, or destroy others at your pleasure. You would regard yourself as the only one of your kind, the only one whose well-being really matters. If it would be bad to literally be the only one of your kind, the last surviving person, then it's bad to live as if you were. The good of moral behavior toward others, for each of us, is the good of being part of a richer world, in which there are many beings with independent importance.

Morality is good for us because it makes us less alone—it gives me a kind of friendship not just with my *friends* but with everyone. If friendship strikes you as an obvious good, then this explanation will satisfy you. But what if it doesn't? There is this also to say: there is something painfully limited about our lives. You can only live one life—here, not there; now, not in the past or the future; doing this, not that. We break through these limits by identifying with hungry people on the other side of the globe or with the inhabitants of a polluted, over-heated world in the next century. We become (a bit) *them*. Ethical concern is something of a cure for our sense of finitude. It's good to do the right thing because it gives you an expanded life, one that encompasses not just your own feelings and satisfactions and accomplishments, but those of other people (and possibly animals as well). . . .

A list of four necessities—happiness, autonomy, self-expression, and morality—is admirably tidy, but not absurdly restrictive. Each thing on the list is robustly valuable. We certainly act like these things are critically important in our daily lives. Now we enter less certain territory.

Take, to begin with, a woman I will call Constance. She works as a piano teacher, plays Beethoven sonatas splendidly, enjoys going to the symphony. She wears attractive, timeless fashions picked out of the Land's End catalogue and reads the Bible in her spare time. She's a good friend to her neighbors and a generous donor to the American Cancer Society. The problem is that she does exactly these things from the age of 21 to her death at 81. Constance doesn't get better at playing the piano or choose new music. She doesn't grow tired of Land's End fashions. She doesn't get interested in new charities. There is no improvement in any way; there is minimal change. The good she is missing is the good of growth, positive change, progress.

We do seem to value progress itself, and not just the good things that are the outcome of making progress—like greater autonomy, happiness, and accomplishment. Some of the lives we admire most are lives transformed by adversity. Lance Armstrong would impress us if he won the Tour de France over and over again. He impresses us far more because he progressed from cancer survivor to race winner. We're impressed no matter what by a person who is highly autonomous, but we're especially impressed by the great abolitionist Frederick Douglass, who started off as a slave and fought his way to autonomy. Since cancer and slavery are very bad things, and undoubtedly detracted from these two lives, we must accord progress itself a very high value, considering that these lives strike us as being especially good.

We want our lives in some way to go from worse to better. We want that to happen over small stretches and large, in minor ways and in major ways. Moving from worse to better might mean fixing the toaster one morning, or learning salsa dancing in the space of a month, or becoming acquainted with Peru over a summer. Or it could mean becoming a better teacher over a 10-year period, or learning to be more compassionate over a lifetime.

But wouldn't it be better to skip "worse" and go directly to "better"— to have the knowledge, or skills, or activities, or experiences that are "better" from the start? Maybe that would be good for another kind of being. God, in our conception, starts off perfect and stays perfect. Absence of change in a supreme being is no flaw at all. But in us, no progress would be a serious flaw. It's not a fixed toaster, or dancing, or familiarity with Peru that really makes a person's life better. It really is precisely the process of going from broken to fixed, from clumsy to competent, from ignorant to familiar. It's exercising the power to go from worse to better.

In his extraordinary memoir, *Angela's Ashes*, Frank McCourt tells the story of a childhood spent in extreme poverty and heartbreak. He lacks just about every good I've discussed at the beginning of his life, and comes to possess everything as an adult. Is this really a better life than one that starts well and ends well? It certainly is puzzling to say that it is. That would imply that to give our children a shot at the best possible lives, we ought to deliberately put ourselves in dire circumstances. Should we?

It's true that you have a shot at the most extraordinary progress only if you start in the deepest trough. But most people who start in the deepest trough stay there. So, no, we shouldn't seek problems so we can rise to their solutions. If progress is a necessity—and I'm going to say it is, with just a dash of uncertainty—the progress we need is moderate. What we must avoid is complete stagnation. Wherever we start, we should aim higher. It's quite ordinary types of change that we can't do without.

WITH A ROSTER OF GOOD things now in place, let's return for a moment to happiness. Happiness is good wherever it comes from, I've argued, and having some is a necessity. But what if all your happiness comes from valueless sources? Maggie works as a nurse in an intensive care unit. Make her the head nurse so that she has plenty of autonomy. She performs her job impeccably and let's also assume she's a supporter of good causes, perhaps a life-long volunteer at the SPCA. Make it up as you like. She's happy and responsible and she's learned and progressed over time. But here's the hitch. Maggie's happiness comes from Magic Drug. Without it she would find her job grueling, she'd fall into dependent relationships, and she'd hate animals. Magic Drug doesn't just help her derive happiness from her life. It's not like the medication that helped William Styron recover from depression, enabling him to once more derive happiness from his writing and friendships and so on. The source of Maggie's happiness is Magic Drug and nothing else.

Maggie's problem takes plenty of real-world forms. Imagine a person with lots of good in his life, who derives happiness only from gambling. When he's with his lovely wife and children, he's not happy with them, he's happy because he's anticipating the next trip to the casino. (Don't think of this person as an addict, or you'll have trouble believing he has autonomy. No, he's in control of himself. It's just that gambling is his sole source of pleasure.) This strikes me as a blight that stops his life from going entirely well. If he were to stop the gambling and begin to derive satisfaction from spending time with his children (let's say), that would make his life go better.

Happiness is good wherever it comes from, but in addition to wanting happiness, we also want our happiness to come at least substantially from things that have value. The good that Maggie is missing is a funny, subtle sort of thing. There's no one word for it; to have it is to be happy *with* the good things in your life. What we want, beyond happiness and the other things I've discussed, is a link between happiness and the other things. There's no reason for every last drop of our happiness to be derived from valuable things—that would be a rather puritanical expectation—but something's amiss when most of it isn't.

Jean Kazez: Necessities

1. Kazez says that "Happiness is a good thing, always." Do you agree? Is the happiness that a sadistic person gets from torturing someone good? Why or why not?
2. Kazez argues that autonomy is necessary for someone to have a good life. Yet she allows that arranged marriages can turn out as well as freely chosen marriages. Do you think that your life could go well if others made all your decisions for you, provided they did a very good job?
3. What does Kazez think is wrong with the life of "Nowhere Man"? Do you agree with her view that such a life would be undesirable, even if it were filled with happiness?
4. Kazez says that "Ethical concern is something of a cure for our sense of finitude." What does she mean by this? Does she succeed in showing that morality is a necessary part of a good life?
5. Kazez thinks that improvement over time can make a life go better. Which would you prefer: a life of constant happiness, or a life that begins miserably and ends in great achievement and contentment?
6. Is all happiness equally valuable, or does the value of happiness depend on its sources (as Kazez claims)?

PART II

Normative Ethics

Theories of Right Conduct

6

Euthyphro
Plato

....

In an early section (omitted here) of this dialogue about the nature of
piety, Socrates bumps into Euthyphro in front of the law courts of
Athens. Socrates is on trial for his life; Euthyphro is there to prosecute
a murderer. It turns out that Euthyphro is prosecuting his own father,
an act that would shock ancient Greek audiences as much as it would
shock us in our own time. When Socrates asks him why he would do
such a thing, Euthyphro replies that he is privy to many secrets of the
gods, and that piety demands that he seek his father's conviction.

Our excerpt picks up at this point. Socrates immediately begs
Euthyphro to reveal the essence of piety, its true nature, so that Socrates
and others may live more pious lives. Euthyphro first provides some
examples of pious actions, but this is not what Socrates is after. He
wants to know what is common to all instances of piety. Euthyphro
then says that piety is what the gods love.

Socrates then asks what has since come to be known as the Euthyphro Question: are acts pious because the gods love them, or do the
gods love actions because they are pious? We can modify the question
a bit to get the following puzzle: is an action morally right because God
commands it, or does God command an action because it is right?

Many who think that religion is essential to morality endorse the
first option—God's commands are what make actions right, so that if

From *Five Dialogues*, 2nd ed., trans. G. M. A. Grube, rev. by John Cooper (Indianapolis:
Hackett Publishers 2002), pp. 7–14.

God does not exist, or does not issue commands, then nothing is morally right. Plato's arguments are designed to cast doubt on this view.

....

SOCRATES: . . . So tell me now, by Zeus, what you just now maintained you clearly knew: what kind of thing do you say that godliness and ungodliness are, both as regards murder and other things; or is the pious not the same and alike in every action, and the impious the opposite of all that is pious and like itself, and everything that is to be impious presents us with one form or appearance insofar as it is impious?

EUTHYPHRO: Most certainly, Socrates.

SOCRATES: Tell me then, what is the pious, and what the impious, do you say?

EUTHYPHRO: I say that the pious is to do what I am doing now, to prosecute the wrongdoer, be it about murder or temple robbery or anything else, whether the wrongdoer is your father or your mother or anyone else; not to prosecute is impious. And observe, Socrates, that I can cite powerful evidence that the law is so. I have already said to others that such actions are right, not to favor the ungodly, whoever they are. These people themselves believe that Zeus is the best and most just of the gods, yet they agree that he bound his father because he unjustly swallowed his sons, and that he in turn castrated his father for similar reasons. But they are angry with me because I am prosecuting my father for his wrongdoing. They contradict themselves in what they say about the gods and about me. . . .

SOCRATES: And do you believe that there really is war among the gods, and terrible enmities and battles, and other such things as are told by the poets, and other sacred stories such as are embroidered by good writers and by representations of which the robe of the goddess is adorned when it is carried up to the Acropolis? Are we to say these things are true, Euthyphro?

EUTHYPHRO: Not only these, Socrates, but, as I was saying just now, I will, if you wish, relate many other things about the gods which I know will amaze you.

SOCRATES: I should not be surprised, but you will tell me these at leisure some other time. For now, try to tell me more clearly what I was asking just now, for, my friend, you did not teach me adequately when

I asked you what the pious was, but you told me that what you are doing now, in prosecuting your father for murder, is pious.

EUTHYPHRO: And I told the truth, Socrates.

SOCRATES: Perhaps. You agree, however, that there are many other pious actions.

EUTHYPHRO: There are.

SOCRATES: Bear in mind then that I did not bid you tell me one or two of the many pious actions but that form itself that makes all pious actions pious, for you agreed that all impious actions are impious and all pious actions pious through one form, or don't you remember?

EUTHYPHRO: I do.

SOCRATES: Tell me then what this form itself is, so that I may look upon it and, using it as a model, say that any action of yours or another's that is of that kind is pious, and if it is not that it is not.

EUTHYPHRO: If that is how you want it, Socrates, that is how I will tell you.

SOCRATES: That is what I want.

EUTHYPHRO: Well then, what is dear to the gods is pious, what is not is impious.

SOCRATES: Splendid, Euthyphro! You have now answered in the way I wanted. Whether your answer is true I do not know yet, but you will obviously show me that what you say is true.

EUTHYPHRO: Certainly.

SOCRATES: Come then, let us examine what we mean. An action or a man dear to the gods is pious, but an action or a man hated by the gods is impious. They are not the same, but quite opposite, the pious and the impious. Is that not so?

EUTHYPHRO: It is indeed.

SOCRATES: And that seems to be a good statement?

EUTHYPHRO: I think so, Socrates.

SOCRATES: We have also stated that the gods are in a state of discord, that they are at odds with each other, Euthyphro, and that they are at enmity with each other. Has that, too, been said?

EUTHYPHRO: It has.

SOCRATES: What are the subjects of difference that cause hatred and anger? Let us look at it this way. If you and I were to differ about numbers as to which is the greater, would this difference make us enemies and angry with each other, or would we proceed to count and soon resolve our difference about this?

EUTHYPHRO: We would certainly do so.

SOCRATES: Again, if we differed about the larger and the smaller, we would turn to measurement and soon cease to differ.

EUTHYPHRO: That is so.

SOCRATES: And about the heavier and the lighter, we would resort to weighing and be reconciled.

EUTHYPHRO: Of course.

SOCRATES: What subject of difference would make us angry and hostile to each other if we were unable to come to a decision? Perhaps you do not have an answer ready, but examine as I tell you whether these subjects are the just and the unjust, the beautiful and the ugly, the good and the bad. Are these not the subjects of difference about which, when we are unable to come to a satisfactory decision, you and I and other men become hostile to each other whenever we do?

EUTHYPHRO: That is the difference, Socrates, about those subjects.

SOCRATES: What about the gods, Euthyphro? If indeed they have differences, will it not be about these same subjects?

EUTHYPHRO: It certainly must be so.

SOCRATES: Then according to your argument, my good Euthyphro, different gods consider different things to be just, beautiful, ugly, good, and bad, for they would not be at odds with one another unless they differed about these subjects, would they?

EUTHYPHRO: You are right.

SOCRATES: And they like what each of them considers beautiful, good, and just, and hate the opposites of these?

EUTHYPHRO: Certainly.

SOCRATES: But you say that the same things are considered just by some gods and unjust by others, and as they dispute about these things they are at odds and at war with each other. Is that not so?

EUTHYPHRO: It is.

SOCRATES: The same things then are loved by the gods and hated by the gods, and would be both god-loved and god-hated.

EUTHYPHRO: It seems likely.

SOCRATES: And the same things would be both pious and impious, according to this argument?

EUTHYPHRO: I'm afraid so.

SOCRATES: So you did not answer my question, you surprising man. I did not ask you what same thing is both pious and impious, and it appears that what is loved by the gods is also hated by them. So it is in no way surprising if your present action, namely punishing your father, may be pleasing to Zeus but displeasing to Cronus and Uranus, pleasing to Hephaestus but displeasing to Hera, and so with any other gods who differ from each other on this subject.

EUTHYPHRO: I think, Socrates, that on this subject no gods would differ from one another, that whoever has killed anyone unjustly should pay the penalty.

SOCRATES: Well now, Euthyphro, have you ever heard any man maintaining that one who has killed or done anything else unjustly should not pay the penalty?

EUTHYPHRO: They never cease to dispute on this subject, both elsewhere and in the courts, for when they have committed many wrongs they do and say anything to avoid the penalty.

SOCRATES: Do they agree they have done wrong, Euthyphro, and in spite of so agreeing do they nevertheless say they should not be punished?

EUTHYPHRO: No, they do not agree on that point.

SOCRATES: So they do not say or do just anything. For they do not venture to say this, or dispute that they must not pay the penalty if they have done wrong, but I think they deny doing wrong. Is that not so?

EUTHYPHRO: That is true.

SOCRATES: Then they do not dispute that the wrongdoer must be punished, but they may disagree as to who the wrongdoer is, what he did, and when.

EUTHYPHRO: You are right.

SOCRATES: Do not the gods have the same experience, if indeed they are at odds with each other about the just and the unjust, as your argument maintains? Some assert that they wrong one another, while others deny it, but no one among gods or men ventures to say that the wrongdoer must not be punished.

EUTHYPHRO: Yes, that is true, Socrates, as to the main point.

SOCRATES: And those who disagree, whether men or gods, dispute about each action, if indeed the gods disagree. Some say it is done justly, others unjustly. Is that not so?

EUTHYPHRO: Yes, indeed.

SOCRATES: Come now, my dear Euthyphro, tell me, too, that I may become wiser, what proof you have that all the gods consider that man to have been killed unjustly who became a murderer while in your service, was bound by the master of his victim, and died in his bonds before the one who bound him found out from the seers what was to be done with him, and that it is right for a son to denounce and to prosecute his father on behalf of such a man. Come, try to show me a clear sign that all the gods definitely believe this action to be right. If you can give me adequate proof of this, I shall never cease to extol your wisdom.

EUTHYPHRO: This is perhaps no light task, Socrates, though I could show you very clearly.

SOCRATES: I understand that you think me more dull-witted than the jury, as you will obviously show them that these actions were unjust and that all the gods hate such actions.

EUTHYPHRO: I will show it to them clearly, Socrates, if only they will listen to me.

SOCRATES: They will listen if they think you show them well. But this thought came to me as you were speaking, and I am examining it, saying to myself: "If Euthyphro shows me conclusively that all the gods consider such a death unjust, to what greater extent have I learned from him the nature of piety and impiety? This action would then, it seems, be hated by the gods, but the pious and the impious were not thereby now defined, for what is hated by the gods has also been shown to be loved by them." So I will not insist on this point; let us assume, if you wish, that all the gods consider this unjust and that they all hate it. However, is this the correction we are making in our discussion, that what all the gods hate is impious, and what they all love is pious, and that what some gods love and others hate is neither or both? Is that how you now wish us to define piety and impiety?

EUTHYPHRO: What prevents us from doing so, Socrates?

SOCRATES: For my part nothing, Euthyphro, but you look whether on your part this proposal will enable you to teach me most easily what you promised.

EUTHYPHRO: I would certainly say that the pious is what all the gods love, and the opposite, what all the gods hate, is the impious.

SOCRATES: Then let us again examine whether that is a sound statement, or do we let it pass, and if one of us, or someone else, merely says that something is so, do we accept that it is so? Or should we examine what the speaker means?

EUTHYPHRO: We must examine it, but I certainly think that this is now a fine statement.

SOCRATES: We shall soon know better whether it is. Consider this: Is the pious being loved by the gods because it is pious, or is it pious because it is being loved by the gods?

EUTHYPHRO: I don't know what you mean, Socrates.

SOCRATES: I shall try to explain more clearly: we speak of something carried and something carrying, of something led and something leading, of something seen and something seeing, and you understand that these things are all different from one another and how they differ?

EUTHYPHRO: I think I do.

SOCRATES: So there is also something loved and—a different thing—something loving.

EUTHYPHRO: Of course.

SOCRATES: Tell me then whether the thing carried is a carried thing because it is being carried, or for some other reason?

EUTHYPHRO: No, that is the reason.

SOCRATES. And the thing led is so because it is being led, and the thing seen because it is being seen?

EUTHYPHRO: Certainly.

SOCRATES: It is not being seen because it is a thing seen but on the contrary it is a thing seen because it is being seen; nor is it because it is something led that it is being led but because it is being led that it is something led; nor is something being carried because it is something carried, but it is something carried because it is being carried. Is what I want to say clear, Euthyphro? I want to say this, namely, that if anything is being changed or is being affected in any way, it is not being changed because it is something changed, but rather it is something changed because it is being changed; nor is it being affected because it is something affected, but it is something affected because it is being affected. Or do you not agree?

EUTHYPHRO: I do.

SOCRATES: Is something loved either something changed or something affected by something?

EUTHYPHRO: Certainly.

SOCRATES: So it is in the same case as the things just mentioned; it is not being loved by those who love it because it is something loved, but it is something loved because it is being loved by them?

EUTHYPHRO: Necessarily.

SOCRATES: What then do we say about the pious, Euthyphro? Surely that it is being loved by all the gods, according to what you say?

EUTHYPHRO: Yes.

SOCRATES: Is it being loved because it is pious, or for some other reason?

EUTHYPHRO: For no other reason.

SOCRATES: It is being loved then because it is pious, but it is not pious because it is being loved?

EUTHYPHRO: Apparently.

SOCRATES: And yet it is something loved and god-loved because it is being loved by the gods?

EUTHYPHRO: Of course.

SOCRATES: Then the god-loved is not the same as the pious, Euthyphro, nor the pious the same as the god-loved, as you say it is, but one differs from the other.

EUTHYPHRO: How so, Socrates?

SOCRATES: Because we agree that the pious is being loved for this reason, that it is pious, but it is not pious because it is being loved. Is that not so?

EUTHYPHRO: Yes.

SOCRATES: And that the god-loved, on the other hand, is so because it is being loved by the gods, by the very fact of being loved, but it is not being loved because it is god-loved.

EUTHYPHRO: True.

SOCRATES: But if the god-loved and the pious were the same, my dear Euthyphro, then if the pious was being loved because it was pious, the god-loved would also be being loved because it was god-loved; and if the god-loved was god-loved because it was being loved by the gods, then the pious would also be pious because it was being loved by the gods. But now you see that they are in opposite cases as being altogether different from each other: the one is such as to be loved because it is being loved, the other is being loved because it is such as to be loved. I'm afraid, Euthyphro, that when you were asked what piety is, you did not wish to make its nature clear to me, but you told me an affect or a quality of it, that the pious has the quality of being loved by all the gods, but you have not yet told me what the pious is.

Plato: Euthyphro

1. What is Euthyphro's first answer to Socrates's question about the nature of piety? Why does Socrates find this answer to be inadequate?
2. In his second attempt to answer Socrates's question, Euthyphro suggests that "what is dear to the gods is pious, what is not is impious." Socrates points out that the gods sometimes disagree (according to the traditional religious views of ancient Greece). Why does this raise a

problem for the view in question? Is there any analogous problem for the monotheistic theory that what God commands is morally right?

3. The most famous question of the dialogue comes when Socrates asks: "Is the pious being loved by the gods because it is pious, or is it pious because it is being loved by the gods?" How does Socrates attempt to explain this question when Euthyphro does not understand? What exactly does the question mean?

4. When Euthyphro suggests that the gods love the pious because it is pious, Socrates responds with the complaint, "you have not yet told me what the pious is." Why does Socrates say this? Is he correct?

5. Suppose Euthyphro were to claim that the pious is pious because it is loved by the gods. What objections might Socrates raise to this proposal?

7

Natural Goodness

Philippa Foot

In this excerpt from her book *Natural Goodness* (2001), Philippa Foot (1920–2010) argues that we can derive moral norms from so-called natural norms—those that tell us how things ought to be, given insights about their nature. Foot argues that we have no reservations about assessing plants and animals as better or worse members of their species, depending on how well they measure up to natural norms. A deer's nature, for instance, includes, among other things, an ability to run swiftly; a male peacock is, by nature, able to fan its tail in a bright, attractive way. Such natural norms enable us to assess a deer as deficient if it can only hobble along, and a male peacock as doing well if it is, indeed, able to offer an attractive display.

Foot suggests that things are essentially the same when it comes to human beings. The natural norms that apply to us, of course, will not be just the same as those that apply to plants and animals. Still, we can derive standards for how we ought to be, and what we ought to do, based on insights about human nature. This places her latest views within a long tradition of natural law thinkers, who have sought to base morality on features of human nature.

Philippa Foot, from *Natural Goodness* (2001), pp. 26–34, 41–44, 47. By permission of Oxford University Press.

Natural Norms

Judgements of goodness and badness can have, it seems, a special 'grammar' when the subject belongs to a living thing, whether plant, animal, or human being. This, at least, is what I argue in this book. I think that this special category of goodness is easily overlooked; perhaps because we make so many evaluations of other kinds, as when we assess non-living things in the natural world, such as soil or weather, or again assess artefacts either made by humans as are houses and bridges, or made by animals as are the nests of birds or beavers' dams. But the goodness predicated in these latter cases, like goodness predicated to living things when they are evaluated in a relationship to members of species other than their own, is what I should like to call secondary goodness. It is in this derivative way that we can speak of the goodness of, for example, soil or weather, as such things are related to plants, to animals, or to us. And we also ascribe this secondary goodness to living things, as, for instance, to specimens of plants that grow as we want them to grow, or to horses that carry us as we want to be carried, while artefacts are often named and evaluated by the need or interest that they chiefly serve. By contrast, 'natural' goodness, as I define it, which is attributable only to living things themselves and to their parts, characteristics, and operations, is intrinsic or 'autonomous' goodness in that it depends directly on the relation of an individual to the 'life form' of its species. On barren Mars there is no natural goodness, and even secondary goodness can be attributed to things on that planet only by relating them to our own lives, or to living things existing elsewhere. . . .

My belief is that for all the differences that there are, as we shall see, between the evaluation of plants and animals and their parts and characteristics on the one hand, and the moral evaluation of humans on the other, we shall find that these evaluations share a basic logical structure and status. I want to suggest that moral defect is a form of natural defect not as different as is generally supposed from defect in sub-rational living things. So this is what I shall go on to argue, after a discussion of 'natural goodness' as it is found in sub-rational living things.

Firstly, therefore, I shall explore natural goodness in plants and in animals other than human beings. For help I shall turn to a paper published by Michael Thompson: a paper I admire very much.

Michael Thompson's subject in this paper, which is called 'The Representation of Life', is the description of living things. His thesis is that to understand certain distinctive ways in which we describe individual organisms, we must recognize the logical dependence of these descriptions on the nature of the species to which the individual belongs. Species-dependence is his leitmotif. For this reason he concerns himself with propositions of the form 'S's are F' or 'The S is F', where 'S' holds a place for the name of a species (or 'life form' as he is ready to say for the sake of those who want to give 'species' a technical definition) and 'F' a place for a predicate; so that a representative sentence would be 'Rabbits are herbivores' or 'The rabbit is a herbivore'. He contrasts the logical form of the sentences

> S's are F   (Rabbits are herbivores)
> S's do V   (Rabbits eat grass)

with

> N.N. is F   (Mrs Muff is a rabbit)
> N.N. is doing V (Mrs Muff is eating grass).

He points out, referring back to an early article by Elizabeth Anscombe, a peculiarity of the *logical form* of the first pair of sentences: that they are logically unquantifiable.[1] They do not speak of an individual rabbit, though the same verbal form can of course be used with that reference, as when the conjurer says to his wife 'The rabbit does not look well.' Nor, of course, do the propositions that interest Michael Thompson predicate something of every member of the species: 'Cats are four-legged but Tibbles may have only three.' Elizabeth Anscombe's original example concerned the number of teeth that human beings have—which is 32, though most human beings have lost quite a few and some never had the full complement. It is arguable that if 'The S is F' (understood in this way) is true then at least some S's must be F. But even if this is so, 'Some S's are F' is clearly not the whole of what such a proposition asserts. Thompson speaks in this context of a 'natural-history account' of the life form or species: of how creatures of this kind live. And he points out, as part of his insistence on the way in which descriptions of individuals depend on the species to which they belong, that without this reference, 'life activities' such as eating or reproducing cannot even be identified in an individual. Eating, for instance, is essentially, conceptually, related to nourishment, and could not be conclusively identified by a story about the taking in, crushing, transforming, and spewing out of substances since, for all that, its purpose might be not

---

1 Anscombe, "Modern Moral Philosophy," in *Collected Philosophical Papers*, pp. 111, 38.

the maintenance of tissue but, say, skunk-like defence. Mitosis occurs in amoebae and human beings, and is given a uniform description in textbooks: in the first, however, it is reproduction of an individual organism, but in the second not.[2]

Thompson also points out peculiarities of the time references found within such propositions. It is said for instance that certain animals mate at a certain time of the year, and give birth, or lay eggs, so many weeks or months later; but this is 'typically a matter of before and after—"in the spring", "in the fall" . . . and not of now and then . . . and when I was young and so forth.'[3] Natural-history sentences, which Thompson also calls 'Aristotelian categoricals', speak of the life cycle of individuals of a given species.[4] In one way, therefore, this is the time-span with which they have to do. In another way, however, a longer time reference is needed, since we must speak of *reproduction*, and the characteristics of a single individual cannot determine what will count as *another of the same*.

It will no doubt be objected here that reproduction is in fact not fixed, since species themselves are subject to change. This is of course important, and it means that Aristotelian categoricals must take account of sub-species adapted to local conditions. The history of a species is not, however, the subject with which Aristotelian categoricals deal. Their truth is truth about a species at a given historical time, and it is only the relative stability of at least the most general features of the different species of living things that makes these propositions possible at all. They tell how a kind of plant or animal, considered at a particular time and in its natural habitat, develops, sustains itself, defends itself, and reproduces. It is only in so far as 'stills' can be made from the moving picture of the evolution of species that we can have a natural history account of the life of a particular kind of living thing. And it is only in so far as we have a 'natural history account' that we can have a 'vital description' of individuals here and now.

Let us now ask how all this is relevant to the normative judgements that we make about plants and animals when we say, for instance, that a plant in our garden is diseased, or not growing properly, or that a certain lioness is a neglectful parent, or a particular rabbit not as reproductive as a rabbit should be. Thompson suggests that the relation between the Aristotelian categorical and the evaluative assessment is very close indeed. In

---

2 Thompson, "The Representation of Life," pp. 272–273.

3 Ibid., p. 282.

4 Ibid., p. 267.

fact, he says that if we have a true natural-history proposition to the effect that S's are F, then if a certain individual S—the individual here and now or then and there—is not F it is therefore not as it should be, but rather weak, diseased, or in some other way defective.[5] The evaluative assessment is the product of propositions of the two logically different kinds.

Essentially, I think that Thompson is right about this, although I seem to see a gap in his account of Aristotelian categoricals that has to be filled in here. For I think he has not said enough to isolate the kind of proposition that will yield evaluations of individual organisms. His talk of 'natural-history propositions' was perhaps misleading in that it did not explicitly separate out what I would like to call the teleological from the non-teleological attachment of predicates to a subject term that is the name of a species. Consider, for instance, a sentence such as 'The blue tit has a round blue patch on its head.' This is superficially like 'The male peacock has a brightly coloured tail', but in a way of course it is not. For, on the assumption that colour of head plays no part in the life of the blue tit, it is in this respect quite unlike the colour of the male peacock's tail: there would be nothing wrong with the blue tit in my garden *in that* it had a drab-coloured head; and the peculiarity might or might not accompany a defect. So how are we to distinguish these two types of propositions? Or how, again, are we to distinguish the case of leaves rustling when it is windy from that of flowers opening when the sun comes out? It is natural to say that the rustling of its leaves plays no part in the life of a tree, whereas pollination is gained by a display of scent and colours in sunshine. But then we must ask what we mean by 'playing a part in the life' of a living thing. What counts as 'its life' in this context? And what is 'playing a part'?

There emerges here the special link, mentioned but not explored by Thompson, between his 'Aristotelian categoricals' and teleology in living things. Aristotelian categoricals are propositions having to do with the way that certain features appear or that certain things are done in organisms of a given species either by the whole organism or by their characteristics or parts. But, speaking now for myself rather than for Thompson, I should say that to obtain the connection between Aristotelian categoricals and evaluation another move must be made. I should say that in plants and non-human animals these things all have to do, directly or indirectly, with self-maintenance, as by defence and the obtaining of nourishment, or with the reproduction of the individual, as by the building of nests. This is

---

5 Ibid., p. 295.

'the life' characteristic of the kind of animal with which the categoricals here have to do. What 'plays a part' in this life is that which is causally and teleologically related to it, as putting out roots is related to obtaining nourishment, and attracting insects is related to reproduction in plants.

We start from the fact that there is a basis for the Aristotelian categorical that does not come from the counting of heads. What is this basis? In what was said about the blue tits and the peacocks it was suggested that some but not all general propositions about a species have to do with the teleology of living things of this kind. There is an Aristotelian categorical about the species *peacock* to the effect that the male peacock displays his brilliant tail *in order to* attract a female during the mating season. The display serves this purpose. Let us call such language, purposive language. But be careful here! Where something that S's do is, in this sense, purposive we should beware of slipping over into saying of an individual S that it *has* this purpose when it does this thing. Plants grow upwards in order to get to the light, but it is fanciful to say that that is what my honeysuckle is trying to do or that that is 'its end'. Migrating birds flying off in order to reach the southern insects do not *have* this as their end or purpose even though it could be said to be the end or purpose of the operation. What is crucial to all teleological propositions is the expectation of an answer to the question 'What part does it play in the life cycle of things of the species S?' In other words, 'What is its function?' or 'What good does it do?' . . .

Thus, evaluation of an individual living thing in its own right, with no reference to our interests or desires, is possible where there is intersection of two types of propositions: on the one hand, Aristotelian categoricals (life-form descriptions relating to the species), and on the other, propositions about particular individuals that are the subject of evaluation.

It will be useful to remind ourselves at this point of the elements that came to light in the earlier discussion of 'good' and 'bad' as applied to characteristics and operations of plants and animals.

(a) There was the life cycle, which in those cases consisted roughly of self-maintenance and reproduction.

(b) There was the set of propositions saying *how* for a certain species this was achieved: how nourishment was obtained, how development took place, what defences were available, and how reproduction was secured.

(c) From all this, *norms* were derived, requiring, for instance, a certain degree of swiftness in the deer, night vision in the owl, and cooperative hunting in the wolf.

(d) By the application of these norms to an individual member of the relevant species it (this individual) was judged to be as it should be or, by contrast, to a lesser or greater degree defective in a certain respect.

There are here many details that are not germane to the aim of this book. But something more must be said about the way in which Aristotelian categoricals about the 'how and what' of the life cycle determine normative assessments of individual living things in the here and now or there and then of historical place and time.

As illustration let us consider the Aristotelian categorical stating that the deer is an animal whose form of defence is flight. From this we know that it is a defect, a weakness, in an individual deer if it is slow of foot. Swiftness, as opposed to fierceness or camouflage, is what fits it to escape from its predators. But two remarks must be added about this. In the first place, swiftness does no more than *fit* it to survive: in some circumstances even the greatest speed possible for this type of animal would not be enough. Moreover, by chance it may sometimes be that the fastest deer fleeing from one predator is the very one that gets caught in a trap.[5] Secondly, what is excellence, and what defect, is relative to the natural habitat of the species. Even in a zoo a fleeing animal like a deer that cannot run well is so far forth defective and not as it should be, in spite of the fact that, as this particular individual is by chance placed, this may be no disadvantage for defence or feeding or mating or rearing the young. . . .

Transition to Human Beings

The idea that any features and operations of humans could be evaluated in the same way as those of plants and animals may provoke instant opposition. For to say that this is possible is to imply that some at least of our judgements of goodness and badness in human beings are given truth or falsity by the conditions of human life. And even if it is allowed that certain evaluations of this kind are possible—those vaguely thought of perhaps as 'merely biological'—there is bound to be scepticism about the possibility that 'moral evaluation' could be like this. Surely, it will be urged, we must start afresh when thinking about the subject of moral philosophy. I believe, however, that this is only partly true.

The question remains, however, as to whether once we have made the transition from sub-rational to rational beings we may not need a new

---

5   As it may be the skillful archer who fails to hit a target in the presence of a freak gust of wind.

theory of evaluation. Surely, my critics will say, it must be so, given the part that the life cycle of a plant or animal rightly played in Michael Thompson's account of the conceptual structure within which the evaluation of properties and operations of individual organisms had a place. For such an evaluation is based on the general relation of this kind of feature to the pattern of life that is the *good of* creatures of this species. But how could we possibly see human good in the same terms? The life cycle of a plant or animal ultimately has to do with what is involved in development, self-sustenance, and reproduction. Are we really going to suggest that human strengths and weaknesses, and even virtues and vices, are to be identified by reference to such 'biological' cycles?

This challenge, ill-conceived as it is in suggesting that the natural-history account of human beings could be explained in terms of a merely animal life, raises a most important and difficult topic. For it is true that in the course of describing 'natural goodness' in plants and animals we have implicitly adverted to the idea of the good of a living thing as well as its goodness in various respects, and the two ideas, though related, are distinct. That this is so can be seen if we think about what it means to benefit a plant or an animal. Very often, to be sure, a living thing is benefited by itself being made better, and there must be a systematic connection between natural goodness and benefit—whether reflexive or other-related as in the case of the stinging bees. But it does not follow that benefit of either kind follows goodness whatever circumstance an individual happens to be in. In our earlier example it was the swiftest deer, ahead of the others, that fell into the hunter's trap; and the properly acting bee that stings a gardener may well bring about the destruction of the nest.

Whether an individual plant or animal actually succeeds in living the life that it is its good to live depends on chance as well as on its own qualities. But its own goodness or defect is conceptually determined by the interaction of natural habitat and natural (species-general) 'strategies' for survival and reproduction. What conceptually determines goodness in a feature or operation is the relation, for the species, of that feature or operation to survival and reproduction, because it is in that that good lies in the botanical and zoological worlds. At that point questions of 'How?' and 'Why?' and 'What for?' come to an end. But clearly this is not true when we come to human beings.

Take reproduction, for instance. Lack of capacity to reproduce is a defect in a human being. But choice of childlessness and even celibacy is not thereby shown to be defective choice, because human good is not the same as plant or animal good. The bearing and rearing of children is not an ultimate good in human life, because other elements of good such as the demands of work to be done may give a man or woman reason to renounce family life. And the great (if often troubling) good of having children has to do with the love and ambition of parents for children, the special role of grandparents, and many other things that simply do not belong to animal life.

Moreover, the good of survival itself is something more complex for human beings than for animals; even for the animals closest to us. The human desire to live is, of course, instinctual, but it often also has to do with a desperate hope that something may yet turn out well in the future. And it seems that the preciousness of the unique memories that each person has is part of what he or she may cling to even in the most terrible of circumstances. In other words, the teleological story goes beyond a reference to survival itself.

The idea of human good is deeply problematic. One may be inclined to think of it as happiness, but much would have to be said before that could be so understood as to be true, and I shall discuss this in a later chapter. Here I want only to recall that Wittgenstein famously said on his deathbed, 'Tell them I have had a wonderful life.' The example should teach us not to be too ready to speak of every good life as 'a happy life': Wittgenstein surely did not have a happy life, being too tormented and self-critical for that.

Thus the idea of a good life for a human being, and the question of its relation to happiness, is each deeply problematic. And, moreover, there is so much diversity in human beings and human cultures that the schema of natural normativity may seem to be inapplicable from the start. Nevertheless, for all the diversities of human life, it is possible to give some quite general account of human necessities, that is, of what is quite generally needed for human good, if only by starting from the negative idea of human deprivation. For then we see at once that human good depends on many characteristics and capacities that are not needed even by animals, never mind by plants. There are, for instance, physical properties such as the kind of larynx that allows of the myriad sounds that make up human language, as well as the kind of hearing that can distinguish them. Moreover, human beings need the mental capacity for learning language; they also need powers of imagination that allow them to understand stories, to join in songs and dances—and to laugh at jokes. Without such things human beings may survive and reproduce themselves, but they are deprived. And what could be more natural than to say on this account that we have introduced the subject of possible human defects; calling them 'natural defects' as we used these terms in the discussion of plant and animal life?

We can see, moreover, that, as with animals, some defects have as we might say 'a reflexive role', in that the deprivation comes primarily to the defective individual; but that there are some that chiefly or at least most directly affect other people. We might think here, for instance, of the failure of maternal affection, or of (non-iterated) 'prisoner's dilemma' cases where each person gains from the action of others but loses through his own. The way of solving the dilemma, however we should understand its details, depends on our human way of thinking. We act within a language that allows us to say 'I owe it to him' or 'I suppose I should play my part' (as we nowadays think, for instance, of taking a bus rather than a car, to reduce traffic on the road, knowing that we ourselves may need to get somewhere urgently by car some other time). There are also human enjoyments such as songs and ceremonials that need cooperative participation. And, further, human societies depend on especially talented individuals playing special roles in a society's life. As some species of animals need a lookout, or as herds of elephants need an old she-elephant to lead them to a watering hole, so human societies need leaders, explorers, and artists. Failure to perform a special role can here be a defect in a man or woman who is not ready to contribute what he or she alone—or best—can give. There is also something wrong with the rest of us if we do not support those of genius, or even special talent, in their work.

In spite of the diversity of human goods—the elements that can make up good human lives—it is therefore possible that the concept of a good human life plays the same part in determining goodness of human characteristics and operations that the concept of flourishing plays in the determination of goodness in plants and animals. So far the conceptual structure seems to be intact. Nor is there any reason to think that it could not be in place even in the evaluations that are nowadays spoken of as the special domain of morality. This special domain—and more generally that of goodness of the will—will be discussed in detail in the next two chapters. But if we ask whether Geach was right to say that human beings need virtues as bees need stings . . . , the answer is surely that he was. Men and women need to be industrious and tenacious of purpose not only so as to be able to house, clothe, and feed themselves, but also to pursue human ends having to do with love and friendship. They need the ability to form family ties, friendships, and special relations with neighbours. They also need codes of conduct. And how could they have all these things without virtues such as loyalty, fairness, kindness, and in certain circumstances obedience? . . .

Thus the structure of the derivation is the same whether we derive an evaluation of the roots of a particular tree or the action of a particular human being. The meaning of the words 'good' and 'bad' is not different when used of features of plants on the one hand and humans on the other, but is rather the same as applied, in judgements of natural goodness and defect, in the case of all living things.

Philippa Foot: Natural Goodness

1. What is the difference, according to Foot, between "natural goodness" and "secondary goodness"?
2. Consider the sentence "Cats are four-legged." Foot points out that such a sentence doesn't claim that *all* cats have four legs. Yet it also claims more than the sentence "Some cats are four-legged." What, then, does such a sentence mean?
3. Foot says that a creature is *defective* if it does not possess the traits that "fit it to survive" in its "natural habitat." It follows that a deer is defective if it is unable to run very fast, even if that deer is in a zoo and doesn't need to run from any predators. Is this a plausible claim?
4. What is Foot's objection to the view that a good life is just a happy life? Do you find this objection persuasive?
5. Foot says that the words "good" and "bad" mean the same thing when applied to plants as when applied to humans. What does she mean by this claim? Do you agree with her?

8

Extreme and Restricted Utilitarianism

J. J. C. Smart

J. J. C. Smart here introduces us to two forms of utilitarianism, extreme and restricted, which nowadays go by the name of act and rule utilitarianism, respectively. Extreme utilitarianism makes the morality of actions depend entirely on their results, requiring us always to do that action, among all available to us at the time, which will yield the greatest overall happiness. Restricted (i.e., rule) utilitarianism, by contrast, assesses the rightness of actions based on whether they adhere to rules that, if embraced by all, would yield optimal happiness.

Smart himself endorses extreme utilitarianism, and presents a criticism of restricted utilitarianism that has been very influential. Suppose that we are faced with a situation in which we must break a moral rule in order to maximize happiness. Since the goal of such rules, from a utilitarian standpoint, is to maximize the world's happiness, the only rational thing to do is to break that rule. And yet restricted utilitarians insist that we honor the rule, even when doing so undermines the ultimate utilitarian goal. That is irrational, says Smart, and gives us decisive reason to prefer the extreme version of utilitarianism.

1

Utilitarianism is the doctrine that the rightness of actions is to be judged by their consequences. What do we mean by "actions" here? Do we mean particular actions or do we mean classes of actions? According to which way we interpret the word "actions" we get two different theories, both of which merit the appellation "utilitarian."

(1) If by "actions" we mean particular individual actions we get the sort of doctrine held by Bentham, Sidgwick, and Moore. According to this doctrine we test individual actions by their consequences, and general rules, like "keep promises," are mere rules of thumb which we use only to avoid the necessity of estimating the probable consequences of our actions at every step. The rightness or wrongness of keeping a promise on a particular occasion depends only on the goodness or badness of the consequences of keeping or of breaking the promise on that particular occasion. Of course part of the consequences of breaking the promise, and a part to which we will normally ascribe decisive importance, will be the weakening of faith in the institution of promising. However, if the goodness of the consequences of breaking the rule is *in toto* greater than the goodness of the consequences of keeping it, then we must break the rule, irrespective of whether the goodness of the consequences *of everybody's* obeying the rule is or is not greater than the consequences of *everybody's* breaking it. To put it shortly, rules do not matter, save *per accidens* as rules of thumb and as *de facto* social institutions with which the utilitarian has to reckon when estimating consequences. I shall call this doctrine "extreme utilitarianism."

(2) A more modest form of utilitarianism has recently become fashionable. The doctrine is to be found in Toulmin's book *The Place of Reason in Ethics*, in Nowell-Smith's *Ethics* (though I think Nowell-Smith has qualms), in John Austin's *Lectures on Jurisprudence* (Lecture II), and even in J. S. Mill, if Urmson's interpretation of him is correct (*Philosophical Quarterly*, vol. 3, pp. 33–9, 1953). Part of its charm is that it appears to resolve the dispute in moral philosophy between intuitionists and utilitarians in a way which is very neat. The above philosophers hold, or seem to hold, that moral rules are more than rules of thumb. In general the rightness of an action is *not* to be tested by evaluating its consequences but only by considering whether or not it falls under a certain rule. Whether the rule is to be considered an acceptable moral rule, is, however, to be decided by considering the consequences of adopting the rule.

Broadly, then, actions are to be tested by rules and rules by consequences. The only cases in which we must test an individual action directly by its consequences are (a) when the action comes under two different rules, one of which enjoins it and one of which forbids it, and (b) when there is no rule whatever that governs the given case. I shall call this doctrine "restricted utilitarianism."

2

For an extreme utilitarian moral rules are rules of thumb. In practice the extreme utilitarian will mostly guide his conduct by appealing to the rules ("do not lie," "do not break promises," etc.) of common sense morality. This is not because there is anything sacrosanct in the rules themselves but because he can argue that probably he will most often act in an extreme utilitarian way if he does not think as a utilitarian. For one thing, actions have frequently to be done in a hurry. Imagine a man seeing a person drowning. He jumps in and rescues him. There is no time to reason the matter out, but usually this will be the course of action which an extreme utilitarian would recommend if he did reason the matter out. If, however, the man drowning had been drowning in a river near Berchtesgaden in 1938, and if he had had the well known black forelock and moustache of Adolf Hitler, an extreme utilitarian would, if he had time, work out the probability of the man's being the villainous dictator, and if the probability were high enough he would, on extreme utilitarian grounds, leave him to drown. The rescuer, however, has not time. He trusts to his instincts and dives in and rescues the man. And this trusting to instincts and to moral rules can be justified on extreme utilitarian grounds. Furthermore, an extreme utilitarian who knew that the drowning man was Hitler would nevertheless praise the rescuer, not condemn him. For by praising the man he is strengthening a courageous and benevolent disposition of mind, and in general this disposition has great positive utility. (Next time, perhaps, it will be Winston Churchill that the man saves!) We must never forget that an extreme utilitarian may praise actions which he knows to be wrong. Saving Hitler was wrong, but it was a member of a class of actions which are generally right, and the motive to do actions of this class is in general an optimific one. In considering questions of praise and blame it is not the expediency of the praised or blamed action that is at issue, but the expediency of the praise. It can be expedient to praise an inexpedient action and inexpedient to praise an expedient one.

Lack of time is not the only reason why an extreme utilitarian may, on extreme utilitarian principles, trust to rules of common sense morality. He knows that in particular cases where his own interests are involved his calculations are likely to be biased in his own favor. Suppose that he is unhappily married and is deciding whether to get divorced. He will in all probability greatly exaggerate his own unhappiness (and possibly his wife's) and greatly underestimate the harm done to his children by the break up of the family. He will probably also underestimate the likely harm done by the weakening of the general faith in marriage vows. So probably he will come to the correct extreme utilitarian conclusion if he does not in this instance think as an extreme utilitarian but trusts to common sense morality.

There are many more and subtle points that could be made in connection with the relation between extreme utilitarianism and the morality of common sense. All those that I have just made and many more will be found in Book IV Chapters 3–5 of Sidgwick's *Methods of Ethics*. I think that this book is the best book ever written on ethics, and that these chapters are the best chapters of the book. As they occur so near the end of a very long book they are unduly neglected. I refer the reader, then, to Sidgwick for the classical exposition of the relation between (extreme) utilitarianism and the morality of common sense. One further point raised by Sidgwick in this connection is whether an (extreme) utilitarian ought on (extreme) utilitarian principles to propagate (extreme) utilitarianism among the public. As most people are not very philosophical and not good at empirical calculations, it is probable that they will most often act in an extreme utilitarian way if they do not try to think as extreme utilitarians. We have seen how easy it would be to misapply the extreme utilitarian criterion in the case of divorce. Sidgwick seems to think it quite probable that an extreme utilitarian should not propagate his doctrine too widely. However, the great danger to humanity comes nowadays on the plane of public morality—not private morality. There is a greater danger to humanity from the hydrogen bomb than from an increase of the divorce rate, regrettable though that might be, and there seems no doubt that extreme utilitarianism makes for good sense in international relations. When France walked out of the United Nations because she did not wish Morocco discussed, she said that she was within her rights because Morocco and Algiers are part of her metropolitan territory and nothing to do with UN. This was clearly a legalistic if not superstitious argument. We should not be concerned with the so-called "rights" of

France or any other country but with whether the cause of humanity would best be served by discussing Morocco in UN. (I am not saying that the answer to this is "Yes." There are good grounds for supposing that more harm than good would come by such a discussion.) I myself have no hesitation in saying that on extreme utilitarian principles we ought to propagate extreme utilitarianism as widely as possible. But Sidgwick had respectable reasons for suspecting the opposite.

The extreme utilitarian, then, regards moral rules as rules of thumb and as sociological facts that have to be taken into account when deciding what to do, just as facts of any other sort have to be taken into account. But in themselves they do not justify any action.

3

The restricted utilitarian regards moral rules as more than rules of thumb for short-circuiting calculations of consequences. Generally, he argues, consequences are not relevant at all when we are deciding what to do in a particular case. In general, they are relevant only to deciding what rules are good reasons for acting in a certain way in particular cases. This doctrine is possibly a good account of how the modern unreflective twentieth century Englishman often thinks about morality, but surely it is monstrous as an account of how it is most rational to think about morality. Suppose that there is a rule *R* and that in 99% of cases the best possible results are obtained by acting in accordance with *R*. Then clearly *R* is a useful rule of thumb; if we have not time or are not impartial enough to assess the consequences of an action it is an extremely good bet that the thing to do is to act in accordance with *R*. But is it not monstrous to suppose that if we *have* worked out the consequences and if we have perfect faith in the impartiality of our calculations, and if we *know* that in this instance to break *R* will have better results than to keep it, we should nevertheless obey the rule? Is it not to erect *R* into a sort of idol if we keep it when breaking it will prevent, say, some avoidable misery? Is not this a form of superstitious rule-worship (easily explicable psychologically) and not the rational thought of a philosopher?

The point may be made more clearly if we consider Mill's comparison of moral rules to the tables in the nautical almanac (*Utilitarianism*, Everyman Edition, pp. 22–3). This comparison of Mill's is adduced by Urmson as evidence that Mill was a restricted utilitarian, but I do not think that it will bear this interpretation at all. (Though I quite agree with Urmson that many other things said by Mill are in harmony with restricted rather than extreme utilitarianism. Probably Mill had never thought very much about the distinction and was arguing for utilitarianism, restricted or extreme, against other and quite non-utilitarian forms of moral argument.) Mill says: "Nobody argues that the art of navigation is not founded on astronomy, because sailors cannot wait to calculate the Nautical Almanac. Being rational creatures, they go out upon the sea of life with their minds made up on the common questions of right and wrong, as well as on many of the far more difficult questions of wise and foolish. . . . Whatever we adopt as the fundamental principle of morality, we require subordinate principles to apply it by." Notice that this is, as it stands, only an argument for subordinate principles as rules of thumb. The example of the nautical almanac is misleading because the information given in the almanac is in all cases the same as the information one would get if one made a long and laborious calculation from the original astronomical data on which the almanac is founded. Suppose, however, that astronomy were different. Suppose that the behavior of the sun, moon and planets was very nearly as it is now, but that on rare occasions there were peculiar irregularities and discontinuities, so that the almanac gave us rules of the form "in 99% of cases where the observations are such and such you can deduce that your position is so and so." Furthermore, let us suppose that there were methods which enabled us, by direct and laborious calculation from the original astronomical data, not using the rough and ready tables of the almanac, to get our correct position in 100% of cases. Seafarers might use the almanac because they never had time for the long calculations and they were content with a 99% chance of success in calculating their positions. Would it not be absurd, however, if they *did* make the direct calculation, and finding that it disagreed with the almanac calculation, nevertheless they ignored it and stuck to the almanac conclusion? Of course the case would be altered if there were a high enough probability of making slips in the direct calculation: then we might stick to the almanac result, liable to error though we knew it to be, simply because the direct calculation would be open to error for a different reason, the fallibility of the computer. This would be analogous to the case of the extreme utilitarian who abides by the conventional rule against the dictates of his utilitarian calculations simply because he thinks that his calculations are probably affected by personal bias. But if the navigator were sure of his direct calculations would he not be foolish to abide by his almanac? I conclude, then, that if we change our suppositions about astronomy and the almanac (to which there are no exceptions) to bring the case into line with that of morality (to whose rules there are exceptions), Mill's example loses its appearance of supporting the restricted form of utilitarianism. Let me say once more that I am not here concerned with how ordinary men think about morality but with how they ought to think. We could quite well imagine a race of sailors who acquired a superstitious reverence for their almanac, even though it was only right in 99% of cases, and who indignantly threw overboard any man who mentioned the possibility of a direct calculation. But would this behavior of the sailors be rational?

Let us consider a much discussed sort of case in which the extreme utilitarian might go against the conventional moral rule. I have promised to a friend, dying on a desert island from which I am subsequently rescued, that I will see that his fortune (over which I have control) is given to a jockey club. However, when I am rescued I decide that it would be better to give the money to a hospital, which can do more good with it. It may be argued that I am wrong to give the money to the hospital. But why? (*a*) The hospital can do more good with the money than the jockey club can. (*b*) The present case is unlike most cases of promising in that no one except me knows about the promise. In breaking the promise I am doing so with complete secrecy and am doing nothing to weaken the general faith in promises. That is, a factor, which would normally keep the extreme utilitarian from promise breaking even in otherwise unoptimific cases, does not at present operate. (*c*) There is no doubt a slight weakening in my own character as an habitual promise keeper, and moreover psychological tensions will be set up in me every time I am asked what the man made me promise him to do. For clearly I shall have to say that he made me promise to give the money to the hospital, and, since I am an habitual truth teller, this will go very much against the grain with me. Indeed I am pretty sure that in practice I myself would keep the promise. But we are not discussing what my moral habits would probably make me do; we are discussing what I ought to do. Moreover, we must not forget that even if it would be most rational of me to give the money to the hospital it would also be most rational of you to punish or condemn me if you did, most improbably, find out the truth (e.g. by finding a note washed ashore in a bottle). Furthermore, I would agree that though it was most rational of me to give the money to the hospital it would be most rational of you to condemn me for it. We revert again to Sidgwick's distinction between the utility of the action and the utility of the praise of it.

Many such issues are discussed by A. K. Stout[1] . . . It will be useful . . . to consider one . . . example that he gives. Suppose that during hot weather there is an edict that no water must be used for watering gardens. I have a garden and I reason that most people are sure to obey the edict, and that as the amount of water that I use will be by itself negligible no harm will be done if I use the water secretly. So I do use the water, thus producing some lovely flowers which give happiness to various people. Still, you may say, though the action was perhaps optimific, it was unfair and wrong.

There are several matters to consider. Certainly my action should be condemned. We revert once more to Sidgwick's distinction. A right action may be rationally condemned. Furthermore, this sort of offense is normally found out. If I have a wonderful garden when everybody else's is dry and brown there is only one explanation. So if I water my garden I am weakening my respect for law and order, and as this leads to bad results an extreme utilitarian would agree that I was wrong to water the garden. Suppose now that the case is altered and that I can keep the thing secret: there is a secluded part of the garden where I grow flowers which I give away anonymously to a home for old ladies. Are you still so sure that I did the wrong thing by watering my garden? However, this is still a weaker case than that of the hospital and the jockey club. There will be tensions set up within myself: my secret knowledge that I have broken the rule will make it hard for me to exhort others to keep the rule. These psychological ill effects in myself may be not inconsiderable: directly and indirectly they may lead to harm which is at least of the same order as the happiness that the old ladies get from the flowers. You can see that on an extreme utilitarian view there are two sides to the question.

So far I have been considering the duty of an extreme utilitarian in a predominantly non-utilitarian society. . . . I now pass on to a type of case which may be thought to be the trump card of restricted utilitarianism. Consider the rule of the road. It may be said that since all that matters is that everyone should do the same it is indifferent which rule we have, "go on the left hand side" or "go on the right hand side." Hence the only *reason* for going on the left hand side in British countries is that this is the rule. Here the rule does seem to be a reason, in itself, for acting in a certain way. I wish to argue against this. The rule in itself is not a reason for our actions. We would be perfectly justified in going on the right hand side if (*a*) we knew that the rule was to go on the left hand side, and (*b*) we were in a

---

1   "But Suppose Everybody Did the Same?," *Australasian Journal of Philosophy* vol. 32, pp. 1–29.

country peopled by super-anarchists who always on principle did the opposite of what they were told. This shows that the rule does not give us a reason for acting so much as an indication of the probable actions of others, which helps us to find out what would be our own most rational course of action. If we are in a country not peopled by anarchists, but by non-anarchist extreme Utilitarians, we expect, other things being equal, that they will keep rules laid down for them. Knowledge of the rule enables us to predict their behavior and to harmonize our own actions with theirs. The rule "keep to the left hand side," then, is not a logical *reason* for action but an anthropological *datum* for planning actions.

I conclude that in every case if there is a rule R the keeping of which is in general optimific, but such that in a special sort of circumstances the optimific behavior is to break R, then in these circumstances we should break R. Of course we must consider all the less obvious effects of breaking R, such as reducing people's faith in the moral order, before coming to the conclusion that to break R is right: in fact we shall rarely come to such a conclusion. Moral rules, on the extreme utilitarian view, are rules of thumb only, but they are not bad rules of thumb. But if we *do* come to the conclusion that we should break the rule and if we have weighed in the balance our own fallibility and liability to personal bias, what good reason remains for keeping the rule? I can understand "it is optimific" as a reason for action, but why should "it is a member of a class of actions which are usually optimific" or "it is a member of a class of actions which as a class are more optimific than any alternative general class" be a good reason? You might as well say that a person ought to be picked to play for Australia just because all his brothers have been, or that the Australian team should be composed entirely of the Harvey family because this would be better than composing it entirely of any other family. The extreme utilitarian does not appeal to artificial feelings, but only to our feelings of benevolence, and what better feelings can there be to appeal to? Admittedly we can have a pro-attitude to anything, even to rules, but such artificially begotten pro-attitudes smack of superstition. Let us get down to realities, human happiness and misery, and make these the objects of our pro-attitudes and anti-attitudes.

The restricted utilitarian might say that he is talking only of *morality*, not of such things as rules of the road. I am not sure how far this objection, if valid, would affect my argument, but in any case I would reply that as a philosopher I conceive of ethics as the study of how it would be *most rational* to act. If my opponent wishes to restrict the word "morality" to a narrower use he can have the word. The fundamental question is the question of rationality of action *in general*. Similarly if the restricted utilitarian were to appeal to ordinary usage and say "it might be most rational to leave Hitler to drown but it would surely not be *wrong* to rescue him," I should again let him have the words "right" and "wrong" and should stick to "rational" and "irrational." We already saw that it would be rational to praise Hitler's rescuer, even though it would have been most rational not to have rescued Hitler. In ordinary language, no doubt, "right" and "wrong" have not only the meaning "most rational to do" and "not most rational to do" but also have the meaning "praiseworthy" and "not praiseworthy." Usually to the utility of an action corresponds utility of praise of it, but as we saw, this is not always so. Moral language could thus do with tidying up, for example by reserving "right" for "most rational" and "good" as an epithet of praise for the motive from which the action sprang. It would be more becoming in a philosopher to try to iron out illogicalities in moral language and to make suggestions for its reform than to use it as a court of appeal whereby to perpetuate confusions.

J.J.C. Smart: Extreme and Restricted Utilitarianism

1. Extreme utilitarians hold that moral rules are "mere rules of thumb," while restricted utilitarians think that the rightness of an action is determined by "whether or not it falls under a certain rule." What exactly is the difference between these two views of moral rules?
2. According to Smart, we should sometimes praise actions we know to be wrong, and condemn actions we know to be right. Why does he think this? Do you agree?
3. Smart claims that restricted utilitarianism amounts to "superstitious rule-worship." What does he mean by this? Do you think he is correct?
4. Extreme utilitarians think that we ought to break our promises whenever doing so will bring about a better outcome than keeping the promise. Are we obligated to keep our promises, even if we could bring about more good by breaking them?
5. In his example of the gardener, Smart suggests that it is sometimes morally acceptable to secretly break the law, even if the law is perfectly just. Do you agree with him?

9

The Good Will and the Categorical Imperative

Immanuel Kant

Immanuel Kant (1724–1804) was the greatest German philosopher who ever lived. In this excerpt from his *Groundwork of the Metaphysics of Morals*, Kant introduces two key elements of his moral philosophy. According to Kant, the first of these, the *good will*, is the only thing possessed of unconditional value: it is valuable in its own right, in every possible circumstance. The good will is the steady commitment to do our duty for its own sake. Our actions possess moral worth if, but only if, they are prompted by the good will.

The second important element is the *categorical imperative*, Kant's term for a requirement of reason that applies to us regardless of what we care about. Moral requirements are categorical imperatives—we must, for instance, sometimes give help to others in need, even if we don't want to, and even if such help gets us nothing that we care about. Kant believed that moral action is rational action. Each of us has a compelling reason to obey morality, even when doing so only frustrates our deepest desires.

Kant here sets out two tests for morally acceptable action. The first says that actions are morally acceptable only when the principles that inspire them can be acted on by everyone consistently. The second requires us to treat humanity always as an end in itself, and

From *Groundwork of the Metaphysics of Morals*, trans. Mary Gregor (1998). Reprinted with the permission of Cambridge University Press.

never as a mere means. Kant realizes that such formulations are somewhat abstract, and so here offers us a number of illustrations that are meant to help us understand and apply them.

....

The Good Will

It is impossible to think of anything at all in the world, or indeed even beyond it, that could be considered good without limitation except a **good will**. Understanding, wit, judgment and the like, whatever such *talents* of mind may be called, or courage, resolution, and perseverance in one's plans, as qualities of *temperament*, are undoubtedly good and desirable for many purposes, but they can also be extremely evil and harmful if the will which is to make use of these gifts of nature, and whose distinctive constitution is therefore called *character*, is not good. It is the same with *gifts of fortune*. Power, riches, honor, even health and that complete well-being and satisfaction with one's condition called *happiness*, produce boldness and thereby often arrogance as well unless a good will is present which corrects the influence of these on the mind and, in so doing, also corrects the whole principle of action and brings it into conformity with universal ends—not to mention that an impartial rational spectator can take no delight in seeing the uninterrupted prosperity of a being graced with no feature of a pure and good will, so that a good will seems to constitute the indispensable condition even of worthiness to be happy.

Some qualities are even conducive to this good will itself and can make its work much easier; despite this, however, they have no inner unconditional worth but always presuppose a good will, which limits the esteem one otherwise rightly has for them and does not permit their being taken as absolutely good. Moderation in affects and passions, self-control, and calm reflection are not only good for all sorts of purposes but even seem to constitute a part of the *inner* worth of a person; but they lack much that would be required to declare them good without limitation (however unconditionally they were praised by the ancients); for, without the basic principles of a good will they can become extremely evil, and the coolness of a scoundrel makes him not only far more dangerous but also immediately more abominable in our eyes than we would have taken him to be without it.

A good will is not good because of what it effects or accomplishes, because of its fitness to attain some proposed end, but only because of its volition, that is, it is good in itself and, regarded for itself, is to be valued incomparably higher than all that could merely be brought about by it in favor of some inclination and indeed, if you will, of the sum of all inclinations. Even if, by a special disfavor of fortune or by the niggardly provision of a stepmotherly nature, this will should wholly lack the capacity to carry out its purpose—if with its greatest efforts it should yet achieve nothing and only the good will were left (not, of course, as a mere wish but as the summoning of all means insofar as they are in our control)—then, like a jewel, it would still shine by itself, as something that has its full worth in itself. Usefulness or fruitlessness can neither add anything to this worth nor take anything away from it. Its usefulness would be, as it were, only the setting to enable us to handle it more conveniently in ordinary commerce or to attract to it the attention of those who are not yet expert enough, but not to recommend it to experts or to determine its worth. . . .

We have, then, to explicate the concept of a will that is to be esteemed in itself and that is good apart from any further purpose, as it already dwells in natural sound understanding and needs not so much to be taught as only to be clarified—this concept that always takes first place in estimating the total worth of our actions and constitutes the condition of all the rest. In order to do so, we shall set before ourselves the concept of **duty**, which contains that of a good will though under certain subjective limitations and hindrances, which, however, far from concealing it and making it unrecognizable, rather bring it out by contrast and make it shine forth all the more brightly.

I here pass over all actions that are already recognized as contrary to duty, even though they may be useful for this or that purpose; for in their case the question whether they might have been done *from duty* never arises, since they even conflict with it. I also set aside actions that are really in conformity with duty but to which human beings have *no inclination* immediately and which they still perform because they are impelled to do so through another inclination. For in this case it is easy to distinguish whether an action in conformity with duty is done *from duty* or from a self-seeking purpose. It is much more difficult to note this distinction when an action conforms with duty and the subject has, besides, an *immediate* inclination to it. For example, it certainly conforms with duty that a shopkeeper not overcharge an inexperienced customer, and where there is a good deal of trade a prudent merchant does not overcharge but keeps a fixed general price for everyone, so that a child can buy from him as well as everyone else. People are thus served *honestly*; but this is not nearly enough for us to believe that the merchant acted in this way from duty and basic principles of honesty; his advantage required it; it cannot be assumed here that he had, besides, an immediate inclination toward his customers, so as from love, as it were, to give no one preference over another in the matter of price. Thus the action was done neither from duty nor from immediate inclination but merely for purposes of self-interest.

On the other hand, to preserve one's life is a duty, and besides everyone has an immediate inclination to do so. But on this account the often anxious care that most people take of it still has no inner worth and their maxim has no moral content. They look after their lives *in conformity with duty* but not *from duty*. On the other hand, if adversity and hopeless grief have quite taken away the taste for life; if an unfortunate man, strong of soul and more indignant about his fate than despondent or dejected, wishes for death and yet preserves his life without loving it, not from inclination or fear but from duty, then his maxim has moral content.

To be beneficent where one can is a duty, and besides there are many souls so sympathetically attuned that, without any other motive of vanity or self-interest they find an inner satisfaction in spreading joy around them and can take delight in the satisfaction of others so far as it is their own work. But I assert that in such a case an action of this kind, however it may conform with duty and however amiable it may be, has nevertheless no true moral worth but is on the same footing with other inclinations, for example, the inclination to honor, which, if it fortunately lights upon what is in fact in the common interest and in conformity with duty and hence honorable, deserves praise and encouragement but not esteem; for the maxim lacks moral content, namely that of doing such actions not from inclination but *from duty*. Suppose, then, that the mind of this philanthropist were overclouded by his own grief, which extinguished all sympathy with the fate of others, and that while he still had the means to benefit others in distress their troubles did not move him because he had enough to do with his own; and suppose that now, when no longer incited to it by any inclination, he nevertheless tears himself out of this deadly insensibility and does the action without any inclination, simply from duty; then the action first has its genuine moral worth.

Still further: if nature had put little sympathy in the heart of this or that man; if (in other respects an honest man) he is by temperament cold and indifferent to the sufferings of others, perhaps because he himself is provided with the special gift of patience and endurance toward his own sufferings and presupposes the same in every other or even requires it; if nature had not properly fashioned such a man (who would in truth not be its worst product) for a philanthropist, would he not still find within himself a source from which to give himself a far higher worth than what a mere good-natured temperament might have? By all means! It is just then that the worth of character comes out, which is moral and incomparably the highest, namely that he is beneficent not from inclination but from duty. . . .

Thus the moral worth of an action does not lie in the effect expected from it and so too does not lie in any principle of action that needs to borrow its motive from this expected effect. For, all these effects (agreeableness of one's condition, indeed even promotion of others' happiness) could have been also brought about by other causes, so that there would have been no need, for this, of the will of a rational being, in which, however, the highest and unconditional good alone can be found. Hence nothing other than the *representation of the law* in itself, *which can of course occur only in a rational being*, insofar as it and not the hoped-for effect is the determining ground of the will, can constitute the preeminent good we call moral, which is already present in the person himself who acts in accordance with this representation and need not wait upon the effect of his action.

But what kind of law can that be, the representation of which must determine the will, even without regard for the effect expected from it, in order for the will to be called good absolutely and without limitation? Since I have deprived the will of every impulse that could arise for it from obeying some law, nothing is left but the conformity of actions as such with universal law, which alone is to serve the will as its principle, that is, *I ought never to act except in such a way that I could also will that my maxim should become a universal law.* Here mere conformity to law as such, without having as its basis some law determined for certain actions, is what serves the will as its principle, and must so serve it, if duty is not to be everywhere an empty delusion and a chimerical concept. Common human reason also agrees completely with this in its practical appraisals and always has this principle before its eyes. Let the question be, for example: may I, when hard pressed, make a promise with the intention not to keep it? Here I easily distinguish two significations the question can have: whether it is prudent or whether it is in conformity with duty to make a false promise. The first can undoubtedly often be the case. I see very well that it is not enough to get out of a present difficulty by means of this subterfuge but that I must reflect carefully whether this lie may later give rise to much greater inconvenience for me than that from which I now extricate myself; and since, with all my supposed *cunning*, the results cannot be so easily foreseen but that once confidence in me is lost this could be far more prejudicial to me than all the troubles I now think to avoid, I must reflect whether the matter might be handled *more prudently* by proceeding on a general maxim and making it a habit to promise nothing except with the intention of keeping it. But it is soon clear to me that such a maxim will still be based only on results feared. To be truthful from duty, however, is something entirely different from being truthful from anxiety about detrimental results, since in the first case the concept of the action in itself already contains a law for me while in the second I must first look about elsewhere to see what effects on me might be combined with it. For, if I deviate from the principle of duty this is quite certainly evil; but if I am unfaithful to my maxim of prudence this can sometimes be very advantageous to me, although it is certainly safer to abide by it. However, to inform myself in the shortest and yet infallible way about the answer to this problem, whether a lying promise is in conformity with duty, I ask myself: would I indeed be content that my maxim (to get myself out of difficulties by a false promise) should hold as a universal law (for myself as well as for others)? and could I indeed say to myself that every one may make a false promise when he finds himself in a difficulty he can get out of in no other way? Then I soon become aware that I could indeed will the lie, but by no means a universal law to lie; for in accordance with such a law there would properly be no promises at all, since it would be futile to avow my will with regard to my future actions to others who would not believe this avowal or, if they rashly did so, would pay me back in like coin; and thus my maxim, as soon as it were made a universal law, would have to destroy itself.

I do not, therefore, need any penetrating acuteness to see what I have to do in order that my volition be morally good. Inexperienced in the course of the world, incapable of being prepared for whatever might come to pass in it, I ask myself only: can you also will that your maxim become a universal law? If not, then it is to be repudiated, and that not because of a disadvantage to you or even to others forthcoming from it but because it cannot fit as a principle into a possible giving of universal law, for which lawgiving reason, however, forces from me immediate respect. Although I do not yet *see* what this respect is based upon (this the philosopher may investigate), I at least understand this much: that it is an estimation of a worth that far outweighs any worth of what is recommended by inclination, and that the necessity of my action from *pure* respect for the practical law is what constitutes duty, to which every other motive must give way because it is the condition of a will good *in itself*, the worth of which surpasses all else. . . .

The Categorical Imperative

Now, all imperatives command either *hypothetically* or *categorically*. The former represent the practical necessity of a possible action as a means to achieving something else that one wills (or that it is at least possible for one to will). The categorical imperative would be that which represented an action as objectively necessary of itself, without reference to another end.

Since every practical law represents a possible action as good and thus as necessary for a subject practically determinable by reason, all imperatives are formulae for the determination of action that is necessary in accordance with the principle of a will which is good in some way. Now, if the action would be good merely as a means *to something else* the imperative is *hypothetical*; if the action is represented as *in itself* good, hence as necessary in a will in itself conforming to reason, as its principle, *then it is categorical.* . . .

There is one imperative that, without being based upon and having as its condition any other purpose to be attained by certain conduct, commands this conduct immediately. This imperative is **categorical**. It has to do not with the matter of the action and what is to result from it, but with the form and the principle from which the action itself follows; and the essential good in the action consists in the disposition, let the result be what it may. This imperative may be called the imperative **of morality.** . . .

When I think of a *hypothetical* imperative in general I do not know beforehand what it will contain; I do not know this until I am given the condition. But when I think of a *categorical* imperative I know at once what it contains. For, since the imperative contains, beyond the law, only the necessity that the maxim[1] be in conformity with this law, while the law contains no condition to which it would be limited, nothing is left with which the maxim of action is to conform but the universality of a law as such; and this conformity alone is what the imperative properly represents as necessary.

There is, therefore, only a single categorical imperative and it is this: *act only in accordance with that maxim through which you can at the same time will that it become a universal law.*

Now, if all imperatives of duty can be derived from this single imperative as from their principle, then, even though we leave it undecided whether what is called duty is not as such an empty concept, we shall at least be able to show what we think by it and what the concept wants to say.

Since the universality of law in accordance with which effects take place constitutes what is properly called *nature* in the most general sense (as regards its form)—that is, the existence of things insofar as it is determined in accordance with universal laws—the universal imperative of duty can also go as follows: *act as if the maxim of your action were to become by your will a* **universal law of nature**.

We shall now enumerate a few duties in accordance with the usual division of them into duties to ourselves and to other human beings and into perfect and imperfect duties.[2]

(1) Someone feels sick of life because of a series of troubles that has grown to the point of despair, but is still so far in possession of his reason that he can ask himself whether it would not be contrary to his duty to himself to take his own life. Now he inquires whether the maxim of his action could indeed become a universal law of nature. His maxim, however, is: from self-love I make it my principle to shorten my life when its longer duration threatens more troubles than it promises agreeableness. The only further question is whether this principle of self-love could become a universal law of nature. It is then seen at once that a nature

---

1 A maxim is the subjective principle of acting, and must be distinguished from the objective principle, namely the practical law. The former contains the practical rule determined by reason conformably with the conditions of the subject (often his ignorance or also his inclinations), and is therefore the principle in accordance with which the subject acts; but the law is the objective principle valid for every rational being, and the principle in accordance with which he ought to act, i.e., an imperative.

2 ... I understand here by a perfect duty one that admits no exception in favor of inclination.

whose law it would be to destroy life itself by means of the same feeling whose destination is to impel toward the furtherance of life would contradict itself and would therefore not subsist as nature; thus that maxim could not possibly be a law of nature and, accordingly, altogether opposes the supreme principle of all duty.

(2) Another finds himself urged by need to borrow money. He well knows that he will not be able to repay it but sees also that nothing will be lent him unless he promises firmly to repay it within a determinate time. He would like to make such a promise, but he still has enough conscience to ask himself: is it not forbidden and contrary to duty to help oneself out of need in such a way? Supposing that he still decided to do so, his maxim of action would go as follows: when I believe myself to be in need of money I shall borrow money and promise to repay it, even though I know that this will never happen. Now this principle of self-love or personal advantage is perhaps quite consistent with my whole future welfare, but the question now is whether it is right. I therefore turn the demand of self-love into a universal law and put the question as follows: how would it be if my maxim became a universal law? I then see at once that it could never hold as a universal law of nature and be consistent with itself, but must necessarily contradict itself. For, the universality of a law that everyone, when he believes himself to be in need, could promise whatever he pleases with the intention of not keeping it would make the promise and the end one might have in it itself impossible, since no one would believe what was promised him but would laugh at all such expressions as vain pretenses.

(3) A third finds in himself a talent that by means of some cultivation could make him a human being useful for all sorts of purposes. However, he finds himself in comfortable circumstances and prefers to give himself up to pleasure than to trouble himself with enlarging and improving his fortunate natural predispositions. But he still asks himself whether his maxim of neglecting his natural gifts, besides being consistent with his propensity to amusement, is also consistent with what one calls duty. He now sees that a nature could indeed always subsist with such a universal law, although (as with the South Sea Islanders) the human being should let his talents rust and be concerned with devoting his life merely to idleness, amusement, procreation—in a word, to enjoyment; only he cannot possibly will that this become a universal law or be put in us as such by means of natural instinct. For, as a rational being he necessarily wills that all the capacities in him be developed, since they serve him and are given to him for all sorts of possible purposes.

(4) Yet a *fourth*, for whom things are going well while he sees that others (whom he could very well help) have to contend with great hardships, thinks: what is it to me? let each be as happy as heaven wills or as he can make himself; I shall take nothing from him nor even envy him; only I do not care to contribute anything to his welfare or to his assistance in need! Now, if such a way of thinking were to become a universal law the human race could admittedly very well subsist, no doubt even better than when everyone prates about sympathy and benevolence and even exerts himself to practice them occasionally, but on the other hand also cheats where he can, sells the right of human beings or otherwise infringes upon it. But although it is possible that a universal law of nature could very well subsist in accordance with such a maxim, it is still impossible to will that such a principle hold everywhere as a law of nature. For, a will that decided this would conflict with itself, since many cases could occur in which one would need the love and sympathy of others and in which, by such a law of nature arisen from his own will, he would rob himself of all hope of the assistance he wishes for himself. . . .

If we now attend to ourselves in any transgression of a duty, we find that we do not really will that our maxim should become a universal law, since that is impossible for us, but that the opposite of our maxim should instead remain a universal law, only we take the liberty of making an *exception* to it for ourselves (or just for this once) to the advantage of our inclination. Consequently, if we weighed all cases from one and the same point of view, namely that of reason, we would find a contradiction in our own will, namely that a certain principle be objectively necessary as a universal law and yet subjectively not hold universally but allow exceptions. . . .

Suppose there were something the *existence of which in itself* has an absolute worth, something which as *an end in itself* could be a ground of determinate laws; then in it, and in it alone, would lie the ground of a possible categorical imperative, that is, of a practical law.

Now I say that the human being and in general every rational being *exists* as an end in itself, *not merely as a means* to be used by this or that will at its discretion; instead he must in all his actions, whether directed to himself or also to other rational beings, always be regarded *at the same time as an end*. All objects of the inclinations have only a conditional worth; for, if there were not inclinations and the needs based on them, their object would be without worth. But the inclinations themselves, as sources of needs, are so far from having an absolute worth, so as to make one wish to have them, that it must instead be the universal wish of every rational being to be altogether free from them. Thus the worth of any object *to be acquired* by our action is always conditional. Beings the existence of which rests not on our will but on nature, if they are beings without reason, still have only a relative worth, as means, and are therefore called *things*, whereas rational beings are called *persons* because their nature already marks them out as an end in itself, that is, as something that may not be used merely as a means, and hence so far limits all choice (and is an object of respect). These, therefore, are not merely subjective ends, the existence of which as an effect of our action has a worth *for us*, but rather *objective ends*, that is, beings the existence of which is in itself an end, and indeed one such that no other end, to which they would serve *merely* as means, can be put in its place, since without it nothing of *absolute worth* would be found anywhere; but if all worth were conditional and therefore contingent, then no supreme practical principle for reason could be found anywhere.

If, then, there is to be a supreme practical principle and, with respect to the human will, a categorical imperative, it must be one such that, from the representation of what is necessarily an end for everyone because it is an *end in itself*, it constitutes an *objective* principle of the will and thus can serve as a universal practical law. The ground of this principle is: *rational nature exists as an end in itself*. The human being necessarily represents his own existence in this way; so far it is thus a *subjective* principle of human actions. But every other rational being also represents his existence in this way consequent on just the same rational ground that also holds for me; thus it is at the same time an *objective* principle from which, as a supreme practical ground, it must be possible to derive all laws of the will. The practical imperative will therefore be the following: *So act that you use humanity, whether in your own person or in the person of any other, always at the same time as an end, never merely as a means.* We shall see whether this can be carried out.

To keep to the preceding examples:

First, as regards the concept of necessary duty to oneself, someone who has suicide in mind will ask himself whether his action can be consistent with the idea of humanity *as an end in itself.* If he destroys himself in order to escape from a trying condition he makes use of a person *merely as a means* to maintain a tolerable condition up to the end of life. A human being, however, is not a thing and hence not something that can be used *merely* as a means, but must in all his actions always be regarded as an end in itself. I cannot, therefore, dispose of a human being in my own person by maiming, damaging or killing him. (I must here pass over a closer determination of this principle that would prevent any misinterpretation, e.g., as to having limbs amputated in order to preserve myself, or putting my life in danger in order to preserve my life, and so forth; that belongs to morals proper.)

Second, as regards necessary duty to others or duty owed them, he who has it in mind to make a false promise to others sees at once that he wants to make use of another human being *merely as a means,* without the other at the same time containing in himself the end. For, he whom I want to use for my purposes by such a promise cannot possibly agree to my way of behaving toward him, and so himself contain the end of this action. This conflict with the principle of other human beings is seen more distinctly if examples of assaults on the freedom and property of others are brought forward. For then it is obvious that he who transgresses the rights of human beings intends to make use of the person of others merely as means, without taking into consideration that, as rational beings, they are always to be valued at the same time as ends, that is, only as beings who must also be able to contain in themselves the end of the very same action.

Third, with respect to contingent (meritorious) duty to oneself, it is not enough that the action does not conflict with humanity in our person as an end in itself; it must also *harmonize with it.* Now there are in humanity predispositions to greater perfection, which belong to the end of nature with respect to humanity in our subject; to neglect these might admittedly be consistent with the *preservation* of humanity as an end in itself but not with the *furtherance* of this end.

Fourth, concerning meritorious duty to others, the natural end that all human beings have is their own happiness. Now, humanity might indeed subsist if no one contributed to the happiness of others but yet did not intentionally withdraw anything from it; but there is still only a negative and not a positive agreement with *humanity as an end in itself* unless everyone also tries, as far as he can, to further the ends of others. For, the ends of a subject who is an end in itself must as far as possible be also *my* ends, if that representation is to have its *full* effect in me. . . .

Immanuel Kant: The Good Will and the Categorical Imperative

1. Kant claims that a good will is the only thing that can be considered "good without limitation." What does he mean by this? Do you find this claim plausible?
2. Unlike hedonists, Kant believes that happiness is not always good. What reasons does he give for thinking this? Do you agree with him?
3. What is the difference between doing something "in conformity with duty" and doing something "from duty"? Is Kant correct in saying that only actions done *from duty* have moral worth?
4. Kant claims to have discovered a *categorical imperative*, a moral requirement that we have reason to follow regardless of what we happen to desire. Can people have reasons for action that are completely independent of their desires?
5. According to Kant, it is morally permissible to act on a particular principle (or "maxim") only if "you can at the same time will that it become a universal law." Do you think this is a good test of whether an action is morally permissible? Can you think of any immoral actions that would pass this test, or any morally permissible actions that would fail it?
6. Kant later gives another formulation of the categorical imperative: "So act that you use humanity, whether in your own person or in the person of any other, always at the same time as an end, never merely as a means." What does it mean to treat someone as an end? Are we always morally required to treat humans in this way?

10

Leviathan

Thomas Hobbes

Thomas Hobbes (1588–1679) is the most brilliant of the modern social contract theorists. His theory, important in both ethics and political philosophy, views the basic moral rules of society as ones that rational people would adopt in order to protect their own interests. Without obedience to such rules, the situation deteriorates into a "war of all against all, in which the life of man is solitary, poor, nasty, brutish and short."

Hobbes was an ethical egoist—someone who thinks that our fundamental duty is to look after our own interests—as well as a social contract theorist. Many commentators have found a tension in this combination. See for yourself whether Hobbes succeeded in justifying the basic moral rules by reference to self-interest.

Among the many interesting features in this excerpt from Hobbes's classic *Leviathan* is his discussion of the fool. The fool is someone who allows that breaking one's promises is unjust, but who thinks that it may sometimes be rational to do so anyway. Hobbes resists this idea. He wants to show that it is always rational to do one's duty—to live by the laws of cooperation that would be accepted by free and rational people. His overall view is motivated by the thought that moral duties must provide each of us with excellent reasons to obey them, and that these reasons must ultimately stem from self-interest. As a result, Hobbes's discussion casts fascinating light on the perennial question of why we should be moral.

Of the Natural Condition of Mankind as Concerning Their Felicity and Misery

Nature hath made men so equal in the faculties of body and mind as that, though there be found one man sometimes manifestly stronger in body or of quicker mind than another, yet when all is reckoned together the difference between man and man is not so considerable as that one man can thereupon claim to himself any benefit to which another may not pretend as well as he. For as to the strength of body, the weakest has strength enough to kill the strongest, either by secret machination or by confederacy with others that are in the same danger with himself.

And as to the faculties of the mind, setting aside the arts grounded upon words, and especially that skill of proceeding upon general and infallible rules, called science, which very few have and but in few things, as being not a native faculty born with us, nor attained, as prudence, while we look after somewhat else, I find yet a greater equality amongst men than that of strength. For prudence is but experience, which equal time equally bestows on all men in those things they equally apply themselves unto. That which may perhaps make such equality incredible is but a vain conceit of one's own wisdom, which almost all men think they have in a greater degree than the vulgar; that is, than all men but themselves, and a few others, whom by fame, or for concurring with themselves, they approve. For such is the nature of men that howsoever they may acknowledge many others to be more witty, or more eloquent or more learned, yet they will hardly believe there be many so wise as themselves; for they see their own wit at hand, and other men's at a distance. But this proveth rather that men are in that point equal, than unequal. For there is not ordinarily a greater sign of the equal distribution of anything than that every man is contented with his share.

From this equality of ability ariseth equality of hope in the attaining of our ends. And therefore if any two men desire the same thing, which nevertheless they cannot both enjoy, they become enemies; and in the way to their end (which is principally their own conservation, and sometimes their delectation only) endeavour to destroy or subdue one another. And from hence it comes to pass that where an invader hath no more to fear than another man's single power, if one plant, sow, build, or possess a convenient seat, others may probably be expected to come prepared with forces united to dispossess and deprive him, not only of the fruit of his labour, but also of his life or liberty. And the invader again is in the like danger of another.

And from this diffidence of one another, there is no way for any man to secure himself so reasonable as anticipation; that is, by force, or wiles, to master the persons of all men he can so long till he see no other power great enough to endanger him: and this is no more than his own conservation requireth, and is generally allowed. Also, because there be some that, taking pleasure in contemplating their own power in the acts of conquest, which they pursue farther than their security requires, if others, that otherwise would be glad to be at ease within modest bounds, should not by invasion increase their power, they would not be able, long time, by standing only on their defence, to subsist. And by consequence, such augmentation of dominion over men being necessary to a man's conservation, it ought to be allowed him.

Again, men have no pleasure (but on the contrary a great deal of grief) in keeping company where there is no power able to overawe them all. For every man looketh that his companion should value him at the same rate he sets upon himself, and upon all signs of contempt or undervaluing naturally endeavours, as far as he dares (which amongst them that have no common power to keep them in quiet is far enough to make them destroy each other), to extort a greater value from his contemners, by damage; and from others, by the example.

So that in the nature of man, we find three principal causes of quarrel. First, competition; secondly, diffidence; thirdly, glory.

The first maketh men invade for gain; the second, for safety; and the third, for reputation. The first use violence, to make themselves masters of other men's persons, wives, children, and cattle; the second, to defend them; the third, for trifles, as a word, a smile, a different opinion, and any other sign of undervalue, either direct in their persons or by reflection in their kindred, their friends, their nation, their profession, or their name.

Hereby it is manifest that during the time men live without a common power to keep them all in awe, they are in that condition which is called war; and such a war as is of every man against every man. For war consisteth not in battle only, or the act of fighting, but in a tract of time, wherein the will to contend by battle is sufficiently known: and therefore the notion of time is to be considered in the nature of war, as it is in the nature of weather. For as the nature of foul weather lieth not in a shower or two of rain, but in an inclination thereto of many days together: so the nature of war consisteth not in actual fighting, but in the known disposition thereto during all the time there is no assurance to the contrary. All other time is peace.

Whatsoever therefore is consequent to a time of war, where every man is enemy to every man, the same consequent to the time wherein men live without other security than what their own strength and their own invention shall furnish them withal. In such condition there is no place for industry, because the fruit thereof is uncertain: and consequently no culture of the earth; no navigation, nor use of the commodities that may be imported by sea; no commodious building; no instruments of moving and removing such things as require much force; no knowledge of the face of the earth; no account of time; no arts; no letters; no society; and which is worst of all, continual fear, and danger of violent death; and the life of man, solitary, poor, nasty, brutish, and short.

It may seem strange to some man that has not well weighed these things that Nature should thus dissociate and render men apt to invade and destroy one another: and he may therefore, not trusting to this inference, made from the passions, desire perhaps to have the same confirmed by experience. Let him therefore consider with himself: when taking a journey, he arms himself and seeks to go well accompanied; when going to sleep, he locks his doors; when even in his house he locks his chests; and this when he knows there be laws and public officers, armed, to revenge all injuries shall be done him; what opinion he has of his fellow subjects, when he rides armed; of his fellow citizens, when he locks his doors; and of his children, and servants, when he locks his chests. Does he not there as much accuse mankind by his actions as I do by my words? But neither of us accuse man's nature in it. The desires, and other passions of man, are in themselves no sin. No more are the actions that proceed from those passions till they know a law that forbids them; which till laws be made they cannot know, nor can any law be made till they have agreed upon the person that shall make it.

It may peradventure be thought there was never such a time nor condition of war as this; and I believe it was never generally so, over all the world: but there are many places where they live so now. For the savage people in many places of America, except the government of small families, the concord whereof dependeth on natural lust, have no government at all, and live at this day in that brutish manner, as I said before. Howsoever, it may be perceived what manner of life there would be, where there were no common power to fear, by the manner of life which men that have formerly lived under a peaceful government use to degenerate into a civil war.

But though there had never been any time wherein particular men were in a condition of war one against another, yet in all times kings and persons of sovereign authority, because of their independency, are in continual jealousies, and in the state and posture of gladiators, having their weapons pointing, and their eyes fixed on one another; that is, their forts, garrisons, and guns upon the frontiers of their kingdoms, and continual spies upon their neighbours, which is a posture of war. But because they uphold thereby the industry of their subjects, there does not follow from it that misery which accompanies the liberty of particular men.

To this war of every man against every man, this also is consequent; that nothing can be unjust. The notions of right and wrong, justice and injustice, have there no place. Where there is no common power, there is no law; where no law, no injustice. Force and fraud are in war the two cardinal virtues. Justice and injustice are none of the faculties neither of the body nor mind. If they were, they might be in a man that were alone in the world, as well as his senses and passions. They are qualities that relate to men in society, not in solitude. It is consequent also to the same condition that there be no propriety, no dominion, no mine and thine distinct; but only that to be every man's that he can get, and for so long as he can keep it. And thus much for the ill condition which man by mere nature is actually placed in; though with a possibility to come out of it, consisting partly in the passions, partly in his reason.

The passions that incline men to peace are: fear of death; desire of such things as are necessary to commodious living; and a hope by their industry to obtain them. And reason suggesteth convenient articles of peace upon which men may be drawn to agreement. These articles are they which otherwise are called the laws of nature, whereof I shall speak more particularly in the two following chapters.

Of the First and Second Natural Laws, and of Contracts

The right of nature, which writers commonly call *jus naturale*, is the liberty each man hath to use his own power as he will himself for the preservation of his own nature; that is to say, of his own life; and consequently, of doing anything which, in his own judgement and reason, he shall conceive to be the aptest means thereunto.

By liberty is understood, according to the proper signification of the word, the absence of external impediments; which impediments may oft take away part of a man's power to do what he would, but cannot hinder him from using the power left him according as his judgement and reason shall dictate to him.

A law of nature, *lex naturalis*, is a precept, or general rule, found out by reason, by which a man is forbidden to do that which is destructive of his life, or taketh away the means of preserving the same, and to omit that by which he thinketh it may be best preserved.

And because the condition of man . . . is a condition of war of every one against every one, in which case every one is governed by his own reason, and there is nothing he can make use of that may not be a help unto him in preserving his life against his enemies; it followeth that in such a condition every man has a right to every thing, even to one another's body. And therefore, as long as this natural right of every man to every thing endureth, there can be no security to any man, how strong or wise soever he be, of living out the time which nature ordinarily alloweth men to live. And consequently it is a precept, or general rule of reason: that every man ought to endeavour peace, as far as he has hope of obtaining it; and when he cannot obtain it, that he may seek and use all helps and advantages of war. The first branch of which rule containeth the first and fundamental law of nature, which is: to seek peace and follow it. The second, the sum of the right of nature, which is: by all means we can to defend ourselves.

From this fundamental law of nature, by which men are commanded to endeavour peace, is derived this second law: that a man be willing, when others are so too, as far forth as for peace and defence of himself he shall think it necessary, to lay down this right to all things; and be contented with so much liberty against other men as he would allow other men against himself. For as long as every man holdeth this right, of doing anything he liketh; so long are all men in the condition of war. But if other men will not lay down their right, as well as he, then there is no reason for anyone to divest himself of his: for that were to expose himself to prey, which no man is bound to, rather than to dispose himself to peace. This is that law of the gospel: Whatsoever you require that others should do to you, that do ye to them.

Whensoever a man transferreth his right, or renounceth it, it is either in consideration of some right reciprocally transferred to himself, or for some other good he hopeth for thereby. For it is a voluntary act: and of the voluntary acts of every man, the object is some good to himself. And therefore there be some rights which no man can be understood by any words, or other signs, to have abandoned or transferred. As first a man cannot lay down the right of resisting them that assault him by force to take away his life, because he cannot be understood to aim thereby at any good to himself.

The same may be said of wounds, and chains, and imprisonment, both because there is no benefit consequent to such patience, as there is to the patience of suffering another to be wounded or imprisoned, as also because a man cannot tell when he seeth men proceed against him by violence whether they intend his death or not. And lastly the motive and end for which this renouncing and transferring of right is introduced is nothing else but the security of a man's person, in his life, and in the means of so preserving life as not to be weary of it. And therefore if a man by words, or other signs, seem to despoil himself of the end for which those signs were intended, he is not to be understood as if he meant it, or that it was his will, but that he was ignorant of how such words and actions were to be interpreted.

The mutual transferring of right is that which men call contract. . . .

Signs of contract are either express or by inference. Express are words spoken with understanding of what they signify: and such words are either of the time present or past; as, I give, I grant, I have given, I have granted, I will that this be yours: or of the future; as, I will give, I will grant, which words of the future are called promise.

Signs by inference are sometimes the consequence of words; sometimes the consequence of silence; sometimes the consequence of actions; sometimes the consequence of forbearing an action: and generally a sign by inference, of any contract, is whatsoever sufficiently argues the will of the contractor.

Words alone, if they be of the time to come, and contain a bare promise, are an insufficient sign of a free gift and therefore not obligatory. For if they be of the time to come, as, tomorrow I will give, they are a sign I have not given yet, and consequently that my right is not transferred, but remaineth till I transfer it by some other act. . . .

If a covenant be made wherein neither of the parties perform presently, but trust one another, in the condition of mere nature (which is a condition of war of every man against every man) upon any reasonable suspicion, it is void: but if there be a common power set over them both, with right and force sufficient to compel performance, it is not void. For he that performeth first has no assurance the other will perform after, because the bonds of words are too weak to bridle men's ambition, avarice, anger, and other passions, without the fear of some coercive power; which in the condition of mere nature, where all men are equal, and judges of the justness of their own fears, cannot possibly be supposed. And therefore he which performeth first does but betray himself to his enemy, contrary to the right he can never abandon of defending his life and means of living.

But in a civil estate, where there is a power set up to constrain those that would otherwise violate their faith, that fear is no more reasonable; and for that cause, he which by the covenant is to perform first is obliged so to do.

Of Other Laws of Nature

From that law of nature by which we are obliged to transfer to another such rights as, being retained, hinder the peace of mankind, there followeth a third; which is this: that men perform their covenants made; without which covenants are in vain, and but empty words; and the right of all men to all things remaining, we are still in the condition of war.

And in this law of nature consisteth the fountain and original of justice. For where no covenant hath preceded, there hath no right been transferred, and every man has right to everything and consequently, no action can be unjust. But when a covenant is made, then to break it is unjust and the definition of injustice is no other than the not performance of covenant. And whatsoever is not unjust is just.

But because covenants of mutual trust, where there is a fear of not performance on either part (as hath been said in the former chapter), are invalid, though the original of justice be the making of covenants, yet injustice actually there can be none till the cause of such fear be taken away; which, while men are in the natural condition of war, cannot be done. Therefore before the names of just and unjust can have place, there must be some coercive power to compel men equally to the performance of their covenants, by the terror of some punishment greater than the benefit they expect by the breach of their covenant, and to make good that propriety which by mutual contract men acquire in recompense of the universal right they abandon: and such power there is none before the erection of a Commonwealth. And this is also to be gathered out of the ordinary definition of justice in the Schools, for they say that justice is the constant will of giving to every man his own. And therefore where there is no own, that is, no propriety, there is no injustice; and where there is no coercive power erected, that is, where there is no Commonwealth, there is no propriety, all men having right to all things: therefore where there is no Commonwealth, there nothing is unjust. So that the nature of justice consisteth in keeping of valid covenants, but the validity of covenants begins not but with the constitution of a civil power sufficient to compel men to keep them: and then it is also that propriety begins.

The fool hath said in his heart, there is no such thing as justice, and sometimes also with his tongue, seriously alleging that every man's conservation and contentment being committed to his own care, there could be no reason why every man might not do what he thought conduced thereunto: and therefore also to make, or not make; keep, or not keep, covenants was not against reason when it conduced to one's benefit. He does not therein deny that there be covenants; and that they are sometimes broken, sometimes kept; and that such breach of them may be called injustice, and the observance of them justice: but he questioneth whether injustice, taking away the fear of God (for the same fool hath said in his heart there is no God), may not sometimes stand with that reason which dictateth to every man his own good; and particularly then, when it conduceth to such a benefit as shall put a man in a condition to neglect not only the dispraise and revilings, but also the power of other men. The kingdom of God is gotten by violence: but what if it could be gotten by unjust violence? Were it against reason so to get it, when it is impossible to receive hurt by it? And if it be not against reason, it is not against justice: or else justice is not to be approved for good. From such reasoning as this, successful wickedness hath obtained the name of virtue: and some that in all other things have disallowed the violation of faith, yet have allowed it when it is for the getting of a kingdom. And the heathen that believed that Saturn was deposed by his son Jupiter believed nevertheless the same Jupiter to be the avenger of injustice, somewhat like to a piece of law in Coke's Commentaries on Littleton; where he says if the right heir of the crown be attainted of treason, yet the crown shall descend to him, and *eo instante* the attainder be void: from which instances a man will be very prone to infer that when the heir apparent of a kingdom shall kill him that is in possession, though his father, you may call it injustice, or by what other name you will; yet it can never be against reason, seeing all the voluntary actions of men tend to the benefit of themselves; and those actions are most reasonable that conduce most to their ends. This specious reasoning is nevertheless false.

For the question is not of promises mutual, where there is no security of performance on either side, as when there is no civil power erected over the parties promising; for such promises are no covenants: but either where one of the parties has performed already, or where there is a power to make him perform, there is the question whether it be against reason; that is, against the benefit of the other to perform, or not. And I say it is not against reason. For the manifestation whereof we are to consider; first, that when a man doth a thing, which notwithstanding anything can be foreseen and reckoned on tendeth to his own destruction, howsoever some accident, which he could not expect, arriving may turn it to his benefit; yet such events do not make it reasonably or wisely done. Secondly, that in a condition of war, wherein every man to every man, for want of a common power to keep them all in awe, is an enemy, there is no man can hope by his own strength, or wit, to defend himself from destruction without the help of confederates; where every one expects the same defence by the confederation that any one else does: and therefore he which declares he thinks it reason to deceive those that help him can in reason expect no other means of safety than what can be had from his own single power. He, therefore, that breaketh his covenant, and consequently declareth that he thinks he may with reason do so, cannot be received into any society that unite themselves for peace and defence but by the error of them that receive him; nor when he is received be retained in it without seeing the danger of their error; which errors a man cannot reasonably reckon upon as the means of his security: and therefore if he be left, or cast out of society, he perisheth; and if he live in society, it is by the errors of other men, which he could not foresee nor reckon upon, and consequently against the reason of his preservation; and so, as all men that contribute not to his destruction forbear him only out of ignorance of what is good for themselves.

As for the instance of gaining the secure and perpetual felicity of heaven by any way, it is frivolous; there being but one way imaginable, and that is not breaking, but keeping of covenant.

And for the other instance of attaining sovereignty by rebellion; it is manifest that, though the event follow, yet because it cannot reasonably be expected, but rather the contrary, and because by gaining it so, others are taught to gain the same in like manner, the attempt thereof is against reason. Justice therefore, that is to say, keeping of covenant, is a rule of reason by which we are forbidden to do anything destructive to our life, and consequently a law of nature.

Thomas Hobbes: Leviathan

1. At the beginning of the selection, Hobbes argues that all humans are fundamentally equal. In what ways does Hobbes claim that we are equal? Do you agree with him?
2. Hobbes claims that without a government to enforce law and order, we would find ourselves in a "war . . . of every man against every man." What reasons does he give for believing this? Do you think he is right?

3. According to Hobbes, if there were no governments to establish laws, nothing would be just or unjust. Does this seem plausible? Would some actions be unjust, even if there were no authority around to punish those who committed them?

4. Hobbes says, "Of the voluntary acts of every man, the object is some good to himself." Is Hobbes correct in thinking that self-interest is what motivates every voluntary action?

5. Hobbes claims that it is always unjust to violate our covenants (or contracts), provided that there is a government with the power to enforce them. He also claims that any action that does not violate a covenant is just. Can you think of any counterexamples to either of these claims?

6. The "fool" claims that it is rational to unjustly break one's covenants in cases where doing so promotes one's self-interest. How does Hobbes respond to this claim? Do you find Hobbes's replies convincing?

11

What Makes Right Acts Right?

W. D. Ross

W. D. Ross (1877–1971) developed a truly novel moral theory in his book *The Right and the Good* (1930), from which this selection is taken. He found something attractive about both utilitarianism and Kantianism, the major theoretical competitors of his day, but found that each had a major flaw. Ross applauded utilitarianism's emphasis on benevolence, but rejected its idea that maximizing goodness is our sole moral duty. Kantianism, on the other hand, preserved the attractive idea that justice is independently important, but erred in claiming that the moral rules that specified such duties were absolute (never to be broken).

Ross created a kind of compromise theory, in which he identified a number of distinct grounds for moral duty (benevolence, fidelity to promises, truth-telling, avoiding harm, gratitude, justice, reparation). Each of these is a basis for a *prima facie duty*—an always-important reason that generates an "all-things-considered" duty, provided that no other reason or set of reasons is weightier in the situation. In other words, it is sometimes acceptable to violate a prima facie duty.

But when? We cannot offer a permanent ranking of these prima facie duties. Sometimes, for instance, it is right to promote the general happiness even if we have to commit an injustice to do so. But at other times, the balance should be struck in the opposite way.

W. D. Ross, "What Makes Right Acts Right?" from *The Right and the Good* (1930), pp. 16–32. By permission of Oxford University Press, Inc.

Ross insisted that these prima facie duties are self-evident. Here he offers some very influential (and controversial) remarks on how we can gain moral knowledge, both of the moral principles themselves and of the correct verdicts to reach in particular cases.

....

The point at issue is that to which we now pass, viz. whether there is any general character which makes right acts right, and if so, what it is. Among the main historical attempts to state a single characteristic of all right actions which is the foundation of their rightness are those made by egoism and utilitarianism. But I do not propose to discuss these, not because the subject is unimportant, but because it has been dealt with so often and so well already, and because there has come to be so much agreement among moral philosophers that neither of these theories is satisfactory. A much more attractive theory has been put forward by Professor Moore: that what makes actions right is that they are productive of more *good* than could have been produced by any other action open to the agent.

This theory is in fact the culmination of all the attempts to base rightness on productivity of some sort of result. The first form this attempt takes is the attempt to base rightness on conduciveness to the advantage or pleasure of the agent. This theory comes to grief over the fact, which stares us in the face, that a great part of duty consists in an observance of the rights and a furtherance of the interests of others, whatever the cost to ourselves may be. Plato and others may be right in holding that a regard for the rights of others never in the long run involves a loss of happiness for the agent, that 'the just life profits a man'. But this, even if true, is irrelevant to the rightness of the act. As soon as a man does an action *because* he thinks he will promote his own interests thereby, he is acting not from a sense of its rightness but from self-interest.

To the egoistic theory hedonistic utilitarianism supplies a much-needed amendment. It points out correctly that the fact that a certain pleasure will be enjoyed by the agent is no reason why he ought to bring it into being rather than an equal or greater pleasure to be enjoyed by another, though, human nature being what it is, it makes it not unlikely that he will try to bring it into being. But hedonistic utilitarianism in its turn needs a correction. On reflection it seems clear that pleasure is not the only thing in life that we think good in itself, that for instance we think the possession of a good character, or an intelligent understanding of the world, as good or better. A great advance is made by the substitution of 'productive of the greatest good' for 'productive of the greatest pleasure'.

Not only is this theory more attractive than hedonistic utilitarianism, but its logical relation to that theory is such that the latter could not be true unless it were true, while it might be true though hedonistic utilitarianism were not. It is in fact one of the logical bases of hedonistic utilitarianism. For the view that what produces the maximum pleasure is right has for its bases the views (1) that what produces the maximum good is right, and (2) that pleasure is the only thing good in itself. If, therefore, it can be shown that productivity of the maximum good is not what makes all right actions right, we shall *a fortiori* have refuted hedonistic utilitarianism.

When a plain man fulfils a promise because he thinks he ought to do so, it seems clear that he does so with no thought of its total consequences, still less with any opinion that these are likely to be the best possible. He thinks in fact much more of the past than of the future. What makes him think it right to act in a certain way is the fact that he has promised to do so—that and, usually, nothing more. That his act will produce the best possible consequences is not his reason for calling it right. What lends colour to the theory we are examining, then, is not the actions (which form probably a great majority of our actions) in which some such reflection as 'I have promised' is the only reason we give ourselves for thinking a certain action right, but the exceptional cases in which the consequences of fulfilling a promise (for instance) would be so disastrous to others that we judge it right not to do so. It must of course be admitted that such cases exist. If I have promised to meet a friend at a particular time for some trivial purpose, I should certainly think myself justified in breaking my engagement if by doing so I could prevent a serious accident or bring relief to the victims of one. And the supporters of the view we are examining hold that my thinking so is due to my thinking that I shall bring more good into existence by the one action than by the other. A different account may, however, be given of the matter, an account which will, I believe, show itself to be the true one. It may be said that besides the duty of fulfilling promises I have and recognize a duty of relieving distress, and that when I think it right to do the latter at the cost of not doing the former, it is not because I think I shall produce more good thereby but because I think it the duty which is in the circumstances more of a duty. This account surely corresponds much more closely with what we really think in such a situation.

If, so far as I can see, I could bring equal amounts of good into being by fulfilling my promise and by helping some one to whom I had made no promise, I should not hesitate to regard the former as my duty. Yet on the view that what is right is right because it is productive of the most good I should not so regard it.

There are two theories, each in its way simple, that offer a solution of such cases of conscience. One is the view of Kant, that there are certain duties of perfect obligation, such as those of fulfilling promises, of paying debts, of telling the truth, which admit of no exception whatever in favour of duties of imperfect obligation, such as that of relieving distress. The other is the view of, for instance, Professor Moore and Dr. Rashdall, that there is only the duty of producing good, and that all 'conflicts of duties' should be resolved by asking 'by which action will most good be produced?' But it is more important that our theory fit the facts than that it be simple, and the account we have given above corresponds (it seems to me) better than either of the simpler theories with what we really think, viz. that normally promise-keeping, for example, should come before benevolence, but that when and only when the good to be produced by the benevolent act is very great and the promise comparatively trivial, the act of benevolence becomes our duty.

In fact the theory of 'ideal utilitarianism', if I may for brevity refer so to the theory of Professor Moore, seems to simplify unduly our relations to our fellows. It says, in effect, that the only morally significant relation in which my neighbours stand to me is that of being possible beneficiaries by my action. They do stand in this relation to me, and this relation is morally significant. But they may also stand to me in the relation of promisee to promiser, of creditor to debtor, of wife to husband, of child to parent, of friend to friend, of fellow countryman to fellow countryman, and the like; and each of these relations is the foundation of a *prima facie* duty, which is more or less incumbent on me according to the circumstances of the case. When I am in a situation, as perhaps I always am, in which more than one of these *prima facie* duties is incumbent on me, what I have to do is to study the situation as fully as I can until I form the considered opinion (it is never more) that in the circumstances one of them is more incumbent than any other; then I am bound to think that to do this *prima facie* duty is my duty *sans phrase* in the situation.

I suggest '*prima facie* duty' or 'conditional duty' as a brief way of referring to the characteristic (quite distinct from that of being a duty proper) which an act has, in virtue of being of a certain kind (e.g. the keeping of a promise), of being an act which would be a duty proper if it were not at the same time of another kind which is morally significant. Whether an act is a duty proper or actual duty depends on *all* the morally significant kinds it is an instance of.

The phrase '*prima facie* duty' must be apologized for, since (1) it suggests that what we are speaking of is a certain kind of duty, whereas it is in fact not a duty, but something related in a special way to duty. Strictly speaking, we want not a phrase in which duty is qualified by an adjective, but a separate noun. (2) '*Prima*' *facie* suggests that one is speaking only of an appearance which a moral situation presents at first sight, and which may turn out to be illusory; whereas what I am speaking of is an objective fact involved in the nature of the situation, or more strictly in an element of its nature, though not, as duty proper does, arising from its whole nature.

There is nothing arbitrary about these *prima facie* duties. Each rests on a definite circumstance which cannot seriously be held to be without moral significance. Of *prima facie* duties I suggest, without claiming completeness or finality for it, the following division.

1. Some duties rest on previous acts of my own. These duties seem to include two kinds.
   A. Those resting on a promise or what may fairly be called an implicit promise, such as the implicit undertaking not to tell lies which seems to be implied in the act of entering into conversation (at any rate by civilized men), or of writing books that purport to be history and not fiction. These may be called the duties of fidelity.
   B. Those resting on a previous wrongful act. These may be called the duties of reparation.
2. Some rest on previous acts of other men, i.e. services done by them to me. These may be loosely described as the duties of gratitude.
3. Some rest on the fact or possibility of a distribution of pleasure or happiness (or of the means thereto) which is not in accordance with the merit of the persons concerned; in such cases there arises a duty to upset or prevent such a distribution. These are the duties of justice.
4. Some rest on the mere fact that there are beings in the world whose condition we can make better in respect of virtue, or of intelligence, or of pleasure. These are the duties of beneficence.

5. Some rest on the fact that we can improve our own condition in respect of virtue or of intelligence. These are the duties of self-improvement.

6. I think that we should distinguish from (4) the duties that may be summed up under the title of 'not injuring others'. No doubt to injure others is incidentally to fail to do them good; but it seems to me clear that non-maleficence is apprehended as a duty distinct from that of beneficence, and as a duty of a more stringent character.

The essential defect of the 'ideal utilitarian' theory is that it ignores, or at least does not do full justice to, the highly personal character of duty. If the only duty is to produce the maximum of good, the question who is to have the good—whether it is myself, or my benefactor, or a person to whom I have made a promise to confer that good on him, or a mere fellow man to whom I stand in no such special relation—should make no difference to my having a duty to produce that good. But we are all in fact sure that it makes a vast difference.

If the objection be made, that this catalogue of the main types of duty is an unsystematic one resting on no logical principle, it may be replied, first, that it makes no claim to being ultimate. It is a *prima facie* classification of the duties which reflection on our moral convictions seems actually to reveal. And if these convictions are, as I would claim that they are, of the nature of knowledge, and if I have not misstated them, the list will be a list of authentic conditional duties, correct as far as it goes though not necessarily complete. The list of *goods* put forward by the rival theory is reached by exactly the same method—the only sound one in the circumstances—viz. that of direct reflection on what we really think. Loyalty to the facts is worth more than a symmetrical architectonic or a hastily reached simplicity. If further reflection discovers a perfect logical basis for this or for a better classification, so much the better.

It may, again, be objected that our theory that there are these various and often conflicting types of *prima facie* duty leaves us with no principle upon which to discern what is our actual duty in particular circumstances. But this objection is not one which the rival theory is in a position to bring forward. For when we have to choose between the production of two heterogeneous goods, say knowledge and pleasure, the 'ideal utilitarian' theory can only fall back on an opinion, for which no logical basis can be offered, that one of the goods is the greater; and this is no better than a similar opinion that one of two duties is the more urgent. And again, when we consider the infinite variety of the effects of our actions in the way of pleasure, it must surely be admitted that the claim which *hedonism* sometimes makes, that it offers a readily applicable criterion of right conduct, is quite illusory.

I am unwilling, however, to content myself with an *argumentum ad hominem*, and I would contend that in principle there is no reason to anticipate that every act that is our duty is so for one and the same reason. Why should two sets of circumstances, or one set of circumstances, not possess different characteristics, any one of which makes a certain act our *prima facie* duty? When I ask what it is that makes me in certain cases sure that I have a *prima facie* duty to do so and so, I find that it lies in the fact that I have made a promise; when I ask the same question in another case, I find the answer lies in the fact that I have done a wrong. And if on reflection I find (as I think I do) that neither of these reasons is reducible to the other, I must not on any *a priori* ground assume that such a reduction is possible.

It is necessary to say something by way of clearing up the relation between *prima facie* duties and the actual or absolute duty to do one particular act in particular circumstances. If, as almost all moralists except Kant are agreed, and as most plain men think, it is sometimes right to tell a lie or to break a promise, it must be maintained that there is a difference between *prima facie* duty and actual or absolute duty. When we think ourselves justified in breaking, and indeed morally obliged to break, a promise in order to relieve some one's distress, we do not for a moment cease to recognize a *prima facie* duty to keep our promise, and this leads us to feel, not indeed shame or repentance, but certainly compunction, for behaving as we do; we recognize, further, that it is our duty to make up somehow to the promisee for the breaking of the promise. We have to distinguish from the characteristic of being our duty that of tending to be our duty. Any act that we do contains various elements in virtue of which it falls under various categories. In virtue of being the breaking of a promise, for instance, it tends to be wrong; in virtue of being an instance of relieving distress it tends to be right.

Something should be said of the relation between our apprehension of the *prima facie* rightness of certain types of act and our mental attitude towards particular acts. It is proper to use the word 'apprehension' in the former case and not in the latter. That an act, *qua* fulfilling a promise, or *qua* effecting a just distribution of good, or *qua* returning services rendered, or *qua* promoting the good of others, or *qua* promoting the virtue or insight of the agent, is *prima facie* right, is self-evident; not in the sense that it is evident from the beginning of our lives, or as soon as we attend to the proposition for the first time, but in the sense that when we have reached sufficient mental maturity and have given sufficient attention to the proposition it is evident without any need of proof, or of evidence beyond itself. It is self-evident just as a mathematical axiom, or the validity of a form of inference, is evident. The moral order expressed in these propositions is just as much part of the fundamental nature of the universe (and, we may add, of any possible universe in which there were moral agents at all) as is the spatial or numerical structure expressed in the axioms of geometry or arithmetic. In our confidence that these propositions are true there is involved the same trust in our reason that is involved in our confidence in mathematics; and we should have no justification for trusting it in the latter sphere and distrusting it in the former. In both cases we are dealing with propositions that cannot be proved, but that just as certainly need no proof.

Our judgements about our actual duty in concrete situations have none of the certainty that attaches to our recognition of the general principles of duty. A statement is certain, i.e. is an expression of knowledge, only in one or other of two cases: when it is either self-evident, or a valid conclusion from self-evident premises. And our judgements about our particular duties have neither of these characters. (1) They are not self-evident. Where a possible act is seen to have two characteristics, in virtue of one of which it is *prima facie* right, and in virtue of the other *prima facie* wrong, we are (I think) well aware that we are not certain whether we ought or ought not to do it; that whether we do it or not, we are taking a moral risk. We come in the long run, after consideration, to think one duty more pressing than the other, but we do not feel certain that it is so. And though we do not always recognize that a possible act has two such characteristics, and though there may be cases in which it has not, we are never certain that any particular possible act has not, and therefore never certain that it is right, nor certain that it is wrong. For, to go no further in the analysis, it is enough to point out that any particular act will in all probability in the course of time contribute to the bringing about of good or of evil for many human beings, and thus have a *prima facie* rightness or wrongness of which we know nothing. (2) Again, our judgements about our particular duties are not logical conclusions from self-evident premisses. The only possible premisses would be the general principles stating their *prima facie* rightness or wrongness *qua* having the different characteristics they do have; and even if we could (as we cannot) apprehend the extent to which an act will tend on the one hand, for example, to bring about advantages for our benefactors, and on the other hand to bring about disadvantages for fellow men who are not our benefactors, there is no principle by which we can draw the conclusion that it is on the whole right or on the whole wrong. In this respect the judgement as to the rightness of a particular act is just like the judgement as to the beauty of a particular natural object or work of art. A poem is, for instance, in respect of certain qualities beautiful and in respect of certain others not beautiful; and our judgement as to the degree of beauty it possesses on the whole is never reached by logical reasoning from the apprehension of its particular beauties or particular defects. Both in this and in the moral case we have more or less probable opinions which are not logically justified conclusions from the general principles that are recognized as self-evident.

There is therefore much truth in the description of the right act as a fortunate act. If we cannot be certain that it is right, it is our good fortune if the act we do is the right act. This consideration does not, however, make the doing of our duty a mere matter of chance. There is a parallel here between the doing of duty and the doing of what will be to our personal advantage. We never *know* what act will in the long run be to our advantage. Yet it is certain that we are more likely in general to secure our advantage if we estimate to the best of our ability the probable tendencies of our actions in this respect, than if we act on caprice. And similarly we are more likely to do our duty if we reflect to the best of our ability on the *prima facie* rightness or wrongness of various possible acts in virtue of the characteristics we perceive them to have, than if we act without reflection. With this greater likelihood we must be content.

The general principles of duty are obviously not self-evident from the beginning of our lives. How do they come to be so? The answer is, that they come to be self-evident to us just as mathematical axioms do. We find by experience that this couple of matches and that couple make four matches, that this couple of balls on a wire and that couple make four balls: and by reflection on these and similar discoveries we come to see that it is of the nature of two and two to make four. In a precisely similar way, we see the *prima facie* rightness of an act which would be the fulfilment of a particular promise, and of another which would be the fulfilment of another promise, and when we have reached sufficient maturity to think in general terms, we apprehend *prima facie* rightness to belong to the nature of any fulfilment of promise. What comes first in time is the apprehension of the self-evident *prima facie* rightness of an individual act of a particular type. From this we come by reflection to apprehend the self-evident general principle of *prima facie* duty. From this, too, perhaps along with the apprehension of the self-evident *prima facie* rightness of the same act in virtue of its having another characteristic as well, and perhaps in spite of the apprehension of its *prima facie* wrongness in virtue of its having some third characteristic, we come to believe something not self-evident at all, but an object of probable opinion, viz. that this particular act is (not *prima facie* but) actually right.

In what has preceded, a good deal of use has been made of 'what we really think' about moral questions; a certain theory has been rejected because it does not agree with what we really think. It might be said that this is in principle wrong; that we should not be content to expound what our present moral consciousness tells us but should aim at a criticism of our existing moral consciousness in the light of theory. Now I do not doubt that the moral consciousness of men has in detail undergone a good deal of modification as regards the things we think right, at the hands of moral theory. But if we are told, for instance, that we should give up our view that there is a special obligatoriness attaching to the keeping of promises because it is self-evident that the only duty is to produce as much good as possible, we have to ask ourselves whether we really, when we reflect, are convinced that this is self-evident, and whether we really can get rid of our view that promise-keeping has a bindingness independent of productiveness of maximum good. In my own experience I find that I cannot, in spite of a very genuine attempt to do so; and I venture to think that most people will find the same.

I would maintain, in fact, that what we are apt to describe as 'what we think' about moral questions contains a considerable amount that we do not think but know, and that this forms the standard by reference to which the truth of any moral theory has to be tested, instead of having itself to be tested by reference to any theory. I hope that I have in what precedes indicated what in my view these elements of knowledge are that are involved in our ordinary moral consciousness.

It would be a mistake to found a natural science on 'what we really think', i.e. on what reasonably thoughtful and well-educated people think about the subjects of the science before they have studied them scientifically. For such opinions are interpretations, and often misinterpretations, of sense-experience; and the man of science must appeal from these to sense-experience itself, which furnishes his real data. In ethics no such appeal is possible. We have no more direct way of access to the facts about rightness and goodness and about what things are right or good, than by thinking about them; the moral convictions of thoughtful and well-educated people are the data of ethics just as sense-perceptions are the data of a natural science. Just as some of the latter have to be rejected as illusory, so have some of the former; but as the latter are rejected only when they are in conflict with other more accurate sense-perceptions, the former are rejected only when they are in conflict with other convictions which stand better the test of reflection. The existing body of moral convictions of the best people is the cumulative product of the moral reflection of many generations, which has developed an extremely delicate power of appreciation of moral distinctions; and this the theorist cannot afford to treat with anything other than the greatest respect. The verdicts of the moral consciousness of the best people are the foundation on which he must build; though he must first compare them with one another and eliminate any contradictions they may contain.

W. D. Ross: What Makes Right Acts Right?

1. Ross begins by considering the view that the right action is the one that is "productive of more *good* than could have been produced by any other action open to the agent." What objections does he offer to this view? Do you think they are good ones?

2. Ross also considers Kant's view, according to which there are certain moral rules that must be followed without exception. What does Ross think is wrong with this theory? Do you agree with his criticism?

3. What does Ross mean by "*prima facie* duties," and how do these differ from "duty proper"? How does he think we should use our knowledge of prima facie duties to determine what our duty is in a particular situation?

4. How does Ross think we come to know prima facie duties? Do you find his view plausible?

5. What reasons does Ross give for his claim that we can never be certain about what the right thing to do is in a particular situation? Do you agree with him about this?

6. Ross claims that "the moral convictions of thoughtful and well-educated people are the data of ethics just as sense-perceptions are the data of a natural science." Is beginning with our own moral convictions the best way of doing ethics, or do you think there is a better way?

12

Nicomachean Ethics

Aristotle

....

Aristotle (384–322 BCE) was perhaps the greatest philosopher who ever lived. He worked in a variety of philosophical areas (logic, metaphysics, philosophy of mind, epistemology, ethics, rhetoric), and in each field produced work that exerted an influence across many centuries.

His seminal work in moral philosophy is *Nicomachean Ethics*, believed to be a set of carefully recorded lecture notes taken down by Aristotle's students. In this excerpt, from book 2 of the *Nicomachean Ethics*, Aristotle discusses the nature of virtue, its role in a good human life, and its relation to happiness and to "the golden mean." Aristotle's thoughts on the virtues have served as the basis of almost every version of virtue ethics developed in Western philosophy over the past two millennia.

....

Aristotle, from *Nicomachean Ethics* (1998), trans. W. D. Ross, pp. 28–47. By permission of Oxford University Press.

Moral Virtue

Moral Virtue, How Produced, in What Medium and in What Manner Exhibited

Moral virtue, like the arts, is acquired by repetition of the corresponding acts

VIRTUE, . . . being of two kinds, intellectual and moral, intellectual virtue in the main owes both its birth and its growth to teaching (for which reason it requires experience and time), while moral virtue comes about as a result of habit, whence also its name (ἠθική) is one that is formed by a slight variation from the word 'ἔθος (habit). From this it is also plain that none of the moral virtues arises in us by nature; for nothing that exists by nature can form a habit contrary to its nature. For instance the stone which by nature moves downwards cannot be habituated to move upwards, not even if one tries to train it by throwing it up ten thousand times; nor can fire be habituated to move downwards, nor can anything else that by nature behaves in one way be trained to behave in another. Neither by nature, then, nor contrary to nature do the virtues arise in us; rather we are adapted by nature to receive them, and are made perfect by habit.

Again, of all the things that come to us by nature we first acquire the potentiality and later exhibit the activity (this is plain in the case of the senses; for it was not by often seeing or often hearing that we got these senses, but on the contrary we had them before we used them, and did not come to have them by using them); but the virtues we get by first exercising them, as also happens in the case of the arts as well. For the things we have to learn before we can do them, we learn by doing them, e.g. men become builders by building and lyre-players by playing the lyre; so too we become just by doing just acts, temperate by doing temperate acts, brave by doing brave acts.

These acts cannot be prescribed exactly, but must avoid excess and defect

Since, then, the present inquiry does not aim at theoretical knowledge like the others (for we are inquiring not in order to know what virtue is, but in order to become good, since otherwise our inquiry would have been of no use), we must examine the nature of actions, namely how we ought to do them; for these determine also the nature of the states of character that are produced, as we have said. Now, that we must act according to the right rule is a common principle and must be assumed—it will be discussed later, i.e. both what the right rule is, and how it is related to the other virtues. But this must be agreed upon beforehand, that the whole account of matters of conduct must be given in outline and not precisely, . . . that the accounts we demand must be in accordance with the subject-matter; matters concerned with conduct and questions of what is good for us have no fixity, any more than matters of health. The general account being of this nature, the account of particular cases is yet more lacking in exactness; for they do not fall under any art or precept, but the agents themselves must in each case consider what is appropriate to the occasion, as happens also in the art of medicine or of navigation.

But though our present account is of this nature we must give what help we can. First, then, let us consider this, that it is the nature of such things to be destroyed by defect and excess, as we see in the case of strength and of health (for to gain light on things imperceptible we must use the evidence of sensible things); exercise either excessive or defective destroys the strength, and similarly drink or food which is above or below a certain amount destroys the health, while that which is proportionate both produces and increases and preserves it. So too is it, then, in the case of temperance and courage and the other virtues. For the man who flies from and fears everything and does not stand his ground against anything becomes a coward, and the man who fears nothing at all but goes to meet every danger becomes rash; and similarly the man who indulges in every pleasure and abstains from none becomes self-indulgent, while the man who shuns every pleasure, as boors do, becomes in a way insensible; temperance and courage, then, are destroyed by excess and defect, and preserved by the mean.

But not only are the sources and causes of their origination and growth the same as those of their destruction, but also the sphere of their actualization will be the same; for this is also true of the things which are more evident to sense, e.g. of strength; it is produced by taking much food and undergoing much exertion, and it is the strong man that will be most able to do these things. So too is it with the virtues; by abstaining from pleasures we become temperate, and it is when we have become so that we are most able to abstain from them; and similarly too in the case of courage; for by being habituated to despise things that are fearful and to stand our ground against them we become brave, and it is when we have become so that we shall be most able to stand our ground against them.

Pleasure in doing virtuous acts is a sign that the virtuous
disposition has been acquired: a variety of considerations
show the essential connexion of moral virtue with
pleasure and pain

We must take as a sign of states of character the pleasure or pain that supervenes upon acts; for the man who abstains from bodily pleasures and delights in this very fact is temperate, while the man who is annoyed at it is self-indulgent, and he who stands his ground against things that are terrible and delights in this or at least is not pained is brave, while the man who is pained is a coward. For moral excellence is concerned with pleasures and pains; it is on account of the pleasure that we do bad things, and on account of the pain that we abstain from noble ones. Hence we ought to have been brought up in a particular way from our very youth, as Plato says, so as both to delight in and to be pained by the things that we ought; this is the right education.

We assume, then, that this kind of excellence tends to do what is best with regard to pleasures and pains, and vice does the contrary.

That virtue, then, is concerned with pleasures and pains, and that by the acts from which it arises it is both increased and, if they are done differently, destroyed, and that the acts from which it arose are those in which it actualizes itself—let this be taken as said.

The actions that produce moral virtue are not good in the same
sense as those that flow from it: the latter must
fulfil certain conditions not necessary
inthe case of the arts

The question might be asked, what we mean by saying that we must become just by doing just acts, and temperate by doing temperate acts; for if men do just and temperate acts, they are already just and temperate, exactly as, if they do what is in accordance with the laws of grammar and of music, they are grammarians and musicians.

Or is this not true even of the arts? It is possible to do something that is in accordance with the laws of grammar, either by chance or under the guidance of another. A man will be a grammarian, then, only when he has both said something grammatical and said it grammatically; and this means doing it in accordance with the grammatical knowledge in himself.

Again, the case of the arts and that of the virtues are not similar; for the products of the arts have their goodness in themselves, so that it is enough that they should have a certain character, but if the acts that are in accordance with the virtues have themselves a certain character it does not follow that they are done justly or temperately. The agent also must be in a certain condition when he does them; in the first place he must have knowledge, secondly he must choose the acts, and choose them for their own sakes, and thirdly his action must proceed from a firm and unchangeable character. These are not reckoned in as conditions of the possession of the arts except the bare knowledge; but as a condition of the possession of the virtues knowledge has little or no weight, while the other conditions count not for a little but for everything, i.e. the very conditions which result from often doing just and temperate acts.

Actions, then, are called just and temperate when they are such as the just or the temperate man would do; but it is not the man who does these that is just and temperate, but the man who also does them *as* just and temperate men do them. It is well said, then, that it is by doing just acts that the just man is produced, and by doing temperate acts the temperate man; without doing these no one would have even a prospect of becoming good.

Definition of Moral Virtue

The genus of moral virtue: it is a state of character,
not a passion, nor a faculty

Next we must consider what virtue is. Since things that are found in the soul are of three kinds—passions, faculties, states of character—virtue must be one of these. By passions I mean appetite, anger, fear, confidence, envy, joy, friendly feeling, hatred, longing, emulation, pity, and in general the feelings that are accompanied by pleasure or pain; by faculties the things in virtue of which we are said to be capable of feeling these, e.g. of becoming angry or being pained or feeling pity; by states of character the things in virtue of which we stand well or badly with reference to the passions, e.g. with reference to anger we stand badly if we feel it violently or too weakly, and well if we feel it moderately; and similarly with reference to the other passions.

Now neither the virtues nor the vices are *passions*, because we are not called good or bad on the ground of our passions, but are so called on the ground of our virtues and our vices, and because we are neither praised nor blamed for our passions (for the man who feels fear or anger is not praised, nor is the man who simply feels anger blamed, but the man who feels it in a certain way), but for our virtues and our vices we *are* praised or blamed.

Again, we feel anger and fear without choice, but the virtues are modes of choice or involve choice. Further, in respect of the passions we are said to be moved, but in respect of the virtues and the vices we are said not to be moved but to be disposed in a particular way.

For these reasons also they are not *faculties*; for we are neither called good or bad, nor praised or blamed, for the simple capacity of feeling the passions; again, we have the faculties by nature, but we are not made good or bad by nature; we have spoken of this before.

If, then, the virtues are neither passions nor faculties, all that remains is that they should be *states of character*.

Thus we have stated what virtue is in respect of its genus.

The differentia of moral virtue: it is a disposition to choose the mean

We must, however, not only describe virtue as a state of character, but also say what sort of state it is. We may remark, then, that every virtue or excellence both brings into good condition the thing of which it is the excellence and makes the work of that thing be done well; e.g. the excellence of the eye makes both the eye and its work good; for it is by the excellence of the eye that we see well. Similarly the excellence of the horse makes a horse both good in itself and good at running and at carrying its rider and at awaiting the attack of the enemy. Therefore, if this is true in every case, the virtue of man also will be the state of character which makes a man good and which makes him do his own work well.

How this is to happen we have stated already, but it will be made plain also by the following consideration of the specific nature of virtue. In everything that is continuous and divisible it is possible to take more, less, or an equal amount, and that either in terms of the thing itself or relatively to us; and the equal is an intermediate between excess and defect. By the intermediate in the object I mean that which is equidistant from each of the extremes, which is one and the same for all men; by the intermediate relatively to us that which is neither too much nor too little—and this is not one, nor the same for all. For instance, if ten is many and two is few, six is the intermediate, taken in terms of the object; for it exceeds and is exceeded by an equal amount; this is intermediate according to arithmetical proportion. But the intermediate relatively to us is not to be taken so; if ten pounds are too much for a particular person to eat and two too little, it does not follow that the trainer will order six pounds; for this also is perhaps too much for the person who is to take it, or too little—too little for Milo, too much for the beginner in athletic exercises. The same is true of running and wrestling. Thus a master of any art avoids excess and defect, but seeks the intermediate and chooses this—the intermediate not in the object but relatively to us.

If it is thus, then, that every art does its work well—by looking to the intermediate and judging its works by this standard (so that we often say of good works of art that it is not possible either to take away or to add anything, implying that excess and defect destroy the goodness of works of art, while the mean preserves it; and good artists, as we say, look to this in their work), and if, further, virtue is more exact and better than any art, as nature also is, then virtue must have the quality of aiming at the intermediate. I mean moral virtue; for it is this that is concerned with passions and actions, and in these there is excess, defect, and the intermediate. For instance, both fear and confidence and appetite and anger and pity and in general pleasure and pain may be felt both too much and too little, and in both cases not well; but to feel them at the right times, with reference to the right objects, towards the right people, with the right motive, and in the right way, is what is both intermediate and best, and this is characteristic of virtue. Similarly with regard to actions also there is excess, defect, and the intermediate. Now virtue is concerned with passions and actions, in which excess is a form of failure, and so is defect, while the intermediate is praised and is a form of success; and being praised and being successful are both characteristics of virtue. Therefore virtue is a kind of mean, since, as we have seen, it aims at what is intermediate.

Again, it is possible to fail in many ways (for evil belongs to the class of the unlimited, as the Pythagoreans conjectured, and good to that of the limited), while to succeed is possible only in one way (for which reason also one is easy and the other difficult—to miss the mark easy, to hit it difficult); for these reasons also, then, excess and defect are characteristic of vice, and the mean of virtue;

For men are good in but one way, but bad in many.

Virtue, then, is a state of character concerned with choice, lying in a mean, i.e. the mean relative to us, this being determined by a rational principle, and by that principle by which the man of practical wisdom would determine it. Now it is a mean between two vices, that which depends on excess and that which depends on defect; and again it is a mean because the vices respectively fall short of or exceed what is right in both passions and actions, while virtue both finds and chooses that which is intermediate. Hence in respect of what it is, i.e. the definition which states its essence, virtue is a mean, with regard to what is best and right an extreme.

But not every action nor every passion admits of a mean; for some have names that already imply badness, e.g. spite, shamelessness, envy, and in the case of actions adultery, theft, murder; for all of these and suchlike things imply by their names that they are themselves bad, and not the excesses or deficiencies of them. It is not possible, then, ever to be right with regard to them; one must always be wrong. Nor does goodness or badness with regard to such things depend on committing adultery with the right woman, at the right time, and in the right way, but simply to do any of them is to go wrong. It would be equally absurd, then, to expect that in unjust, cowardly, and voluptuous action there should be a mean, an excess, and a deficiency; for at that rate there would be a mean of excess and of deficiency, an excess of excess, and a deficiency of deficiency. But as there is no excess and deficiency of temperance and courage because what is intermediate is in a sense an extreme, so too of the actions we have mentioned there is no mean nor any excess and deficiency, but however they are done they are wrong; for in general there is neither a mean of excess and deficiency, nor excess and deficiency of a mean.

The above proposition illustrated by reference to particular virtues

We must, however, not only make this general statement, but also apply it to the individual facts. For among statements about conduct those which are general apply more widely, but those which are particular are more true, since conduct has to do with individual cases, and our statements must harmonize with the facts in these cases. We may take these cases from our table. With regard to feelings of fear and confidence courage is the mean; of the people who exceed, he who exceeds in fearlessness has no name (many of the states have no name), while the man who exceeds in confidence is rash, and he who exceeds in fear and falls short in confidence is a coward. With regard to pleasures and pains—not all of them, and not so much with regard to the pains—the mean is temperance, the excess self-indulgence. Persons deficient with regard to the pleasures are not often found; hence such persons also have received no name. But let us call them 'insensible'.

With regard to giving and taking of money the mean is liberality, the excess and the defect prodigality and meanness. In these actions people exceed and fall short in contrary ways; the prodigal exceeds in spending and falls short in taking, while the mean man exceeds in taking and falls short in spending. (At present we are giving a mere outline or summary, and are satisfied with this; later these states will be more exactly determined.) With regard to money there are also other dispositions—a mean, magnificence (for the magnificent man differs from the liberal man; the former deals with large sums, the latter with small ones), an excess, tastelessness and vulgarity, and a deficiency, niggardliness; these differ from the states opposed to liberality, and the mode of their difference will be stated later.

With regard to honour and dishonour the mean is proper pride, the excess is known as a sort of 'empty vanity', and the deficiency is undue humility; and as we said liberality was related to magnificence, differing from it by dealing with small sums, so there is a state similarly related to proper pride, being concerned with small honours while that is concerned with great. For it is possible to desire honour as one ought, and more than one ought, and less, and the man who exceeds in his desires is called ambitious, the man who falls short unambitious, while the intermediate person has no name. The dispositions also are nameless, except that that of the ambitious man is called ambition. Hence the people who are at the extremes lay claim to the middle place; and we ourselves sometimes call the intermediate person ambitious and sometimes unambitious, and sometimes praise the ambitious man and sometimes the unambitious. The reason of our doing this will be stated in what follows; but now let us speak of the remaining states according to the method which has been indicated.

With regard to anger also there is an excess, a deficiency, and a mean. Although they can scarcely be said to have names, yet since we call the intermediate person good-tempered let us call the mean good temper; of the persons at the extremes let the one who exceeds be called irascible, and his vice irascibility, and the man who falls short an unirascible sort of person, and the deficiency unirascibility.

Characteristics of the Extreme and Mean States: Practical Corollaries

The extremes are opposed to each other and to the mean
There are three kinds of disposition, then, two of them vices, involving excess and deficiency respectively, and one a virtue, viz. the mean, and all are in a sense opposed to all; for the extreme states are contrary both

to the intermediate state and to each other, and the intermediate to the extremes; as the equal is greater relatively to the less, less relatively to the greater, so the middle states are excessive relatively to the deficiencies, deficient relatively to the excesses, both in passions and in actions. For the brave man appears rash relatively to the coward, and cowardly relatively to the rash man; and similarly the temperate man appears self-indulgent relatively to the insensible man, insensible relatively to the self-indulgent, and the liberal man prodigal relatively to the mean man, mean relatively to the prodigal. Hence also the people at the extremes push the intermediate man each over to the other, and the brave man is called rash by the coward, cowardly by the rash man, and correspondingly in the other cases.

These states being thus opposed to one another, the greatest contrariety is that of the extremes to each other, rather than to the intermediate; for these are further from each other than from the intermediate, as the great is further from the small and the small from the great than both are from the equal. Again, to the intermediate some extremes show a certain likeness, as that of rashness to courage and that of prodigality to liberality; but the extremes show the greatest unlikeness to each other; now contraries are defined as the things that are furthest from each other, so that things that are further apart are more contrary.

To the mean in some cases the deficiency, in some the excess, is more opposed; e.g. it is not rashness, which is an excess, but cowardice, which is a deficiency, that is more opposed to courage, and not insensibility, which is a deficiency, but self-indulgence, which is an excess, that is more opposed to temperance. This happens from two reasons, one being drawn from the thing itself; for because one extreme is nearer and liker to the intermediate, we oppose not this but rather its contrary to the intermediate. E.g., since rashness is thought liker and nearer to courage, and cowardice more unlike, we oppose rather the latter to courage; for things that are further from the intermediate are thought more contrary to it. This, then, is one cause, drawn from the thing itself; another is drawn from ourselves; for the things to which we ourselves more naturally tend seem more contrary to the intermediate. For instance, we ourselves tend more naturally to pleasures, and hence are more easily carried away towards self-indulgence than towards propriety. We describe as contrary to the mean, then, rather the directions in which we more often go to great lengths; and therefore self-indulgence, which is an excess, is the more contrary to temperance.

The mean is hard to attain, and is grasped by perception,
not by reasoning

That moral virtue is a mean, then, and in what sense it is so, and that it is
a mean between two vices, the one involving excess, the other deficiency,
and that it is such because its character is to aim at what is intermediate
in passions and in actions, has been sufficiently stated. Hence also it is no
easy task to be good. For in everything it is no easy task to find the middle, e.g. to find the middle of a circle is not for everyone but for him who
knows; so, too, anyone can get angry—that is easy—or give or spend
money; but to do this to the right person, to the right extent, at the right
time, with the right motive, and in the right way, *that* is not for everyone,
nor is it easy; wherefore goodness is both rare and laudable and noble.

Hence he who aims at the intermediate must first depart from what is
the more contrary to it, as Calypso advises—

Hold the ship out beyond that surf and spray.

For of the extremes one is more erroneous, one less so; therefore, since
to hit the mean is hard in the extreme, we must as a second best, as people
say, take the least of the evils; and this will be done best in the way we
describe.

But we must consider the things towards which we ourselves also are
easily carried away; for some of us tend to one thing, some to another; and
this will be recognizable from the pleasure and the pain we feel. We must
drag ourselves away to the contrary extreme; for we shall get into the intermediate state by drawing well away from error, as people do in straighten-
ing sticks that are bent.

Now in everything the pleasant or pleasure is most to be guarded
against; for we do not judge it impartially. We ought, then, to feel towards
pleasure as the elders of the people felt towards Helen, and in all circumstances repeat their saying; for if we dismiss pleasure thus we are less likely
to go astray. It is by doing this, then, (to sum the matter up) that we shall
best be able to hit the mean.

But this is no doubt difficult, and especially in individual cases; for it
is not easy to determine both how and with whom and on what provocation and how long one should be angry; for we too sometimes praise those
who fall short and call them good-tempered, but sometimes we praise
those who get angry and call them manly. The man, however, who deviates
little from goodness is not blamed, whether he do so in the direction of the

more or of the less, but only the man who deviates more widely; for *he* does not fail to be noticed. But up to what point and to what extent a man must deviate before he becomes blameworthy it is not easy to determine by reasoning, any more than anything else that is perceived by the senses; such things depend on particular facts, and the decision rests with perception. So much, then, is plain, that the intermediate state is in all things to be praised, but that we must incline sometimes towards the excess, sometimes towards the deficiency; for so shall we most easily hit the mean and what is right.

Aristotle: Nicomachean Ethics

1. Some philosophers have maintained that people are naturally morally good, while others have held that people are naturally wicked. Aristotle takes a middle ground, saying, "Neither by nature, then, nor contrary to nature do the virtues arise in us." Which view do you think is correct, and why?
2. What do you think Aristotle means when he says that "matters concerned with conduct and questions of what is good for us have no fixity"? Do you agree with this statement?
3. What is the difference, according to Aristotle, between performing virtuous actions and being a virtuous person? Do you agree with him that the latter is more valuable?
4. Aristotle says that virtue is a "mean" between extremes. For instance, the virtue of courage consists of the disposition to feel neither too much nor too little fear, but rather some appropriate amount in between. Is this consistent with his claim that some actions (such as stealing or adultery) are always wrong in all circumstances?
5. What advice does Aristotle give regarding how we should go about seeking the mean between extremes? Do you think this is good advice?

13

What Is Feminist Ethics?

Hilde Lindemann

Hilde Lindemann offers us a brief overview of feminist ethics in this
selection. She first discusses the nature of feminism and identifies
some of the various ways that people have defined it. Lindemann
argues against thinking of feminism as focused primarily on equality,
women, or the differences between the sexes. She instead invites us to
think of feminism as based on considerations of gender—specifically,
considerations to do with the lesser degree of power that women have,
largely the world over, as compared with men.

Lindemann proceeds to discuss the sex/gender distinction and to
identify the central tasks of feminist ethics: to understand, criticize,
and correct the inaccurate gender assumptions that underlie our moral
thinking and behavior. An important approach of most feminists is a
kind of skepticism about the ability to distinguish political commitments from intellectual ones. Lindemann concludes by discussing this
skepticism and its implications for feminist thought.

A few years ago, a dentist in Ohio was convicted of having sex with
his female patients while they were under anesthesia. I haven't
been able to discover whether he had to pay a fine or do jail time,

Hilde Lindemann, "What Is Feminist Ethics?" from *An Invitation to Feminist Ethics* (2004),
pp. 2–3, 6–16. Reproduced with the permission of The McGraw-Hill Companies.

but I do remember that the judge ordered him to take a course in ethics. And I recall thinking how odd that order was. Let's suppose, as the judge apparently did, that the dentist really and truly didn't know it was wrong to have sex with anesthetized patients (this will tax your imagination, but try to suppose it anyway). Can we expect—again, as the judge apparently did—that on completing the ethics course, the dentist would be a better, finer man?

Hardly. If studying ethics could make you good, then the people who have advanced academic degrees in the subject would be paragons of moral uprightness. I can't speak for all of them, of course, but though the ones I know are nice enough, they're no more moral than anyone else. Ethics doesn't improve your character. Its *subject* is morality, but its relationship to morality is that of a scholarly study to the thing being studied. In that respect, the relationship is a little like the relationship between grammar and language.

Let's explore that analogy. People who speak fluent English don't have to stop and think about the correctness of the sentence "He gave it to *her.*" But here's a harder one. Should you say, "He gave it to *her* who must be obeyed?" or "He gave it to *she* who must be obeyed?" To sort this out, it helps to know a little grammar—the systematic, scholarly description of the structure of the language and the rules for speaking and writing in it. According to those rules, the object of the preposition "to" is the entire clause that comes after it, and the subject of that clause is "she." So, even though it sounds peculiar, the correct answer is "He gave it to she who must be obeyed."

In a roughly similar vein, morally competent adults don't have to stop and think about whether it's wrong to have sex with one's anesthetized patients. But if you want to understand whether it's wrong to have large signs in bars telling pregnant women not to drink, or to sort out the conditions under which it's all right to tell a lie, it helps to know a little ethics. The analogy between grammar and ethics isn't exact, of course. For one thing, there's considerably more agreement about what language is than about what morality is. For another, grammarians are concerned only with the structure of language, not with the meaning or usage of particular words. In both cases, however, the same point can be made: You already have to know quite a lot about how to behave—linguistically or morally—before there's much point in studying either grammar or ethics. . . .

What Is Feminism?

What, then, is feminism? As a social and political movement with a long, intermittent history, feminism has repeatedly come into public awareness, generated change, and then disappeared again. As an eclectic body of theory, feminism entered colleges and universities in the early 1970s as a part of the women's studies movement, contributing to scholarship in every academic discipline, though probably most heavily in the arts, social sciences, literature, and the humanities in general. Feminist ethics is a part of the body of theory that is being developed primarily in colleges and universities.

Many people in the United States think of feminism as a movement that aims to make women the social equals of men, and this impression has been reinforced by references to feminism and feminists in the newspapers, on television, and in the movies. But bell hooks has pointed out in *Feminist Theory from Margin to Center* (1984, 18–19) that this way of defining feminism raises some serious problems. Which men do women want to be equal to? Women who are socially well off wouldn't get much advantage from being the equals of the men who are poor and lower class, particularly if they aren't white. hooks's point is that there are no women and men in the abstract. They are poor, black, young, Latino/a, old, gay, able-bodied, upper class, down on their luck, Native American, straight, and all the rest of it. When a woman doesn't think about this, it's probably because she doesn't have to. And that's usually a sign that her own social position is privileged. In fact, privilege often means that there's something uncomfortable going on that others have to pay attention to but you don't. So, when hooks asks which men women want to be equal to, she's reminding us that there's an unconscious presumption of privilege built right in to this sort of demand for equality.

There's a second problem with the equality definition. Even if we could figure out which men are the ones to whom women should be equal, that way of putting it suggests that the point of feminism is somehow to get women to measure up to what (at least some) men already are. Men remain the point of reference; theirs are the lives that women would naturally want. If the first problem with the equality definition is "Equal to *which* men?" the second problem could be put as "Why equal to *any* men?" Reforming a system in which men are the point of reference by allowing women to perform as their equals "forces women to focus on men and address men's conceptions of women rather than creating and developing women's values about themselves," as Sarah Lucia Hoagland puts it in *Lesbian Ethics* (1988, 57). For that reason, Hoagland and some other feminists believe that feminism is first and foremost about women.

But characterizing feminism as about women has its problems too. What, after all, is a woman? In her 1949 book, *The Second Sex*, the French feminist philosopher Simone de Beauvoir famously observed, "One is not born, but becomes a woman. No biological, psychological, or economic fate determines the figure that the human female presents in society: it is civilization as a whole that produces this creature, intermediate between male and eunuch, which is described as feminine" (Beauvoir 1949, 301). Her point is that while plenty of human beings are born female, 'woman' is not a natural fact about them—it's a social invention. According to that invention, which is widespread in "civilization as a whole," man represents the positive, typical human being, while woman represents only the negative, the not-man. She is the Other against whom man defines himself—he is all the things that she is not. And she exists only in relation to him. In a later essay called "One Is Not Born a Woman," the lesbian author and theorist Monique Wittig (1981, 49) adds that because women belong to men sexually as well as in every other way, women are necessarily heterosexual. For that reason, she argued, lesbians aren't women.

But, you are probably thinking, everybody knows what a woman is, and lesbians certainly *are* women. And you're right. These French feminists aren't denying that there's a perfectly ordinary use of the word *woman* by which it means exactly what you think it means. But they're explaining what this comes down to, if you look at it from a particular point of view. Their answer to the question "What is a woman?" is that women are different from men. But they don't mean this as a trite observation. They're saying that 'woman' refers to *nothing but* difference from men, so that apart from men, women aren't anything. 'Man' is the positive term, 'woman' is the negative one, just like 'light' is the positive term and 'dark' is nothing but the absence of light.

A later generation of feminists have agreed with Beauvoir and Wittig that women are different from men, but rather than seeing that difference as simply negative, they put it in positive terms, affirming feminine qualities as a source of personal strength and pride. For example, the philosopher Virginia Held thinks that women's moral experience as mothers, attentively nurturing their children, may serve as a better model for social relations than the contract model that the free market provides. The poet Adrienne Rich celebrated women's passionate nature (as opposed, in stereotype, to the rational nature of men), regarding the emotions as morally valuable rather than as signs of weakness.

But defining feminism as about the positive differences between men and women creates yet another set of problems. In her 1987 *Feminism Unmodified*, the feminist legal theorist Catharine A. MacKinnon points out that this kind of difference, as such, is a symmetrical relationship: If I am different from you, then you are different from me in exactly the same respects and to exactly the same degree. "Men's differences from women are equal to women's differences from men," she writes. "There is an *equality* there. Yet the sexes are not socially equal" (MacKinnon 1987, 37). No amount of attention to the differences between men and women explains why men, as a group, are more socially powerful, valued, advantaged, or free than women. For that, you have to see differences as counting in certain ways, and certain differences being created precisely because they give men *power* over women.

Although feminists disagree about this, my own view is that feminism isn't—at least not directly—about equality, and it isn't about women, and it isn't about difference. It's about power. Specifically, it's about the social pattern, widespread across cultures and history, that distributes power asymmetrically to favor men over women. This asymmetry has been given many names, including the subjugation of women, sexism, male dominance, patriarchy, systemic misogyny, phallocracy, and the oppression of women. A number of feminist theorists simply call it gender, and throughout this book, I will too.

What Is Gender?

Most people think their gender is a natural fact about them, like their hair and eye color: "Jones is 5 foot 8, has red hair, and is a man." But gender is a *norm*, not a fact. It's a prescription for how people are supposed to act; what they must or must not wear; how they're supposed to sit, walk, or stand; what kind of person they're supposed to marry; what sorts of things they're supposed to be interested in or good at; and what they're entitled to. And because it's an *effective* norm, it creates the differences between men and women in these areas.

Gender doesn't just tell women to behave one way and men another, though. It's a *power* relation, so it tells men that they're entitled to things that women aren't supposed to have, and it tells women that they are supposed to defer to men and serve them. It says, for example, that men are supposed to occupy positions of religious authority and women are supposed to run the church suppers. It says that mothers are supposed to take care of their children but fathers have more important things to do. And it says that the things associated with femininity are supposed to take a back seat to the things that are coded masculine. Think of the many tax dollars allocated to the military as compared with the few tax dollars allocated to the arts. Think about how kindergarten teachers are paid as compared to how stockbrokers are paid. And think about how many presidents of the United States have been women. Gender operates through social institutions (like marriage and the law) and practices (like education and medicine) by disproportionately conferring entitlements and the control of resources on men, while disproportionately assigning women to subordinate positions in the service of men's interests.

To make this power relation seem perfectly natural—like the fact that plants grow up instead of down, or that human beings grow old and die—gender constructs its norms for behavior around what is supposed to be the natural biological distinction between the sexes. According to this distinction, people who have penises and testicles, XY chromosomes, and beards as adults belong to the male sex, while people who have clitorises and ovaries, XX chromosomes, and breasts as adults belong to the female sex, and those are the only sexes there are. Gender, then, is the complicated set of cultural meanings that are constructed around the two sexes. Your sex is either male or female, and your gender—either masculine, or feminine—corresponds socially to your sex.

As a matter of fact, though, sex isn't quite so simple. Some people with XY chromosomes don't have penises and never develop beards, because they don't have the receptors that allow them to make use of the male hormones that their testicles produce. Are they male or female? Other people have ambiguous genitals or internal reproductive structures that don't correspond in the usual manner to their external genitalia. How should we classify them? People with Turner's syndrome have XO chromosomes instead of XX. People with Klinefelter's syndrome have three sex chromosomes: XXY. Nature is a good bit looser in its categories than the simple male/female distinction acknowledges. Most human beings can certainly be classified as one sex or the other, but a considerable number of them fall somewhere in between.

The powerful norm of gender doesn't acknowledge the existence of the in-betweens, though. When, for example, have you ever filled out an application for a job or a driver's license or a passport that gave you a choice other than M or F? Instead, by basing its distinction between masculine and feminine on the existence of two and only two sexes, gender makes the inequality of power between men and women appear natural and therefore legitimate.

Gender, then, is about power. But it's not about the power of just one group over another. Gender always interacts with other social markers—such as race, class, level of education, sexual orientation, age, religion, physical and mental health, and ethnicity—to distribute power unevenly among women positioned differently in the various social orders, and it does the same to men. A man's social status, for example, can have a great deal to do with the extent to which he's even perceived as a man. There's a wonderful passage in the English travel writer Frances Trollope's *Domestic Manners of the Americans* (1831), in which she describes the exaggerated delicacy of middle-class young ladies she met in Kentucky and Ohio. They wouldn't dream of sitting in a chair that was still warm from contact with a gentleman's bottom, but thought nothing of getting laced into their corsets in front of a male house slave. The slave, it's clear, didn't count as a man—not in the relevant sense, anyway. Gender is the force that makes it matter whether you are male or female, but it always works hand in glove with all the other things about you that matter at the same time. It's one power relation intertwined with others in a complex social system that distinguishes your betters from your inferiors in all kinds of ways and for all kinds of purposes.

Power and Morality

If feminism is about gender, and gender is the name for a social system that distributes power unequally between men and women, then you'd expect feminist ethicists to try to *understand, criticize,* and *correct* how gender operates within our moral beliefs and practices. And they do just that. In the first place, they challenge, on moral grounds, the powers men have over women, and they claim for women, again on moral grounds, the powers that gender denies them. As the moral reasons for opposing gender are similar to the moral reasons for opposing power systems based on social markers other than gender, feminist ethicists also offer moral arguments against systems based on class, race, physical or mental ability, sexuality, and age. And because all these systems, including gender, are powerful enough to *conceal* many of the forces that keep them in place, it's often necessary to make the forces visible by explicitly identifying—and condemning—the various ugly ways they allow some people to treat others. This is a central task for feminist ethics.

Feminist ethicists also produce theory about the moral meaning of various kinds of *legitimate* relations of unequal power, including relationships of dependency and vulnerability, relationships of trust, and relationships based on something other than choice. Parent–child relationships, for example, are necessarily unequal and for the most part unchosen. Parents can't help having power over their children, and while they may have chosen to have children, most don't choose to have the particular children they do, nor do children choose their parents. This raises questions about the responsible use of parental power and the nature of involuntary obligations, and these are topics for feminist ethics. Similarly, when you trust someone, that person has power over you. Whom should you trust, for what purposes, and when is trust not warranted? What's involved in being trustworthy, and what must be done to repair breaches of trust? These too are questions for feminist ethics.

Third, feminist ethicists look at the various forms of power that are required for morality to operate properly at all. How do we learn right from wrong in the first place? We usually learn it from our parents, whose power to permit and forbid, praise and punish, is essential to our moral training. For whom or what are we ethically responsible? Often this depends on the kind of power we have over the person or thing in question. If, for instance, someone is particularly vulnerable to harm because of something I've done, I might well have special duties toward that person. Powerful social institutions—medicine, religion, government, and the market, to take just a few examples—typically dictate what is morally required of us and to whom we are morally answerable. Relations of power set the terms for who must answer to whom, who has authority over whom, and who gets excused from certain kinds of accountability to whom. But because so many of these power relations are illegitimate, in that they're instances of gender, racism, or other kinds of bigotry, figuring out which ones are morally justified is a task for feminist ethics.

Description and Prescription

So far it sounds as if feminist ethics devotes considerable attention to *description*—as if feminist ethicists were like poets or painters who want to show you something about reality that you might otherwise have missed. And indeed, many feminist ethicists emphasize the importance of understanding how social power actually works, rather than concentrating solely on how it ought to work. But why, you might ask, should ethicists worry about how power operates within societies? Isn't it up to sociologists and political scientists to describe how things *are*, while ethicists concentrate on how things *ought* to be?

As the philosopher Margaret Urban Walker has pointed out in *Moral Contexts*, there is a tradition in Western philosophy, going all the way back to Plato, to the effect that morality is something ideal and that ethics, being the study of morality, properly examines only that ideal. According to this tradition, notions of right and wrong as they are found in the world are unreliable and shadowy manifestations of something lying outside of human experience—something to which we ought to aspire but can't hope to reach. Plato's Idea of the Good, in fact, is precisely not of this earth, and only the gods could truly know it. Christian ethics incorporates Platonism into its insistence that earthly existence is fraught with sin and error and that heaven is our real home. Kant too insists that moral judgments transcend the histories and circumstances of people's actual lives, and most moral philosophers of the twentieth century have likewise shown little interest in how people really live and what it's like for them to live that way. "They think," remarks Walker (2001), "that there is little to be learned from what is about what ought to be" (3).

In Chapter Four [omitted here—ed.] we'll take a closer look at what goes wrong when ethics is done that way, but let me just point out here that if you don't know how things are, your prescriptions for how things ought to be won't have much practical effect. Imagine trying to sail a ship without knowing anything about the tides or where the hidden rocks and shoals lie. You might have a very fine idea of where you are trying to go, but if you don't know the waters, at best you are likely to go off course, and at worst you'll end up going down with all your shipmates. If, as many feminists have noted, a crucial fact about human selves is that they are always embedded in a vast web of relationships, then the forces at play within those relationships must be understood. It's knowing how people are situated with respect to these forces, what they are going through as they are subjected to them, and what life is like in the face of them, that lets us decide which of the forces are morally justified. Careful description of how things are is a crucial part of feminist methodology, because the power that puts certain groups of people at risk of physical harm, denies them full access to the good things their society has to offer, or treats them as if they were useful only for other people's purposes is often hidden and hard to see. If this power isn't seen, it's likely to remain in place, doing untold amounts of damage to great numbers of people.

All the same, feminist ethics is *normative* as well as descriptive. It's fundamentally about how things ought to be, while description plays the crucial but secondary role of helping us to figure that out. Normative language is the language of "ought" instead of "is," the language of "worth" and "value," "right" and "wrong," "good" and "bad." Feminist ethicists differ on a number of normative issues, but as the philosopher Alison Jaggar (1991) has famously put it, they all share two moral commitments: "that the subordination of women is morally wrong and that the moral experience of women is worthy of respect" (95). The first commitment—that women's interests ought not systematically to be set in the service of men's—can be understood as a moral challenge to power under the guise of gender. The second commitment—that women's experience must be taken seriously—can be understood as a call to acknowledge how that power operates. These twin commitments are the two normative legs on which any feminist ethics stands. . . .

Morality and Politics

If the idealization of morality goes back over two thousand years in Western thought, a newer tradition, only a couple of centuries old, has split off morality from politics. According to this tradition, which can be traced to Kant and some other Enlightenment philosophers, morality concerns the relations between persons, whereas politics concerns the relations among nation-states, or between a state and its citizens. So, as Iris Marion Young (1990) puts it, ethicists have tended to focus on intentional actions by individual persons, conceiving of moral life as "conscious, deliberate, a rational weighing of alternatives," whereas political philosophers have focused on impersonal governmental systems, studying "laws, policies, the large-scale distribution of social goods, countable quantities like votes and taxes" (149).

For feminists, though, the line between ethics and political theory isn't quite so bright as this tradition makes out. It's not always easy to tell where feminist ethics leaves off and feminist political theory begins. There are two reasons for this. In the first place, while ethics certainly concerns personal behavior, there is a long-standing insistence on the part of feminists that the personal *is* political. In a 1970 essay called "The Personal Is Political," the political activist Carol Hanisch observed that "personal problems are political problems. There are no personal solutions at this time" (204–205). What Hanisch meant is that even the most private areas of everyday life, including such intensely personal areas as sex, can function to maintain abusive power systems like gender. If a heterosexual woman believes, for example, that contraception is primarily her responsibility because she'll have to take care of the baby if she gets pregnant, she is propping up a system that lets men evade responsibility not only for pregnancy, but for their own offspring as well. Conversely, while unjust social arrangements such as gender and race invade every aspect of people's personal lives, "there are no personal solutions," either when Hanisch wrote those words or now, because to shift dominant understandings of how certain groups may be treated, and what other groups are entitled to expect of them, requires concerted political action, not just personal good intentions.

The second reason why it's hard to separate feminist ethics from feminist politics is that feminists typically subject the ethical theory they produce to critical political scrutiny, not only to keep untoward political biases out, but also to make sure that the work accurately reflects their feminist politics. Many nonfeminist ethicists, on the other hand, don't acknowledge that their work reflects their politics, because they don't think it should. Their aim, by and large, has been to develop ideal moral theory that applies to all people, regardless of their social position or experience of life, and to do that objectively, without favoritism, requires them to leave their own personal politics behind. The trouble, though, is that they aren't really leaving their own personal politics behind. They're merely refusing to notice that their politics is inevitably built right in to their theories. (This is an instance of Lindemann's ad hoc rule Number 22: Just because you think you are doing something doesn't mean you're actually doing it.) Feminists, by contrast, are generally skeptical of the idealism nonfeminists favor, and they're equally doubtful that objectivity can be achieved by stripping away what's distinctive about people's experiences or commitments. Believing that it's no wiser to shed one's political allegiances in the service of ethics than it would be to shed one's moral allegiances, feminists prefer to be transparent about their politics as a way of keeping their ethics intellectually honest. . . .

Hilde Lindemann: What Is Feminist Ethics?

1. Near the beginning of her piece, Lindemann claims that "studying ethics doesn't improve your character." Do you think she is right about this? If so, what is the point of studying ethics?
2. What problems does Lindemann raise for the view that feminism is fundamentally about equality between men and women? Can these problems be overcome, or must we admit that feminism is concerned with equality?
3. What is the difference between sex and gender? Why does Lindemann think that gender is essentially about power? Do you think she is right about this?
4. Lindemann claims that feminist ethics is "*normative* as well as descriptive." What does she mean by this? In what ways is feminist ethics more descriptive than other approaches to ethics? Do you see this as a strength or a weakness?
5. What is meant by the slogan "the personal is political?" Do you agree with the slogan?
6. Lindemann claims that one should not set aside one's political views when thinking about ethical issues. What reasons does she give for thinking this? Do you agree with her?

For Further Reading

Baier, Annette. 1994. *Moral Prejudices: Essays on Ethics.* Cambridge, MA: Harvard University Press.

Beauvoir, Simone de. 1949 [1974]. *The Second Sex.* Trans. and ed. H. M. Parshley. New York: Modern Library.

Hanisch, Carol. 1970. "The Personal Is Political." In *Notes from the Second Year.* New York: Radical Feminism.

Hoagland, Sarah Lucia. 1988. *Lesbian Ethics: Toward New Value.* Palo Alto, CA: Institute of Lesbian Studies.

hooks, bell. 1984. *Feminist Theory from Margin to Center.* Boston: South End Press.

Jaggar, Alison. 1991. "Feminist Ethics: Projects, Problems, Prospects." In *Feminist Ethics*, ed. Claudia Card. Lawrence: University Press of Kansas.

MacKinnon, Catharine A. 1987. *Feminism Unmodified*. Cambridge, MA: Harvard University Press.

Plumwood, Val. 2002. *Environmental Culture: The Ecological Crisis of Reason*. London: Routledge.

Walker, Margaret Urban. 2001. "Seeing Power in Morality: A Proposal for Feminist Naturalism in Ethics." In *Feminists Doing Ethics*, ed. Peggy DesAutels and Joanne Waugh. Lanham, MD: Rowman & Littlefield.

———. 2003. *Moral Contexts*. Lanham, MD: Rowman & Littlefield.

Wittig, Monique. 1981. "One Is Not Born a Woman." *Feminist Issues* 1, no. 2.

Young, Iris Marion. 1990. *Justice and the Politics of Difference*. Princeton, NJ: Princeton University Press.

PART III

Metaethics

The Status of Morality

====== ❧ ======

14

Moral Distinctions
Not Derived from Reason

David Hume

....

David Hume (1711–1776) sought to offer a wholly naturalistic account of the nature and origins of morality. He rejected the idea of eternal moral truths, graspable by reason alone. He thought that morality is essentially a way of organizing our emotional responses to a value-free world. In this excerpt from his first masterpiece, *A Treatise of Human Nature* (1737), Hume offers several influential arguments against moral rationalism—the idea that reason is the basis of morality, our primary means of gaining moral knowledge, and the source of moral motivation. Also included here is perhaps his most famous claim about morality, namely, that one cannot derive an *ought* from an *is*. According to Hume, it is impossible to substantiate a claim about what ought to be done, or ought to be the case, solely from claims about how the world actually is. Since reason is confined to telling us what is the case, it cannot, by itself, supply us with advice about our duty, or about which ideals we should aspire to.

....

. . . It has been observed, that nothing is ever present to the mind but its perceptions; and that all the actions of seeing, hearing, judging, loving, hating, and thinking, fall under this denomination. The mind can never exert itself in any action which we may not comprehend under the term of *perception*; and consequently that term is no less applicable to those judgments by which we distinguish moral good and evil, than to every other operation of the mind. To approve of one character, to condemn another, are only so many different perceptions.

Now, as perceptions resolve themselves into two kinds, viz. *impressions* and *ideas*, this distinction gives rise to a question, with which we shall open up our present inquiry concerning morals, *whether it is by means of our* ideas *or* impressions *we distinguish betwixt vice and virtue, and pronounce an action blamable or praise-worthy?* This will immediately cut off all loose discourses and declamations, and reduce us to something precise and exact on the present subject.

Those who affirm that virtue is nothing but a conformity to reason; that there are eternal fitnesses and unfitnesses of things, which are the same to every rational being that considers them; that the immutable measure of right and wrong impose an obligation, not only on human creatures, but also on the Deity himself: all these systems concur in the opinion, that morality, like truth, is discerned merely by ideas, and by their juxtaposition and comparison. In order, therefore, to judge of these systems, we need only consider whether it be possible from reason alone, to distinguish betwixt moral good and evil, or whether there must concur some other principles to enable us to make that distinction.

If morality had naturally no influence on human passions and actions, it were in vain to take such pains to inculcate it; and nothing would be more fruitless than that multitude of rules and precepts with which all moralists abound. Philosophy is commonly divided into *speculative* and *practical*; and as morality is always comprehended under the latter division, it is supposed to influence our passions and actions, and to go beyond the calm and indolent judgments of the understanding. And this is confirmed by common experience, which informs us that men are often governed by their duties, and are deterred from some actions by the opinion of injustice, and impelled to others by that of obligation.

Since morals, therefore, have an influence on the actions and affections, it follows that they cannot be derived from reason; and that because reason alone, as we have already proved, can never have any such influence. Morals excite passions, and produce or prevent actions. Reason of itself is utterly impotent in this particular. The rules of morality, therefore, are not conclusions of our reason.

No one, I believe, will deny the justness of this inference; nor is there any other means of evading it, than by denying that principle on which it is founded. As long as it is allowed, that reason has no influence on our passions and actions, it is in vain to pretend that morality is discovered only by a deduction of reason. An active principle can never be founded on an inactive; and if reason be inactive in itself, it must remain so in all its shapes and appearances, whether it exerts itself in natural or moral subjects, whether it considers the powers of external bodies, or the actions of rational beings.

It would be tedious to repeat all the arguments by which I have proved that reason is perfectly inert, and can never either prevent or produce any action or affection. It will be easy to recollect what has been said upon that subject. I shall only recall on this occasion one of these arguments, which I shall endeavour to render still more conclusive, and more applicable to the present subject.

Reason is the discovery of truth or falsehood. Truth or falsehood consists in an agreement or disagreement either to the *real* relations of ideas, or to *real* existence and matter of fact. Whatever therefore is not susceptible of this agreement or disagreement, is incapable of being true or false, and can never be an object of our reason. Now, it is evident our passions, volitions, and actions, are not susceptible of any such agreement or disagreement; being original facts and realities, complete in themselves, and implying no reference to other passions, volitions, and actions. It is impossible, therefore, they can be pronounced either true or false, and be either contrary or conformable to reason.

This argument is of double advantage to our present purpose. For it proves *directly*, that actions do not derive their merit from a conformity to reason, nor their blame from a contrariety to it; and it proves the same truth more *indirectly*, by showing us, that as reason can never immediately prevent or produce any action by contradicting or approving of it, it cannot be the source of moral good and evil, which are found to have that influence. Actions may be laudable or blamable; but they cannot be reasonable or unreasonable: laudable or blamable, therefore, are not the same with reasonable or unreasonable. The merit and demerit of actions frequently contradict, and sometimes control our natural propensities. But reason has no such influence. Moral distinctions, therefore, are not the offspring of reason. Reason is wholly inactive, and can never be the source of so active a principle as conscience, or a sense of morals.

But perhaps it may be said, that though no will or action can be immediately contradictory to reason, yet we may find such a contradiction in some of the attendants of the actions, that is, in its causes or effects. The action may cause a judgment, or may be *obliquely* caused by one, when the judgment concurs with a passion; and by an abusive way of speaking, which philosophy will scarce allow of, the same contrariety may, upon that account, be ascribed to the action. How far this truth or falsehood may be the source of morals, it will now be proper to consider.

It has been observed that reason, in a strict and philosophical sense, can have an influence on our conduct only after two ways: either when it excites a passion, by informing us of the existence of something which is a proper object of it; or when it discovers the connection of causes and effects, so as to afford us means of exerting any passion. These are the only kinds of judgment which can accompany our actions, or can be said to produce them in any manner; and it must be allowed, that these judgments may often be false and erroneous. A person may be affected with passion, by supposing a pain or pleasure to lie in an object which has no tendency to produce either of these sensations, or which produces the contrary to what is imagined. A person may also take false measures for the attaining of his end, and may retard, by his foolish conduct, instead of forwarding the execution of any object. These false judgments may be thought to affect the passions and actions, which are connected with them, and may be said to render them unreasonable, in a figurative and improper way of speaking. But though this be acknowledged, it is easy to observe, that these errors are so far from being the source of all immorality, that they are commonly very innocent, and draw no manner of guilt upon the person who is so unfortunate as to fall into them. They extend not beyond a mistake of *fact*, which moralists have not generally supposed criminal, as being perfectly involuntary. I am more to be lamented than blamed, if I am mistaken with regard to the influence of objects in producing pain or pleasure, or if I know not the proper means of satisfying my desires. No one can ever regard such errors as a defect in my moral character. A fruit, for instance, that is really disagreeable, appears to me at a distance, and, through mistake, I fancy it to be pleasant and delicious. Here is one error. I choose certain means of reaching this fruit, which are not proper for my end. Here is a second error; nor is there any third one, which can ever possibly enter into our reasonings concerning actions. I ask, therefore, if a man in this situation, and guilty of these two errors, is to be regarded as vicious and criminal, however unavoidable they might have been? Or if it be possible to imagine that such errors are the sources of all immorality?

And here it may be proper to observe, that if moral distinctions be derived from the truth or falsehood of those judgments, they must take place wherever we form the judgments; nor will there be any difference, whether the question be concerning an apple or a kingdom, or whether the error be avoidable or unavoidable.

For as the very essence of morality is supposed to consist in an agreement or disagreement to reason, the other circumstances are entirely arbitrary, and can never either bestow on any action the character of virtuous or vicious, or deprive it of that character. To which we may add, that this agreement or disagreement, not admitting of degrees, all virtues and vices would of course be equal.

Should it be pretended, that though a mistake of *fact* be not criminal, yet a mistake of *right* often is; and that this may be the source of immorality: I would answer, that it is impossible such a mistake can ever be the original source of immorality, since it supposes a real right and wrong; that is, a real distinction in morals, independent of these judgments. A mistake, therefore, of right, may become a species of immorality; but it is only a secondary one, and is founded on some other antecedent to it.

As to those judgments which are the *effects* of our actions, and which, when false, give occasion to pronounce the actions contrary to truth and reason; we may observe, that our actions never cause any judgment, either true or false, in ourselves, and that it is only on others they have such an influence. It is certain that an action, on many occasions, may give rise to false conclusions in others; and that a person, who, through a window, sees any lewd behaviour of mine with my neighbour's wife, may be so simple as to imagine she is certainly my own. In this respect my action resembles somewhat a lie or falsehood; only with this difference, which is material, that I perform not the action with any intention of giving rise to a false judgment in another, but merely to satisfy my lust and passion. It causes, however, a mistake and false judgment by accident; and the falsehood of its effects may be ascribed, by some odd figurative way of speaking, to the action itself. But still I can see no pretext of reason for asserting, that the tendency to cause such an error is the first spring or original source of all immorality.

Thus, upon the whole, it is impossible that the distinction betwixt moral good and evil can be made by reason; since that distinction has an influence upon our actions, of which reason alone is incapable. Reason and judgment may, indeed, be the mediate cause of an action, by prompting or by directing a passion; but it is not pretended that a judgment of this kind, either in its truth or falsehood, is attended with virtue or vice. And as to the judgments, which are caused by our judgments, they can still less bestow those moral qualities on the actions which are their causes.

But, to be more particular, and to show that those eternal immutable fitnesses and unfitnesses of things cannot be defended by sound philosophy, we may weigh the following considerations.

If the thought and understanding were alone capable of fixing the boundaries of right and wrong, the character of virtuous and vicious either must lie in some relations of objects, or must be a matter of fact which is discovered by our reasoning. This consequence is evident. As the operations of human understanding divide themselves into two kinds, the comparing of ideas, and the inferring of matter of fact, were virtue discovered by the understanding, it must be an object of one of these operations; nor is there any third operation of the understanding which can discover it. There has been an opinion very industriously propagated by certain philosophers, that morality is susceptible of demonstration; and though no one has ever been able to advance a single step in those demonstrations, yet it is taken for granted that this science may be brought to an equal certainty with geometry or algebra. Upon this supposition, vice and virtue must consist in some relations; since it is allowed on all hands, that no matter of fact is capable of being demonstrated. Let us therefore begin with examining this hypothesis, and endeavour, if possible, to fix those moral qualities which have been so long the objects of our fruitless researches; point out distinctly the relations which constitute morality or obligation, that we may know wherein they consist, and after what manner we must judge of them.

If you assert that vice and virtue consist in relations susceptible of certainty and demonstration, you must confine yourself to those *four* relations which alone admit of that degree of evidence; and in that case you run into absurdities from which you will never be able to extricate yourself. For as you make the very essence of morality to lie in the relations, and as there is no one of these relations but what is applicable, not only to an irrational but also to an inanimate object, it follows that even such objects must be susceptible of merit or demerit. *Resemblance, contrariety, degrees in quality*, and *proportions in quantity and number*; all these relations belong as properly to matter as to our actions, passions, and volitions. It is unquestionable, therefore, that morality lies not in any of these relations, nor the sense of it in their discovery.

Should it be asserted, that the sense of morality consists in the discovery of some relation distinct from these, and that our enumeration was not complete when we comprehended all demonstrable relations under four general heads; to this I know not what to reply, till some one be so good as to point out to me this new relation. It is impossible to refute a system which has never yet been explained. In such a manner of fighting in the dark, a man loses his blows in the air, and often places them where the enemy is not present.

I must therefore, on this occasion, rest contented with requiring the two following conditions of any one that would undertake to clear up this system. *First*, as moral good and evil belong only to the actions of the mind, and are derived from our situation with regard to external objects, the relations from which these moral distinctions arise must lie only betwixt internal actions and external objects, and must not be applicable either to internal actions, compared among themselves, or to external objects, when placed in opposition to other external objects. For as morality is supposed to attend certain relations, if these relations could belong to internal actions considered singly, it would follow, that we might be guilty of crimes in ourselves, and independent of our situation with respect to the universe; and in like manner, if these moral relations could be applied to external objects, it would follow that even inanimate beings would be susceptible of moral beauty and deformity. Now, it seems difficult to imagine that any relation can be discovered betwixt our passions, volitions, and actions, compared to external objects, which relation might not belong either to these passions and volitions, or to these external objects, compared among *themselves*.

But it will be still more difficult to fulfil the *second* condition, requisite to justify this system. According to the principles of those who maintain an abstract rational difference betwixt moral good and evil, and a natural fitness and unfitness of things, it is not only supposed, that these relations, being eternal and immutable, are the same, when considered by every rational creature, but their *effects* are also supposed to be necessarily the same; and it is concluded they have no less, or rather a greater, influence in directing the will of the Deity, than in governing the rational and virtuous of our own species. These two particulars are evidently distinct. It is one thing to know virtue, and another to conform the will to it. In order, therefore, to prove that the measures of right and wrong are eternal laws, *obligatory* on every rational mind, it is not sufficient to show the relations upon which they are founded: we must also point out the connection betwixt the relation and the will; and must prove that this connection is so necessary, that in every well-disposed mind, it must take place and have its influence; though the difference betwixt these minds be in other respects immense and infinite. Now, besides what I have already proved, that even in human nature no relation can ever alone produce any action; besides this, I say, it has been shown, in treating of the understanding, that there is no connection of cause and effect, such as this is supposed to be, which is discoverable otherwise than by experience, and of which we can pretend to have any security by the simple consideration of the objects. All beings in the universe, considered in themselves, appear entirely loose and independent of each other. It is only by experience we learn their influence and connection; and this influence we ought never to extend beyond experience.

Thus it will be impossible to fulfil the *first* condition required to the system of eternal rational measures of right and wrong; because it is impossible to show those relations, upon which such a distinction may be founded: and it is as impossible to fulfil the *second* condition: because we cannot prove *a priori*, that these relations, if they really existed and were perceived, would be universally forcible and obligatory. . . .

Nor does this reasoning only prove, that morality consists not in any relations that are the objects of science; but if examined, will prove with equal certainty, that it consists not in any *matter of fact*, which can be discovered by the understanding. This is the *second* part of our argument; and if it can be made evident, we may conclude that morality is not an object of reason. But can there be any difficulty in proving that vice and virtue are not matters of fact, whose existence we can infer by reason? Take any action allowed to be vicious; wilful murder, for instance. Examine it in all lights, and see if you can find that matter of fact, or real existence, which you call *vice*. In whichever way you take it, you find only certain passions, motives, volitions, and thoughts. There is no other matter of fact in the case. The vice entirely escapes you, as long as you consider the object. You never can find it, till you turn your reflection into your own breast, and find a sentiment of disapprobation, which arises in you, towards this action. Here is a matter of fact; but it is the object of feeling, not of reason. It lies in yourself, not in the object. So that when you pronounce any action or character to be vicious, you mean nothing, but that from the constitution of your nature you have a feeling or sentiment of blame from the contemplation of it. Vice and virtue, therefore, may be compared to sounds, colours, heat, and cold, which, according to modern philosophy, are not qualities in objects, but perceptions in the mind: and this discovery in morals, like that other in physics, is to be regarded as a considerable advancement of the speculative sciences; though, like that too, it has little or no influence on practice. Nothing can be more real, or concern us more, than our own sentiments of pleasure and uneasiness; and if these be favourable to virtue, and unfavourable to vice, no more can be requisite to the regulation of our conduct and behaviour.

I cannot forbear adding to these reasonings an observation, which may, perhaps, be found of some importance. In every system of morality which I have hitherto met with, I have always remarked, that the author proceeds for some time in the ordinary way of reasoning, and establishes the being of a God, or makes observations concerning human affairs; when of a sudden I am surprised to find, that instead of the usual copulations of propositions, *is*, and *is not*, I meet with no proposition that is not connected with an *ought*, or an *ought not*. This change is imperceptible; but is, however, of the last consequence. For as this *ought*, or *ought not*, expresses some new relation or affirmation, it is necessary that it should be observed and explained; and at the same time that a reason should be given, for what seems altogether inconceivable, how this new relation can be a deduction from others, which are entirely different from it. But as authors do not commonly use this precaution, I shall presume to recommend it to the readers; and am persuaded, that this small attention would subvert all the vulgar systems of morality, and let us see that the distinction of vice and virtue is not founded merely on the relations of objects, nor is perceived by reason.

David Hume: Moral Distinctions Not Derived from Reason

1. According to Hume, "reason has no influence on our actions and passions." What does Hume mean by this? Do you think he is right?
2. Hume claims that the rules of morality "are not conclusions of our reason." How does he argue for this? Do you find his argument convincing?
3. Hume admits that "false judgments" may influence our behavior, but argues that the truth of our judgments does not determine whether actions are morally right or wrong. What is his argument for thinking this?
4. According to Hume, to say that an action is wrong is equivalent to saying that "from the constitution of your nature you have a feeling or sentiment of blame from the contemplation of it." Is this a plausible account of what we mean when we say that an action is wrong? Does this imply

that different actions are wrong for different people, depending on how they feel?

5. Hume claims it is "inconceivable" that we can deduce claims about what *ought* to be the case from claims about what *is* the case. What exactly does he mean by this? Do you think there are any counterexamples to this claim?

15

A Critique of Ethics

A. J. Ayer

....

In this excerpt from his important book *Language, Truth and Logic*, English philosopher A. J. Ayer (1910–1989) offers his arguments on behalf of the theory known as *emotivism*. Emotivism is the view that moral judgments essentially express our emotions, rather than describing the way the world is. Moral judgments are not in the business of reporting any facts, but rather are intended to vent one's feelings and persuade others to share them. As such, they are neither true nor false. When we say, for instance, that genocide is immoral, we are not describing genocide, but only expressing our opposition to it. It's as if we were saying: "Genocide–boo!" Such an expression isn't false. But neither is it true.

Ayer's central argument relies on the *verifiability criterion of meaning*. This criterion says that a claim can be meaningful only if it is empirically verifiable (i.e., can be confirmed by means of evidence gathered through our five senses) or is true by definition (e.g., "All bachelors are unmarried"). But, says Ayer, moral claims are not empirically verifiable, and they are not true by definition. Therefore they are meaningless. Like all meaningless claims, they cannot be true (or false).

If there is no truth in ethics, then there can be no ethical knowledge. Ayer accepts this. He also claims that since there is no moral truth awaiting our discovery, there is nothing for moral philosophers to do.

A. J. Ayer, "A Critique of Ethics," from *Language, Truth and Logic* (NY: Dover Publications, 1952), pp. 102–114.

No view is morally better than another, since there are no standards of correctness in ethics. The only interesting question of ethics is psychological: Why do we hold the moral views we do?

....

There is still one objection to be met before we can claim to have justified our view that all synthetic propositions are empirical hypotheses. This objection is based on the common supposition that our speculative knowledge is of two distinct kinds—that which relates to questions of empirical fact, and that which relates to questions of value. It will be said that "statements of value" are genuine synthetic propositions, but that they cannot with any show of justice be represented as hypotheses, which are used to predict the course of our sensations; and, accordingly, that the existence of ethics and aesthetics as branches of speculative knowledge presents an insuperable objection to our radical empiricist thesis.

In face of this objection, it is our business to give an account of "judgements of value" which is both satisfactory in itself and consistent with our general empiricist principles. We shall set ourselves to show that in so far as statements of value are significant, they are ordinary "scientific" statements; and that in so far as they are not scientific, they are not in the literal sense significant, but are simply expressions of emotion which can be neither true nor false. In maintaining this view, we may confine ourselves for the present to the case of ethical statements. What is said about them will be found to apply, *mutatis mutandis*, to the case of aesthetic statements also.

The ordinary system of ethics, as elaborated in the works of ethical philosophers, is very far from being a homogeneous whole. Not only is it apt to contain pieces of metaphysics, and analyses of non-ethical concepts: its actual ethical contents are themselves of very different kinds. We may divide them, indeed, into four main classes. There are, first of all, propositions which express definitions of ethical terms, or judgements about the legitimacy or possibility of certain definitions. Secondly, there are propositions describing the phenomena of moral experience, and their causes. Thirdly, there are exhortations to moral virtue. And, lastly, there are actual ethical judgements. It is unfortunately the case that the distinction between these four classes, plain as it is, is commonly ignored by ethical philosophers; with the result that it is often very difficult to tell from their works what it is that they are seeking to discover or prove.

In fact, it is easy to see that only the first of our four classes, namely that which comprises the propositions relating to the definitions of ethical terms, can be said to constitute ethical philosophy. The propositions which describe the phenomena of moral experience, and their causes, must be assigned to the science of psychology, or sociology. The exhortations to moral virtue are not propositions at all, but ejaculations or commands which are designed to provoke the reader to action of a certain sort. Accordingly, they do not belong to any branch of philosophy or science. As for the expressions of ethical judgements, we have not yet determined how they should be classified. But inasmuch as they are certainly neither definitions nor comments upon definitions, nor quotations, we may say decisively that they do not belong to ethical philosophy. A strictly philosophical treatise on ethics should therefore make no ethical pronouncements. But it should, by giving an analysis of ethical terms, show what is the category to which all such pronouncements belong. And this is what we are now about to do.

A question which is often discussed by ethical philosophers is whether it is possible to find definitions which would reduce all ethical terms to one or two fundamental terms. But this question, though it undeniably belongs to ethical philosophy, is not relevant to our present enquiry. We are not now concerned to discover which term, within the sphere of ethical terms, is to be taken as fundamental; whether, for example, "good" can be defined in terms of "right" or "right" in terms of "good," or both in terms of "value." What we are interested in is the possibility of reducing the whole sphere of ethical terms to non-ethical terms. We are enquiring whether statements of ethical value can be translated into statements of empirical fact.

That they can be so translated is the contention of those ethical philosophers who are commonly called subjectivists, and of those who are known as utilitarians. For the utilitarian defines the rightness of actions, and the goodness of ends, in terms of the pleasure, or happiness, or satisfaction, to which they give rise; the subjectivist, in terms of the feelings of approval which a certain person, or group of people, has towards them. Each of these types of definition makes moral judgements into a sub-class of psychological or sociological judgements; and for this reason they are very attractive to us. For, if either was correct, it would follow that ethical assertions were not generically different from the factual assertions which are ordinarily contrasted with them; and the account which we have already given of empirical hypotheses would apply to them also.

Nevertheless we shall not adopt either a subjectivist or a utilitarian analysis of ethical terms. We reject the subjectivist view that to call an action right, or a thing good, is to say that it is generally approved of, because it is not self-contradictory to assert that some actions which are generally approved of are not right, or that some things which are generally approved of are not good. And we reject the alternative subjectivist view that a man who asserts that a certain action is right, or that a certain thing is good, is saying that he himself approves of it, on the ground that a man who confessed that he sometimes approved of what was bad or wrong would not be contradicting himself. And a similar argument is fatal to utilitarianism. We cannot agree that to call an action right is to say that of all the actions possible in the circumstances it would cause, or be likely to cause, the greatest happiness, or the greatest balance of pleasure over pain, or the greatest balance of satisfied over unsatisfied desire, because we find that it is not self-contradictory to say that it is sometimes wrong to perform the action which would actually or probably cause the greatest happiness, or the greatest balance of pleasure over pain, or of satisfied over unsatisfied desire. And since it is not self-contradictory to say that some pleasant things are not good, or that some bad things are desired, it cannot be the case that the sentence "x is good" is equivalent to "x is pleasant," or to "x is desired." And to every other variant of utilitarianism with which I am acquainted the same objection can be made. And therefore we should, I think, conclude that the validity of ethical judgements is not determined by the felicific tendencies of actions, any more than by the nature of people's feelings; but that it must be regarded as "absolute" or "intrinsic," and not empirically calculable.

If we say this, we are not, of course, denying that it is possible to invent a language in which all ethical symbols are definable in non-ethical terms, or even that it is desirable to invent such a language and adopt it in place of our own; what we are denying is that the suggested reduction of ethical to non-ethical statements is consistent with the conventions of our actual language. That is, we reject utilitarianism and subjectivism, not as proposals to replace our existing ethical notions by new ones, but as analyses of our existing ethical notions. Our contention is simply that, in our language, sentences which contain normative ethical symbols are not equivalent to sentences which express psychological propositions, or indeed empirical propositions of any kind.

It is advisable here to make it plain that it is only normative ethical symbols, and not descriptive ethical symbols, that are held by us to be indefinable in factual terms. There is a danger of confusing these two types of symbols, because they are commonly constituted by signs of the same sensible form. Thus a complex sign of the form "*x* is wrong" may constitute a sentence which expresses a moral judgement concerning a certain type of conduct, or it may constitute a sentence which states that a certain type of conduct is repugnant to the moral sense of a particular society. In the latter case, the symbol "wrong" is a descriptive ethical symbol, and the sentence in which it occurs expresses an ordinary sociological proposition; in the former case, the symbol "wrong" is a normative ethical symbol, and the sentence in which it occurs does not, we maintain, express an empirical proposition at all. It is only with normative ethics that we are at present concerned; so that whenever ethical symbols are used in the course of this argument without qualification, they are always to be interpreted as symbols of the normative type.

In admitting that normative ethical concepts are irreducible to empirical concepts, we seem to be leaving the way clear for the "absolutist" view of ethics—that is, the view that statements of value are not controlled by observation, as ordinary empirical propositions are, but only by a mysterious "intellectual intuition." A feature of this theory, which is seldom recognized by its advocates, is that it makes statements of value unverifiable. For it is notorious that what seems intuitively certain to one person may seem doubtful, or even false, to another. So that unless it is possible to provide some criterion by which one may decide between conflicting intuitions, a mere appeal to intuition is worthless as a test of a proposition's validity. But in the case of moral judgements, no such criterion can be given. Some moralists claim to settle the matter by saying that they "know" that their own moral judgements are correct. But such an assertion is of purely psychological interest, and has not the slightest tendency to prove the validity of any moral judgement. For dissentient moralists may equally well "know" that their ethical views are correct. And, as far as subjective certainty goes, there will be nothing to choose between them. When such differences of opinion arise in connection with an ordinary empirical proposition, one may attempt to resolve them by referring to, or actually carrying out, some relevant empirical test. But with regard to ethical statements, there is, on the "absolutist" or "intuitionist" theory, no relevant empirical test. We are therefore justified in saying that on this theory ethical statements are held to be unverifiable. They arc, of course, also held to be genuine synthetic propositions.

Considering the use which we have made of the principle that a synthetic proposition is significant only if it is empirically verifiable, it is clear that the acceptance of an "absolutist" theory of ethics would undermine the whole of our main argument. And as we have already rejected the "naturalistic" theories which are commonly supposed to provide the only alternative to "absolutism" in ethics, we seem to have reached a difficult position. We shall meet the difficulty by showing that the correct treatment of ethical statements is afforded by a third theory, which is wholly compatible with our radical empiricism.

We begin by admitting that the fundamental ethical concepts are unanalysable, inasmuch as there is no criterion by which one can test the validity of the judgements in which they occur. So far we are in agreement with the absolutists. But, unlike the absolutists, we are able to give an explanation of this fact about ethical concepts. We say that the reason why they are unanalysable is that they are mere pseudo-concepts. The presence of an ethical symbol in a proposition adds nothing to its factual content. Thus if I say to someone, "You acted wrongly in stealing that money," I am not stating anything more than if I had simply said, "You stole that money." In adding that this action is wrong I am not making any further statement about it. I am simply evincing my moral disapproval of it. It is as if I had said, "You stole that money," in a peculiar tone of horror, or written it with the addition of some special exclamation marks. The tone, or the exclamation marks, adds nothing to the literal meaning of the sentence. It merely serves to show that the expression of it is attended by certain feelings in the speaker.

If now I generalise my previous statement and say, "Stealing money is wrong," I produce a sentence which has no factual meaning—that is, expresses no proposition which can be either true or false. It is as if I had written "Stealing money!!"—where the shape and thickness of the exclamation marks show, by a suitable convention, that a special sort of moral disapproval is the feeling which is being expressed. It is clear that there is nothing said here which can be true or false. Another man may disagree with me about the wrongness of stealing, in the sense that he may not have the same feelings about stealing as I have, and he may quarrel with me on account of my moral sentiments. But he cannot, strictly speaking, contradict me. For in saying that a certain type of action is right or wrong, I am not making any factual statement, not even a statement about my own state of mind. I am merely expressing certain moral sentiments. And the man who is ostensibly contradicting me is merely expressing his moral sentiments. So that there is plainly no sense in asking which of us is in the right. For neither of us is asserting a genuine proposition.

What we have just been saying about the symbol "wrong" applies to all normative ethical symbols. Sometimes they occur in sentences which record ordinary empirical facts besides expressing ethical feeling about those facts: sometimes they occur in sentences which simply express ethical feeling about a certain type of action, or situation, without making any statement of fact. But in every case in which one would commonly be said to be making an ethical judgement, the function of the relevant ethical word is purely "emotive." It is used to express feeling about certain objects, but not to make any assertion about them.

It is worth mentioning that ethical terms do not serve only to express feeling. They are calculated also to arouse feeling, and so to stimulate action. Indeed some of them are used in such a way as to give the sentences in which they occur the effect of commands. Thus the sentence "It is your duty to tell the truth" may be regarded both as the expression of a certain sort of ethical feeling about truthfulness and as the expression of the command "Tell the truth." The sentence "You ought to tell the truth" also involves the command "Tell the truth," but here the tone of the command is less emphatic. In the sentence "It is good to tell the truth" the command has become little more than a suggestion. And thus the "meaning" of the word "good," in its ethical usage, is differentiated from that of the word "duty" or the word "ought." In fact we may define the meaning of the various ethical words in terms both of the different feelings they are ordinarily taken to express, and also the different responses which they are calculated to provoke.

We can now see why it is impossible to find a criterion for determining the validity of ethical judgements. It is not because they have an "absolute" validity which is mysteriously independent of ordinary sense-experience, but because they have no objective validity whatsoever. If a sentence makes no statement at all, there is obviously no sense in asking whether what it says is true or false. And we have seen that sentences which simply express moral judgements do not say anything. They are pure expressions of feeling and as such do not come under the category of truth and falsehood. They are unverifiable for the same reason as a cry of pain or a word of command is unverifiable—because they do not express genuine propositions.

Thus, although our theory of ethics might fairly be said to be radically subjectivist, it differs in a very important respect from the orthodox subjectivist theory. For the orthodox subjectivist does not deny, as we do, that the sentences of a moralizer express genuine propositions. All he denies is that they express propositions of a unique non-empirical character. His own view is that they express propositions about the speaker's feelings. If this were so, ethical judgements clearly would be capable of being true or false. They would be true if the speaker had the relevant feelings, and false if he had not. And this is a matter which is, in principle, empirically verifiable. Furthermore they could be significantly contradicted. For if I say, "Tolerance is a virtue," and someone answers, "You don't approve of it," he would, on the ordinary subjectivist theory, be contradicting me. On our theory, he would not be contradicting me, because, in saying that tolerance was a virtue, I should not be making any statement about my own feelings or about anything else. I should simply be evincing my feelings, which is not at all the same thing as saying that I have them.

The distinction between the expression of feeling and the assertion of feeling is complicated by the fact that the assertion that one has a certain feeling often accompanies the expression of that feeling, and is then, indeed, a factor in the expression of that feeling. Thus I may simultaneously express boredom and say that I am bored, and in that case my utterance of the words, "I am bored," is one of the circumstances which make it true to say that I am expressing or evincing boredom. But I can express boredom without actually saying that I am bored. I can express it by my tone and gestures, while making a statement about something wholly unconnected with it, or by an ejaculation, or without uttering any words at all. So that even if the assertion that one has a certain feeling always involves the expression of that feeling, the expression of a feeling assuredly does not always involve the assertion that one has it. And this is the important point to grasp in considering the distinction between our theory and the ordinary subjectivist theory. For whereas the subjectivist holds that ethical statements actually assert the existence of certain feelings, we hold that ethical statements are expressions and excitants of feeling which do not necessarily involve any assertions.

We have already remarked that the main objection to the ordinary subjectivist theory is that the validity of ethical judgements is not determined by the nature of their author's feelings. And this is an objection which our theory escapes. For it does not imply that the existence of any feelings is a necessary and sufficient condition of the validity of an ethical judgement. It implies, on the contrary, that ethical judgements have no validity.

There is, however, a celebrated argument against subjectivist theories which our theory does not escape. It has been pointed out by Moore that if ethical statements were simply statements about the speaker's feelings, it would be impossible to argue about questions of value. To take a typical example: if a man said that thrift was a virtue, and another replied that it was a vice, they would not, on this theory, be disputing with one another. One would be saying that he approved of thrift, and the other that *he* didn't; and there is no reason why both these statements should not be true. Now Moore held it to be obvious that we do dispute about questions of value, and accordingly concluded that the particular form of subjectivism which he was discussing was false.

It is plain that the conclusion that it is impossible to dispute about questions of value follows from our theory also. For as we hold that such sentences as "Thrift is a virtue" and "Thrift is a vice" do not express propositions at all, we clearly cannot hold that they express incompatible propositions. We must therefore admit that if Moore's argument really refutes the ordinary subjectivist theory, it also refutes ours. But, in fact, we deny that it does refute even the ordinary subjectivist theory. For we hold that one really never does dispute about questions of value.

This may seem, at first sight, to be a very paradoxical assertion. For we certainly do engage in disputes which are ordinarily regarded as disputes about questions of value. But, in all such cases, we find, if we consider the matter closely, that the dispute is not really about a question of value, but about a question of fact. When someone disagrees with us about the moral value of a certain action or type of action, we do admittedly resort to argument in order to win him over to our way of thinking. But we do not attempt to show by our arguments that he has the "wrong" ethical feeling towards a situation whose nature he has correctly apprehended. What we attempt to show is that he is mistaken about the facts of the case. We argue that he has misconceived the agent's motive: or that he has misjudged the effects of the action, or its probable effects in view of the agent's knowledge; or that he has failed to take into account the special circumstances in which the agent was placed. Or else we employ more general arguments about the effects which actions of a certain type tend to produce, or the qualities which are usually manifested in their performance. We do this in the hope that we have only to get our opponent to agree with us about the nature of the empirical facts for him to adopt the same moral attitude towards them as we do. And as the people with whom we argue have generally received the same moral education as ourselves, and live in the same social order, our expectation is usually justified. But if our opponent happens to have undergone a different process of moral "conditioning" from ourselves, so that, even when he acknowledges all the facts, he still disagrees with us about the moral value of the actions under discussion, then we abandon the attempt to convince him by argument. We say that it is impossible to argue with him because he has a distorted or undeveloped moral sense; which signifies merely that he employs a different set of values from our own. We feel that our own system of values is superior, and therefore speak in such derogatory terms of his. But we cannot bring forward any arguments to show that our system is superior. For our judgement that it is so is itself a judgement of value, and accordingly outside the scope of argument. It is because argument fails us when we come to deal with pure questions of value, as distinct from questions of fact, that we finally resort to mere abuse.

In short, we find that argument is possible on moral questions only if some system of values is presupposed. If our opponent concurs with us in expressing moral disapproval of all actions of a given type *t*, then we may get him to condemn a particular action A, by bringing forward arguments to show that A is of type *t*. For the question whether A does or does not belong to that type is a plain question of fact. Given that a man has certain moral principles, we argue that he must, in order to be consistent, react morally to certain things in a certain way. What we do not and cannot argue about is the validity of these moral principles. We merely praise or condemn them in the light of our own feelings.

If anyone doubts the accuracy of this account of moral disputes, let him try to construct even an imaginary argument on a question of value which does not reduce itself to an argument about a question of logic or about an empirical matter of fact. I am confident that he will not succeed in producing a single example. And if that is the case, he must allow that its involving the impossibility of purely ethical arguments is not, as Moore thought, a ground of objection to our theory, but rather a point in favour of it.

Having upheld our theory against the only criticism which appeared to threaten it, we may now use it to define the nature of all ethical enquiries. We find that ethical philosophy consists simply in saying that ethical concepts are pseudo-concepts and therefore unanalysable. The further task of describing the different feelings that the different ethical terms are used to express, and the different reactions that they customarily provoke, is a task for the psychologist. There cannot be such a thing as ethical science, if by ethical science one means the elaboration of a "true" system of morals. For we have seen that, as ethical judgements are mere expressions of feeling, there can be no way of determining the validity of any ethical system, and, indeed, no sense in asking whether any such system is true. All that one may legitimately enquire in this connection is, What are the moral habits of a given person or group of people, and what causes them to have precisely those habits and feelings? And this enquiry falls wholly within the scope of the existing social sciences.

It appears, then, that ethics, as a branch of knowledge, is nothing more than a department of psychology and sociology. And in case anyone thinks that we are overlooking the existence of casuistry, we may remark that casuistry is not a science, but is a purely analytical investigation of the structure of a given moral system. In other words, it is an exercise in formal logic.

When one comes to pursue the psychological enquiries which constitute ethical science, one is immediately enabled to account for the Kantian and hedonistic theories of morals. For one finds that one of the chief causes of moral behaviour is fear, both conscious and unconscious, of a god's displeasure, and fear of the enmity of society. And this, indeed, is the reason why moral precepts present themselves to some people as "categorical" commands. And one finds, also, that the moral code of a society is partly determined by the beliefs of that society concerning the conditions of its own happiness—or, in other words, that a society tends to encourage or discourage a given type of conduct by the use of moral sanctions according as it appears to promote or detract from the contentment of the society as a whole. And this is the reason why altruism is recommended in most moral codes and egotism condemned. It is from the observation of this connection between morality and happiness that hedonistic or eudaemonistic theories of morals ultimately spring, just as the moral theory of Kant is based on the fact, previously explained, that moral precepts have for some people the force of inexorable commands. As each of these theories ignores the fact which lies at the root of the other, both may be criticized as being one-sided; but this is not the main objection to either of them. Their essential defect is that they treat propositions which refer to the causes and attributes of our ethical feelings as if they were definitions of ethical concepts. And thus they fail to recognise that ethical concepts are pseudo-concepts and consequently indefinable.

As we have already said, our conclusions about the nature of ethics apply to aesthetics also. Aesthetic terms are used in exactly the same way as ethical terms. Such aesthetic words as "beautiful" and "hideous" are employed, as ethical words are employed, not to make statements of fact, but simply to express certain feelings and evoke a certain response. It follows, as in ethics, that there is no sense in attributing objective validity to aesthetic judgements, and no possibility of arguing about questions of value in aesthetics, but only about questions of fact. A scientific treatment of aesthetics would show us what in general were the causes of aesthetic feeling, why various societies produced and admired the works of art they did, why taste varies as it does within a given society, and so forth. And these are ordinary psychological or sociological questions. They have, of course, little or nothing to do with aesthetic criticism as we understand it. But that is because the purpose of aesthetic criticism is not so much to give knowledge as to communicate emotion. The critic, by calling attention to certain features of the work under review, and expressing his own feelings about them, endeavours to make us share his attitude towards the work as a whole. The only relevant propositions that he formulates are propositions describing the nature of the work. And these are plain records of fact. We conclude, therefore, that there is nothing in aesthetics, any more than there is in ethics, to justify the view that it embodies a unique type of knowledge.

It should now be clear that the only information which we can legitimately derive from the study of our aesthetic and moral experiences is information about our own mental and physical make-up. We take note of these experiences as providing data for our psychological and sociological generalisations. And this is the only way in which they serve to increase our knowledge. It follows that any attempt to make our use of ethical and aesthetic concepts the basis of a metaphysical theory concerning the existence of a world of values, as distinct from the world of facts, involves a false analysis of these concepts.

A.J. Ayer: A Critique of Ethics

1. Ayer claims that "a strictly philosophical treatise on ethics" should "make no ethical pronouncements." What does he mean by this, and why does he say it?

2. According to Ayer, claims of the form "x is wrong" usually do not express anything that can be true or false, but there are some exceptions to this. Under what circumstances does Ayer think that such claims express genuine propositions?

3. Ayer's view is similar to the subjectivist view that to call an action right is merely to say that one approves of it. Why does Ayer reject this subjectivist view, and how is his own view different?

4. In what ways does Ayer agree with what he calls the "absolutist" view of ethics? In what ways does he disagree with it?

5. One of the consequences of Ayer's theory is the view that "it is impossible to dispute about questions of value." Do you find such a claim to be plausible? Why or why not?

16

The Subjectivity of Values

J. L. Mackie

....

J. L. Mackie (1917–1981), who taught for many years at Oxford University, regarded all ethical views as bankrupt. In this excerpt from his book *Ethics: Inventing Right and Wrong* (1977), Mackie outlines the basic ideas and the central motivating arguments for his *error theory*—the view that all positive moral claims are mistaken. All moral talk, as Mackie sees it, is based on a false assumption: that there are objective moral values. This fundamental error infects the entire system of morality. The foundations are corrupt, and so the entire moral edifice must come tumbling down.

    Mackie offers a number of important arguments to substantiate his critique of morality. The argument from relativity claims that the extent of moral disagreement is best explained by the claim that there are no objective values. The argument from queerness contends that objective moral values would be objectionably different from any other kind of thing in the universe, possessed of strange powers that are best rejected. Mackie concludes with his account of why so many people, for so long, have fallen into error by succumbing to the temptation to think of morality as objective.

....

Moral Scepticism

There are no objective values. This is a bald statement of the thesis of this chapter, but before arguing for it I shall try to clarify and restrict it in ways that may meet some objections and prevent some misunderstanding. . . .

The claim that values are not objective, are not part of the fabric of the world, is meant to include not only moral goodness, which might be most naturally equated with moral value, but also other things that could be more loosely called moral values or disvalues—rightness and wrongness, duty, obligation, an action's being rotten and contemptible, and so on. It also includes non-moral values, notably aesthetic ones, beauty and various kinds of artistic merit. I shall not discuss these explicitly, but clearly much the same considerations apply to aesthetic and to moral values, and there would be at least some initial implausibility in a view that gave the one a different status from the other. . . .

The claim to objectivity, however ingrained in our language and thought, is not self-validating. It can and should be questioned. But the denial of objective values will have to be put forward not as the result of an analytic approach, but as an 'error theory', a theory that although most people in making moral judgements implicitly claim, among other things, to be pointing to something objectively prescriptive, these claims are all false. It is this that makes the name 'moral scepticism' appropriate.

But since this is an error theory, since it goes against assumptions ingrained in our thought and built into some of the ways in which language is used, since it conflicts with what is sometimes called common sense, it needs very solid support. It is not something we can accept lightly or casually and then quietly pass on. If we are to adopt this view, we must argue explicitly for it. Traditionally it has been supported by arguments of two main kinds, which I shall call the argument from relativity and the argument from queerness. . . .

The Argument from Relativity

The argument from relativity has as its premiss the well-known variation in moral codes from one society to another and from one period to another, and also the differences in moral beliefs between different groups and classes within a complex community. Such variation is in itself merely a truth of descriptive morality, a fact of anthropology which entails neither first order nor second order ethical views. Yet it may indirectly support second order subjectivism: radical differences between first order moral judgements make it difficult to treat those judgements as apprehensions of objective truths. But it is not the mere occurrence of disagreements that tells against the objectivity of values. Disagreement on questions in history or biology or cosmology does not show that there are no objective issues in these fields for investigators to disagree about. But such scientific disagreement results from speculative inferences or explanatory hypotheses based on inadequate evidence, and it is hardly plausible to interpret moral disagreement in the same way. Disagreement about moral codes seems to reflect people's adherence to and participation in different ways of life. The causal connection seems to be mainly that way round: it is that people approve of monogamy because they participate in a monogamous way of life rather than that they participate in a monogamous way of life because they approve of monogamy. Of course, the standards may be an idealization of the way of life from which they arise: the monogamy in which people participate may be less complete, less rigid, than that of which it leads them to approve. This is not to say that moral judgements are purely conventional. Of course there have been and are moral heretics and moral reformers, people who have turned against the established rules and practices of their own communities for moral reasons, and often for moral reasons that we would endorse. But this can usually be understood as the extension, in ways which, though new and unconventional, seemed to them to be required for consistency, of rules to which they already adhered as arising out of an existing way of life. In short, the argument from relativity has some force simply because the actual variations in the moral codes are more readily explained by the hypothesis that they reflect ways of life than by the hypothesis that they express perceptions, most of them seriously inadequate and badly distorted, of objective values.

But there is a well-known counter to this argument from relativity, namely to say that the items for which objective validity is in the first place to be claimed are not specific moral rules or codes but very general basic principles which are recognized at least implicitly to some extent in all society—such principles as provide the foundations of what Sidgwick has called different methods of ethics: the principle of universalizability, perhaps, or the rule that one ought to conform to the specific rules of any way of life in which one takes part, from which one profits, and on which one relies, or some utilitarian principle of doing what tends, or seems likely, to promote the general happiness. It is easy to show that such general principles, married with differing concrete circumstances, different existing social patterns or different preferences, will beget different specific moral rules; and there is some plausibility in the claim that the specific rules thus generated will vary from community to community or from group to group in close agreement with the actual variations in accepted codes.

The argument from relativity can be only partly countered in this way. To take this line the moral objectivist has to say that it is only in these principles that the objective moral character attaches immediately to its descriptively specified ground or subject: other moral judgements are objectively valid or true, but only derivatively and contingently—if things had been otherwise, quite different sorts of actions would have been right. And despite the prominence in recent philosophical ethics of universalization, utilitarian principles, and the like, these are very far from constituting the whole of what is actually affirmed as basic in ordinary moral thought. Much of this is concerned rather with what Hare calls 'ideals' or, less kindly, 'fanaticism'. That is, people judge that some things are good or right, and others are bad or wrong, not because—or at any rate not only because—they exemplify some general principle for which widespread implicit acceptance could be claimed, but because something about those things arouses certain responses immediately in them, though they would arouse radically and irresolvably different responses in others. 'Moral sense' or 'intuition' is an initially more plausible description of what supplies many of our basic moral judgements than 'reason'. With regard to all these starting points of moral thinking the argument from relativity remains in full force.

The Argument from Queerness

Even more important, however, and certainly more generally applicable, is the argument from queerness. This has two parts, one metaphysical, the other epistemological. If there were objective values, then they would be entities or qualities or relations of a very strange sort, utterly different from anything else in the universe. Correspondingly, if we were aware of them, it would have to be by some special faculty of moral perception or intuition, utterly different from our ordinary ways of knowing everything else. These points were recognized by Moore when he spoke of non-natural qualities, and by the intuitionists in their talk about a 'faculty of moral intuition'. Intuitionism has long been out of favour, and it is indeed easy to point out its implausibilities. What is not so often stressed, but is more important, is that the central thesis of intuitionism is one to which any objectivist view of values is in the end committed: intuitionism merely makes unpalatably plain what other forms of objectivism wrap up. Of course the suggestion that moral judgements are made or moral problems solved by just sitting down and having an ethical intuition is a travesty of actual moral thinking. But, however complex the real process, it will require (if it is to yield authoritatively prescriptive conclusions) some input of this distinctive sort, either premises or forms of argument or both. When we ask the awkward question, how we can be aware of this authoritative prescriptivity, of the truth of these distinctively ethical premises or of the cogency of this distinctively ethical pattern of reasoning, none of our ordinary accounts of sensory perception or introspection or the framing and confirming of explanatory hypotheses or inference or logical construction or conceptual analysis, or any combination of these, will provide a satisfactory answer; 'a special sort of intuition' is a lame answer, but it is the one to which the clear-headed objectivist is compelled to resort.

Indeed, the best move for the moral objectivist is not to evade this issue, but to look for companions in guilt. For example, Richard Price argues that it is not moral knowledge alone that such an empiricism as those of Locke and Hume is unable to account for, but also our knowledge and even our ideas of essence, number, identity, diversity, solidity, inertia, substance, the necessary existence and infinite extension of time and space, necessity and possibility in general, power, and causation. If the understanding, which Price defines as the faculty within us that discerns truth, is also a source of new simple ideas of so many other sorts, may it not also be a power of immediately perceiving right and wrong, which yet are real characters of actions?

This is an important counter to the argument from queerness. The only adequate reply to it would be to show how, on empiricist foundations, we can construct an account of the ideas and beliefs and knowledge that we have of all these matters. I cannot even begin to do that here, though I have undertaken some parts of the task elsewhere. I can only state my belief that satisfactory accounts of most of these can be given in empirical terms. If some supposed metaphysical necessities or essences resist such treatment, then they too should be included, along with objective values, among the targets of the argument from queerness.

This queerness does not consist simply in the fact that ethical statements are 'unverifiable'. Although logical positivism with its verifiability theory of descriptive meaning gave an impetus to non-cognitive accounts of ethics, it is not only logical positivists but also empiricists of a much more liberal sort who should find objective values hard to accommodate. Indeed, I would not only reject the verifiability principle but also deny the conclusion commonly drawn from it, that moral judgements lack descriptive meaning. The assertion that there are objective values or intrinsically prescriptive entities or features of some kind, which ordinary moral judgements presuppose, is, I hold, not meaningless but false.

Plato's Forms give a dramatic picture of what objective values would have to be. The Form of the Good is such that knowledge of it provides the knower with both a direction and an overriding motive; something's being good both tells the person who knows this to pursue it and makes him pursue it. An objective good would be sought by anyone who was acquainted with it, not because of any contingent fact that this person, or every person, is so constituted that he desires this end, but just because the end has to-be-pursuedness somehow built into it. Similarly, if there were objective principles of right and wrong, any wrong (possible) course of action would have not-to-be-doneness somehow built into it. Or we should have something like Clarke's necessary relations of fitness between situations and actions, so that a situation would have a demand for such-and-such an action somehow built into it.

The need for an argument of this sort can be brought out by reflection on Hume's argument that 'reason'—in which at this stage he includes all sorts of knowing as well as reasoning—can never be an 'influencing motive of the will'. Someone might object that Hume has argued unfairly from the lack of influencing power (not contingent upon desires) in ordinary objects of knowledge and ordinary reasoning, and might maintain that values differ from natural objects precisely in their power, when known, automatically to influence the will. To this Hume could, and would need to, reply that this objection involves the postulating of value-entities or value-features of quite a different order from anything else with which we are acquainted, and of a corresponding faculty with which to detect them. That is, he would have to supplement his explicit argument with what I have called the argument from queerness.

Another way of bringing out this queerness is to ask, about anything that is supposed to have some objective moral quality, how this is linked with its natural features. What is the connection between the natural fact that an action is a piece of deliberate cruelty—say, causing pain just for fun—and the moral fact that it is wrong? It cannot be an entailment, a logical or semantic necessity. Yet it is not merely that the two features occur together. The wrongness must somehow be 'consequential' or 'supervenient'; it is wrong because it is a piece of deliberate cruelty. But just what *in the world* is signified by this 'because'? And how do we know the relation that it signifies, if this is something more than such actions being socially condemned, and condemned by us too, perhaps through our having absorbed attitudes from our social environment? It is not even sufficient to postulate a faculty which 'sees' the wrongness: something must be postulated which can see at once the natural features that constitute the cruelty, and the wrongness, and the mysterious consequential link between the two. Alternatively, the intuition required might be the perception that wrongness is a higher order property belonging to certain natural properties; but what is this belonging of properties to other properties, and how can we discern it? How much simpler and more comprehensible the situation would be if we could replace the moral quality with some sort of subjective response which could be causally related to the detection of the natural features on which the supposed quality is said to be consequential.

It may be thought that the argument from queerness is given an unfair start if we thus relate it to what are admittedly among the wilder products of philosophical fancy—Platonic Forms, non-natural qualities, self-evident relations of fitness, faculties of intuition, and the like. Is it equally forceful if applied to the terms in which everyday moral judgements are more likely to be expressed—though still, as has been argued in the original work, with a claim to objectivity—'you must do this', 'you can't do that', 'obligation', 'unjust', 'rotten', 'disgraceful', 'mean', or talk about good reasons for or against possible actions? Admittedly not; but that is because the objective prescriptivity, the element a claim for whose authoritativeness is embedded in ordinary moral thought and language, is not yet isolated in these forms of speech, but is presented along with relations to desires and feelings, reasoning about the means to desired ends, interpersonal demands, the injustice which consists in the violation of what are in the context the accepted standards of merit, the psychological constituents of meanness, and so on. There is nothing queer about any of these, and under cover of them the claim for moral authority may pass unnoticed. But if I am right in arguing that it is ordinarily there, and is therefore very likely to be incorporated almost automatically in philosophical accounts of ethics which systematize our ordinary thought even in such apparently innocent terms as these, it needs to be examined, and for this purpose it needs to be isolated and exposed as it is by the less cautious philosophical reconstructions.

Patterns of Objectification

Considerations of these kinds suggest that it is in the end less paradoxical to reject than to retain the common-sense belief in the objectivity of moral values, provided that we can explain how this belief, if it is false, has become established and is so resistant to criticisms. This proviso is not difficult to satisfy.

On a subjectivist view, the supposedly objective values will be based in fact upon attitudes which the person has who takes himself to be recognizing and responding to those values. If we admit what Hume calls the mind's 'propensity to spread itself on external objects', we can understand the supposed objectivity of moral qualities as arising from what we can call the projection or objectification of moral attitudes. This would be analogous to what is called the 'pathetic fallacy', the tendency to read our feelings into their objects. If a fungus, say, fills us with disgust, we may be inclined to ascribe to the fungus itself a non-natural quality of foulness. But in moral contexts there is more than this propensity at work. Moral attitudes themselves are at least partly social in origin: socially established—and socially necessary—patterns of behaviour put pressure on individuals, and each individual tends to internalize these pressures and to join in requiring these patterns of behaviour of himself and of others. The attitudes that are objectified into moral values have indeed an external source, though not the one assigned to them by the belief in their absolute authority. Moreover, there are motives that would support objectification. We need morality to regulate interpersonal relations, to control some of the ways in which people behave towards one another, often in opposition to contrary inclinations. We therefore want our moral judgements to be authoritative for other agents as well as for ourselves: objective validity would give them the authority required. Aesthetic values are logically in the same position as moral ones; much the same metaphysical and epistemological considerations apply to them. But aesthetic values are less strongly objectified than moral ones; their subjective status, and an 'error theory' with regard to such claims to objectivity as are incorporated in aesthetic judgements, will be more readily accepted, just because the motives for their objectification are less compelling.

But it would be misleading to think of the objectification of moral values as primarily the projection of feelings, as in the pathetic fallacy.

More important are wants and demands. As Hobbes says, 'whatsoever is the object of any man's Appetite or Desire, that is it, which he for his part calleth *Good* '; and certainly both the adjective 'good' and the noun 'goods' are used in non-moral contexts of things because they are such as to satisfy desires. We get the notion of something's being objectively good, or having intrinsic value, by reversing the direction of dependence here, by making the desire depend upon the goodness, instead of the goodness on the desire. And this is aided by the fact that the desired thing will indeed have features that make it desired, that enable it to arouse a desire or that make it such as to satisfy some desire that is already there. It is fairly easy to confuse the way in which a thing's desirability is indeed objective with its having in our sense objective value. The fact that the word 'good' serves as one of our main moral terms is a trace of this pattern of objectification. . . .

J. L. Mackie: The Subjectivity of Values

1. Why does Mackie refer to his view as an "error theory"? What is the "error" that Mackie takes himself to be pointing out?
2. Mackie cites widespread disagreement about morality as evidence for his view that there are no objective moral values. Yet he admits that the existence of scientific disagreement does not suggest that there are no objective scientific truths. Why does Mackie think that ethics is different from science in this regard? Do you think he is right about this?
3. One might object to Mackie's argument from disagreement by noting that some moral prohibitions (against killing innocent people, against adultery, etc.) are widely shared across cultures. Does this show that there is something wrong with the argument from disagreement? How do you think Mackie would respond to such an objection?
4. Mackie claims that objective values, if they existed, would be entities "of a very strange sort, utterly different from anything else in the universe." What feature of moral values would make them so strange? Do you agree with Mackie that the "queerness" of moral properties is a good reason to deny their existence?
5. Mackie suggests that his view is "simpler and more comprehensible" than accepting objective values. In what ways is his view simpler? Is this a good reason to reject the existence of objective values?
6. Mackie thinks that for his error theory to succeed, he must explain how people come to think that there are objective moral values in the first place. How does he attempt to do so? Do you think he is successful?

17

Cultural Relativism

Harry Gensler

In this essay, Harry Gensler presents and evaluates the doctrine known as *cultural relativism*. This is the view that social approval is the ultimate measure of morality. Those acts approved of by society are good; those that are socially frowned on are bad.

Cultural relativists believe that morality is like the law, or other social conventions. Just as what is legal varies from society to society, so too does what is moral. There are no objective moral standards that apply universally. Rather, what is right or wrong depends entirely on the customs that have arisen in different societies. Different customs mean different moral standards, none of which is uniquely correct for all people at all times.

Though many people are attracted to relativism because it appears to be soundly based on the fact of wide cultural differences and on the importance of tolerating diverse customs, Gensler argues that relativism is deeply problematic. He cites four reasons that cast doubt on the doctrine.

First, relativism cannot allow for consistent disagreement with one's own social code. So long as a society can make moral mistakes, then its approval is not enough to show that something is morally good.

Second, relativism is a very poor basis for defending tolerance. If a society favors intolerance, as many societies do, then relativism tells us that intolerance within those societies is a good thing.

Third, relativism is a counsel of conformity. When trying to morally educate children, relativism tells us to be uncritical of the norms of our society, since they are, by relativist definition, always correct.

Fourth, relativism offers us poor advice about what to do in a situation that is increasingly common. Many of us are members of subcultures situated within larger groups. When we belong to more than one social group, then what do we do if the norms of these groups conflict? Relativism gives us either no advice at all, or conflicting advice.

Gensler concludes by trying to show why considerations that have led many people to relativism are compatible with antirelativist, objective views of ethics.

....

Cultural relativism (CR) says that good and bad are relative to culture. What is "good" is what is "socially approved" in a given culture. Our moral principles describe social conventions and must be based on the norms of our society.

We'll begin by listening to the fictional Ima Relativist explain her belief in cultural relativism. As you read this and similar accounts, reflect on how plausible you find the view and how well it harmonizes with your own thinking. After listening to Ima, we'll consider various objections to CR.

Ima Relativist

My name is Ima Relativist. I've embraced cultural relativism as I've come to appreciate the deeply cultural basis for morality.

I was brought up to believe that morality is about objective facts. Just as snow is white, so also infanticide is wrong. But attitudes vary with time and place. The norms that I was taught are the norms of my own society; other societies have different ones. Morality is a cultural construct. Just as societies create different styles of food and clothing, so too they create different moral codes. I've learned about these in my anthropology class and experienced them as an exchange student in Mexico.

Consider my belief that infanticide is wrong. I was taught this as if it were an objective standard. But it isn't; it's just what my society holds. When I say "Infanticide is wrong," this just means that my society disapproves of it. For the ancient Romans, on the other hand, infanticide was all right. There's no sense in asking which side here is "correct." Their view is true relative to their culture, and our view is true relative to ours. There are no objective truths about right or wrong. When we claim otherwise, we're just imposing our culturally taught attitudes as the "objective truth."

"Wrong" is a relative term. Let me explain what this means. Something isn't "to the left" absolutely, but only "to the left *of*" this or that. Similarly, something isn't "wrong" absolutely, but only "wrong *in*" this or that society. Infanticide might be wrong in one society but right in another.

We can express CR most clearly as a definition: "X is good" means "The majority (of the society in question) approves of X." Other moral terms, like "bad" and "right," can be defined in a similar way. Note the reference to a specific society. Unless otherwise specified, the society in question is that of the person making the judgment. When I say "Hitler acted *wrongly*," I mean "according to the standards of *my* society."

The myth of objectivity says that things can be good or bad "absolutely"—not relative to this or that culture. But how can we know what is good or bad absolutely? How can we argue about this without just presupposing the standards of our own society? People who speak of good or bad absolutely are absolutizing the norms of their own society. They take the norms that they were taught to be objective facts. Such people need to study anthropology, or to live for a time in another culture.

As I've come to believe in cultural relativism, I've grown in my acceptance of other cultures. Like many exchange students, I used to have this "we're right and they're wrong" attitude. I struggled against this. I came to realize that the other side isn't "wrong" but just "different." We have to see others from their point of view; if we criticize them, we're just imposing the standards of our own society. We cultural relativists are more tolerant.

Through cultural relativism I've also come to be more accepting of the norms of my own society. CR gives a basis for a common morality within a culture—a democratic basis that pools everyone's ideas and insures that the norms have wide support. So I can feel solidarity with my own people, even though other groups have different values.

Objections to CR

Ima has given us a clear formulation of an approach that many find attractive. She's thought a lot about morality, and we can learn from her. Yet I'm convinced that her basic perspective on morality is wrong. Ima will likely come to agree as she gets clearer in her thinking.

Let me point out the biggest problem. CR forces us to conform to society's norms—or else we contradict ourselves. If "good" and "socially approved" meant the same thing, then whatever was one would have to be the other. So this reasoning would be valid:

Such and such is socially approved.
∴ Such and such is good.

If CR were true, then we couldn't consistently disagree with the values of our society. But this is an absurd result. We surely can consistently disagree with the values of our society. We can consistently affirm that something is "socially approved" but deny that it is "good." This would be impossible if CR were true.

Ima could bite the bullet (accept the implausible consequence), and say that it *is* self-contradictory to disagree morally with the majority. But this would be a difficult bullet for her to bite. She'd have to hold that civil rights leaders contradicted themselves when they disagreed with accepted views on segregation. And she'd have to accept the majority view on all moral issues—even if she sees that the majority is ignorant.

Suppose that Ima learned that most people in her society approve of displaying intolerance and ridicule toward people of other cultures. She'd then have to conclude that such intolerance is good (even though this goes against her new insights):

Intolerance is socially approved.
∴ Intolerance is good.

She'd have to either accept the conclusion (that intolerance is good) or else reject cultural relativism. Consistency would require that she change at least one of her views.

Here's a bigger bullet for Ima to bite. Imagine that Ima meets a figure skater named Lika Rebel, who is on tour from a Nazi country. In Lika's homeland, Jews and critics of the government are put in concentration camps. The majority of the people, since they are kept misinformed, support these policies. Lika dissents. She says that these policies are supported by the majority but are wrong. If Ima applied CR to this case, she'd have to say something like this to Lika:

Lika, your word "good" refers to what is approved in your culture. Since your culture approves of racism and oppression, you must accept that these are good. You can't think otherwise. The minority view is always wrong—since what is "good" is by definition what the majority approves.

CR is intolerant toward minority views (which are automatically wrong) and would force Lika to accept racism and oppression as good. These results follow from CR's definition of "good" as "socially approved." Once Ima sees these results, she'll likely give up CR.

Racism is a good test case for ethical views. A satisfying view should give some way to attack racist actions. CR fails at this, since it holds that racist actions are good in a society if they're socially approved. If Lika followed CR, she'd have to agree with a racist majority, even if they're misinformed and ignorant. CR is very unsatisfying here.

Moral education gives another test case for ethical views. If we accepted CR, how would we bring up our children to think about morality? We'd teach them to think and live by the norms of their society—whatever these were. We'd teach conformity. We'd teach that these are examples of correct reasoning:

- "My society approves of A, so A is good."
- "My peer-group society approves of getting drunk on Friday night and then driving home, so this is good."
- "My Nazi society approves of racism, so racism is good."

CR would make us uncritical about the norms of our society. These norms can't be in error—even if they come from stupidity and ignorance. Likewise, the norms of another society (even Lika's Nazi homeland) can't be in error or be criticized. Thus CR goes against the critical spirit that characterizes philosophy.

Moral Diversity

CR sees the world as neatly divided into distinct societies. Each one has little or no moral disagreement, since the majority view determines what is right or wrong in that society. But the world isn't like that. Instead, the world is a confusing mixture of overlapping societies and groups; and individuals don't necessarily follow the majority view.

CR ignores the subgroup problem. We all belong to overlapping groups. I'm part of a specific nation, state, city, and neighborhood. And I'm also part of various family, professional, religious, and peer groups.

These groups often have conflicting values. According to CR, when I say "Racism is wrong" I mean "My society disapproves of racism." But *which* society does this refer to? Maybe most in my national and religious societies disapprove of racism, while most in my professional and family societies approve of it. CR could give us clear guidance only if we belonged to just one society. But the world is more complicated than that. We're all multicultural to some extent.

CR doesn't try to establish common norms *between* societies. As technology shrinks the planet, moral disputes between societies become more important. Nation A approves of equal rights for women (or for other races or religions), but nation B disapproves. What is a multinational corporation that works in both societies to do? Or societies A and B have value conflicts that lead to war. Since CR helps very little with such problems, it gives a poor basis for life in the twenty-first century.

How do we respond to moral diversity between societies? Ima rejects the dogmatic "we're right and they're wrong" attitude. And she stresses the need to understand the other side from their point of view. These are positive ideas. But Ima then says that neither side can be wrong. This limits our ability to learn. If our society can't be wrong, then it can't learn from its mistakes. Understanding the norms of another culture can't then help us to correct errors in our own norms.

Those who believe in objective values see the matter differently. They might say something like this:

> There's a truth to be found in moral matters, but no culture has a monopoly on this truth. Different cultures need to learn from each other. To see the errors and blind spots in our own values, we need to see how other cultures do things, and how they react to what we do. Learning about other cultures can help us to correct our cultural biases and move closer to the truth about how we ought to live.

Objective Values

We need to talk more about the objectivity of values. . . . The objective view (also called moral realism) claims that some things are objectively right or wrong, independently of what anyone may think or feel. Dr Martin Luther King, for example, claimed that racist actions were objectively wrong. The wrongness of racism was a fact. Any person or culture that approved of racism was mistaken. In saying this, King wasn't absolutizing the norms of his society; instead, he disagreed with accepted norms. He appealed to a higher truth about right and wrong, one that didn't depend on human thinking or feeling. He appealed to objective values.

Ima rejects this belief in objective values and calls it "the myth of objectivity." On her view, things are good or bad only relative to this or that culture. Things aren't good or bad objectively, as King thought. But are objective values really a "myth"? Let's examine Ima's reasoning.

Ima had three arguments against objective values. There can't be objective moral truths, she thought, because

1. morality is a product of culture,
2. cultures disagree widely about morality, and
3. there's no clear way to resolve moral differences.

But these arguments fall apart if we examine them carefully.

(1) "Since morality is a product of culture, there can't be objective moral truths." The problem with this reasoning is that a product of culture can express objective truths. Every book is a product of culture; and yet many books express objective truths. So too, a moral code could be a product of culture and yet still express objective truths about how people ought to live.

(2) "Since cultures disagree widely about morality, there can't be objective moral truths." But the mere fact of disagreement doesn't show that there's no truth of the matter, that neither side is right or wrong. Cultures disagree widely about anthropology or religion or even physics. Yet there may still be a truth of the matter about these subjects. So a wide disagreement on moral issues wouldn't show that there's no truth of the matter on moral issues.

We might also question whether cultures differ so deeply about morality. Most cultures have fairly similar norms against killing, stealing, and lying. Many moral differences can be explained as the application of similar basic values to differing situations. The golden rule, "Treat others as you want to be treated," is almost universally accepted across the world. And the diverse cultures that make up the United Nations have agreed to an extensive statement on basic human rights.

(3) "Since there's no clear way to resolve moral differences, there can't be objective moral truths." But there may be clear ways to resolve at least many moral differences. We need a way to reason about ethics that would appeal to intelligent and open-minded people of all cultures—and that would do for ethics what scientific method does for science. . . .

Even if there were no solid way to know moral truths, it wouldn't follow that there are no such truths. There may be truths that we have no solid way of knowing about. Did it rain on this spot 500 years ago today? There's some truth about this, but we'll never know it. Only a small percentage of all truths are knowable. So there could be objective moral truths, even if we had no solid way to know them.

So Ima's attack on objective values fails. But this isn't the end of the matter, for there are further arguments on the issue. The dispute over objective values is important, and we'll talk more about it later. But before leaving this section, let me clarify some related points.

The objective view says that *some* things are objectively right or wrong, independently of what anyone may think or feel; but it still could accept much relativity in other areas. Many social rules clearly are determined by local standards:

- Local law: "Right turns on a red light are forbidden."
- Local rule of etiquette: "Use the fork only in your left hand."

We need to respect such local rules; otherwise, we may hurt people, either by crashing their cars or by hurting their feelings. On the objective view, the demand that we not hurt people is a rule of a different sort—a *moral* rule—and *not* determined by local customs. Moral rules are seen as more authoritative and objective than government laws or rules of etiquette; they are rules that *any* society must follow if it is to survive and prosper. If we go to a place where local standards permit hurting people for trivial reasons, then the local standards are mistaken. Cultural relativists would dispute this. They insist that local standards determine even basic moral principles; so hurting others for trivial reasons would be good if it were socially approved.

Respecting a range of cultural differences doesn't make you a cultural relativist. What makes you a cultural relativist is the claim that *anything* that is socially approved must thereby be good.

Harry Gensler: Cultural Relativism

1. What is Gensler's definition of cultural relativism? What analogies does he use to establish the idea of the relativity of morality? Can you think of other analogies that might convey cultural relativism's central idea?
2. Many people endorse cultural relativism because they think that it naturally supports tolerance toward the moral standards of different

societies. Gensler rejects this thought. Explain how he does so, and then assess his reasoning.

3. Can societies make moral mistakes? If so, can cultural relativism allow for that?

4. What is the correct attitude to have toward one's own society's moral norms? Can cultural relativism support this attitude? Why or why not?

5. Cultures sometimes disagree about morality. Does this support cultural relativism? Gensler denies that it does. Is his reasoning plausible?

18

Why I Am an Objectivist about
Ethics (And Why You Are, Too)

David Enoch

David Enoch claims that almost all of us are committed to the
objectivity of ethics. When we reflect on our attitudes toward ethical
claims and ethical practices, it is clear that we are assuming that there
are correct answers to moral questions, and correct standards of moral
evaluation, whose truth and authority do not depend on our beliefs or
attitudes about them. In the first half of his paper, Enoch presents
three tests that attempt to reveal our commitment to moral objectivity.
Even if these tests succeed in their aim—and Enoch thinks that they
clearly do—he realizes that this is not enough to prove that morality is
objective. For as he says, religious commitments also aspire to
objectivity. And yet this does not show that any religious claim is
objectively true (or true at all).

Still, the compelling appearance of objectivity in morality gives us
good reason to think that morality is indeed objective—unless, of
course, there are even stronger arguments that undermine this appearance. Enoch devotes the second half of his paper to considering a few
of the most important of these arguments. Some critics argue that the
extent of moral disagreement undermines moral objectivity. Critics
also argue that those who defend the existence of objective truths need
to provide a way of coming to know them, but that there is no plausible
way to gain moral knowledge, if morality is indeed objective. Critics also
worry that ethical objectivity supports intolerance and dogmatism.

Enoch carefully presents each criticism and then offers sharp replies to the objections.

....

Y ou may think that you're a moral relativist or subjectivist—many people today seem to. But I don't think you are. In fact, when we start doing metaethics—when we start, that is, thinking philosophically about our moral discourse and practice—thoughts about morality's objectivity become almost irresistible. Now, as is always the case in philosophy, that some thoughts seem irresistible is only the starting point for the discussion, and under argumentative pressure we may need to revise our relevant beliefs. Still, it's important to get the starting points right. So it's important to understand the deep ways in which rejecting morality's objectivity is unappealing. What I want to do, then, is to highlight the ways in which accepting morality's objectivity is appealing, and to briefly address some common worries about it, worries that may lead some to reject—or to think they reject—such objectivity. In the final section, I comment on the (not obvious) relation between the underlying concerns about morality's objectivity and the directions in which current discussion in metaethics are developing. As it will emerge, things are not (even) as simple as the discussion below seems to suggest. This is just one reason why metaethics is so worth doing.

Why Objectivity? Three (Related) Reasons

In the next section we're going to have to say a little more about what objectivity is. But sometimes it's helpful to start by engaging the underlying concerns, and return to more abstract, perhaps conceptual, issues later on.

The Spinach Test

Consider the following joke (which I borrow from Christine Korsgaard): A child hates spinach. He then reports that he's glad he hates spinach. To the question "Why?" he responds: "Because if I liked it, I would have eaten it, and it's yucky!"

In a minute we're going to have to annoyingly ask why the joke is funny. For now, though, I want to highlight the fact that similar jokes are not always similarly funny. Consider, for instance, someone who grew up in the twentieth-century West and who believes that the earth revolves around the sun. Also, she reports to be happy she wasn't born in the Middle Ages, "because had I grown up in the Middle Ages, I would have believed that the earth is in the center of the universe, and that belief is false!"

To my ears, the joke doesn't work in this latter version (try it on your friends!). The response in the earth-revolves-around-the-sun case sounds perfectly sensible, precisely in a way in which the analogous response does not sound sensible in the spinach case.

We need one last case. Suppose someone grew up in the United States in the late twentieth century and rejects any manifestation of racism as morally wrong. He then reports that he's happy that that's when and where he grew up, "because had I grown up in the eighteenth century, I would have accepted slavery and racism. And these things are wrong!" How funny is this third, last version of the joke? To my ears, it's about as (un)funny as the second one, and nowhere nearly as amusing as the first. The response to the question in this last case (why he is happy that he grew up in the twentieth century) seems to me to make perfect sense, and I suspect it makes sense to you too. And this is why there's nothing funny about it.

OK, then, why is the spinach version funny and the others are not? Usually, our attitude towards our own likings and dislikings (when it comes to food, for instance) is that it's all about us. If you don't like spinach, the reason you shouldn't have it is precisely that you don't like it. So if we're imagining a hypothetical scenario in which you do like it, then you no longer have any reason not to eat it. This is what the child in the first example gets wrong: he's holding fixed his dislike for spinach, even in thinking about the hypothetical case in which he likes spinach. But because these issues are all about him and what he likes and dislikes, this makes no sense.

But physics is different: What we want, believe or do—none of this affects the earth's orbit. The fact that the earth revolves around the sun is just not about us at all. So it makes sense to hold this truth fixed even when thinking about hypothetical cases in which you don't believe it. And so it makes sense to be happy that you aren't in the Middle Ages, since you'd then be in a situation in which your beliefs about the earth's orbit would be false (even if you couldn't know that they were). And because this makes sense, the joke isn't funny.

And so we have the spinach test: About any relevant subject matter, formulate an analogue of the spinach joke. If the joke works, this seems to indicate that the subject matter is all about us and our responses, our likings and dislikings, our preferences, and so on. If the joke doesn't work, the subject matter is much more objective than that, as in the astronomy case. And when we apply the spinach test to a moral issue (like the moral status of racism), it seems to fall squarely on the objective side.

(Exercise: Think about your taste in music, and formulate the spinach test for it. Is the joke funny?)

Disagreement and Deliberation

We sometimes engage in all sorts of disagreements. Sometimes, for instance, we may engage in a disagreement about even such silly things as whether bitter chocolate is better than milk chocolate. Sometimes we disagree about such things as whether human actions influence global warming. But these two kinds of disagreement are very different. One way of seeing this is thinking about what it feels like from the inside to engage in such disagreements. In the chocolate case, it feels like stating one's own preference, and perhaps trying to influence the listener into getting his own preferences in line. In the global warming case, though, it feels like trying to get at an objective truth, one that is there anyway, independently of our beliefs and preferences. (Either human actions contribute to global warming, or they don't, right?)

And so another test suggests itself, a test having to do with what it *feels like* to engage in disagreement (or, as we sometimes say, with the *phenomenology* of disagreement).

But now think of some serious moral disagreement—about the moral status of abortion, say. Suppose, then, that you are engaged in such disagreement. (It's important to imagine this from the inside, as it were. Don't imagine looking from the outside at two people arguing over abortion; think what it's like to be engaged in such argument yourself—if not about abortion, then about some other issue you care deeply about.) Perhaps you think that there is nothing wrong with abortion, and you're arguing with someone who thinks that abortion is morally wrong. What does such disagreement feel like? In particular, does it feel more like disagreeing over which chocolate is better, or like disagreeing over factual matters (such as whether human actions contribute to global warming)?

Because this question is a phenomenological one (that is, it's about what something feels like from the inside), I can't answer this question for you. You have to think about what it feels like for you when you are engaged in moral disagreement. But I can say that in my case such moral disagreement feels exactly like the one about global warming—it's about an objective matter of fact, that exists independently of us and our disagreement. It is in no way like disagreeing over the merits of different kinds of chocolate. And I think I can rather safely predict that this is how it feels for you too.

So on the phenomenology-of-disagreement test as well, morality seems to fall on the objective side.

In fact, we may be able to take disagreement out of the picture entirely. Suppose there is no disagreement—perhaps because you're all by yourself trying to make up your mind about what to do next. In one case, you're thinking about what kind of chocolate to get. In another, you're choosing between buying a standard car and a somewhat more expensive hybrid car (whose effect on global warming, if human actions contribute to global warming, is less destructive). Here, too, there's a difference. In the first case, you seem to be asking questions about yourself and what you like more (in general, or right now). In the second case, you need to make up your mind about your own action, of course, but you're asking yourself questions about objective matters of fact that do not depend on you at all—in particular, about whether human actions affect global warming.

Now consider a third case, in which you're trying to make up your mind about having an abortion, or advising a friend who is considering an abortion. So you're wondering whether abortion is wrong. Does it feel like asking about your own preferences or like an objective matter of fact? Is it more like the chocolate case or like the hybrid car case? If, like me, you answer that it's much more like the hybrid car case, then you think, like me, that the phenomenology of deliberation too indicates that morality is objective.

(Exercise: think about your taste in music again. In terms of the phenomenology of disagreement and deliberation, is it on the objective side?)

Would It Still Have Been Wrong If…?

Top hats are out of fashion. This may be an interesting, perhaps even practically relevant, fact—it may, for instance, give you reason to wear a top hat (if you want to be special) or not to (if not). But think about the following question: Had our fashion practices been very different—had we all worn top hats, thought they were cool, and so on—would it still have been true that top hats are out of fashion? The answer, it seems safe to assume, is "no."

Smoking causes cancer. This is an interesting, practically relevant, fact—it most certainly gives you a reason not to smoke, or perhaps to stop smoking. Now, had our relevant practices and beliefs regarding smoking been different—had we been OK with it, had we not banned it, had we thought smoking was actually quite harmless—would it still have been true that smoking causes cancer? I take it to be uncontroversial that the answer is "yes." The effects of smoking on our health do not depend on our beliefs and practices in anything like the way in which the fashionability of top hats does. Rather, it is an objective matter of fact.

And so we have a third objectivity test, one in terms of the relevant "what if" sentences (or *counterfactuals*, as they are often called), such as "Had our beliefs and practices been very different, would it still have been true that so-and-so?" Let's apply this test to morality.

Gender-based discrimination is wrong. I hope you agree with me on this (if you don't, replace this with a moral judgment you're rather confident in). Would it still have been wrong had our relevant practices and beliefs been different? Had we been all for gender-based discrimination, would that have made gender-based discrimination morally acceptable? Of course, in such a case we would have *believed* that there's nothing wrong with gender-based discrimination. But would it *be* wrong? To me it seems very clear that the answer is "Yes!" Gender-based discrimination is just as wrong in a society where everyone believes it's morally permissible. (This, after all, is why we would want such a society to change, and why, if we are members, we would fight for reform.) The problem in such a society is precisely that its members miss something so important—namely, the wrongness of gender-based discrimination. Had we thought gender-based discrimination was okay, we would have been mistaken. The morality of such discrimination does not depend on our opinion of it. The people in that hypothetical society may accept gender-based discrimination, but that doesn't make such discrimination acceptable.

In this respect too, then, morality falls on the objective side. When it comes to the counterfactual test, moral truths behave more like objective, factual truths (like whether smoking causes cancer) than like purely subjective, perhaps conventional claims (say, that top hats are unfashionable).

(Exercises: Can you see how the counterfactual test relates to the spinach test? And think about your favorite music, the kind of music that you don't just like, but that you think is *good*. Had you not liked it, would it still have been good?)

What's At Issue?

We have, then, three tests for objectivity—the spinach test, the phenomenology-of-disagreement-and-deliberation test, and the counterfactual test. And though we haven't yet said much about what objectivity comes to, these tests test for something that is recognizably in the vicinity of what we're after with our term "objectivity."

Objectivity, like many interesting philosophical terms, can be understood in more than one way. As a result, when philosophers affirm or deny the objectivity of some subject matter, it's not to be taken for granted that they're asserting or denying the same thing. But we don't have to go through a long list of what may be meant by morality's objectivity. It will be more productive, I think, to go about things in a different way. We can start by asking, why does it matter whether morality is objective? If we have a good enough feel for the answer to this question, we can then use it to find the sense of objectivity that we care about.

I suggest that we care about the objectivity of morality for roughly the reasons specified in the previous section. We want morality's objectivity to support our responses in those cases. We want morality's objectivity to vindicate the phenomenology of deliberation and disagreement, and our relevant counterfactual judgments. We want morality's objectivity to explain why the moral analogue of the spinach test isn't funny.

Very well, then, in what sense must morality be objective in order for the phenomenology of disagreement and deliberation and our counterfactual judgments to be justified? The answer, it seems to me, is that a subject matter is objective if the truths or facts in it exist independently of what we think or feel about them.

This notion of objectivity nicely supports the counterfactual test. If a certain truth (say, that smoking causes cancer) doesn't depend on our views about it, then it would have been true even had we not believed it. Not so for truths that do depend on our beliefs, practices, or emotions (such as the truth that top hats are unfashionable). And if moral truths are similarly independent of our beliefs, desires, preferences, emotions, points of view, and so on—if, as is sometimes said, moral truths are *response-independent*—then it's clear why gender-based discrimination would have been wrong even had we approved of it.

Similarly, if it's our responses that make moral claims true, then in a case of disagreement, it seems natural to suppose that both sides may be right. Perhaps, in other words, your responses make it the case that abortion is morally permissible ("for you," in some sense of this very weird phrase?), and your friend's responses make it the case that abortion is morally wrong ("for her"?). But if the moral status of abortion is response-*in*dependent, we understand why moral disagreement feels like factual disagreement—only one of you is right, and it's important to find out who.

And of course, the whole point of the spinach test was to distinguish between caring about things just because we care about them (such as not eating spinach, if you find it yucky) and caring about things that seem to us important independently of us caring about them (such as the wrongness of racism).

Another way of making the same point is as follows: Objective facts are those we seek to discover, not those we make true. And in this respect too, when it comes to moral truths, we are in a position more like that of the scientist who tries to discover the laws of nature (which exist independently of her investigations) than that of the legislator (who creates laws).

Now, in insisting that morality is objective in this sense—for instance, by relying on the reasons given in the previous section—it's important to see what has and what has not been established. In order to see this, it may help to draw an analogy with religious discourse. So think of your deeply held religious beliefs, if you have any. (If, like me, you do not, try to think what it's like to be deeply committed to a religious belief, or perhaps think of your commitment to atheism.) And try to run our tests—does it make sense to be happy that you were brought up under the religion in which you deeply believe, even assuming that with a different education you would have believed another religion, or no religion at all? What do you think of the phenomenology of religious deliberation and disagreement? And had you stopped believing, would the doctrines of your faith still have been true?

Now, perhaps things are not obvious here, but it seems to me that for many religious people, religious discourse passes all these objectivity tests. But from this it does not follow that atheism is false, much less that a specific religion is true. When they are applied to some specific religious discourse, the objectivity tests show that such discourse *aspires* to objectivity. In other words, the tests show what the world must be like for the commitments of the discourse to be vindicated: if (say) a Catholic's religious beliefs are to be true, what must be the case is that the doctrines of the Catholic Church hold objectively, that is, response-independently. This leaves entirely open the question whether these doctrines do in fact hold.

Back to morality, then. Here too, what the discussion of objectivity (tentatively) establishes is just something about the *aspirations* of moral discourse: namely, that it aspires to objectivity. If our moral judgments are to be true, it must be the case that things have value, that people have rights and duties, that there are better and worse ways to live our lives—and all of this must hold objectively, that is, response-independently. But establishing that moral discourse *aspires* to objectivity is one thing. Whether *there actually are* objective moral truths is quite another.

And now you may be worried. Why does it matter, you may wonder, what morality's aspirations are, if (for all I've said so far) they may not be met? I want to offer two replies here. First, precisely in order to check whether morality's aspirations are in fact fulfilled, we should understand them better. If you are trying to decide, for instance, whether the commitments of Catholicism are true, you had better understand them first. Second, and more importantly, one of the things we are trying to do here is to gain a better understanding of what we are already committed to. You may recall that I started with the hypothesis that you may think you're a relativist or a subjectivist. But if the discussion so far gets things right (if, that is, morality aspires to this kind of objectivity), and if you have any moral beliefs at all (don't you think that some things are wrong? do we really need to give gruesome examples?), then it follows that you yourself are already committed to morality's objectivity. And this is already an interesting result, at least for you.

That morality aspires in this way to objectivity also has the implication that any full metaethical theory—any theory, that is, that offers a full description and explanation of moral discourse and practice—has to take this aspiration into account. Most likely, it has to accommodate it. Less likely, but still possibly, such a theory may tell us that this aspiration is futile, explaining why even though morality is not objective, we tend to think that it is, why it manifests the marks of objectivity that the tests above catch on, and so on. What no metaethical theory can do, however, is ignore the very strong appearance that morality is objective. I get back to this in the final section, below.

Why Not?

As I already mentioned, we cannot rule out the possibility that under argumentative pressure we're going to have to revise even some of our most deeply held beliefs. Philosophy, in other words, is hard. And as you can imagine, claims about morality's objectivity have not escaped criticism. Indeed, perhaps some such objections have already occurred to you. In this section, I quickly mention some of them, and hint at the ways in which I think they can be coped with. But let me note how incomplete the discussion here is. There are, of course, other objections, objections that I don't discuss here. More importantly, there are many more things to say—on both sides—regarding the objections that I do discuss. The discussion here is meant as an introduction to these further discussions, no more than that. (Have I mentioned that philosophy is hard?)

Disagreement

I have been emphasizing ways in which moral disagreement may motivate the thought that morality is objective. But it's very common to think that something about moral disagreement actually goes the other way. For if there are perfectly objective moral truths, why is there so much disagreement about them? Wouldn't we expect, if there are such objective truths, to see everyone converging on them? Perhaps such convergence cannot be expected to be perfect and quick, but still—why is there so much persistent, apparently irreconcilable disagreement in morality, but not in subject matters whose objectivity is less controversial? If there is no answer to this question, doesn't this count heavily against morality's objectivity?

It is not easy to see exactly what this objection comes to. (Exercise: Can you try and formulate a precise argument here?) It may be necessary to distinguish between several possible arguments. Naturally, different ways of understanding the objection will call for different responses. But there are some things that can be said in general here. First, the objection seems to underrate the extent of disagreement in subject matters whose objectivity is pretty much uncontroversial (think of the causes and effects of global warming again). It may also overrate the extent of disagreement in morality. Still, the requirement to explain the scope and nature of moral disagreements seems legitimate. But objectivity-friendly explanations seem possible.

Perhaps, for instance, moral disagreement is sometimes best explained by noting that people tend to accept the moral judgments that it's in their interest to accept, or that tend to show their lives and practices in good light. Perhaps this is why the poor tend to believe in the welfare state, and the rich tend to believe in property rights.

Perhaps the most important general lesson here is that not all disagreements count against the objectivity of the relevant discourse. So what we need is a criterion to distinguish between objectivity-undermining and non-objectivity-undermining disagreements. And then we need an argument showing that moral disagreement is of the former kind. I don't know of a fully successful way of filling in these details here.

Notice, by the way, that such attempts are going to have to overcome a natural worry about *self-defeat*. Some theories defeat themselves, that is, roughly, fail even by their own lights. Consider, for instance, the theory "All theories are false," or the belief "No belief is justified." (Exercise: Can you think of other self-defeating theories?) Now, disagreement in philosophy has many of the features that moral disagreement seems to have. In particular, so does metaethical disagreement. Even more in particular, so does disagreement about *whether disagreement undermines objectivity*. If moral disagreement undermines the objectivity of moral conclusions, metaethical disagreement seems to undermine the objectivity of metaethical conclusions, including the conclusion that disagreement of this kind undermines objectivity. And this starts to look like self-defeat. So if some disagreement-objection to the objectivity of morality is going to succeed, it must show how moral disagreement undermines the objectivity of morality, but metaethical disagreement does *not* undermine the objectivity of metaethical claims. Perhaps it's possible to do so. But it's not going to be easy.

But How Do We Know?

Even if there are these objective moral truths—for instance, the kind of objective moral truth that both sides to a moral disagreement typically lay a claim to—how can we ever come to know them? In the astronomical case of disagreement about the relative position and motion of the earth and the sun, there are things we can say in response to a similar question— we can talk about perception, and scientific methodology, and progress. Similarly in other subject matters where we are very confident that objective truths await our discovery. Can anything at all be said in the moral case? We do not, after all, seem to possess something worth calling moral perception, a direct perception of the moral status of things. And in the moral case it's hard to argue that we have an established, much less uncontroversial, methodology either. (Whether there is moral progress is, I'm sure you've already realized, highly controversial.)

In other words, what we need is a moral epistemology, an account of how moral knowledge is possible, of how moral beliefs can be more or less justified, and the like. And I do not want to belittle the need for a moral epistemology, in particular an epistemology that fits well with an objectivist understanding of moral judgments. But the objectivist is not without resources here. After all, morality is not the only subject matter where perception and empirical methodology do not seem to be relevant. Think, for instance, of mathematics, and indeed of philosophy. But we do not often doubt the reality of mathematical knowledge. (Philosophical knowledge is a harder case, perhaps. Exercise: Can you see how claiming that we do not have philosophical knowledge may again give rise to a worry about self-defeat?)

Perhaps, then, what is really needed is a general epistemology of the a priori—of those areas, roughly, where the empirical method seems out of place. And perhaps it's not overly optimistic to think that any plausible epistemology of the a priori will vindicate moral knowledge as well.

Also, to say that there is no methodology of doing ethics is at the very least an exaggeration. Typically, when facing a moral question, we do not just stare at it helplessly. Perhaps we're not always very good at morality. But this doesn't mean that we never are. And perhaps at our best, when we employ our best ways of moral reasoning, we manage to attain moral knowledge.

(Exercise: There is no *uncontroversial* method of doing ethics. What, if anything, follows from this?)

Who Decides?

Still, even if moral knowledge is not especially problematic, even if moral disagreement can be explained in objectivity-friendly ways, and even if there are perfectly objective moral truths, what should we do in cases of disagreement and conflict? Who gets to decide what the right way of proceeding is? Especially in the case of intercultural disagreement and conflict, isn't saying something like "We're right and you're wrong about what is objectively morally required" objectionably dogmatic, intolerant, perhaps an invitation to fanaticism?

Well, in a sense, no one decides. In another sense, everyone does. The situation here is precisely as it is everywhere else: no one gets to decide whether smoking causes cancer, whether human actions contribute to global warming, whether the earth revolves around the sun. Our decisions do not make these claims true or false. But everyone gets (roughly speaking) to decide what they are going to believe about these matters. And this is so for moral claims as well.

How about intolerance and fanaticism? If the worry is that people are likely to become dangerously intolerant if they believe in objective morality, then first, such a prediction would have to be established. After all, many social reformers (think, for instance, of Martin Luther King, Jr.) who fought *against* intolerance and bigotry seem to have been inspired by the thought that their vision of equality and justice was objectively correct. Further, even if it's very dangerous for people to believe in the objectivity of their moral convictions, this doesn't mean that morality isn't objective. Such danger would give us reasons not to let people know about morality's objectivity. It would not give us a reason to believe that morality is not objective. (Compare: even if it were the case that things would go rapidly downhill if atheism were widely believed, this wouldn't prove that atheism is false.)

More importantly, though, it's one thing to believe in the objectivity of morality, it's quite another to decide what to do about it. And it's quite possible that the right thing to do, given morality's objectivity, is hardly ever to respond with "I am simply right and you are simply wrong!" or to be intolerant. In fact, if you think that it's wrong to be intolerant, aren't you committed to the objectivity of this very claim? (Want to run the three tests again?) So it seems as if the only way of accommodating the importance of toleration is actually to *accept* morality's objectivity, not to *reject* it.

Conclusion

As already noted, much more can be said—about what objectivity is, about the reasons to think that morality is objective, and about these (and many other) objections to morality's objectivity. Much more work remains to be done.

And one of the ways in which current literature addresses some of these issues may sound surprising, for a major part of the debate *assumes* something like morality's aspiration to objectivity in the sense above, but refuses to infer from such observations quick conclusions about the nature of moral truths and facts. In other words, many metaethicists today deny the most straightforward objectivist view of morality, according to which moral facts are a part of response-independent reality, much like mathematical and physical facts. But they do not deny morality's objectivity—they care, for instance, about passing the three tests above. And so they attempt to show how even on other metaethical views, morality's objectivity can be accommodated. As you can imagine, philosophers disagree about the success (actual and potential) of such accommodation projects.

Naturally, such controversies also lead to attempts to better understand what the objectivity at stake exactly is, and why it matters (if it matters) whether morality is objective. As is often the case, attempts to evaluate answers to a question make us better understand—or wonder about—the question itself.

Nothing here, then, is simple. But I hope that you now see how you are probably a moral objectivist, at least in your intuitive starting point. Perhaps further philosophical reflection will require that you abandon this starting point. But this will be an *abandoning*, and a very strong reason is needed to justify it. Until we get such a conclusive argument against moral objectivity, then, objectivism should be the view to beat.

David Enoch: Why I Am an Objectivist about Ethics (And Why You Are, Too)

1. In what ways does our attitude to morality seem to be different from our attitude to matters of taste?
2. In what ways does our attitude to morality seem to be different from our attitude to matters of convention, like fashion?
3. How can the phenomenon of moral disagreement count against the objectivity of morality?
4. Can the dangerousness of belief in moral objectivity give us reason to believe that morality is not after all objective? If so, how? If not, why not?
5. In what ways do we treat our aesthetic commitments and our moral ones on a par? In what ways do they seem to differ?

PART IV

Moral Problems

19

Why Shouldn't Tommy and Jim Have Sex? A Defense of Homosexuality

John Corvino

....

In this article, John Corvino considers and rejects each of the four most popular kinds of arguments that seek to establish the immorality of homosexuality. The first of these arguments claims that homosexuality is unnatural, and is therefore immoral. Corvino distinguishes five different senses in which things can be unnatural, and concludes, for each of these meanings, that homosexuality is either perfectly natural or, if unnatural, is not unnatural in a way that makes it immoral.

The second kind of argument against homosexuality is that it is harmful, either to homosexuals themselves or to third parties. Corvino thinks that the harm-to-others charge would be very serious if it could be sustained. But he argues that it fails, as does the claim that partners in homosexual relations are likelier to harm other people than those involved in heterosexual relations.

The third argument is one based on biblical teaching. The Hebrew scriptures appear to contain explicit condemnations of male homosexual conduct, and both Jewish and Christian traditions have long

---

"Why Shouldn't Tommy and Jim Have Sex?" from *Same Sex: Debating the Ethics, Science and Culture of Homosexuality*, ed. John Corvino (1997). Reprinted with permission of Rowman & Littlefield.

condemned homosexuality. Corvino argues that a plausible interpretive principle for ancient texts enables us to justify a position, within these religious frameworks, that puts these condemnations in context and enables believers, in good faith, to emerge with a view that finds homosexuality morally acceptable.

The last argument takes the form of a slippery slope: If homosexuality is morally permitted, then so, too, are bestiality and polygamy. But these are immoral, and therefore so too is homosexuality. Corvino thinks that we can resist the slippery slope, because (as he argues) there are special reasons to condemn bestiality and polygamy that do not apply to the case of homosexuality.

....

T ommy and Jim are a homosexual couple I know. Tommy is an accountant; Jim is a botany professor. They are in their forties and have been together fourteen years, the last five of which they've lived in a Victorian house that they've lovingly restored. Although their relationship has had its challenges, each has made sacrifices for the sake of the other's happiness and the relationship's long-term success.

I assume that Tommy and Jim have sex with each other (although I've never bothered to ask). Furthermore, I contend that they probably *should* have sex with each other. For one thing, sex is pleasurable. But it is also much more than that: a sexual relationship can unite two people in a way that virtually nothing else can. It can be an avenue of growth, of communication, and of lasting interpersonal fulfillment. These are reasons why most heterosexual couples have sex even if they don't want children, don't want children yet, or don't want additional children. And if these reasons are good enough for most heterosexual couples, then they should be good enough for Tommy and Jim.

Of course, having a reason to do something does not preclude there being an even better reason for not doing it. Tommy might have a good reason for drinking orange juice (it's tasty and nutritious) but an even better reason for not doing so (he's allergic). The point is that one would need a pretty good reason for denying a sexual relationship to Tommy and Jim, given the intense benefits widely associated with such relationships. The question I shall consider in this paper is thus quite simple: Why shouldn't Tommy and Jim have sex?

Homosexual Sex Is "Unnatural"

Many contend that homosexual sex is "unnatural." But what does that mean? Many things that people value—clothing, houses, medicine, and government, for example—are unnatural in some sense. On the other hand, many things that people detest—disease, suffering, and death, for example—are "natural" in the sense that they occur "in nature." If the unnaturalness charge is to be more than empty rhetorical flourish, those who levy it must specify what they mean. Borrowing from Burton Leiser, I will examine several possible meanings of "unnatural."[1]

What Is Unusual or Abnormal Is Unnatural

One meaning of "unnatural" refers to that which deviates from the norm, that is, from what most people do. Obviously, most people engage in heterosexual relationships. But does it follow that it is wrong to engage in homosexual relationships? Relatively few people read Sanskrit, pilot ships, play the mandolin, breed goats, or write with both hands, yet none of these activities is immoral simply because it is unusual. As the Ramsey Colloquium, a group of Jewish and Christian scholars who oppose homosexuality, writes, "The statistical frequency of an act does not determine its moral status."[2] So while homosexuality might be unnatural in the sense of being unusual, that fact is morally irrelevant.

What Is Not Practiced by Other Animals Is Unnatural

Some people argue, "Even animals know better than to behave homosexually; homosexuality must be wrong." This argument is doubly flawed. First it rests on a false premise. Numerous studies—including Anne Perkins's study of "gay" sheep and George and Molly Hunt's study of "lesbian" seagulls—have shown that some animals do form homosexual pairbonds. Second, even if animals did not behave homosexually, that fact would not prove that homosexuality is immoral. After all, animals don't cook their food, brush their teeth, participate in religious worship, or attend college; human beings do all of these without moral censure.

---

1 Burton M. Leiser, *Liberty, Justice, and Morals: Contemporary Value Conflicts* (New York: Macmillan, 1986), pp. 51–57.

2 The Ramsey Colloquium, "The Homosexual Movement," *First Things* (March 1994), pp. 15–20.

Indeed, the idea that animals could provide us with our standards—especially our sexual standards—is simply amusing.

What Does Not Proceed from Innate Desires Is Unnatural

Recent studies suggesting a biological basis for homosexuality have resulted in two popular positions. One side proposes that homosexual people are "born that way" and that it is therefore natural (and thus good) for them to form homosexual relationships. The other side maintains that homosexuality is a lifestyle choice, which is therefore unnatural (and thus wrong). Both sides assume a connection between the origin of homosexual orientation, on the one hand, and the moral value of homosexual activity, on the other. And insofar as they share that assumption, both sides are wrong.

Consider first the pro-homosexual side: "They are born that way; therefore it's natural and good." This inference assumes that all innate desires are good ones (i.e., that they should be acted upon). But that assumption is clearly false. Research suggests that some people are born with a predisposition toward violence, but such people have no more right to strangle their neighbors than anyone else. So while people like Tommy and Jim may be born with homosexual tendencies, it doesn't follow that they ought to act on them. Nor does it follow that they ought *not* to act on them, even if the tendencies are not innate. I probably do not have any innate tendency to write with my left hand (since I, like everyone else in my family, have always been right-handed), but it doesn't follow that it would be immoral for me to do so. So simply asserting that homosexuality is a lifestyle choice will not show that it is an immoral lifestyle choice.

Do people "choose" to be homosexual? People certainly don't seem to choose their sexual *feelings*, at least not in any direct or obvious way. (Do you? Think about it.) Rather, they find certain people attractive and certain activities arousing, whether they "decide" to or not. Indeed, most people at some point in their lives wish that they could control their feelings more—for example, in situations of unrequited love—and find it frustrating that they cannot. What they *can* control to a considerable degree is how and when they act upon those feelings. In that sense, both homosexuality and heterosexuality involve lifestyle choices. But in either case, determining the origin of the feelings will not determine whether it is moral to act on them.

What Violates an Organ's Principal Purpose Is Unnatural

Perhaps when people claim that homosexual sex is unnatural they mean that it cannot result in procreation. The idea behind the argument is that human organs have various natural purposes: eyes are for seeing, ears are for hearing, genitals are for procreating. According to this argument, it is immoral to use an organ in a way that violates its particular purpose. Many of our organs, however, have multiple purposes. Tommy can use his mouth for talking, eating, breathing, licking stamps, chewing gum, kissing women, or kissing Jim; and it seems rather arbitrary to claim that all but the last use are "natural." (And if we say that some of the other uses are "unnatural, but not immoral," we have failed to specify a morally relevant sense of the term "natural.")

Just because people can and do use their sexual organs to procreate, it does not follow that they should not use them for other purposes. Sexual organs seem very well suited for expressing love, for giving and receiving pleasure, and for celebrating, replenishing, and enhancing a relationship—even when procreation is not a factor. Unless opponents of homosexuality are prepared to condemn heterosexual couples who use contraception or individuals who masturbate, they must abandon this version of the unnaturalness argument. Indeed, even the Roman Catholic Church, which forbids contraception and masturbation, approves of sex for sterile couples and of sex during pregnancy, neither of which can lead to procreation. The Church concedes here that intimacy and pleasure are morally legitimate purposes for sex, even in cases where procreation is impossible. But since homosexual sex can achieve these purposes as well, it is inconsistent for the Church to condemn it on the grounds that it is not procreative.

One might object that sterile heterosexual couples do not *intentionally* turn away from procreation, whereas homosexual couples do. But this distinction doesn't hold. It is no more possible for Tommy to procreate with a woman whose uterus has been removed than it is for him to procreate with Jim. By having sex with either one, he is intentionally engaging in a non-procreative sexual act.

Yet one might press the objection further and insist that Tommy and the woman *could* produce children if the woman were fertile: whereas homosexual relationships are essentially infertile, heterosexual relationships are only incidentally so. But what does that prove? Granted, it might require less of a miracle for a woman without a uterus to become pregnant than for Jim to become pregnant, but it would require a miracle nonetheless. Thus it seems that the real difference here is not that one couple is fertile and the other not, nor that one couple "could" be fertile (with the help of a miracle) and the other not, but rather that one couple is male-female and the other male-male. In other words, sex between Tommy and Jim is wrong because it's male-male—i.e., because it's homosexual. But that, of course, is no argument at all.

What Is Disgusting or Offensive Is Unnatural

It often seems that when people call homosexuality "unnatural" they really just mean that it's disgusting. But plenty of morally neutral activities—handling snakes, eating snails, performing autopsies, cleaning toilets, and so on—disgust people. Indeed, for centuries, most people found interracial relationships disgusting, yet that feeling—which has by no means disappeared—hardly proves that such relationships are wrong. In sum, the charge that homosexuality is unnatural, at least in its most common forms, is longer on rhetorical flourish than on philosophical cogency. At best it expresses an aesthetic judgment, not a moral judgment.

Homosexual Sex Is Harmful

One might instead argue that homosexuality is harmful. The Ramsey Colloquium, for instance, argues that homosexuality leads to the breakdown of the family and, ultimately, of human society, and it points to the "alarming rates of sexual promiscuity, depression, and suicide and the ominous presence of AIDS within the homosexual subculture."[3] Thomas Schmidt marshals copious statistics to show that homosexual activity undermines physical and psychological health.[4] Such charges, if correct, would seem to provide strong evidence against homosexuality. But are the charges correct? And do they prove what they purport to prove?

One obvious (and obviously problematic) way to answer the first question is to ask people like Tommy and Jim. It would appear that no one is in a better position to judge the homosexual lifestyle than those who know it firsthand. Yet it is unlikely that critics would trust their testimony. Indeed, the more homosexual people try to explain their lives, the more critics accuse them of deceitfully promoting an agenda. (It's like trying to

---

3 The Ramsey Colloquium, "Homosexual Movement," p. 19.

4 Thomas Schmidt, "The Price of Love" in *Straight and Narrow? Compassion and Clarity in the Homosexuality Debate* (Downers Grove, IL: InterVarsity Press, 1995), chap. 6.

prove that you're not crazy. The more you object, the more people think, "That's exactly what a crazy person would say.")

One might instead turn to statistics. An obvious problem with this tack is that both sides of the debate bring forth extensive statistics and "expert" testimony, leaving the average observer confused. There is a more subtle problem as well. Because of widespread antigay sentiment, many homosexual people won't acknowledge their romantic feelings to themselves, much less to researchers. I have known a number of gay men who did not "come out" until their forties and fifties, and no amount of professional competence on the part of interviewers would have been likely to open their closets sooner. Such problems compound the usual difficulties of finding representative population samples for statistical study.

Yet even if the statistical claims of gay rights opponents were true, they would not prove what they purport to prove, for several reasons. First, as any good statistician realizes, correlation does not equal cause. Even if homosexual people were more likely to commit suicide, be promiscuous, or contract AIDS than the general population, it would not follow that their homosexuality causes them to do these things. An alternative—and very plausible—explanation is that these phenomena, like the disproportionately high crime rates among African Americans, are at least partly a function of society's treatment of the group in question. Suppose you were told from a very early age that the romantic feelings that you experienced were sick, unnatural, and disgusting. Suppose further that expressing these feelings put you at risk of social ostracism or, worse yet, physical violence. Is it not plausible that you would, for instance, be more inclined to depression than you would be without such obstacles? And that such depression could, in its extreme forms, lead to suicide or other self-destructive behaviors? (It is indeed remarkable that couples like Tommy and Jim continue to flourish in the face of such obstacles.)

A similar explanation can be given for the alleged promiscuity of homosexuals. The denial of legal marriage, the pressure to remain in the closet, and the overt hostility toward homosexual relationships are all more conducive to transient, clandestine encounters than they are to long-term unions. As a result, that which is challenging enough for heterosexual couples—settling down and building a life together—becomes far more challenging for homosexual couples. . . .

But what about AIDS? Opponents of homosexuality sometimes claim that even if homosexual sex is not, strictly speaking, immoral, it is still a bad idea, since it puts people at risk for AIDS and other sexually transmitted diseases. But that claim is misleading: it is infinitely more risky for Tommy to have sex with a woman who is HIV-positive than with Jim, who is HIV-negative. Obviously, it's not homosexuality that's harmful, it's the virus; and the virus may be carried by both heterosexual and homosexual people.

Now it may be true (in the United States, at least) that homosexual males are statistically more likely to carry the virus than heterosexual females and thus that homosexual sex is *statistically* more risky than heterosexual sex (in cases where the partner's HIV status is unknown). But opponents of homosexuality need something stronger than this statistical claim. For if it is wrong for men to have sex with men because their doing so puts them at a higher AIDS risk than heterosexual sex, then it is also wrong for women to have sex with men because their doing so puts them at a higher AIDS risk than homosexual sex (lesbians as a group have the lowest incidence of AIDS). Purely from the standpoint of AIDS risk, women ought to prefer lesbian sex.

If this response seems silly, it is because there is obviously more to choosing a romantic or sexual partner than determining AIDS risk. And a major part of the decision, one that opponents of homosexuality consistently overlook, is considering whether one can have a mutually fulfilling relationship with the partner. For many people like Tommy and Jim, such fulfillment—which most heterosexuals recognize to be an important component of human flourishing—is only possible with members of the same sex. . . .

In sum, there is nothing *inherently* risky about sex between persons of the same gender. It is only risky under certain conditions: for instance, if they exchange diseased bodily fluids or if they engage in certain "rough" forms of sex that could cause tearing of delicate tissue. Heterosexual sex is equally risky under such conditions. Thus, even if statistical claims like those of Schmidt and the Ramsey Colloquium were true, they would not prove that homosexuality is immoral. At best, they would prove that homosexual people—like everyone else—ought to take great care when deciding to become sexually active.

Of course, there's more to a flourishing life than avoiding harm. One might argue that even if Tommy and Jim are not harming each other by their relationship, they are still failing to achieve the higher level of fulfillment possible in a heterosexual relationship, which is rooted in the complementarity of male and female. But this argument just ignores the facts: Tommy and Jim are homosexual *precisely because* they find relationships with men (and, in particular, with each other) more fulfilling than relationships with women. Even evangelicals (who have long advocated "faith healing" for homosexuals) are beginning to acknowledge that the choice for most homosexual people is not between homosexual relationships and heterosexual relationships, but rather between homosexual relationships and celibacy. What the critics need to show, therefore, is that no matter how loving, committed, mutual, generous, and fulfilling the relationship may be, Tommy and Jim would flourish more if they were celibate. Given the evidence of their lives (and of others like them), this is a formidable task indeed.

Thus far I have focused on the allegation that homosexuality harms those who engage in it. But what about the allegation that homosexuality harms other, nonconsenting parties? Here I will briefly consider two claims: that homosexuality threatens children and that it threatens society.

Those who argue that homosexuality threatens children may mean one of two things. First, they may mean that homosexual people are child molesters. Statistically, the vast majority of reported cases of child sexual abuse involve young girls and their fathers, stepfathers, or other familiar (and presumably heterosexual) adult males. But opponents of homosexuality argue that when one adjusts for relative percentage in the population, homosexual males appear more likely than heterosexual males to be child molesters. As I argued above, the problems with obtaining reliable statistics on homosexuality render such calculations difficult. Fortunately, they are also unnecessary.

Child abuse is a terrible thing. But when a heterosexual male molests a child (or rapes a woman or commits assault), the act does not reflect upon all heterosexuals. Similarly, when a homosexual male molests a child, there is no reason why that act should reflect upon all homosexuals. Sex with adults of the same sex is one thing; sex with *children* of the same sex is quite another. Conflating the two not only slanders innocent people, it also misdirects resources intended to protect children. Furthermore, many men convicted of molesting young boys are sexually attracted to adult women and report no attraction to adult men. To call such men "homosexual," or even "bisexual," is probably to stretch such terms too far.

Alternatively, those who charge that homosexuality threatens children might mean that the increasing visibility of homosexual relationships makes children more likely to become homosexual. The argument for this view is patently circular. One cannot prove that doing X is bad by arguing that it causes other people to do X, which is bad. One must first establish independently that X is bad. That said, there is not a shred of evidence to demonstrate that exposure to homosexuality leads children to become homosexual.

But doesn't homosexuality threaten society? A Roman Catholic priest once put the argument to me as follows: "Of course homosexuality is bad for society. If everyone were homosexual, there would be no society." Perhaps it is true that if everyone were homosexual, there would be no society. But if everyone were a celibate priest, society would collapse just as surely, and my friend the priest didn't seem to think that he was doing anything wrong simply by failing to procreate. . . .

I have argued that Tommy and Jim's sexual relationship harms neither them nor society. On the contrary, it benefits both. It benefits them because it makes them happier—not merely in a short-term, hedonistic sense, but in a long-term, "big picture" sort of way. And, in turn, it benefits society, since it makes Tommy and Jim more stable, more productive, and more generous than they would otherwise be. In short, their relationship—including its sexual component—provides the same kinds of benefits that infertile heterosexual relationships provide (and perhaps other benefits as well). Nor should we fear that accepting their relationship and others like it will cause people to flee in droves from the institution of heterosexual marriage. After all . . . the usual response to a gay person is not "How come *he* gets to be gay and I don't?"

Homosexuality Violates Biblical Teaching

At this point in the discussion, many people turn to religion. "If the secular arguments fail to prove that homosexuality is wrong," they say, "so much the worse for secular ethics. This failure only proves that we need God for morality." Since people often justify their moral beliefs by appeal to religion, I will briefly consider the biblical position.

At first glance, the Bible's condemnation of homosexual activity seems unequivocal. Consider, for example, the following two passages, one from the "Old" Testament and one from the "New":

> You shall not lie with a male as with a woman; it is an abomination. (Lev. 18:22)
>
> For this reason God gave them up to degrading passions. Their women exchanged natural intercourse for unnatural, and in the same way also the men, giving up natural intercourse with women, were

consumed with passion for one another. Men committed shameless acts with men and received in their own persons the due penalty for their error. (Rom. 1:26–27)

Note, however, that these passages are surrounded by other passages that relatively few people consider binding. For example, Leviticus also declares,

The pig . . . is unclean for you. Of their flesh you shall not eat, and their carcasses you shall not touch; they are unclean for you. (11:7–8)

Taken literally, this passage not only prohibits eating pork, but also playing football, since footballs are made of pigskin. (Can you believe that the University of Notre Dame so flagrantly violates Levitical teaching?)

Similarly, St. Paul, author of the Romans passage, also writes, "Slaves, obey your earthly masters with fear and trembling, in singleness of heart, as you obey Christ" (Eph. 6:5)—morally problematic advice if there ever were any. Should we interpret this passage (as Southern plantation owners once did) as implying that it is immoral for slaves to escape? After all, God himself says in Leviticus,

[Y]ou may acquire male and female slaves . . . from among the aliens residing with you, and from their families that are with you, who have been born in your land; and they may be your property. You may keep them as a possession for your children after you, for them to inherit as property. (25:44–46)

How can people maintain the inerrancy of the Bible in light of such passages? The answer, I think, is that they learn to interpret the passages *in their historical context.*

Consider the Bible's position on usury, the lending of money for interest (for *any* interest, not just excessive interest). The Bible condemns this practice in no uncertain terms. In Exodus God says that "if you lend money to my people, to the poor among you, you shall not exact interest from them" (22:25). Psalm 15 says that those who lend at interest may not abide in the Lord's tent or dwell on his holy hill (1–5). Ezekiel calls usury "abominable"; compares it to adultery, robbery, idolatry, and bribery; and states that anyone who "takes advanced or accrued interest . . . shall surely die; his blood shall be upon himself" (18:13).

Should believers therefore close their savings accounts? Not necessarily. According to orthodox Christian teaching, the biblical prohibition against usury no longer applies. The reason is that economic conditions have changed substantially since biblical times, such that usury no longer has the same negative consequences it had when the prohibitions were issued. Thus, the practice that was condemned by the Bible differs from contemporary interest banking in morally relevant ways.

Yet are we not in a similar position regarding homosexuality? Virtually all scholars agree that homosexual relations during biblical times were vastly different from relationships like Tommy and Jim's. Often such relations were integral to pagan practices. In Greek society, they typically involved older men and younger boys. If those are the kinds of features that the biblical authors had in mind when they issued their condemnations, and such features are no longer typical, then the biblical condemnations no longer apply. As with usury, substantial changes in cultural context have altered the meaning and consequences—and thus the moral value—of the practice in question. Put another way, using the Bible's condemnations of homosexuality against contemporary homosexuality is like using its condemnations of usury against contemporary banking.

Let me be clear about what I am *not* claiming here. First, I am not claiming that the Bible has been wrong before and therefore may be wrong this time. The Bible may indeed by wrong on some matters, but for the purpose of this argument I am assuming its infallibility. Nor am I claiming that the Bible's age renders it entirely inapplicable to today's issues. Rather, I am claiming that when we do apply it, *we must pay attention to morally relevant cultural differences between biblical times and today*. Such attention will help us distinguish between specific time-bound prohibitions (for example, laws against usury or homosexual relations) and the enduring moral values they represent (for example, generosity or respect for persons). And as the above argument shows, my claim is not very controversial. Indeed, to deny it is to commit oneself to some rather strange views on slavery, usury, women's roles, astronomy, evolution, and the like.

Here, one might also make an appeal to religious pluralism. Given the wide variety of religious beliefs (e.g., the Muslim belief that women should cover their faces, the Orthodox Jewish belief against working on Saturday, the Hindu belief that cows are sacred and should not be eaten), each of us inevitably violates the religious beliefs of others. But we normally don't view such violations as occasions for moral censure, since we distinguish between beliefs that depend on particular revelations and beliefs that can be justified independently (e.g., that stealing is wrong). Without an independent justification for condemning homosexuality, the best one can say is, "My religion says so." But in a society that cherishes religious freedom, that reason alone does not normally provide grounds for moral or legal sanctions. That people still fall back on that reason in discussions of homosexuality suggests that they may not have much of a case otherwise.

Conclusion

As a last resort, opponents of homosexuality typically change the subject: "But what about incest, polygamy, and bestiality? If we accept Tommy and Jim's sexual relationship, why shouldn't we accept those as well?" Opponents of interracial marriage used a similar slippery-slope argument in the 1960s when the Supreme Court struck down antimiscegenation laws.[5] It was a bad argument then, and it is a bad argument now.

Just because there are no good reasons to oppose interracial or homosexual relationships, it does not follow that there are no good reasons to oppose incestuous, polygamous, or bestial relationships. One might argue, for instance, that incestuous relationships threaten delicate familial bonds, or that polygamous relationships result in unhealthy jealousies (and sexism), or that bestial relationships—do I need to say it?—aren't really "relationships" at all, at least not in the sense we've been discussing. Perhaps even better arguments could be offered (given much more space than I have here). The point is that there is no logical connection between homosexuality, on the one hand, and incest, polygamy, and bestiality, on the other.

Why, then, do critics continue to push this objection? Perhaps it's because accepting homosexuality requires them to give up one of their favorite arguments: "It's wrong because we've always been taught that it's wrong." This argument—call it the argument from tradition—has an obvious appeal: people reasonably favor tried-and-true ideas over unfamiliar ones, and they recognize the foolishness of trying to invent morality from scratch. But the argument from tradition is also a dangerous argument, as any honest look at history will reveal.

I conclude that Tommy and Jim's relationship, far from being a moral abomination, is exactly what it appears to be to those who know them: a morally positive influence on their lives and on others. Accepting this conclusion takes courage, since it entails that our moral traditions are fallible. But when these traditions interfere with people's happiness for no sound

---

5 *Loving v. Virginia*, 388 U.S. 1967.

reason, they defeat what is arguably the very point of morality: promoting individual and communal well-being. To put the argument simply, Tommy and Jim's relationship makes them better people. And that's not just good for Tommy and Jim: that's good for everyone.

John Corvino: Why Shouldn't Tommy and Jim Have Sex? A Defense of Homosexuality

1. What reasons do Tommy and Jim have for having sex? Do you agree with Corvino that these are the same reasons that many heterosexual couples have for having sex?
2. What does it mean to say that an activity is "unnatural"? Is the fact that something is unnatural ever a good reason for concluding that it is morally wrong?
3. Is homosexual sex harmful or risky to those who engage in it, in a way that heterosexual sex is not? If so, is this a good reason to think that it is morally wrong?
4. Some people argue that public acceptance of homosexual relationships would make children more likely to become homosexual. Why doesn't Corvino think this is a good argument against homosexual relationships? Do you agree with him?
5. How does Corvino respond to religious arguments against homosexuality? Do you find his responses convincing?
6. What is a "slippery slope" argument? Why does Corvino think that slippery slope arguments against homosexuality are bad arguments? Do you agree with him?

20

The Singer Solution to World Poverty

Peter Singer

....

Peter Singer argues that our ordinary patterns of spending money on ourselves are immoral. Such spending involves the purchase of many things that are not essential to preserving our lives or health. The money we spend on fancy dinners, new clothes, or vacations could instead be sent to relief agencies that save people's lives. We don't know our potential beneficiaries, but that is morally irrelevant. Our decision not to spend money to save their lives is morally inexcusable.

Singer offers us a series of fascinating examples in which people have the opportunity to prevent an innocent person's death but fail to do so. We regard the person in each example as having done something extremely immoral. Singer argues that we who spend money on inessential personal pleasures are no better.

But what if most of the people we know are also failing to give anything to famine relief or aid agencies? That doesn't let us off the hook—it just means that they are also behaving in a deeply immoral way.

Perhaps the money sent overseas will not do as much good as advertised? Singer mentions some very reliable aid agencies (and provides contact information) that will not squander your money. For a couple hundred dollars, you can save a child's life, or purchase a

Reprinted by permission of the author. © Peter Singer, 1999. This article first appeared under the title "The Singer Soultion to World Poverty," *New York Times Magazine* (Sept 5, 1999), pp. 60-63.

few new additions to your wardrobe. If Singer is right, then choosing to spend that money on yourself means knowingly allowing an innocent person to die. Given the relatively small sacrifice you would be making if you sent that money overseas, and given the great benefit you would be providing if you did, morality gives you no choice. World poverty could largely be solved if we in the wealthier nations did our moral duty and gave much more than we currently do to those in greatest need.

....

In the Brazilian film *Central Station*, Dora is a retired schoolteacher who makes ends meet by sitting at the station writing letters for illiterate people. Suddenly she has an opportunity to pocket $1,000. All she has to do is persuade a homeless 9-year-old boy to follow her to an address she has been given. (She is told he will be adopted by wealthy foreigners.) She delivers the boy, gets the money, spends some of it on a television set, and settles down to enjoy her new acquisition. Her neighbor spoils the fun, however, by telling her that the boy was too old to be adopted—he will be killed and his organs sold for transplantation. Perhaps Dora knew this all along, but after her neighbor's plain speaking, she spends a troubled night. In the morning Dora resolves to take the boy back.

Suppose Dora had told her neighbor that it is a tough world, other people have nice new TVs too, and if selling the kid is the only way she can get one, well, he was only a street kid. She would then have become, in the eyes of the audience, a monster. She redeems herself only by being prepared to bear considerable risks to save the boy.

At the end of the movie, in cinemas in the affluent nations of the world, people who would have been quick to condemn Dora if she had not rescued the boy go home to places far more comfortable than her apartment. In fact, the average family in the United States spends almost one-third of its income on things that are no more necessary to them than Dora's new TV was to her. Going out to nice restaurants, buying new clothes because the old ones are no longer stylish, vacationing at beach resorts—so much of our income is spent on things not essential to the preservation of our lives and health. Donated to one of a number of charitable agencies, that money could mean the difference between life and death for children in need.

All of which raises a question: In the end, what is the ethical distinction between a Brazilian who sells a homeless child to organ peddlers and an American who already has a TV and upgrades to a better one—knowing that the money could be donated to an organization that would use it to save the lives of kids in need?

Of course, there are several differences between the two situations that could support different moral judgments about them. For one thing, to be able to consign a child to death when he is standing right in front of you takes a chilling kind of heartlessness; it is much easier to ignore an appeal for money to help children you will never meet. Yet for a utilitarian philosopher like myself—that is, one who judges whether acts are right or wrong by their consequences—if the upshot of the American's failure to donate the money is that one more kid dies on the streets of a Brazilian city, then it is, in some sense, just as bad as selling the kid to the organ peddlers. But one doesn't need to embrace my utilitarian ethic to see that, at the very least, there is a troubling incongruity in being so quick to condemn Dora for taking the child to the organ peddlers while, at the same time, not regarding the American consumer's behavior as raising a serious moral issue.

In his 1996 book, *Living High and Letting Die,* the New York University philosopher Peter Unger presented an ingenious series of imaginary examples designed to probe our intuitions about whether it is wrong to live well without giving substantial amounts of money to help people who are hungry, malnourished or dying from easily treatable illnesses like diarrhea. Here's my paraphrase of one of these examples:

Bob is close to retirement. He has invested most of his savings in a very rare and valuable old car, a Bugatti, which he has not been able to insure. The Bugatti is his pride and joy. In addition to the pleasure he gets from driving and caring for his car, Bob knows that its rising market value means that he will always be able to sell it and live comfortably after retirement. One day when Bob is out for a drive, he parks the Bugatti near the end of a railway siding and goes for a walk up the track. As he does so, he sees that a runaway train, with no one aboard, is running down the railway track. Looking farther down the track, he sees the small figure of a child very likely to be killed by the runaway train. He can't stop the train and the child is too far away to warn of the danger, but he can throw a switch that will divert the train down the siding where his Bugatti is parked. Then nobody will be killed—but the train will destroy his Bugatti. Thinking of his joy in owning the car and the financial security it represents, Bob decides not to throw the switch. The child is killed. For many years to come, Bob enjoys owning his Bugatti and the financial security it represents.

Bob's conduct, most of us will immediately respond, was gravely wrong. Unger agrees. But then he reminds us that we, too, have opportunities to save the lives of children. We can give to organizations like UNICEF or Oxfam America. How much would we have to give one of these organizations to have a high probability of saving the life of a child threatened by easily preventable diseases? (I do not believe that children are more worth saving than adults, but since no one can argue that children have brought their poverty on themselves, focusing on them simplifies the issues.) Unger called up some experts and used the information they provided to offer some plausible estimates that include the cost of raising money, administrative expenses and the cost of delivering aid where it is most needed. By his calculation, $200 in donations would help a sickly 2-year-old transform into a healthy 6-year-old—offering safe passage through childhood's most dangerous years. To show how practical philosophical argument can be, Unger even tells his readers that they can easily donate funds by using their credit card and calling one of these toll-free numbers: (800) 367-5437 for Unicef; (800) 693-2687 for Oxfam America. [http://supportunicef.org/forms/whichcountry2.html for Unicef and http://www.oxfam.org/eng/donate.htm for Oxfam—PS].

Now you, too, have the information you need to save a child's life. How should you judge yourself if you don't do it? Think again about Bob and his Bugatti. Unlike Dora, Bob did not have to look into the eyes of the child he was sacrificing for his own material comfort. The child was a complete stranger to him and too far away to relate to in an intimate, personal way. Unlike Dora, too, he did not mislead the child or initiate the chain of events imperiling him. In all these respects, Bob's situation resembles that of people able but unwilling to donate to overseas aid and differs from Dora's situation.

If you still think that it was very wrong of Bob not to throw the switch that would have diverted the train and saved the child's life, then it is hard to see how you could deny that it is also very wrong not to send money to one of the organizations listed above. Unless, that is, there is some morally important difference between the two situations that I have overlooked.

Is it the practical uncertainties about whether aid will really reach the people who need it? Nobody who knows the world of overseas aid can doubt that such uncertainties exist. But Unger's figure of $200 to save a child's life was reached after he had made conservative assumptions about the proportion of the money donated that will actually reach its target.

One genuine difference between Bob and those who can afford to donate to overseas aid organizations but don't is that only Bob can save the child on the tracks, whereas there are hundreds of millions of people who can give $200 to overseas aid organizations. The problem is that most of them aren't doing it. Does this mean that it is all right for you not to do it?

Suppose that there were more owners of priceless vintage cars—Carol, Dave, Emma, Fred, and so on, down to Ziggy—all in exactly the same situation as Bob, with their own siding and their own switch, all sacrificing the child in order to preserve their own cherished car. Would that make it all right for Bob to do the same? To answer this question affirmatively is to endorse follow-the-crowd ethics—the kind of ethics that led many Germans to look away when the Nazi atrocities were being committed. We do not excuse them because others were behaving no better.

We seem to lack a sound basis for drawing a clear moral line between Bob's situation and that of any reader of this article with $200 to spare who does not donate it to an overseas aid agency. These readers seem to be acting at least as badly as Bob was acting when he chose to let the runaway train hurtle toward the unsuspecting child. In the light of this conclusion, I trust that many readers will reach for the phone and donate that $200. Perhaps you should do it before reading further.

Now that you have distinguished yourself morally from people who put their vintage cars ahead of a child's life, how about treating yourself and your partner to dinner at your favorite restaurant? But wait. The money you will spend at the restaurant could also help save the lives of children overseas! True, you weren't planning to blow $200 tonight, but if you were to give up dining out just for one month, you would easily save that amount. And what is one month's dining out, compared to a child's life? There's the rub. Since there are a lot of desperately needy children in the world, there will always be another child whose life you could save for another $200. Are you therefore obliged to keep giving until you have nothing left? At what point can you stop?

Hypothetical examples can easily become farcical. Consider Bob. How far past losing the Bugatti should he go? Imagine that Bob had got his foot stuck in the track of the siding, and if he diverted the train, then before it rammed the car it would also amputate his big toe. Should he still throw the switch? What if it would amputate his foot? His entire leg?

As absurd as the Bugatti scenario gets when pushed to extremes, the point it raises is a serious one: only when the sacrifices become very significant indeed would most people be prepared to say that Bob does nothing wrong when he decides not to throw the switch. Of course, most people could be wrong; we can't decide moral issues by taking opinion polls. But consider for yourself the level of sacrifice that you would demand of Bob, and then think about how much money you would have to give away in order to make a sacrifice that is roughly equal to that. It's almost certainly much, much more than $200. For most middle-class Americans, it could easily be more like $200,000.

Isn't it counterproductive to ask people to do so much? Don't we run the risk that many will shrug their shoulders and say that morality, so conceived, is fine for saints but not for them? I accept that we are unlikely to see, in the near or even medium-term future, a world in which it is normal for wealthy Americans to give the bulk of their wealth to strangers. When it comes to praising or blaming people for what they do, we tend to use a standard that is relative to some conception of normal behavior. Comfortably off Americans who give, say, 10 percent of their income to overseas aid organizations are so far ahead of most of their equally comfortable fellow citizens that I wouldn't go out of my way to chastise them for not doing more. Nevertheless, they should be doing much more, and they are in no position to criticize Bob for failing to make the much greater sacrifice of his Bugatti.

At this point various objections may crop up. Someone may say: "If every citizen living in the affluent nations contributed his or her share I wouldn't have to make such a drastic sacrifice, because long before such levels were reached, the resources would have been there to save the lives of all those children dying from lack of food or medical care. So why should I give more than my fair share?" Another, related, objection is that the Government ought to increase its overseas aid allocations, since that would spread the burden more equitably across all taxpayers.

Yet the question of how much we ought to give is a matter to be decided in the real world—and that, sadly, is a world in which we know that most people do not, and in the immediate future will not, give substantial amounts to overseas aid agencies. We know, too, that at least in the next year, the United States Government is not going to meet even the very modest United Nations-recommended target of 0.7 percent of gross national product; at the moment it lags far below that, at 0.09 percent, not even half of Japan's 0.22 percent or a tenth of Denmark's 0.97 percent.

Thus, we know that the money we can give beyond that theoretical "fair share" is still going to save lives that would otherwise be lost. While the idea that no one need do more than his or her fair share is a powerful one, should it prevail if we know that others are not doing their fair share and that children will die preventable deaths unless we do more than our fair share? That would be taking fairness too far.

Thus, this ground for limiting how much we ought to give also fails. In the world as it is now, I can see no escape from the conclusion that each one of us with wealth surplus to his or her essential needs should be giving most of it to help people suffering from poverty so dire as to be life-threatening. That's right: I'm saying that you shouldn't buy that new car, take that cruise, redecorate the house or get that pricey new suit. After all, a $1,000 suit could save five children's lives.

So how does my philosophy break down in dollars and cents? An American household with an income of $50,000 spends around $30,000 annually on necessities, according to the Conference Board, a nonprofit economic research organization. Therefore, for a household bringing in $50,000 a year, donations to help the world's poor should be as close as possible to $20,000. The $30,000 required for necessities holds for higher incomes as well. So a household making $100,000 could cut a yearly check for $70,000. Again, the formula is simple: whatever money you're spending on luxuries, not necessities, should be given away.

Now, evolutionary psychologists tell us that human nature just isn't sufficiently altruistic to make it plausible that many people will sacrifice so much for strangers. On the facts of human nature, they might be right, but they would be wrong to draw a moral conclusion from those facts. If it is the case that we ought to do things that, predictably, most of us won't do, then let's face that fact head-on. Then, if we value the life of a child more than going to fancy restaurants, the next time we dine out we will know that we could have done something better with our money. If that makes living a morally decent life extremely arduous, well, then that is the way things are. If we don't do it, then we should at least know that we are failing to live a morally decent life—not because it is good to wallow in guilt but because knowing where we should be going is the first step toward heading in that direction.

When Bob first grasped the dilemma that faced him as he stood by that railway switch, he must have thought how extraordinarily unlucky he was to be placed in a situation in which he must choose between the life of an innocent child and the sacrifice of most of his savings. But he was not unlucky at all. We are all in that situation.

Peter Singer: The Singer Solution to World Poverty

1. Was it morally wrong of Bob to refrain from throwing the switch, thus allowing the child to die? Is there any moral difference between Bob's decision and the decision of well-off people to spend money on luxuries rather than the alleviation of poverty?

2. One difference between the case of Bob and the case of someone not giving to charity is that Bob is the only person in a position to prevent the child's death, while many people are in a position to give to charity. Why doesn't Singer think that this is a morally relevant difference? Do you agree with him?

3. How much of our income does Singer think we are morally required to give away? Do you find his standard reasonable?

4. How does Singer respond to the objection that his theory is too demanding, and that people will never make the sacrifices he suggests? Do you find his response convincing?

5. One might respond to Singer's proposals by claiming that instead of individuals contributing money to alleviate world poverty, governments should be responsible for handling such efforts. Why doesn't Singer think that this undermines his view that middle-class people should give large percentages of their income to charity?

21

Feeding the Hungry

Jan Narveson

....

What obligations do we have to those who are starving? If Jan Narveson is right, the answer is usually: none.

Narveson argues that most of us who are well-fed and relatively comfortable in our lives have no duties at all to relieve the suffering of the poor and hungry. If we are responsible for creating the unfortunate situation in which someone else finds himself impoverished, then we *do* owe him relief and support. But those cases aside, Narveson argues that any help we give to the starving is entirely morally optional. We may give if we like, but such assistance is not morally required.

For Narveson, our moral duties are supplied entirely by the demands of justice. And justice requires only two things. First, we must right the wrongs we have done to others. Second, we must respect the liberty of others to do as they please. In other words, we must not "invade" their liberty by (for instance) robbing or beating or killing them. So long as we respect their liberty, and provide compensation where we have wronged others, then we are completely fulfilling the requirements of justice—and so of morality.

Justice is a matter of respecting everyone's rights. Narveson argues that the poor do not have a right to be fed—the needs of others do not automatically give them a right to your assistance. Suppose you are wealthy and I am poor, and I need money for an operation. This does not by itself give me a right to some of your money. So if you refuse to

---

Reprinted by permission from Jan Narveson, *Moral Matters* (Lewiston, N.Y.: Broadview Press, 1993), pp. 138–150.

help me, then you are not committing an injustice. Of course you are certainly permitted to fund my operation. But that would be charity. And charity is not something that we morally can compel.

For Narveson, we are morally permitted to do anything we like, so long as we do not violate the rights of others. While it would be generous and kind and compassionate of us to feed the hungry, doing so is morally optional, rather than required. It is a matter of charity, not justice.

....

Throughout history it has been the lot of most people to know of others worse off than they, and often enough of others who face starvation. In the contemporary world, television and other mass media enable all of us in the better-off areas to hear about starvation in even the most remote places. What, if any, are our obligations toward victims of starvation?

This can be a rather complex subject in real-world situations. We must begin by distinguishing importantly different cases. For *starve* functions both as a passive verb, indicating something that happens to one, and as an active verb, designating something inflicted by one person on another. In the latter case, starvation is a form of killing, and of course comes under the same strictures that any other method of killing is liable to. But when the problem is plague, crop-failure due to drought, or sheer lack of know-how, there is no obviously guilty party. Then the question is whether we, the amply fed, are guilty parties if we fail to come to the rescue of those victims.

Starvation and Murder

If I lock you in a room with no food and don't let you out, I have murdered you. If group A burns the crops of group B, it has slaughtered the Bs. There is, surely, no genuine *issue* about such cases. It is wrong to kill innocent people, and one way of killing them is as eligible for condemnation by this principle as any other, so far as killing goes. Such cases are happily unusual, and we need say no more about them.

Our interest, then, is in the cases where this is not so, or at least not obviously so. But some writers, such as James Rachels, hold that letting someone die is morally equivalent to killing them. Or "basically" equivalent. Is this so? Most people do not think so; it takes a subtle philosophical argument to persuade them of this. The difference between a bad thing which I intentionally or at least foreseeably brought about, and one which just happened, through no fault of my own, matters to most of us in practice. Is our view sustainable in principle, too? Suppose the case is one I could do something about, as when you are starving and my granary is burgeoning. Does that make a difference?

Duties of Justice and Duties of Charity

Another important question, which has cropped up in some of our other cases too but is nowhere more clearly relevant than here, is the distinction between *justice* and *charity*. By justice I here intend those things which we may, if necessary, be *forced* to do—where our actions can be constrained by others in order to ensure our performance. Charity, on the other hand, comes "from the heart": *charity* means, roughly, *caring*, an emotionally-tinged desire to benefit other people just because they need it.

We should note a special point about this. It is often said that charity "cannot be compelled." Is this true? In one clear sense, it is. For in this sense, charity consists *only* of benefits motivated by love or concern. If instead you regard an act as one that we may forcibly compel people to do, then you are taking that act to be a case of *justice*. Can it at the same time be charity? It can if we detach the motive from the act, and define charity simply as doing good for others. The claim that charity in this second sense cannot be compelled is definitely not true by definition, and is in fact false. People are frequently compelled to do good for others, especially by our government, which taxes us in order to benefit the poor, educate the uneducated, and so on. Whether they *should* be thus compelled is a real moral question, however, and must not be evaded by recourse to semantics. (Whether those programs produce benefits that outweigh their costs is a very complex question; but that they do often produce some benefits, at whatever cost, is scarcely deniable.)

When we ask, then, on which side of the moral divide we should put feeding the hungry—unenforceable charity, to be left to individual consciences, or enforceable justice, perhaps to be handled by governments—is a genuine moral issue, and an important one. We are asking whether feeding the hungry is not only something we ought to do but also something we *must do,* as a matter of justice. It is especially this latter question that concerns us in this chapter.

We should note also the logical possibility that someone might differ so strongly with most of us on this matter as to think it positively *wrong* to feed the hungry. That is a rather extreme view, but it looks rather like the view that some writers, such as Garrett Hardin, defend. However, it is misleading to characterize their view in this way. Hardin thinks that feeding the hungry is an exercise in *misguided* charity, not real charity. In feeding the hungry today, he argues, we merely create a much greater problem tomorrow, for feeding the relatively few now will create an unmanageably large number next time their crops fail, a number we won't be able to feed and who will consequently starve. Thus we actually cause more starvation by feeding people now than we do by not feeding them, hard though that may sound. Hardin, then, is not favouring cruelty toward the weak. The truly charitable, he believes, should be *against* feeding the hungry, at least in some types of cases.

Hardin's argument brings up the need for another distinction, of urgent importance: between *principles* and *policies.* Being in favour of feeding the hungry *in principle* may or may not imply that we should feed the particular persons involved in any specific case. For that may depend on further facts about those cases. For example, perhaps trying to feed *these* hungry people runs into the problem that the government of those hungry people doesn't want you feeding them. If the price of feeding them is that you must go to war, then it may not be the best thing to do. If enormous starvation faces a group in the farther future if the starving among them now are fed now, then a policy of feeding them now may not be recommended by a principle of humanity. And so on. Principles are relatively abstract and may be considered just by considering possibilities; but when it comes to policy pursued in the real world, facts cannot be ignored.

The Basic Issues

Our general question is what sort of moral concerns we have with the starving. The basic question then breaks down into these two: first, is there a *basic duty of justice* to feed the starving? And second, if there isn't, then is there a *basic requirement of charity* that we be disposed to do so, and if so, how strong is that requirement?

Justice and Starvation

Let's begin with the first. Is it *unjust* to let others starve to death? We must distinguish two very different ways in which someone might try to argue for this.

First, there are those who, like Rachels, argue that there is no fundamental distinction between killing and letting die. If that is right, then the duty not to kill is all we need to support the conclusion that there is a duty of justice not to let people starve, and the duty not to kill (innocent) people is uncontroversial. Second, however, some insist that feeding the hungry is a duty of justice even if we don't accept the equivalence of killing and letting-die. They therefore need a different argument, in support of a positive right to be fed. The two different views call for very different discussions.

Starving and Allowing to Starve

Starving and allowing-to-starve are special cases of killing and letting-die. Are they the same, as some *insist?* In *our* discussion of euthanasia, we saw the need for a crucial distinction here: between the view that they are literally indistinguishable, and the view that even though they are logically distinguishable, they are nevertheless morally equivalent. As to the first, the argument for nonidentity of the two is straightforward. When you kill someone, you do an act, *x,* which brings it about that the person is dead *when he would otherwise still be alive.* You induce a *change* (for the worse) in his condition. But when you let someone die, this is not so, for she would have died even if you had, say, been in Australia at the time. How can you be said to be the "cause" of something which would have happened if you didn't exist?

To be sure, we do often attribute causality to human inaction. But the clear cases of such attribution are those where the agent in question had an antecedent *responsibility* to do the thing in question. The geraniums may die because you fail to water them, but to say that you thus *caused* them to die is to imply that you were *supposed* to do so. And of course we may agree that *if* we *have* a duty to feed the poor and we don't feed them, then we are at fault. But the question before us is *whether* we have this duty, and the argument we are examining purports to prove this by showing that even when we do nothing, we still "cause" their deaths. If the argument presupposes that very responsibility, it plainly begs the question rather than giving us a good answer to it. What about the claim that killing and letting die are "morally equivalent"? Here again, there is a danger of begging the question. *If* we have a duty to feed the hungry and we don't, then not doing so might be morally equivalent to killing them, perhaps—though I doubt that any proponent would seriously propose life imprisonment for failing to contribute to the cause of feeding the hungry! But again, the consequence clearly doesn't follow if we don't have that duty, which is in question. Those who think we do not have fundamental duties to take care of each other, but only duties to refrain from killing and the like will deny that they are morally equivalent.

The liberty proponent will thus insist that when Beethoven wrote symphonies instead of using his talents to grow food for the starving, like the peasants he depicted in his Pastorale symphony, he was doing what he had a perfect right to do. A connoisseur of music might go further and hold that he was also *doing the right thing:* that someone with the talents of a Beethoven does more for people by composing great music than by trying to save lives—even if he would have been *successful* in saving those lives, which is not terribly likely anyway!

How do we settle this issue? If we were all connoisseurs, it would be easy: if you know and love great music, you will find it easy to believe that a symphony by Beethoven or Mahler is worth more than prolonging the lives of a few hundred starvelings for another few miserable years. If you are one of those starving persons, your view might be different. (But it might not. Consider the starving artist in his garret, famed in Romantic novels and operas: they lived *voluntarily* in squalor, believing that what they were doing was worth the sacrifice.)

We are not all connoisseurs, nor are most of us starving. Advocates of welfare duties talk glibly as though there were a single point of view ("welfare") that dominates everything else. But it's not true. There are all kinds of points of view, diverse, and to a large extent incommensurable. Uniting them is not as simple as the welfarist or utilitarian may think. It is *not* certain, not obvious, that we "add more to the sum of human happiness" by supporting Oxfam than by supporting the opera. How are we to unite diverse people on these evaluative matters? The most plausible answer, I think, is the point of view that allows different people to live their various lives, by forbidding interference with them. Rather than insisting, with threats to back it up, that I help someone for whose projects and purposes I have no sympathy whatever, let us all agree to respect each other's pursuits. We'll agree to let each person live as that person sees fit, with only our bumpings into each other being subject to public control. To do this, we need to draw a sort of line around each person, and insist that others not cross that line without the permission of the occupant. The rule will be not to forcibly intervene in the lives of others, thus requiring that our relations be mutually agreeable. Enforced feeding of the starving, however, does cross the line, invading the farmer or the merchant, forcing him to part with some of his hard-earned produce and give it without compensation to others. That, says the advocate of liberty, is theft, not charity.

So if someone is starving, we may pity him or we may be indifferent, but the question so far as our *obligations* are concerned is only this: how did he *get* that way? If it was not the result of my previous activities, then I have no obligation to him, and may help him out or not, as I choose. If it was such a result, then of course I must do something. If you live and have long lived downstream from me, and I decide to dam up the river and divert the water elsewhere, then I have deprived you of your water and must compensate you, by supplying you with the equivalent, or else desist. But if you live in the middle of a parched desert and it does not rain, so that you are faced with death from thirst, that is not my doing and I have no compensating to do.

This liberty-respecting idea avoids, by and large, the need to make the sort of utility comparisons essential to the utility or welfare view. If we have no general obligation to manufacture as much utility for others as possible, then we don't have to concern ourselves about measuring that utility. Being free to pursue our own projects, we will evaluate our results as best we may, each in our own way. There is no need to keep a constant check on others to see whether we ought to be doing more for them and less for ourselves.

The Ethics of the Hair Shirt

In stark contrast to the liberty-respecting view stands the idea that we are to count the satisfactions of others as equal in value to our own. If I can create a little more pleasure for some stranger by spending my dollar on him than I would create for myself by spending it on an ice cream cone, I then have a putative *obligation* to spend it on him. Thus I am to continually defer to others in the organization of my activities, and shall be assailed by guilt whenever I am not bending my energies to the relief of those allegedly less fortunate than I. Benefit others, at the expense of yourself—and keep doing it until you are as poor and miserable as those whose poverty and misery you are supposed to be relieving! That is the ethics of the hair shirt.

How should we react to this idea? Negatively, in my view—and, I think, in yours. Doesn't that view really make us the slaves of the (supposedly) less well off? Surely a rule of conduct that permits people to be themselves and to try to live the best and most interesting lives they can is better than one which makes us all, in effect, functionaries in a welfare state? The rule that neither the rich nor the poor ought to be enslaved by the others is surely the better rule. Some, of course, think that the poor are, inherently, the "slaves" of the rich, and the rich inherently their masters. Such is the Marxist line, for instance. It's an important argument, but it's important also to realize that it's simply wrong. The wealthy do not have the right to hold a gun to the head of the nonwealthy and tell them what to do. On the contrary, the wealthy, in countries with reasonably free economies, become wealthy by selling things to others, things that those others voluntarily purchase. This makes the purchaser better off as well as the seller; and of course the employees of the latter become better off in the process of making those things, via their wages. The result of this activity is that there are more goods in the world than there would otherwise be.

This is precisely the opposite of the way the thief makes his money. He expends time and energy depriving someone else, involuntarily, of what his victims worked to produce, rather than devoting his own energies to productive activities. He in consequence leaves the world poorer than it was before he set out on his exploitative ways. The Marxist assimilates the honest accumulator to the thief. Rather than being, as so many seem to think, a profound contribution to social theory, that is a first-rank conceptual error, a failure to appreciate that wealth comes about precisely because of the prohibition of theft, rather than by its wholesale exercise.

Mutual Aid

But the anti-welfarist idea can be taken too far as well. Should people be disposed to assist each other in time of need? Certainly! But the appropriate rule for this is not that each person is duty-bound to minister to the poor until he himself is a pauper or near-pauper as well. Rather, the appropriate rule is what the characterization, "in time of need" more nearly suggests. There are indeed emergencies in life when a modest effort by someone will do a great deal for someone else. People who aren't ready to help others are people who deserve to be avoided when they themselves turn to others in time of need.

But this all assumes that these occasions are, in the first place, relatively unusual, and in the second, that the help offered is genuinely of modest cost to the provider. If a stranger on the street asks for directions, a trifling expenditure of time and effort saves him great frustration, and perhaps also makes for a pleasant encounter with another human (which that other human should try to make so, by being polite and saying "thanks!" for example). But if as I walk down the street I am accosted on all sides by similar requests, then I shall never get my day's work done if I can't just say, "Sorry, I've got to be going!" or merely ignore the questioners and walk right on. If instead I must minister to each, then soon there will be nothing to give, since its existence depends entirely on the activities of people who produce it. If the stranger asks me to drive him around town all day looking for a long-lost friend, for instance, then that's going too far. Though of course we should be free to help him out even to that extent, if we are so inclined.

What about parting with the means for making your sweet little daughter's birthday party a memorable one, in order to *keep* a dozen strangers *alive* on the other side of the *World*? Is this something you are morally required to do? Indeed not. She may well *matter* to you more than they. This illustrates again the fact that people do *not* "count equally" for most of us. Normal people care more about some people than others, and *build* their very *lives* around those carings. It is both absurd and very arrogant *for* theorists, *talking* airily about the equality of all people, to insist on cramming it down our throats— which is how ordinary people do see it.

It is reasonable, then, to arrive at a general understanding that we shall be ready to help when help is urgent and when giving it is not very onerous to us. But a general understanding that we shall help everyone as if they were our spouses or dearest friends is quite another matter. Only a thinker whose heart has been replaced by a calculating machine could suppose that to be reasonable.

Is There a Duty of Charity?

One of the good things we can do in life is to make an effort to care about people about whom we don't ordinarily care or think. This can benefit not only the intended beneficiaries in distant places, but it can also benefit you, by broadening your perspective. There is a place for the enlargement of human sympathies. But then, these are sympathies, matters of the heart; and for such matters, family, friends, colleagues, and co-workers in things are rightly first on your agenda. Why so? First, just because you are you and not somebody else—not, for example, a godlike "impartial observer." But there is another reason of interest, even if you think there is something right about the utilitarian view. This is what amounts to a consideration of *efficiency*. We know ourselves and our loved ones; we do not, by definition, know strangers. We can choose a gift for people we know and love, but are we wise to try to benefit someone of alien culture and diet? If we do a good thing for someone we know well, we make an investment that will be returned as the years go by; but we have little idea of the pay-off from charity for the unknown. Of course, that can be overcome, once in awhile— you might end up pen pals with a peasant in Guatemala, but it would not be wise to count on it.

The tendency and desire to do good for others is a virtue. And it is a *moral* virtue, for we all have an interest in the general acquisition of this quality. Just as anyone can kill anyone else, so anyone can benefit anyone else; and so long as the cost to oneself of participating in the general scheme of helpfulness is low—namely, decidedly less than the return— then it is worth it. But it is not reasonable to take the matter beyond that. In particular, it is not reasonable to become a busybody, or a fanatic like Dickens' character Mrs. Jellyby, who is so busy with her charitable work for the natives in darkest Africa that her own children run around in rags and become the terror of the neighbourhood. Nor is it reasonable to be so concerned for the welfare of distant persons that you resort to armed robbery in your efforts to help them out ("Stick 'em up! I'm collecting for Oxfam!").

Notes on the Real World

If we are persuaded by the above, then as decent human beings we will be concerned about starvation and inclined to do something to help out if we can. This raises two questions. First, what is the situation? Are there lots of people in danger of imminent demise from lack of food? And second, just what should we do about it if there are?

Regarding the first question, one notes that contemporary philosophers and many others talk as though the answer is obviously and overwhelmingly in the affirmative. They write as though people by the million are starving daily. It is of interest to realize that they are, generally speaking, wrong, and in the special cases where there really is hunger, its causes are such as to strikingly affect our answer to the second question.

It turns out that starvation in the contemporary world is *not at all* due to the world's population having outgrown its resources, as Garrett Hardin and so many others seem to think; nor is the world even remotely a "lifeboat," as implied by the title of a famous article by Onora O'Neill ("Lifeboat Earth"). In fact, it has come to be appreciated that the world can support an indefinite number of people, certainly vastly more than there are now. If people have more children, they can be fed, or at least there is no reason why they couldn't be, so far as the actual availability of resources is concerned; nor does anyone in the affluent part of the world need to give up eating meat in order to enable them to do so. In 1970, harbingers of gloom and doom on these matters were reporting that by the 1990s there would be massive starvation in the world unless we got to work right now, clamping birth-control measures on the recalcitrant natives. Now in 1992 there are perhaps a half-billion more people than there were then, and—surprise!—they're all eating, and eating better at that. All, that is, *except* for those being starved at gunpoint by their governments or warring political factions. Meanwhile, Western nations are piling up food surpluses and wondering what to do to keep their farmers from going broke for lack of demand for their burgeoning products.

In fact, all of the incidence of substantial starvation (as opposed to the occasional flood) has been due to politics, not agriculture. In several African countries, in Nicaragua for awhile, in China until not long ago, the regimes in power, propelled by ideology or a desire for cheap votes, imposed artificially low food prices or artificially inefficient agricultural systems, on their people, and thus provided remarkably effective disincentives to their farmers to grow food. Not surprisingly, they responded by not growing it. The cure is to let the farmers farm in peace, and charge whatever they like for their produce; it is astonishing how rapidly they will then proceed to grow food to meet the demand. But the cure isn't to have Western countries send over boatloads of Western wheat. Even if the local government will *let* people have this bounty (they often don't—corrupt officials have been known to go out and privately resell the grain elsewhere instead of distributing it to their starving subjects), providing it indiscriminately hooks them on Western charity instead of enabling them to regain the self-sufficiency they enjoyed in earlier times, before modern Western benefits like "democracy" enabled incompetent local governments to disrupt the food supply.

We must also mention countries with governments that drive people forcibly off their land, burn their crops, and at a minimum steal it from the peasantry, as in Ethiopia and Somalia (at the time of this writing). Governments in those countries have combined such barbarities with the familiar tendency to prevent Western aid from getting to its intended recipients. Nature has nothing to do with starvation in such cases, and improvements in agriculture are not the cure. Improvements in politics are—but will not soon be coming, we may be sure. This means that the would-be charitable person faces a pretty difficult problem when he turns to the second question: What to do? In cases of natural disaster, as when a huge flood inundates the coast of Bangladesh, there will be short-term problems, and charitable agencies are excellent at responding quickly with needed food and medical supplies. Supporting some of those for dealing with such emergencies is likely a good idea. But in many other cases, there is very little that an outside agency can do. Tinpot Marxist dictators are not exactly paradigm cases of sweet reason at work, and only governments normally have the kind of clout that can open doors, even a crack, to the sort of aid we might like to give their beleaguered peoples.

The American Peace Corps and CUSO are two interesting organizations whose enthusiastic volunteers go to third-world communities to try to help them in various ways. To what extent they succeed is very hard to say, especially because the fundamental question of what constitutes "help" is so hard to answer. Do we help a native tribe in Africa that has maintained its way of life for thousands of years when we get their children learning arithmetic and wearing jeans? Or do we only destroy what they have and replace it with something impossible for them to cope with? (As a sobering case in point, the travel-writer Dervla Murphy, in *Muddling Through in Madagascar*, describes how one community was given an efficient modern pump for its communal water supply, which provided lots of clean water and relieved people of long trips to polluted wells. It stopped some years later, by which time the people who installed it had long since gone, and nobody knew how to repair it. But, interestingly, they didn't seem terribly concerned about it and made no effort whatever to get someone to fix it, but simply went back to the old ways, uncomplainingly and inefficiently. Apparently *they* didn't realize how terribly "essential" was this pump. Do we really know better than they? Why are we so sure that we do?)

Helping people who are very different from us is not an easy matter. Did all those missionaries who descended on the hapless Africans in the past centuries do them a lot of good by teaching them Christianity, or by bringing the infant mortality rate way down so that families accustomed to having a manageable number of children surviving to maturity suddenly found themselves with six or seven mouths to feed instead of two? Or by building a road to enable tourists to drive up to the villages and give the natives all sorts of Western diseases for which their immune systems were totally unprepared? There is surely a real question here for thoughtful people. Our efforts could well create disasters for the people we are trying to help, as well as to impose pointless costs on ourselves.

The sober conclusion from all this is that maybe it's better on all counts to spend that money on the opera after all. We are unlikely to act well when we act in ignorance, and when we deal with people vastly different from ourselves, ignorance is almost certain to afflict our efforts.

Summing Up

The basic question of this chapter is whether the hungry have a positive right to be fed. Of course we have a right to feed them if we wish, and they have a negative right to be fed. But may we forcibly impose a duty on others to feed them? We may not. If the fact that others are starving is not our fault, then we do not need to provide for them as a duty of justice. To think otherwise is to suppose that we are, in effect, slaves to the badly off. And so we can in good conscience spend our money on the opera instead of on the poor. Even so, feeding the hungry and taking care of the miserable is a nice thing to do, and is morally recommended. Charity is a virtue. Moreover, starvation turns out to be almost entirely a function of bad governments, rather than nature's inability to accommodate the burgeoning masses. Our charitable instincts can handle easily the problems that are due to natural disaster. We can feed the starving *and* go to the opera!

Jan Narveson: Feeding the Hungry

1. Narveson mentions that there are two ways to argue that it is unjust to let others starve to death. What are they? How does he respond to each? Do you think his response is successful? Why or why not?
2. Under what conditions does Narveson think we are obligated to give to those in need? When does he think it is virtuous to give to those in need? How do facts about the real world affect our obligations and virtues? Do you find his view plausible? Why or why not?

3. Explain Narveson's distinction between justice and charity. When is starvation a matter of justice and when is it a matter of charity? Apply this distinction to another moral issue. Do you think the distinction yields plausible results regarding your issue? Why or why not?

4. Explain what Narveson calls "the ethics of the hair shirt." Why does he think this view is mistaken? Explain one way the hair shirt ethicist might respond. Do you think the response is successful? Why or why not?

5. Explain the "liberty proponent" response to the distinction between starving and allowing to starve. According to the liberty proponent, to what extent is morality up to each individual? Do you find this problematic? Why or why not?

22

===== ❦ =====

The Morality of Euthanasia
James Rachels

....

James Rachels (1941–2003) argues that active euthanasia is sometimes
morally permissible. Active euthanasia occurs when someone (typically
a medical professional) takes action to deliberately end a patient's life,
at the patient's request, for the patient's own good. Rachels argues that
considerations of mercy play a vital role in justifying active euthanasia in
many cases.

He first considers a utilitarian argument on behalf of active euthanasia, but finds problems with utilitarianism that are weighty enough
to undermine this argument. However, Rachels believes that a different
version can succeed. In this one, Rachels claims that any action that
promotes the best interests of all concerned, and that violates no rights,
is morally acceptable. Since, he claims, active euthanasia sometimes
satisfies this description, it is sometimes morally acceptable.

....

The single most powerful argument in support of euthanasia is the
argument from mercy. It is also an exceptionally simple argument,
at least in its main idea, which makes one uncomplicated point.
Terminally ill patients sometimes suffer pain so horrible that it is beyond

From "Euthanasia," in Tom Beauchamp, ed., *Matters of Life and Death*, 2nd ed. (McGraw-Hill, 1986),
pp. 49–52.

the comprehension of those who have not actually experienced it. Their suffering can be so terrible that we do not like even to read about it or think about it; we recoil even from the descriptions of such agony. The argument from mercy says euthanasia is justified because it provides an end to *that*.

The great Irish satirist Jonathan Swift took eight years to die, while, in the words of Joseph Fletcher, "His mind crumbled to pieces." At times the pain in his blinded eyes was so intense he had to be restrained from tearing them out with his own hands. Knives and other potential instruments of suicide had to be kept from him. For the last three years of his life, he could do nothing but sit and drool: and when he finally died it was only after convulsions that lasted thirty-six hours.

Swift died in 1745. Since then, doctors have learned how to eliminate much of the pain that accompanies terminal illness, but the victory has been far from complete. So, here is a more modern example.

Stewart Alsop was a respected journalist who died in 1975 of a rare form of cancer. Before he died, he wrote movingly of his experiences as a terminal patient. Although he had not thought much about euthanasia before, he came to approve of it after rooming briefly with someone he called Jack:

> The third night that I roomed with Jack in our tiny double room in the solid-tumor ward of the cancer clinic of the National Institutes of Health in Bethesda, Md., a terrible thought occurred to me.
>
> Jack had a melanoma in his belly, a malignant solid tumor that the doctors guessed was about the size of a softball. The cancer had started a few months before with a small tumor in his left shoulder, and there had been several operations since. The doctors planned to remove the softball-sized tumor, but they knew Jack would soon die. The cancer had metastasized—it had spread beyond control.
>
> Jack was good-looking, about 28, and brave. He was in constant pain, and his doctor had prescribed an intravenous shot of a synthetic opiate—a pain-killer, or analgesic—every four hours. His wife spent many of the daylight hours with him, and she would sit or lie on his bed and pat him all over, as one pats a child, only more methodically, and this seemed to help control the pain. But at night, when his pretty wife had left (wives cannot stay overnight at the NIH clinic) and darkness fell, the pain would attack without pity.
>
> At the prescribed hour, a nurse would give Jack a shot of the synthetic analgesic, and this would control the pain for perhaps two hours or a bit

more. Then he would begin to moan, or whimper, very low, as though he didn't want to wake me. Then he would begin to howl, like a dog.

When this happened, either he or I would ring for a nurse, and ask for a pain-killer. She would give him some codeine or the like by mouth, but it never did any real good—it affected him no more than half an aspirin might affect a man who had just broken his arm. Always the nurse would explain as encouragingly as she could that there was not long to go before the next intravenous shot—"Only about 50 minutes now." And always poor Jack's whimpers and howls would become more loud and frequent until at last the blessed relief came.

The third night of this routine the terrible thought occurred to me. "If Jack were a dog," I thought, "what would be done with him?" The answer was obvious: the pound, and chloroform. No human being with a spark of pity could let a living thing suffer so, to no good end.

The NIH clinic is, of course, one of the most modern and best-equipped hospitals we have. Jack's suffering was not the result of poor treatment in some backward rural facility; it was the inevitable product of his disease, which medical science was powerless to prevent.

I have quoted Alsop at length not for the sake of indulging in gory details but to give a clear idea of the kind of suffering we are talking about. We should not gloss over these facts with euphemistic language or squeamishly avert our eyes from them. For only by keeping them firmly and vividly in mind can we appreciate the full force of the argument from mercy: If a person prefers—and even begs for—death as the only alternative to lingering on *in this kind of torment*, only to die anyway after a while, then surely it is not immoral to help this person die sooner. As Alsop put it, "No human being with a spark of pity could let a living thing suffer so, to no good end."

The Utilitarian Version of the Argument

In connection with this argument, the utilitarians deserve special mention. They argued that actions and social policies should be judged right or wrong *exclusively* according to whether they cause happiness or misery; and they argued that when judged by this standard, euthanasia turns out to be morally acceptable. The utilitarian argument may be elaborated as follows:

(1) Any action or social policy is morally right if it serves to increase the amount of happiness in the world or to decrease the amount of misery. Conversely, an action or social policy is morally wrong if it serves to decrease happiness or to increase misery.

(2) The policy of killing, at their own request, hopelessly ill patients who are suffering great pain would decrease the amount of misery in the world. (An example could be Alsop's friend Jack.)

(3) Therefore, such a policy would be morally right.

The first premise of this argument, (1), states the Principle of Utility, which is the basic utilitarian assumption. Today most philosophers think that this principle is wrong, because they think that the promotion of happiness and the avoidance of misery are not the *only* morally important things. Happiness, they say, is only one among many values that should be promoted: freedom, justice, and a respect for people's rights are also important. To take one example: people *might* be happier if there were no freedom of religion, for if everyone adhered to the same religious beliefs, there would be greater harmony among people. There would be no unhappiness caused within families by Jewish girls marrying Catholic boys, and so forth. Moreover, if people were brainwashed well enough, no one would mind not having freedom of choice. Thus happiness would be increased. But, the argument continues, even if happiness *could* be increased this way, it would not be right to deny people freedom of religion, because people have a right to make their own choices. Therefore, the first premise of the utilitarian argument is unacceptable.

There is a related difficulty for utilitarianism, which connects more directly with the topic of euthanasia. Suppose a person is leading a miserable life—full of more unhappiness than happiness—but does *not* want to die. This person thinks that a miserable life is better than none at all. Now I assume that we would all agree that the person should not be killed; that would be plain, unjustifiable murder. Yet it *would* decrease the amount of misery in the world if we killed this person—it would lead to an increase in the balance of happiness over unhappiness—and so it is hard to see how, on strictly utilitarian grounds, it could be wrong. Again, the Principle of Utility seems to be an inadequate guide for determining right and wrong. So we are on shaky ground if we rely on *this* version of the argument from mercy for a defense of euthanasia.

Doing What Is in Everyone's Best Interests

Although the foregoing utilitarian argument is faulty, it is nevertheless based on a sound idea. For even if the promotion of happiness and avoidance of misery are not the *only* morally important things, they are still very important. So, when an action or a social policy would decrease misery, that is *a* very strong reason in its favor. In the cases of voluntary euthanasia we are now considering, great suffering is eliminated, and since the patient requests it, there is no question of violating individual rights. That is why, regardless of the difficulties of the Principle of Utility, the utilitarian version of the argument still retains considerable force.

I want now to present a somewhat different version of the argument from mercy, which is inspired by utilitarianism but which avoids the difficulties of the foregoing version by not making the Principle of Utility a premise of the argument. I believe that the following argument is sound and proves that active euthanasia *can* be justified:

1. If an action promotes the best interests of *everyone* concerned and violates *no one's* rights, then that action is morally acceptable.
2. In at least some cases, active euthanasia promotes the best interests of everyone concerned and violates no one's rights.
3. Therefore, in at least some cases, active euthanasia is morally acceptable.

It would have been in everyone's best interests if active euthanasia had been employed in the case of Stewart Alsop's friend Jack. First, and most important, it would have been in Jack's own interests, since it would have provided him with an easier, better death, without pain. (Who among us would choose Jack's death, if we had a choice, rather than a quick painless death?) Second, it would have been in the best interests of Jack's wife. Her misery, helplessly watching him suffer, must have been almost unbearable. Third, the hospital staff's best interests would have been served, since if Jack's dying had not been prolonged, they could have turned their attention to other patients whom they could have helped. Fourth, other patients would have benefited, since medical resources would no longer have been used in the sad, pointless maintenance of Jack's physical existence. Finally, if Jack himself requested to be killed, the act would not have violated his rights. Considering all this, how can active euthanasia in this case be wrong? How can it be wrong to do an action that is merciful, that benefits everyone concerned, and that violates no one's rights?

James Rachels: The Morality of Euthanasia

1. Would someone in circumstances like Jack's be better off dead? That is, would dying quickly and painlessly be in his best interest?
2. What are Rachels's objections to the principle of utility? Do you find them convincing?

3. How does Rachels's second argument differ from the utilitarian argument? Do you agree with Rachels that it is a stronger argument?
4. Rachels claims that euthanasia cannot be said to violate anyone's rights, given that the patient requests it. Do you find this claim plausible? Is it possible to do something that violates someone's rights even if he or she consents to it?
5. Rachels claims that (in some cases) active euthanasia promotes the interests of everyone concerned. If our society were to allow active euthanasia, would this be harmful to anyone's interests? Why or why not?

====== ❧ ======

23

The Survival Lottery

John Harris

....

In this paper, John Harris invites us to consider the merits of a special sort of organ transplant scheme, which he calls the survival lottery. Each year, many thousands of people die because of organ failure and the lack of a suitable donor organ. Harris proposes that we remedy this situation by instituting a lottery among (almost) all citizens. Whenever two or more people are in need of a vital organ, we pick a citizen at random to be vivisected (dissected while alive—though presumably under anesthesia!), so that his or her organs can be distributed to those who need them to survive.

We don't do this with any sort of punitive intent, but rather in order to minimize the number of people who die, through no fault of their own, because of organ failure. True, the organ donor being killed is wholly innocent. But then so are those who are dying for lack of a donor organ.

Harris is well aware that the lottery sounds like outright murder, and he devotes the bulk of the article to presenting, and then countering, a great many objections to it. He acknowledges that there may be problems with making such a system feasible in practice. If these problems could be ironed out, however, Harris thinks that rational and morally enlightened people would endorse this proposal for their own society.

....

John Harris, "The Survival Lottery" from *Philosophy* 50 (1975), pp. 81–87. Reprinted with the permission of Cambridge University Press.

L et us suppose that organ transplant procedures have been perfected; in such circumstances if two dying patients could be saved by organ transplants then, if surgeons have the requisite organs in stock and no other needy patients, but nevertheless allow their patients to die, we would be inclined to say, and be justified in saying, that the patients died because the doctors refused to save them. But if there are no spare organs in stock and none otherwise available, the doctors have no choice, they cannot save their patients and so must let them die. In this case we would be disinclined to say that the doctors are in any sense the cause of their patients' deaths. But let us further suppose that the two dying patients, Y and Z, are not happy about being left to die. They might argue that it is not strictly true that there are no organs which could be used to save them. Y needs a new heart and Z new lungs. They point out that if just one healthy person were to be killed his organs could be removed and both of them be saved. We and the doctors would probably be alike in thinking that such a step, while technically possible, would be out of the question. We would not say that the doctors were killing their patients if they refused to prey upon the healthy to save the sick. And because this sort of surgical Robin Hoodery is out of the question we can tell Y and Z that they cannot be saved, and that when they die they will have died of natural causes and not of the neglect of their doctors. Y and Z do not however agree, they insist that if the doctors fail to kill a healthy man and use his organs to save them, then the doctors will be responsible for their deaths.

Many philosophers have for various reasons believed that we must not kill even if by doing so we could save life. They believe that there is a moral difference between killing and letting die. On this view, to kill A so that Y and Z might live is ruled out because we have a strict obligation not to kill but a duty of some lesser kind to save life. A. H. Clough's dictum "Thou shalt not kill but need'st not strive officiously to keep alive" expresses bluntly this point of view. The dying Y and Z may be excused for not being much impressed by Clough's dictum. They agree that it is wrong to kill the innocent and are prepared to agree to an absolute prohibition against so doing. They do not agree, however, that A is more innocent than they are. Y and Z might go on to point out that the currently acknowledged right of the innocent not to be killed, even where their deaths might give life to others, is just a decision to prefer the lives of the fortunate to those of the unfortunate. A is innocent in the sense that he has done nothing to deserve death, but Y and Z are also innocent in this sense. Why should they be the ones to die simply because they are so unlucky as to have diseased organs?

Why, they might argue, should their living or dying be left to chance when in so many other areas of human life we believe that we have an obligation to ensure the survival of the maximum number of lives possible?

Y and Z argue that if a doctor refuses to treat a patient, with the result that the patient dies, he has killed that patient as sure as shooting, and that, in exactly the same way, if the doctors refuse Y and Z the transplants that they need, then their refusal will kill Y and Z, again as sure as shooting. The doctors, and indeed the society which supports their inaction, cannot defend themselves by arguing that they are neither expected, nor required by law or convention, to kill so that lives may be saved (indeed, quite the reverse) since this is just an appeal to custom or authority. A man who does his own moral thinking must decide whether, in these circumstances, he ought to save two lives at the cost of one, or one life at the cost of two. The fact that so called "third parties" have never before been brought into such calculations, have never before been thought of as being involved, is not an argument against their now becoming so. There are of course, good arguments against allowing doctors simply to haul passers-by off the streets whenever they have a couple of patients in need of new organs. And the harmful side-effects of such a practice in terms of terror and distress to the victims, the witnesses and society generally, would give us further reasons for dismissing the idea. Y and Z realize this and have a proposal, which they will shortly produce, which would largely meet objections to placing such power in the hands of doctors and eliminate at least some of the harmful side-effects.

In the unlikely event of their feeling obliged to reply to the reproaches of Y and Z, the doctors might offer the following argument: they might maintain that a man is only responsible for the death of someone whose life he might have saved, if, in all the circumstances of the case, he ought to have saved the man by the means available. This is why a doctor might be a murderer if he simply refused or neglected to treat a patient who would die without treatment, but not if he could only save the patient by doing something he ought in no circumstances to do—kill the innocent. Y and Z readily agree that a man ought not to do what he ought not to do, but they point out that if the doctors, and for that matter society at large, ought on balance to kill one man if two can thereby be saved, then failure to do so will involve responsibility for the consequent deaths. The fact that Y's and Z's proposal involves killing the innocent cannot be a reason for refusing to consider their proposal, for this would just be a refusal to face the question at issue and so avoid having to make a decision as to what ought to be done in circumstances like these. It is Y's and Z's claim that failure to adopt their plan will also involve killing the innocent, rather more of the innocent than the proposed alternative.

To back up this last point, to remove the arbitrariness of permitting doctors to select their donors from among the chance passers-by outside hospitals, and the tremendous power this would place in doctors' hands, to mitigate worries about side-effects and lastly to appease those who wonder why poor old A should be singled out for sacrifice, Y and Z put forward the following scheme: they propose that everyone be given a sort of lottery number. Whenever doctors have two or more dying patients who could be saved by transplants, and no suitable organs have come to hand through "natural" deaths, they can ask a central computer to supply a suitable donor. The computer will then pick the number of a suitable donor at random and he will be killed so that the lives of two or more others may be saved. No doubt if the scheme were ever to be implemented a suitable euphemism for "killed" would be employed. Perhaps we would begin to talk about citizens being called upon to "give life" to others. With the refinement of transplant procedures such a scheme could offer the chance of saving large numbers of lives that are now lost. Indeed, even taking into account the loss of the lives of donors, the numbers of untimely deaths each year might be dramatically reduced, so much so that everyone's chance of living to a ripe old age might be increased. If this were to be the consequence of the adoption of such a scheme, and it might well be, it could not be dismissed lightly. It might of course be objected that it is likely that more old people will need transplants to prolong their lives than will the young, and so the scheme would inevitably lead to a society dominated by the old. But if such a society is thought objectionable, there is no reason to suppose that a program could not be designed for the computer that would ensure the maintenance of whatever is considered to be an optimum age distribution throughout the population.

Suppose that inter-planetary travel revealed a world of people like ourselves, but who organized their society according to this scheme. No one was considered to have an absolute right to life or freedom from interference, but everything was always done to ensure that as many people as possible would enjoy long and happy lives. In such a world a man who attempted to escape when his number was up or who resisted on the grounds that no one had a right to take his life, might well be regarded as a murderer. We might or might not prefer to live in such a world, but the morality of its inhabitants would surely be one that we could respect. It would not be obviously more barbaric or cruel or immoral than our own.

Y and Z are willing to concede one exception to the universal application of their scheme. They realize that it would be unfair to allow people who have brought their misfortune on themselves to benefit from the lottery. There would clearly be something unjust about killing the abstemious B so that W (whose heavy smoking has given him lung cancer) and X (whose drinking has destroyed his liver) should be preserved to overindulge again.

What objections could be made to the lottery scheme? A first straw to clutch at would be the desire for security. Under such a scheme we would never know when we would hear *them* knocking at the door. Every post might bring a sentence of death, every sound in the night might be the sound of boots on the stairs. But, as we have seen, the chances of actually being called upon to make the ultimate sacrifice might be slimmer than is the present risk of being killed on the roads, and most of us do not lie trembling a-bed, appalled at the prospect of being dispatched on the morrow. The truth is that lives might well be more secure under such a scheme.

If we respect individuality and see every human being as unique in his own way, we might want to reject a society in which it appeared that individuals were seen merely as interchangeable units in a structure, the value of which lies in its having as many healthy units as possible. But of course Y and Z would want to know why A's individuality was more worthy of respect than theirs.

Another plausible objection is the natural reluctance to play God with men's lives, the feeling that it is wrong to make any attempt to re-allot the life opportunities that fate has determined, that the deaths of Y and Z would be "natural," whereas the death of anyone killed to save them would have been perpetrated by men. But if we are able to change things, then to elect not to do so is also to determine what will happen in the world.

Neither does the alleged moral differences between killing and letting die afford a respectable way of rejecting the claims of Y and Z. For if we really want to counter proponents of the lottery, if we really want to answer Y and Z and not just put them off, we cannot do so by saying that the lottery involves killing and object to it for that reason, because to do so would, as we have seen, just beg the question as to whether the failure to save as many people as possible might not also amount to killing.

To opt for the society which Y and Z propose would be then to adopt a society in which saintliness would be mandatory. Each of us would have to recognize a binding obligation to give up his own life for others when called upon to do so. In such a society anyone who reneged upon this duty would be a murderer. The most promising objection to such a society, and indeed to any principle which required us to kill A in order to save Y and Z, is, I suspect, that we are committed to the right of self-defence. If I can kill A to save Y and Z then he can kill me to save P and Q, and it is only if I am prepared to agree to this that I will opt for the lottery or be prepared to agree to a man's being killed if doing so would save the lives of more than one other man. Of course there is something paradoxical about basing objections to the lottery scheme on the right of self-defence since, *ex hypothesi*, each person would have a better chance of living to a ripe old age if the lottery scheme were to be implemented. None the less, the feeling that no man should be required to lay down his life for others makes many people shy away from such a scheme, even though it might be rational to accept it on prudential grounds, and perhaps even mandatory on utilitarian grounds. Again, Y and Z would reply that the right of self-defence must extend to them as much as to anyone else; and while it is true that they can only live if another man is killed, they would claim that it is also true that if they are left to die, then someone who lives on does so over their dead bodies.

It might be argued that the institution of the survival lottery has not gone far to mitigate the harmful side-effects in terms of terror and distress to victims, witnesses and society generally, that would be occasioned by doctors simply snatching passers-by off the streets and disorganizing them for the benefit of the unfortunate. Donors would after all still have to be procured, and this process, however it was carried out, would still be likely to prove distressing to all concerned. The lottery scheme would eliminate the arbitrariness of leaving the life and death decisions to the doctors, and remove the possibility of such terrible power falling into the hands of any individuals, but the terror and distress would remain. The effect of having to apprehend presumably unwilling victims would give us pause. Perhaps only a long period of education or propaganda could remove our abhorrence. What this abhorrence reveals about the rights and wrongs of the situation is however more difficult to assess. We might be inclined to say that only monsters could ignore the promptings of conscience so far as to operate the lottery scheme. But the promptings of conscience are not necessarily the most reliable guide. In the present case Y and Z would argue that such promptings are mere squeamishness, an over-nice self-indulgence that costs lives. Death, Y and Z would remind us, is a distressing experience whenever and to whomever it occurs, so the less it occurs the better. Fewer victims and witnesses will be distressed as part of the side-effects of

the lottery scheme than would suffer as part of the side-effects of not instituting it.

Lastly, a more limited objection might be made, not to the idea of killing to save lives, but to the involvement of "third parties." Why, so the
objection goes, should we not give X's heart to Y or Y's lungs to X, the same
number of lives being thereby preserved and no one else's life set at risk?
Y's and Z's reply to this objection differs from their previous line of argument. To amend their plan so that the involvement of so called "third parties"
is ruled out would, Y and Z claim, violate their right to equal concern and
respect with the rest of society. They argue that such a proposal would
amount to treating the unfortunate who need new organs as a class within
society whose lives are considered to be of less value than those of its more
fortunate members. What possible justification could there be for singling
out one group of people whom we would be justified in using as donors
but not another? The idea in the mind of those who would propose such a
step must be something like the following: since Y and Z cannot survive,
since they are going to die in any event, there is no harm in putting their
names into the lottery, for the chances of their dying cannot thereby be
increased and will in fact almost certainly be reduced. But this is just to
ignore everything that Y and Z have been saying. For if their lottery
scheme is adopted they are not going to die anyway—their chances of
dying are no greater and no less than those of any other participant in the
lottery whose number may come up. This ground for confining selection
of donors to the unfortunate therefore disappears. Any other ground must
discriminate against Y and Z as members of a class whose lives are less
worthy of respect than those of the rest of society.

It might more plausibly be argued that the dying who cannot themselves be saved by transplants, or by any other means at all, should be the
priority selection group for the computer programme. But how far off must
death be for a man to be classified as "dying"? Those so classified might
argue that their last few days or weeks of life are as valuable to them (if not
more valuable) than the possibly longer span remaining to others. The
problem of narrowing down the class of possible donors without discriminating unfairly against some sub-class of society is, I suspect, insoluble.

Such is the case for the survival lottery. Utilitarians ought to be in
favour of it, and absolutists cannot object to it on the ground that it involves
killing the innocent, for it is Y's and Z's case that any alternative must also
involve killing the innocent. If the absolutist wishes to maintain his objection he must point to some morally relevant difference between positive

and negative killing. This challenge opens the door to a large topic with a whole library of literature, but Y and Z are dying and do not have time to explore it exhaustively. In their own case the most likely candidate for some feature which might make this moral difference is the malevolent intent of Y and Z themselves. An absolutist might well argue that while no one intends the deaths of Y and Z, no one necessarily wishes them dead, or aims at their demise for any reason, they do mean to kill A (or have him killed). But Y and Z can reply that the death of A is no part of their plan, they merely wish to use a couple of his organs, and if he cannot live without them . . . *tant pis!* None would be more delighted than Y and Z if artificial organs would do as well, and so render the lottery scheme otiose.

One form of absolutist argument perhaps remains. This involves taking an Orwellian stand on some principle of common decency. The argument would then be that even to enter into the sort of "macabre" calculations that Y and Z propose displays a blunted sensibility, a corrupted and vitiated mind. Forms of this argument have recently been advanced by Noam Chomsky (*American Power and the New Mandarins*) and Stuart Hampshire (*Morality and Pessimism*). The indefatigable Y and Z would of course deny that their calculations are in any sense "macabre," and would present them as the most humane course available in the circumstances. Moreover they would claim that the Orwellian stand on decency is the product of a closed mind, and not susceptible to rational argument. Any reasoned defence of such a principle must appeal to notions like respect for human life, as Hampshire's argument in fact does, and these Y and Z could make conformable to their own position.

Can Y and Z be answered? Perhaps only by relying on moral intuition, on the insistence that we do feel there is something wrong with the survival lottery and our confidence that this feeling is prompted by some morally relevant difference between our bringing about the death of A and our bringing about the deaths of Y and Z. Whether we could retain this confidence in our intuitions if we were to be confronted by a society in which the survival lottery operated, was accepted by all, and was seen to save many lives that would otherwise have been lost, it would be interesting to know.

There would of course be great practical difficulties in the way of implementing the lottery. In so many cases it would be agonizingly difficult to decide whether or not a person had brought his misfortune on himself. There are numerous ways in which a person may contribute to his predicament, and the task of deciding how far, or how decisively, a person is himself responsible for his fate would be formidable. And in those cases where we can be confident that a person is innocent of responsibility for his predicament, can we acquire this confidence in time to save him? The lottery scheme would be a powerful weapon in the hands of someone willing and able to misuse it. Could we ever feel certain the lottery was safe from unscrupulous computer programmers? Perhaps we should be thankful that such practical difficulties make the survival lottery an unlikely consequence of the perfection of transplants. Or perhaps we should be appalled.

It may be that we would want to tell Y and Z that the difficulties and dangers of their scheme would be too great a price to pay for its benefits. It is as well to be clear, however, that there is also a high, perhaps an even higher, price to be paid for the rejection of the scheme. That price is the lives of Y and Z and many like them, and we delude ourselves if we suppose that the reason why we reject their plan is that we accept the sixth commandment.

John Harris: The Survival Lottery

1. What exactly is a survival lottery, and how would it work? Do you think it would be morally permissible to institute one?
2. Some people might object to Harris's proposal by claiming that it is never morally permissible to kill innocent people. Why doesn't Harris think this is a good objection? Do you find his criticisms of this objection convincing?
3. Another objection to the survival lottery claims that any such policy would cause widespread terror, since anyone could be selected to have his or her organs harvested. Is this a good objection? How does Harris respond?
4. Harris allows one exception to the universal application of the survival lottery. What is the exception? Do you agree that these individuals should be excluded from the lottery?
5. Some might think that instituting a survival lottery amounts to "playing God." What does it mean to "play God?" Is it always wrong to do so?
6. What "practical difficulties" does Harris think we would face if we tried to institute a survival lottery? Could these difficulties be overcome?

24

Terrorism: A Critique of Excuses
Michael Walzer

Terrorists target innocent people to further their own political agenda.
Michael Walzer thinks that terrorism can never be justified: it can
never be shown to be, in the end, the morally right thing to do. But can
terrorism ever be excused? Can terrorists, while doing something very
wrong, nonetheless be freed of any moral blame for their actions?

Walzer defends a negative answer to this question by considering
the four most prominent excuses for terrorism. These excuses include
the claim (1) that terrorism is a last resort, chosen when all else fails;
(2) that nothing but terrorism is possible for weak insurgency movements; (3) that terrorism works, and whatever works for a good cause
is itself morally acceptable; and (4) that all politics involves terrorism,
and all political groups practice it. Walzer argues that each of these
excuses fails.

How should we combat terrorism? While Walzer does not offer
anything like a simple solution to this question, he identifies some
constraints that must be met. We must avoid repeating the wrongs of
terrorists when we fight against them. We must not target people
indiscriminately. If we must engage in repression and retaliation, it
must be directed at the terrorists themselves, and never at the people
in whose name the terrorists are acting.

Terrorism is often a response to oppression. While Walzer rejects
the idea that this ever justifies or excuses terrorism, he insists that the

Michael Walzer, "Terrorism: A Critique of Excuses" *from Problems of International Justice*, S. Luper-
Foy, ed. (Westview Press, 1988), pp. 237–247. Reprinted with the permission of Michael Walzer.

oppression should be reduced or (ideally) eliminated. Not all terrorism stems from oppression. And when terror is a response to oppression, it can be very tempting to do nothing about the oppression, or even to increase one's iron grip. But Walzer rejects such responses. Justice requires that we relieve oppression, even when one's enemies are using it to justify terroristic attacks.

....

No one these days advocates terrorism, not even those who regularly practice it. The practice is indefensible now that it has been recognized, like rape and murder, as an attack upon the innocent. In a sense, indeed, terrorism is worse than rape and murder commonly are, for in the latter cases the victim has been chosen for a purpose; he or she is the direct object of attack, and the attack has some reason, however twisted or ugly it may be. The victims of a terrorist attack are third parties, innocent bystanders; there is no special reason for attacking them; anyone else within a large class of (unrelated) people will do as well. The attack is directed indiscriminately against the entire class. Terrorists are like killers on a rampage, except that their rampage is not just expressive of rage or madness; the rage is purposeful and programmatic. It aims at a general vulnerability: Kill these people in order to terrify those. A relatively small number of dead victims makes for a very large number of living and frightened hostages.

This, then, is the peculiar evil of terrorism—not only the killing of innocent people but also the intrusion of fear into everyday life, the violation of private purposes, the insecurity of public spaces, the endless coerciveness of precaution. A crime wave might, I suppose, produce similar effects, but no one plans a crime wave; it is the work of a thousand individual decision-makers, each one independent of the others, brought together only by the invisible hand. Terrorism is the work of visible hands; it is an organizational project, a strategic choice, a conspiracy to murder and intimidate . . . you and me. No wonder the conspirators have difficulty defending, in public, the strategy they have chosen.

The moral difficulty is the same, obviously, when the conspiracy is directed not against you and me but against *them*—Protestants, say, not Catholics; Israelis, not Italians or Germans; blacks, not whites. These "limits" rarely hold for long; the logic of terrorism steadily expands the range of vulnerability. The more hostages they hold, the stronger the terrorists are. No one is safe once whole populations have been put at risk. Even if the risk were contained, however, the evil would be no different. So far as individual Protestants or Israelis or blacks are concerned, terrorism is random, degrading, and frightening. That is its hallmark, and that, again, is why it cannot be defended.

But when moral justification is ruled out, the way is opened for ideological excuse and apology. We live today in a political culture of excuses. This is far better than a political culture in which terrorism is openly defended and justified, for the excuse at least acknowledges the evil. But the improvement is precarious, hard won, and difficult to sustain. It is not the case, even in this better world, that terrorist organizations are without supporters. The support is indirect but by no means ineffective. It takes the form of apologetic descriptions and explanations, a litany of excuses that steadily undercuts our knowledge of the evil. Today that knowledge is insufficient unless it is supplemented and reinforced by a systematic critique of excuses. That is my purpose here. I take the principle for granted: that every act of terrorism is a wrongful act. The wrongfulness of the excuses, however, cannot be taken for granted; it has to be argued. The excuses themselves are familiar enough, the stuff of contemporary political debate. I shall state them in stereotypical form. There is no need to attribute them to this or that writer, publicist, or commentator; my readers can make their own attributions.

The most common excuse for terrorism is that it is a last resort, chosen only when all else fails. The image is of people who have literally run out of options. One by one, they have tried every legitimate form of political and military action, exhausted every possibility, failed everywhere, until no alternative remains but the evil of terrorism. They must be terrorists or do nothing at all. The easy response is to insist that, given this description of their case, they should do nothing at all; they have indeed exhausted their possibilities. But this response simply reaffirms the principle, ignores the excuse; this response does not attend to the terrorists' desperation. Whatever the cause to which they are committed, we have to recognize that, given the commitment, the one thing they cannot do is "nothing at all."

But the case is badly described. It is not so easy to reach the "last resort." To get there, one must indeed try everything (which is a lot of things) and not just once, as if a political party might organize a single demonstration, fail to win immediate victory, and claim that it was now justified in moving on to murder. Politics is an art of repetition. Activists and citizens learn from experience, that is, by doing the same thing over and over again. It is by no means clear when they run out of options, but even under conditions of oppression and war, citizens have a good run short of that. The same argument applies to state officials who claim that they have tried "everything" and are now compelled to kill hostages or bomb peasant villages. Imagine such people called before a judicial tribunal and required to answer the question, What exactly did you try? Does anyone believe that they could come up with a plausible list? "Last resort" has only a notional finality; the resort to terror is ideologically last, not last in an actual series of actions, just last for the sake of the excuse. In fact, most state officials and movement militants who recommend a policy of terrorism recommend it as a first resort; they are for it from the beginning, although they may not get their way at the beginning. If they are honest, then, they must make other excuses and give up the pretense of the last resort.

[Would terrorism be justified in a "supreme emergency" as that condition is described in "Emergency Ethics" (chapter 3)*? It might be, but only if the oppression to which the terrorists claimed to be responding was genocidal in character. Against the imminent threat of political and physical extinction, extreme measures can be defended, assuming that they have some chance of success. But this kind of a threat has not been present in any of the recent cases of terrorist activity. Terrorism has not been a means of avoiding disaster but of reaching for political success.]

The second excuse is designed for national liberation movements struggling against established and powerful states. Now the claim is that nothing else is possible, that no other strategy is available except terrorism. This is different from the first excuse because it does not require would-be terrorists to run through all the available options. Or, the second excuse requires terrorists to run through all the options in their heads, not in the world; notional finality is enough. Movement strategists consider their options and conclude that they have no alternative to terrorism. They think that they do not have the political strength to try anything else, and thus they do not try anything else. Weakness is their excuse.

But two very different kinds of weakness are commonly confused here: the weakness of the movement vis-à-vis the opposing state and the movement's weakness vis-à-vis its own people. This second kind of weakness, the inability of the movement to mobilize the nation, makes

---

* In an earlier chapter, omitted here, Walzer defines a supreme emergency as a situation in which a group is faced with a serious risk of annihilation from a dedicated enemy.—Ed.

terrorism the "only" option because it effectively rules out all the others: nonviolent resistance, general strikes, mass demonstrations, unconventional warfare, and so on.

These options are only rarely ruled out by the sheer power of the state, by the pervasiveness and intensity of oppression. Totalitarian states may be immune to nonviolent or guerrilla resistance, but all the evidence suggests that they are also immune to terrorism. Or, more exactly, in totalitarian states state terror dominates every other sort. Where terrorism is a possible strategy for the oppositional movement (in liberal and democratic states, most obviously), other strategies are also possible if the movement has some significant degree of popular support. In the absence of popular support, terrorism may indeed be the one available strategy, but it is hard to see how its evils can then be excused. For it is not weakness alone that makes the excuse, but the claim of the terrorists to represent the weak; and the particular form of weakness that makes terrorism the only option calls that claim into question.

One might avoid this difficulty with a stronger insistence on the actual effectiveness of terrorism. The third excuse is simply that terrorism works (and nothing else does); it achieves the ends of the oppressed even without their participation. "When the act accuses, the result excuses." This is a consequentialist argument, and given a strict understanding of consequentialism, this argument amounts to a justification rather than an excuse. In practice, however, the argument is rarely pushed so far. More often, the argument begins with an acknowledgment of the terrorists' wrongdoing. Their hands are dirty, but we must make a kind of peace with them because they have acted effectively for the sake of people who could not act for themselves. But, in fact, have the terrorists' actions been effective? I doubt that terrorism has ever achieved national liberation—no nation that I know of owes its freedom to a campaign of random murder— although terrorism undoubtedly increases the power of the terrorists within the national liberation movement. Perhaps terrorism is also conducive to the survival and notoriety (the two go together) of the movement, which is now dominated by terrorists. But even if we were to grant some means-end relationship between terror and national liberation, the third excuse does not work unless it can meet the further requirements of a consequentialist argument. It must be possible to say that the desired end could not have been achieved through any other, less wrongful, means. The third excuse depends, then, on the success of the first or second, and neither of these look likely to be successful.

The fourth excuse avoids this crippling dependency. This excuse does not require the apologist to defend either of the improbable claims that terrorism is the last resort or that it is the only possible resort. The fourth excuse is simply that terrorism is the universal resort. All politics is (really) terrorism. The appearance of innocence and decency is always a piece of deception, more or less convincing in accordance with the relative power of the deceivers. The terrorist who does not bother with appearances is only doing openly what everyone else does secretly.

This argument has the same form as the maxim "All's fair in love and war." Love is always fraudulent, war is always brutal, and political action is always terrorist in character. Political action works (as Thomas Hobbes long ago argued) only by generating fear in innocent men and women. Terrorism is the politics of state officials and movement militants alike. This argument does not justify either the officials or the militants, but it does excuse them all. We hardly can be harsh with people who act the way everyone else acts. Only saints are likely to act differently, and sainthood in politics is supererogatory, a matter of grace, not obligation.

But this fourth excuse relies too heavily on our cynicism about political life, and cynicism only sometimes answers well to experience. In fact, legitimate states do not need to terrorize their citizens, and strongly based movements do not need to terrorize their opponents. Officials and militants who live, as it were, on the margins of legitimacy and strength sometimes choose terrorism and sometimes do not. Living in terror is not a universal experience. The world the terrorists create has its entrances and exits.

If we want to understand the choice of terror, the choice that forces the rest of us through the door, we have to imagine what in fact always occurs, although we often have no satisfactory record of the occurrence: A group of men and women, officials or militants, sits around a table and argues about whether or not to adopt a terrorist strategy. Later on, the litany of excuses obscures the argument. But at the time, around the table, it would have been no use for defenders of terrorism to say, "Everybody does it," because there they would be face to face with people proposing to do something else. Nor is it historically the case that the members of this last group, the opponents of terrorism, always lose the argument. They can win, however, and still not be able to prevent a terrorist campaign; the would-be terrorists (it does not take very many) can always split the movement and go their own way. Or, they can split the bureaucracy or the police or officer corps and act in the shadow of state power. Indeed, terrorism often has its origin in such splits. The first victims are the terrorists' former comrades or colleagues. What reason can we possibly have, then, for equating the two? If we value the politics of the men and women who oppose terrorism, we must reject the excuses of their murderers. Cynicism at such a time is unfair to the victims.

The fourth excuse can also take, often does take, a more restricted form. Oppression, rather than political rule more generally, is always terroristic in character, and thus, we must always excuse the opponents of oppression. When they choose terrorism, they are only reacting to someone else's previous choice, repaying in kind the treatment they have long received. Of course, their terrorism repeats the evil—innocent people are killed, who were never themselves oppressors—but repetition is not the same as initiation. The oppressors set the terms of the struggle. But if the struggle is fought on the oppressors' terms, then the oppressors are likely to win. Or, at least, oppression is likely to win, even if it takes on a new face. The whole point of a liberation movement or a popular mobilization is to change the terms. We have no reason to excuse the terrorism reactively adopted by opponents of oppression unless we are confident of the sincerity of their opposition, the seriousness of their commitment to a nonoppressive politics. But the choice of terrorism undermines that confidence.

We are often asked to distinguish the terrorism of the oppressed from the terrorism of the oppressors. What is it, however, that makes the difference? The message of the terrorist is the same in both cases: a denial of the peoplehood and humanity of the groups among whom he or she finds victims. Terrorism anticipates, when it does not actually enforce, political domination. Does it matter if one dominated group is replaced by another? Imagine a slave revolt whose protagonists dream only of enslaving in their turn the children of their masters. The dream is understandable, but the fervent desire of the children that the revolt be repressed is equally understandable. In neither case does understanding make for excuse—not, at least, after a politics of universal freedom has become possible. Nor does an understanding of oppression excuse the terrorism of the oppressed, once we have grasped the meaning of "liberation."

These are the four general excuses for terror, and each of them fails. They depend upon statements about the world that are false, historical arguments for which there is no evidence, moral claims that turn out to be hollow or dishonest. This is not to say that there might not be more particular excuses that have greater plausibility, extenuating circumstances in particular cases that we would feel compelled to recognize. As with murder, we can tell a story (like the story that Richard Wright tells in *Native Son*, for example) that might lead us, not to justify terrorism, but to excuse this or that individual terrorist. We can provide a personal history, a psychological study, of compassion destroyed by fear, moral reason by hatred and rage, social inhibition by unending violence—the product, an individual driven to kill or readily set on a killing course by his or her political leaders. But the force of this story will not depend on any of the four general excuses, all of which grant what the storyteller will have to deny: that terrorism is the deliberate choice of rational men and women. Whether they conceive it to be one option among others or the only one available, they nevertheless argue and choose. Whether they are acting or reacting, they have made a decision. The human instruments they subsequently find to plant the bomb or shoot the gun may act under some psychological compulsion, but the men and women who choose terror as a policy act "freely." They could not act in any other way, or accept any other description of their action, and still pretend to be the leaders of the movement or the state. We ought never to excuse such leaders.

What follows from the critique of excuses? There is still a great deal of room for argument about the best way of responding to terrorism. Certainly, terrorists should be resisted, and it is not likely that a purely defensive resistance will ever be sufficient. In this sort of struggle, the offense is always ahead. The technology of terror is simple; the weapons are readily produced and easy to deliver. It is virtually impossible to protect people against random and indiscriminate attack. Thus, resistance will have to be supplemented by some combination of repression and retaliation. This is a dangerous business because repression and retaliation so often take terroristic forms and there are a host of apologists ready with excuses that sound remarkably like those of the terrorists themselves. It should be clear by now, however, that counterterrorism cannot be excused merely because it is reactive. Every new actor, terrorist or counterterrorist, claims to be reacting to someone else, standing in a circle and just passing the evil along. But the circle is ideological in character; in fact, every actor is a moral agent and makes an independent decision.

Therefore, repression and retaliation must not repeat the wrongs of terrorism, which is to say that repression and retaliation must be aimed systematically at the terrorists themselves, never at the people for whom the terrorists claim to be acting. That claim is in any case doubtful, even when it is honestly made. The people do not authorize the terrorists to act in their name. Only a tiny number actually participate in terrorist activities; they are far more likely to suffer than to benefit from the terrorist program. Even if they supported the program and hoped to benefit from it, however, they would still be immune from attack—exactly as civilians in time of war who support the war effort but are not themselves part of it are subject to the same immunity. Civilians may be put at risk by attacks on military targets, as by attacks on terrorist targets, but the risk must be kept to a minimum, even at some cost to the attackers. The refusal to make ordinary people into targets, whatever their nationality or even their politics, is the only way to say no to terrorism. Every act of repression and retaliation has to be measured by this standard.

But what if the "only way" to defeat the terrorists is to intimidate their actual or potential supporters? It is important to deny the premise of this question: that terrorism is a politics dependent on mass support. In fact, it is always the politics of an elite, whose members are dedicated and fanatical and more than ready to endure, or to watch others endure, the devastations of a counterterrorist campaign. Indeed, terrorists will welcome counterterrorism; it makes the terrorists' excuses more plausible and is sure to bring them, however many people are killed or wounded, however many are terrorized, the small number of recruits needed to sustain the terrorist activities.

Repression and retaliation are legitimate responses to terrorism only when they are constrained by the same moral principles that rule out terrorism itself. But there is an alternative response that seeks to avoid the violence that these two entail. The alternative is to address directly, ourselves, the oppression the terrorists claim to oppose. Oppression, they say, is the cause of terrorism. But that is merely one more excuse. The real cause of terrorism is the decision to launch a terrorist campaign, a decision made by that group of people sitting around a table whose deliberations I have already described. However, terrorists do exploit oppression, injustice, and human misery generally and look to these at least for their excuses. There can hardly be any doubt that oppression strengthens their hand. Is that a reason for us to come to the defense of the oppressed? It seems to me that we have our own reasons to do that, and do not need this one, or should not, to prod us into action. We might imitate those movement militants who argue against the adoption of a terrorist strategy—although not, as the terrorists say, because these militants are prepared to tolerate oppression. They already are opposed to oppression and now add to that opposition, perhaps for the same reasons, a refusal of terror. So should we have been opposed before, and we should now make the same addition.

But there is an argument, put with some insistence these days, that we should refuse to acknowledge any link at all between terrorism and oppression—as if any defense of oppressed men and women, once a terrorist campaign has been launched, would concede the effectiveness of the campaign. Or, at least, the defense would give terrorism the appearance of effectiveness and so increase the likelihood of terrorist campaigns in the future. Here we have the reverse side of the litany of excuses; we have turned over the record. First oppression is made into an excuse for terrorism, and then terrorism is made into an excuse for oppression. The first is the excuse of the far left; the second is the excuse of the neoconservative right. I doubt that genuine conservatives would think it a good reason for defending the status quo that it is under terrorist attack; they would have independent reasons and would be prepared to defend the status quo against any attack. Similarly, those of us who think that the status quo urgently requires change have our own reasons for thinking so and need not be intimidated by terrorists or, for that matter, anti-terrorists.

If one criticizes the first excuse, one should not neglect the second. But I need to state the second more precisely. It is not so much an excuse for oppression as an excuse for doing nothing (now) about oppression. The claim is that the campaign against terrorism has priority over every other political activity. If the people who take the lead in this campaign are the old oppressors, then we must make a kind of peace with them—temporarily, of course, until the terrorists have been beaten. This is a strategy that denies the possibility of a two-front war. So long as the men and women who pretend to lead the fight against oppression are terrorists, we can concede nothing to their demands. Nor can we oppose their opponents.

But why not? It is not likely in any case that terrorists would claim victory in the face of a serious effort to deal with the oppression of the people they claim to be defending. The effort would merely expose the hollowness of their claim, and the nearer it came to success, the more they would escalate their terrorism. They would still have to be defeated, for what they are after is not a solution to the problem but rather the power to impose their own solution. No decent end to the conflict in Ireland, say, or in Lebanon, or in the Middle East generally, is going to look like a victory for terrorism—if only because the different groups of terrorists are each committed, by the strategy they have adopted, to an indecent end. By working for our own ends, we expose the indecency.

Michael Walzer: Terrorism: A Critique of Excuses

1. Although many people talk of "terrorism" today, the term is seldom explicitly defined. What exactly is terrorism? Are all terrorist acts committed by individuals and private organizations, or can states also engage in terrorism?

2. What is the difference between "advocating" and "excusing" terrorism? Do you agree with Walzer that no one advocates terrorism today?

3. How does Walzer respond to the excuse that terrorism is a last resort, to be chosen only when all else fails or when no other strategies are possible? Do you find his criticisms of this excuse convincing?

4. Some people claim that while terrorism is distasteful, it is sometimes justified because it can attain desirable results. How does Walzer respond to this argument? Do you agree with his response?

5. Should we ever comply with the demands of terrorists? If so, under what conditions? If not, why not?

6. What constraints does Walzer place on responding to terrorism? Should we accept such constraints? Why or why not?

25

Should the Ticking Bomb Terrorist Be Tortured?

Alan Dershowitz

....

In this chapter of his book on terrorism, Harvard law professor Alan Dershowitz argues that we should institute a highly regulated system of torture to obtain information from convicted terrorists. Dershowitz argues for this view by introducing the example of the ticking bomb terrorist—one who knows the location of a bomb that, if detonated, will kill hundreds or thousands of innocent people. Dershowitz claims that if a terrorist like this has been captured, and if no other method of discovering the bomb's location has been successful, then the terrorist will definitely be tortured to obtain that information. Since that is so, says Dershowitz, we ought to devise a system in which we can undertake such torture in a way that respects democratic values as much as possible.

The relevant values are three: (i) preserving the safety and security of citizenry; (ii) respecting civil liberties and human rights, and (iii) maintaining public accountability. We can't always honor all three of these values, and in hard cases, like that of the ticking bomb terrorist, the best we can do is to sacrifice one of them as little as possible.

What Dershowitz recommends is that we preserve the safety and security of our citizens by allowing torture in certain cases. But we must openly acknowledge that we will do this, thereby maintaining

From Alan M. Dershowitz, *Why Terrorism Works: Understanding the Threat, Responding to the Challenge* (New Haven and London: Yale University Press, 2002). Reprinted by permission.

democratic accountability. We must publicly state the conditions under which we are prepared to torture, and we must institute a variety of safeguards to prevent unwarranted torture. Dershowitz allows that this isn't a perfect solution. But he challenges us to come up with a better one. As he sees things, it is far better to confront such difficult choices in advance, and to develop a realistic policy about them, rather than sweeping such difficulties under the rug and dealing with them without the benefit of clear guidance from the law.

....

How I Began Thinking About Torture

In the late 1980s I traveled to Israel to conduct some research and teach a class at Hebrew University on civil liberties during times of crisis. In the course of my research I learned that the Israeli security services were employing what they euphemistically called "moderate physical pressure" on suspected terrorists to obtain information deemed necessary to prevent future terrorist attacks. . . .

In my classes and public lectures in Israel, I strongly condemned these methods as a violation of core civil liberties and human rights. The response that people gave, across the political spectrum from civil libertarians to law-and-order advocates, was essentially the same: but what about the "ticking bomb" case?

The ticking bomb case refers to a scenario that has been discussed by many philosophers, including Michael Walzer, Jean-Paul Sartre, and Jeremy Bentham. Walzer described such a hypothetical case in an article titled "Political Action: The Problem of Dirty Hands." In this case, a decent leader of a nation plagued with terrorism is asked "to authorize the torture of a captured rebel leader who knows or probably knows the location of a number of bombs hidden in apartment buildings across the city, set to go off within the next twenty-four hours. He orders the man tortured, convinced that he must do so for the sake of the people who might otherwise die in the explosions—even though he believes that torture is wrong, indeed abominable, not just sometimes, but always."[1] . . .

---

1 Michael Walzer, "Political Action: The Problem of Dirty Hands," *Philosophy and Public Affairs*, 1973.

The Case for Torturing the Ticking Bomb Terrorist

The arguments in favor of using torture as a last resort to prevent a ticking bomb from exploding and killing many people are both simple and simpleminded. Bentham constructed a compelling hypothetical case to support his utilitarian argument against an absolute prohibition on torture:

> Suppose an occasion were to arise, in which a suspicion is entertained, as strong as that which would be received as a sufficient ground for arrest and commitment as for felony—a suspicion that at this very time a considerable number of individuals are actually suffering, by illegal violence inflictions equal in intensity to those which if inflicted by the hand of justice, would universally be spoken of under the name of torture. For the purpose of rescuing from torture these hundred innocents, should any scruple be made of applying equal or superior torture, to extract the requisite information from the mouth of one criminal, who having it in his power to make known the place where at this time the enormity was practising or about to be practised, should refuse to do so? To say nothing of wisdom, could any pretence be made so much as to the praise of blind and vulgar humanity, by the man who to save one criminal, should determine to abandon 100 innocent persons to the same fate?[2]

If the torture of one guilty person would be justified to prevent the torture of a hundred innocent persons, it would seem to follow—certainly to Bentham—that it would also be justified to prevent the murder of thousands of innocent civilians in the ticking bomb case. . . .

The strongest argument against any resort to torture, even in the ticking bomb case, also derives from Bentham's utilitarian calculus. Experience has shown that if torture, which has been deemed illegitimate by the civilized world for more than a century, were now to be legitimated—even for limited use in one extraordinary type of situation—such legitimation would constitute an important symbolic setback in the worldwide campaign against human rights abuses. Inevitably, the legitimation of torture by the world's leading democracy would provide a welcome justification for its more widespread use in other parts of the world. Two Bentham

---

2 Quoted in W. L. Twining and P. E. Twining, "Bentham on Torture," *Northern Ireland Legal Quarterly*, Autumn 1973, p. 347. Bentham's hypothetical question does not distinguish between torture inflicted by private persons and by governments.

scholars, W. L. Twining and P. E. Twining, have argued that torture is unacceptable even if it is restricted to an extremely limited category of cases:

> There is at least one good practical reason for drawing a distinction between justifying an isolated act of torture in an extreme emergency of the kind postulated above and justifying the *institutionalisation* of torture as a regular practice. The circumstances are so extreme in which most of us would be prepared to justify resort to torture, if at all, the conditions we would impose would be so stringent, the practical problems of devising and enforcing adequate safeguards so difficult and the risks of abuse so great that it would be unwise and dangerous to entrust any government, however enlightened, with such a power. Even an out-and-out utilitarian can support an absolute prohibition against institutionalised torture on the ground that no government in the world can be trusted not to abuse the power and to satisfy in practice the conditions he would impose.[3]

Bentham's own justification was based on *case* or *act* utilitarianism—a demonstration that in a *particular case,* the benefits that would flow from the limited use of torture would outweigh its costs. The argument against any use of torture would derive from *rule* utilitarianism—which considers the implications of establishing a precedent that would inevitably be extended beyond its limited case utilitarian justification to other possible evils of lesser magnitude. Even terrorism itself could be justified by a case utilitarian approach. Surely one could come up with a singular situation in which the targeting of a small number of civilians could be thought necessary to save thousands of other civilians—blowing up a German kindergarten by the relatives of inmates in a Nazi death camp, for example, and threatening to repeat the targeting of German children unless the death camps were shut down.

The reason this kind of single-case utilitarian justification is simple-minded is that it has no inherent limiting principle. If nonlethal torture of one person is justified to prevent the killing of many important people, then what if it were necessary to use lethal torture—or at least torture that posed a substantial risk of death? What if it were necessary to torture the suspect's mother or children to get him to divulge the information?

---

3 Twining and Twining, "Bentham on Torture," pp. 348–49.

What if it took threatening to kill his family, his friends, his entire village? Under a simple-minded quantitative case utilitarianism, anything goes as long as the number of people tortured or killed does not exceed the number that would be saved. This is morality by numbers, unless there are other constraints on what we can properly do. These other constraints can come from rule utilitarianisms or other principles of morality, such as the prohibition against deliberately punishing the innocent. Unless we are prepared to impose some limits on the use of torture or other barbaric tactics that might be of some use in preventing terrorism, we risk hurtling down a slippery slope into the abyss of amorality and ultimately tyranny. Dostoevsky captured the complexity of this dilemma in *The Brothers Karamazov* when he had Ivan pose the following question to Alyosha: "Imagine that you are creating a fabric of human destiny with the object of making men happy in the end, giving them peace at last, but that it was essential and inevitable to torture to death only one tiny creature—that baby beating its breast with its fist, for instance—and to found that edifice on its unavenged tears, would you consent to be the architect on those conditions? Tell me the truth."

A willingness to kill an innocent child suggests a willingness to do anything to achieve a necessary result. Hence the slippery slope.

It does not necessarily follow from this understandable fear of the slippery slope that we can never consider the use of nonlethal infliction of pain, if its use were to be limited by acceptable principles of morality. After all, imprisoning a witness who refuses to testify after being given immunity is designed to be punitive—that is painful. Such imprisonment can, on occasion, produce more pain and greater risk of death than nonlethal torture. Yet we continue to threaten and use the pain of imprisonment to loosen the tongues of reluctant witnesses.

It is commonplace for police and prosecutors to threaten recalcitrant suspects with prison rape. As one prosecutor put it: "You're going to be the boyfriend of a very bad man." The slippery slope is an argument of caution, not a debate stopper, since virtually every compromise with an absolutist approach to rights carries the risk of slipping further. An appropriate response to the slippery slope is to build in a principled break. For example, if nonlethal torture were legally limited to convicted terrorists who had knowledge of future massive terrorist acts, were given immunity, and still refused to provide the information, there might still be objections to the use of torture, but they would have to go beyond the slippery slope argument.

The case utilitarian argument for torturing a ticking bomb terrorist is bolstered by an argument from analogy—an a fortiori argument. What moral principle could justify the death penalty for past individual murders and at the same time condemn nonlethal torture to prevent future mass murders? Bentham posed this rhetorical question as support for his argument. The death penalty is, of course, reserved for convicted murderers. But again, what if torture was limited to convicted terrorists who refused to divulge information about future terrorism? Consider as well the analogy to the use of deadly force against suspects fleeing from arrest for dangerous felonies of which they have not yet been convicted. Or military retaliations that produce the predictable and inevitable collateral killing of some innocent civilians. The case against torture, if made by a Quaker who opposes the death penalty, war, self-defense, and the use of lethal force against fleeing felons, is understandable. But for anyone who justifies killing on the basis of a cost-benefit analysis, the case against the use of nonlethal torture to save multiple lives is more difficult to make. In the end, absolute opposition to torture—even nonlethal torture in the ticking bomb case—may rest more on historical and aesthetic considerations than on moral or logical ones.

In debating the issue of torture, the first question I am often asked is, "Do you want to take us back to the Middle Ages?" The association between any form of torture and gruesome death is powerful in the minds of most people knowledgeable of the history of its abuses. This understandable association makes it difficult for many people to think about nonlethal torture as a technique for *saving* lives.

The second question I am asked is, "What kind of torture do you have in mind?" When I respond by describing the sterilized needle being shoved under the fingernails, the reaction is visceral and often visible—a shudder coupled with a facial gesture of disgust. Discussions of the death penalty on the other hand can be conducted without these kinds of reactions, especially now that we literally put the condemned prisoner "to sleep" by laying him out on a gurney and injecting a lethal substance into his body. There is no breaking of the neck, burning of the brain, bursting of internal organs, or gasping for breath that used to accompany hanging, electrocution, shooting, and gassing. The executioner has been replaced by a paramedical technician, as the aesthetics of death have become more acceptable. All this tends to cover up the reality that death is forever while nonlethal pain is temporary. In our modern age death is underrated, while pain is overrated. . . .

The Three—or Four—Ways

The modern resort to terrorism has renewed the debate over how a rights-based society should respond to the prospect of using nonlethal torture in the ticking bomb situation. In the late 1980s the Israeli government appointed a commission headed by a retired Supreme Court justice to look into precisely that situation. The commission concluded that there are "three ways for solving this grave dilemma between the vital need to preserve the very existence of the state and its citizens, and maintain its character as a law-abiding state." The first is to allow the security services to continue to fight terrorism in "a twilight zone which is outside the realm of law." The second is "the way of the hypocrites: they declare that they abide by the rule of law, but turn a blind eye to what goes on beneath the surface." And the third, "the truthful road of the rule of law," is that the "law itself must insure a proper framework for the activity" of the security services in seeking to prevent terrorist acts.

There is of course a fourth road: namely to forgo any use of torture and simply allow the preventable terrorist act to occur. After the Supreme Court of Israel outlawed the use of physical pressure, the Israeli security services claimed that, as a result of the Supreme Court's decision, at least one preventable act of terrorism had been allowed to take place, one that killed several people when a bus was bombed. Whether this claim is true, false, or somewhere in between is difficult to assess. But it is clear that if the preventable act of terrorism was of the magnitude of the attacks of September 11, there would be a great outcry in any democracy that had deliberately refused to take available preventive action, even if it required the use of torture. During numerous public appearances since September 11, 2001, I have asked audiences for a show of hands as to how many would support the use of nonlethal torture in a ticking bomb case. Virtually every hand is raised. The few that remain down go up when I ask how many believe that torture would actually be used in such a case.

Law enforcement personnel give similar responses. This can be seen in reports of physical abuse directed against some suspects that have been detained following September 11, reports that have been taken quite seriously by at least one federal judge. It is confirmed by the willingness of U.S. law enforcement officials to facilitate the torture of terrorist suspects by repressive regimes allied with our intelligence agencies. As one former CIA operative with thirty years of experience reported: "A lot of people are saying we need someone at the agency who can pull fingernails out.

Others are saying, 'Let others use interrogation methods that we don't use.' The only question then is, do you want to have CIA people in the room?" The real issue, therefore, is not whether some torture would or would not be used in the ticking bomb case—it would. The question is whether it would be done openly, pursuant to a previously established legal procedure, or whether it would be done secretly, in violation of existing law.

Several important values are pitted against each other in this conflict. The first is the safety and security of a nation's citizens. Under the ticking bomb scenario this value may require the use of torture, if that is the only way to prevent the bomb from exploding and killing large numbers of civilians. The second value is the preservation of civil liberties and human rights. This value requires that we not accept torture as a legitimate part of our legal system. In my debates with two prominent civil libertarians, Floyd Abrams and Harvey Silverglate, both have acknowledged that they would want nonlethal torture to be used if it could prevent thousands of deaths, but they did not want torture to be officially recognized by our legal system. As Abrams put it: "In a democracy sometimes it is necessary to do things off the books and below the radar screen." . . .

This understandable approach is in conflict with the third important value: namely, open accountability and visibility in a democracy. "Off-the-book actions below the radar screen" are antithetical to the theory and practice of democracy. Citizens cannot approve or disapprove of governmental actions of which they are unaware. We have learned the lesson of history that off-the-book actions can produce terrible consequences. Richard Nixon's creation of a group of "plumbers" led to Watergate, and Ronald Reagan's authorization of an off-the-books foreign policy in Central America led to the Iran-Contra scandal. And these are only the ones we know about!

Perhaps the most extreme example of such a hypocritical approach to torture comes—not surprisingly—from the French experience in Algeria. The French army used torture extensively in seeking to prevent terrorism during a brutal colonial war from 1955 to 1957. An officer who supervised this torture, General Paul Aussaresses, wrote a book recounting what he had done and seen, including the torture of dozens of Algerians. "The best way to make a terrorist talk when he refused to say what he knew was to torture him," he boasted. Although the book was published decades after the war was over, the general was prosecuted—but not for what he had done to the Algerians. Instead, he was prosecuted for *revealing* what he had done, and seeking to justify it.

In a democracy governed by the rule of law, we should never want our soldiers or our president to take any action that we deem wrong or illegal. A good test of whether an action should or should not be done is whether we are prepared to have it disclosed—perhaps not immediately, but certainly after some time has passed. No legal system operating under the rule of law should ever tolerate an "off-the-books" approach to necessity. Even the defense of necessity must be justified lawfully. The road to tyranny has always been paved with claims of necessity made by those responsible for the security of a nation. Our system of checks and balances requires that all presidential actions, like all legislative or military actions, be consistent with governing law. If it is necessary to torture in the ticking bomb case, then our governing laws must accommodate this practice. If we refuse to change our law to accommodate any particular action, then our government should not take that action.

Only in a democracy committed to civil liberties would a triangular conflict of this kind exist. Totalitarian and authoritarian regimes experience no such conflict, because they subscribe to neither the civil libertarian nor the democratic values that come in conflict with the value of security. The hard question is: which value is to be preferred when an inevitable clash occurs? One or more of these values must inevitably be compromised in making the tragic choice presented by the ticking bomb case. If we do not torture, we compromise the security and safety of our citizens. If we tolerate torture, but keep it off the books and below the radar screen, we compromise principles of democratic accountability. If we create a legal structure for limiting and controlling torture, we compromise our principled opposition to torture in all circumstances and create a potentially dangerous and expandable situation.

In 1678, the French writer François de La Rochefoucauld said that "hypocrisy is the homage that vice renders to virtue." In this case we have two vices: terrorism and torture. We also have two virtues: civil liberties and democratic accountability. Most civil libertarians I know prefer hypocrisy, precisely because it appears to avoid the conflict between security and civil liberties, but by choosing the way of the hypocrite these civil libertarians compromise the value of democratic accountability. Such is the nature of tragic choices in a complex world. As Bentham put it more than two centuries ago: "Government throughout is but a choice of evils." In a democracy, such choices must be made, whenever possible, with openness and democratic accountability, and subject to the rule of law.

Consider another terrible choice of evils that could easily have been presented on September 11, 2001—and may well be presented in the future: a hijacked passenger jet is on a collision course with a densely occupied office building; the only way to prevent the destruction of the building and the killing of its occupants is to shoot down the jet, thereby killing its innocent passengers. This choice now seems easy, because the passengers are certain to die anyway and their somewhat earlier deaths will save numerous lives. The passenger jet must be shot down. But what if it were only *probable*, not certain, that the jet would crash into the building? Say, for example, we know from cell phone transmissions that passengers are struggling to regain control of the hijacked jet, but it is unlikely they will succeed in time. Or say we have no communication with the jet and all we know is that it is off course and heading toward Washington, D.C., or some other densely populated city. Under these more questionable circumstances, the question becomes *who* should make this life and death choice between evils—a decision that may turn out tragically wrong?

No reasonable person would allocate this decision to a fighter jet pilot who happened to be in the area or to a local airbase commander—unless of course there was no time for the matter to be passed up the chain of command to the president or the secretary of defense. A decision of this kind should be made at the highest level possible, with visibility and accountability.

Why is this not also true of the decision to torture a ticking bomb terrorist? Why should that choice of evils be relegated to a local policeman, FBI agent, or CIA operative, rather than to a judge, the attorney general, or the president?

There are, of course, important differences between the decision to shoot down the plane and the decision to torture the ticking bomb terrorist. Having to shoot down an airplane, though tragic, is not likely to be a recurring issue. There is no slope down which to slip. Moreover, the jet to be shot down is filled with our fellow citizens—people with whom we can identify. The suspected terrorist we may choose to torture is a "they"—an enemy with whom we do not identify but with whose potential victims we do identify. The risk of making the wrong decision, or of overdoing the torture, is far greater, since we do not care as much what happens to "them" as to "us." Finally, there is something different about torture—even nonlethal torture—that sets it apart from a quick death. In addition to the horrible history associated with torture, there is also the aesthetic of torture. The very idea of deliberately subjecting a captive human being to excruciating pain violates our sense of what is acceptable. On a purely rational basis, it is far worse to shoot a fleeing felon in the back and kill him, yet every civilized society authorizes shooting such a suspect who poses dangers of committing violent crimes against the police or others. In the United States we execute convicted murderers, despite compelling evidence of the unfairness and ineffectiveness of capital punishment. Yet many of us recoil at the prospect of shoving a sterilized needle under the finger of a suspect who is refusing to divulge information that might prevent multiple deaths. Despite the irrationality of these distinctions, they are understandable, especially in light of the sordid history of torture. . . .

It seems logical that a formal, visible, accountable, and centralized system is somewhat easier to control than an ad hoc, off-the-books, and under-the-radar-screen nonsystem. I believe, though I certainly cannot prove, that a formal requirement of a judicial warrant as a prerequisite to nonlethal torture would decrease the amount of physical violence directed against suspects. At the most obvious level, a double check is always more protective than a single check. In every instance in which a warrant is requested, a field officer has already decided that torture is justified and, in the absence of a warrant requirement, would simply proceed with the torture. Requiring that decision to be approved by a judicial officer will result in fewer instances of torture even if the judge rarely turns down a request. Moreover, I believe that most judges would require compelling evidence before they would authorize so extraordinary a departure from our constitutional norms, and law enforcement officials would be reluctant to seek a warrant unless they had compelling evidence that the suspect had information needed to prevent an imminent terrorist attack. A record would be kept of every warrant granted, and although it is certainly possible that some individual agents might torture without a warrant, they would have no excuse, since a warrant procedure would be available. They could not claim "necessity," because the decision as to whether the torture is indeed necessary has been taken out of their hands and placed in the hands of a judge. In addition, even if torture were deemed totally illegal without any exception, it would still occur, though the public would be less aware of its existence.

I also believe that the rights of the suspect would be better protected with a warrant requirement. He would be granted immunity, told that he was now compelled to testify, threatened with imprisonment if he refused to do so, and given the option of providing the requested information.

Only if he refused to do what he was legally compelled to do—provide necessary information, which could not incriminate him because of the immunity—would he be threatened with torture. Knowing that such a threat was authorized by the law, he might well provide the information. If he still refused to, he would be subjected to judicially monitored physical measures designed to cause excruciating pain without leaving any lasting damage.

Let me cite two examples to demonstrate why I think there would be less torture with a warrant requirement than without one. Recall the case of the alleged national security wiretap placed on the phones of Martin Luther King by the Kennedy administration in the early 1960s. This was in the days when the attorney general could authorize a national security wiretap without a warrant. Today no judge would issue a warrant in a case as flimsy as that one. When Zacarias Moussaoui was detained after raising suspicions while trying to learn how to fly an airplane, the government did not even seek a national security wiretap because its lawyers believed that a judge would not have granted one. If Moussaoui's computer could have been searched without a warrant, it almost certainly would have been.

It should be recalled that in the context of searches, our Supreme Court opted for a judicial check on the discretion of the police, by requiring a search warrant in most cases. The Court has explained the reason for the warrant requirement as follows: "The informed and deliberate determinations of magistrates . . . are to be preferred over the hurried action of officers."[4] Justice Robert Jackson elaborated:

> The point of the Fourth Amendment, which often is not grasped by zealous officers, is not that it denies law enforcement the support of the usual inferences which reasonable men draw from evidence. Its protection consists in requiring that those inferences be drawn by a neutral and detached magistrate instead of being judged by the officer engaged in the often competitive enterprise of ferreting out crime. Any assumption that evidence sufficient to support a magistrate's disinterested determination to issue a search warrant will justify the officers in making a search without a warrant would reduce the Amendment to nullity and leave the people's homes secure only in the discretion of police officers.[5]

---

4 *U.S. v. Lefkowitz*, 285 U.S. 452, 464 (1932).
5 *Johnson v. U.S.* 333 U.S. 10, 13–14 (1948).

Although torture is very different from a search, the policies underlying the warrant requirement are relevant to the question whether there is likely to be more torture or less if the decision is left entirely to field officers, or if a judicial officer has to approve a request for a torture warrant. As Abraham Maslow once observed, to a man with a hammer, everything looks like a nail. If the man with the hammer must get judicial approval before he can use it, he will probably use it less often and more carefully.

There are other, somewhat more subtle, considerations that should be factored into any decision regarding torture. There are some who see silence as a virtue when it comes to the choice among such horrible evils as torture and terrorism. It is far better, they argue, not to discuss or write about issues of this sort, lest they become legitimated. And legitimation is an appropriate concern. Justice Jackson, in his opinion in one of the cases concerning the detention of Japanese-Americans during World War II, made the following relevant observation:

> . . . All who observe the work of courts are familiar with what Judge Cardozo described as "the tendency of a principle to expand itself to the limit of its logic." A military commander may overstep the bounds of constitutionality, and it is an incident. But if we review and approve, that passing incident becomes the doctrine of the Constitution. There it has a generative power of its own, and all that it creates will be in its own image.[6]

A similar argument can be made regarding torture: if an agent tortures, that is "an incident," but if the courts authorize it, it becomes a precedent. There is, however, an important difference between the detention of Japanese-American citizens and torture. The detentions were done openly and with presidential accountability; torture would be done secretly, with official deniability. Tolerating an off-the-book system of secret torture can also establish a dangerous precedent.

A variation on this "legitimation" argument would postpone consideration of the choice between authorizing torture and forgoing a possible tactic necessary to prevent an imminent act of terrorism until after the choice—presumably the choice to torture—has been made. In that way, the discussion would not, in itself, encourage the use of torture. If it were employed, then we could decide whether it was justified, excusable, condemnable, or something in between. The problem with that argument is

---

6 *Korematsu v. U.S.* 323 U.S. 214, 245–46 (1944) (Jackson, J., dissenting).

that no FBI agent who tortured a suspect into disclosing information that prevented an act of mass terrorism would be prosecuted—as the policemen who tortured the kidnapper into disclosing the whereabouts of his victim were not prosecuted. In the absence of a prosecution, there would be no occasion to judge the appropriateness of the torture.

I disagree with these more passive approaches and believe that in a democracy it is always preferable to decide controversial issues in advance, rather than in the heat of battle. I would apply this rule to other tragic choices as well, including the possible use of a nuclear first strike, or retaliatory strikes—so long as the discussion was sufficiently general to avoid giving our potential enemies a strategic advantage by their knowledge of our policy.

Even if government officials decline to discuss such issues, academics have a duty to raise them and submit them to the marketplace of ideas. There may be danger in open discussion, but there is far greater danger in actions based on secret discussion, or no discussion at all.

Alan Dershowitz: Should the Ticking Bomb Terrorist Be Tortured?

1. What is the "ticking bomb" case? Do relevantly similar cases often arise in the real world?
2. What is the difference between act-utilitarianism and rule-utilitarianism? Which does Dershowitz think endorses rare cases of torture, and which opposes it? Do you agree with his conclusions about what these theories recommend?
3. What three values does Dershowitz say are in conflict when making decisions about torture? Why does he claim that a clash between these values is "inevitable"? Do you think he is correct about this?
4. Dershowitz claims that "on a purely rational basis, it is far worse to shoot a fleeing felon in the back and kill him" than to torture someone in a ticking bomb case. Do you agree with this claim? If so, does it follow that torture is sometimes justified?
5. What benefits does Dershowitz claim that requiring warrants for torture would have? Given the safeguards he proposes, would instituting an official government policy of torture in rare cases be morally permissible?

26

=== ❧ ===

Puppies, Pigs and People: Eating Meat and Marginal Cases

Alastair Norcross

....

Alastair Norcross opens his provocative piece with a fictional scenario that is both outrageous and meant to make a very serious philosophical point. As he sees it, current practices of factory farming are deeply immoral. One might think that meat-eaters are exempt from blame, though, since for the most part they are not the ones who are actually perpetrating the harms to animals on the factory farms that process the great majority of animal products. Norcross rejects this thought. As he sees it, meat-eaters—at least those who know of the cruelty of the treatment of factory-farmed animals—are fully blameworthy for their indulgence. The good they get from eating meat—primarily the gustatory pleasure they get from eating meat—is far outweighed by the awful suffering of the animals when confined and killed on factory farms.

Norcross considers a wide variety of replies to his charge. These include the claim that individual meat-eaters are off the moral hook because their purchases are so insignificant that they cannot affect the practices on factory farms. Another reply is that meat-eaters do not intend to harm animals, but only foresee animal harm as a result of contemporary farming practices. Norcross extensively criticizes both replies.

Alastair Norcross, "Puppies, Pigs and People: Eating Meat and Marginal Cases," from *Philosophical Perspectives* 18 (2004), pp. 229–234, 239–244.

He then introduces a very popular argument in the literature on animal welfare: the argument from marginal cases. This argument says that we must treat animals and so-called "marginal" human beings as equals, since such humans have mental lives that are no more developed than those of the animals that are killed and eaten for food. He considers several replies to this argument, and finds fault with each of them. If we are unwilling to cruelly confine, prematurely kill, and eat "marginal" human beings, then we should be equally reluctant to do such things to animals.

Norcross concludes with a discussion of the difference between being a moral agent (i.e., someone who can respond to moral reasons and control her behavior by means of such reasons) and a moral patient (i.e., a being to whom we owe duties, even if that being lacks rights or lacks the cognitive powers needed to be a moral agent). Norcross argues that animals qualify as moral patients, even if, because of their diminished or nonexistent rationality, they cannot qualify as moral agents. We therefore owe them duties of respect, which protect them against the current practices involved in factory farming.

....

1. Fred's Basement

Consider the story of Fred, who receives a visit from the police one day. They have been summoned by Fred's neighbors, who have been disturbed by strange sounds emanating from Fred's basement. When they enter the basement they are confronted by the following scene: Twenty-six small wire cages, each containing a puppy, some whining, some whimpering, some howling. The puppies range in age from newborn to about six months. Many of them show signs of mutilation. Urine and feces cover the bottoms of the cages and the basement floor. Fred explains that he keeps the puppies for twenty-six weeks, and then butchers them while holding them upside-down. During their lives he performs a series of mutilations on them, such as slicing off their noses and their paws with a hot knife, all without any form of anesthesia. Except for the mutilations, the puppies are never allowed out of the cages, which are barely big enough to hold them at twenty-six weeks. The police are horrified, and promptly charge Fred with animal abuse. As details of the case are publicized, the public is outraged. Newspapers are flooded with letters demanding that Fred be severely punished. There are calls for more severe penalties for animal abuse. Fred is denounced as a vile sadist.

Finally, at his trial, Fred explains his behavior, and argues that he is blameless and therefore deserves no punishment. He is, he explains, a great lover of chocolate. A couple of years ago, he was involved in a car accident, which resulted in some head trauma. Upon his release from hospital, having apparently suffered no lasting ill effects, he visited his favorite restaurant and ordered their famous rich dark chocolate mousse. Imagine his dismay when he discovered that his experience of the mousse was a pale shadow of its former self. The mousse tasted bland, slightly pleasant, but with none of the intense chocolaty flavor he remembered so well. The waiter assured him that the recipe was unchanged from the last time he had tasted it, just the day before his accident. In some consternation, Fred rushed out to buy a bar of his favorite Belgian chocolate. Again, he was dismayed to discover that his experience of the chocolate was barely even pleasurable. Extensive investigation revealed that his experience of other foods remained unaffected, but chocolate, in all its forms, now tasted bland and insipid. Desperate for a solution to his problem, Fred visited a renowned gustatory neurologist, Dr. T. Bud. Extensive tests revealed that the accident had irreparably damaged the godiva gland, which secretes cocoamone, the hormone responsible for the experience of chocolate. Fred urgently requested hormone replacement therapy. Dr. Bud informed him that, until recently, there had been no known source of cocoamone, other than the human godiva gland, and that it was impossible to collect cocoamone from one person to be used by another. However, a chance discovery had altered the situation. A forensic veterinary surgeon, performing an autopsy on a severely abused puppy, had discovered high concentrations of cocoamone in the puppy's brain. It turned out that puppies, who don't normally produce cocoamone, could be stimulated to do so by extended periods of severe stress and suffering. The research, which led to this discovery, while gaining tenure for its authors, had not been widely publicized, for fear of antagonizing animal welfare groups. Although this research clearly gave Fred the hope of tasting chocolate again, there were no commercially available sources of puppy-derived cocoamone. Lack of demand, combined with fear of bad publicity, had deterred drug companies from getting into the puppy torturing business. Fred appeals to the court to imagine his anguish, on discovering that a solution to his severe deprivation was possible, but not readily available. But he wasn't inclined to sit around bemoaning his cruel fate. He did what any chocolate lover would do. He read the research, and set up his own cocoamone collection lab in his basement. Six months of intense puppy suffering, followed by a brutal death, produced enough cocoamone to last him a week, hence the twenty-six cages. He isn't a sadist or an animal abuser, he explains. If there were a method of collecting cocoamone without torturing puppies, he would gladly employ it. He derives no pleasure from the suffering of the puppies itself. He sympathizes with those who are horrified by the pain and misery of the animals, but the court must realize that human pleasure is at stake. The puppies, while undeniably cute, are mere animals. He admits that he would be just as healthy without chocolate, if not more so. But this isn't a matter of survival or health. His life would be unacceptably impoverished without the experience of chocolate.

End of story. Clearly, we are horrified by Fred's behavior, and unconvinced by his attempted justification. It is, of course, unfortunate for Fred that he can no longer enjoy the taste of chocolate, but that in no way excuses the imposition of severe suffering on the puppies. I expect near universal agreement with this claim (the exceptions being those who are either inhumanly callous or thinking ahead, and wish to avoid the following conclusion, to which such agreement commits them). No decent person would even contemplate torturing puppies merely to enhance a gustatory experience. However, billions of animals endure intense suffering every year for precisely this end. Most of the chicken, veal, beef, and pork consumed in the US comes from intensive confinement facilities, in which the animals live cramped, stress-filled lives and endure unanaesthetized mutilations. The vast majority of people would suffer no ill health from the elimination of meat from their diets. Quite the reverse. The supposed benefits from this system of factory farming, apart from the profits accruing to agribusiness, are increased levels of gustatory pleasure for those who claim that they couldn't enjoy a meat-free diet as much as their current meat-filled diets. If we are prepared to condemn Fred for torturing puppies merely to enhance his gustatory experiences, shouldn't we similarly condemn the millions who purchase and consume factory-raised meat? Are there any morally significant differences between Fred's behavior and their behavior?

2. Fred's Behavior Compared with Our Behavior

The first difference that might seem to be relevant is that Fred tortures the puppies himself, whereas most Americans consume meat that comes from animals that have been tortured by others. But is this really relevant? What if Fred had been squeamish and had employed someone else to torture the puppies and extract the cocoamone? Would we have thought any better of Fred? Of course not.

Another difference between Fred and many consumers of factory-raised meat is that many, perhaps most, such consumers are unaware of the treatment of the animals, before they appear in neatly wrapped packages on supermarket shelves. Perhaps I should moderate my challenge, then. If we are prepared to condemn Fred for torturing puppies merely to enhance his gustatory experiences, shouldn't we similarly condemn those who purchase and consume factory-raised meat, in full, or even partial, awareness of the suffering endured by the animals? While many consumers are still blissfully ignorant of the appalling treatment meted out to meat, that number is rapidly dwindling, thanks to vigorous publicity campaigns waged by animal welfare groups. Furthermore, any meat-eating readers of this article are now deprived of the excuse of ignorance.

Perhaps a consumer of factory-raised animals could argue as follows: While I agree that Fred's behavior is abominable, mine is crucially different. If Fred did not consume his chocolate, he would not raise and torture puppies (or pay someone else to do so). Therefore Fred could prevent the suffering of the puppies. However, if I did not buy and consume factory-raised meat, no animals would be spared lives of misery. Agribusiness is much too large to respond to the behavior of one consumer. Therefore I cannot prevent the suffering of any animals. I may well regret the suffering inflicted on animals for the sake of human enjoyment. I may even agree that the human enjoyment doesn't justify the suffering. However, since the animals will suffer no matter what I do, I may as well enjoy the taste of their flesh.

There are at least two lines of response to this attempted defense. First, consider an analogous case. You visit a friend in an exotic location, say Alabama. Your friend takes you out to eat at the finest restaurant in Tuscaloosa. For dessert you select the house specialty, "Chocolate Mousse à la Bama," served with a small cup of coffee, which you are instructed to drink before eating the mousse. The mousse is quite simply the most delicious dessert you have ever tasted. Never before has chocolate tasted so rich and satisfying. Tempted to order a second, you ask your friend what makes this mousse so delicious. He informs you that the mousse itself is ordinary, but the coffee contains a concentrated dose of cocoamone, the newly discovered chocolate-enhancing hormone. Researchers at Auburn

University have perfected a technique for extracting cocoamone from the brains of freshly slaughtered puppies, who have been subjected to lives of pain and frustration. Each puppy's brain yields four doses, each of which is effective for about fifteen minutes, just long enough to enjoy one serving of mousse. You are, naturally, horrified and disgusted. You will certainly not order another serving, you tell your friend. In fact, you are shocked that your friend, who had always seemed to be a morally decent person, could have both recommended the dessert to you and eaten one himself, in full awareness of the loathsome process necessary for the experience. He agrees that the suffering of the puppies is outrageous, and that the gain in human pleasure in no way justifies the appalling treatment they have to endure. However, neither he nor you can save any puppies by refraining from consuming cocoamone. Cocoamone production is now Alabama's leading industry, so it is much too large to respond to the behavior of one or two consumers. Since the puppies will suffer no matter what either of you does, you may as well enjoy the mousse.

If it is as obvious as it seems that a morally decent person, who is aware of the details of cocoamone production, couldn't order Chocolate Mousse à la Bama, it should be equally obvious that a morally decent person, who is aware of the details of factory farming, can't purchase and consume factory-raised meat. If the attempted excuse of causal impotence is compelling in the latter case, it should be compelling in the former case. But it isn't.

The second response to the claim of causal impotence is to deny it. Consider the case of chickens, the most cruelly treated of all animals raised for human consumption, with the possible exception of veal calves. In 1998, almost 8 billion chickens were slaughtered in the US, almost all of them raised on factory farms. Suppose that there are 250 million chicken eaters in the US, and that each one consumes, on average, 25 chickens per year (this leaves a fair number of chickens slaughtered for nonhuman consumption, or for export). Clearly, if only one of those chicken eaters gave up eating chicken, the industry would not respond. Equally clearly, if they all gave up eating chicken, billions of chickens (approximately 6.25 billion per year) would not be bred, tortured, and killed. But there must also be some number of consumers, far short of 250 million, whose renunciation of chicken would cause the industry to reduce the number of chickens bred in factory farms. The industry may not be able to respond to each individual's behavior, but it must respond to the behavior of fairly large numbers. Suppose that the industry is sensitive to a reduction in demand for chicken equivalent to 10,000 people becoming vegetarians.

(This seems like a reasonable guess, but I have no idea what the actual numbers are, nor is it important.) For each group of 10,000 who give up chicken, a quarter of a million fewer chickens are bred per year. It appears, then, that if you give up eating chicken, you have only a one in ten thousand chance of making any difference to the lives of chickens, unless it is certain that fewer than 10,000 people will ever give up eating chicken, in which case you have no chance. Isn't a one in ten thousand chance small enough to render your continued consumption of chicken blameless? Not at all. . . . A one in ten thousand chance of saving 250,000 chickens per year from excruciating lives is morally and mathematically equivalent to the certainty of saving 25 chickens per year. We commonly accept that even small risks of great harms are unacceptable. That is why we disapprove of parents who fail to secure their children in car seats or with seat belts, who leave their small children unattended at home, or who drink or smoke heavily during pregnancy. Or consider commercial aircraft safety measures. The chances that the oxygen masks, the lifejackets, or the emergency exits on any given plane will be called on to save any lives in a given week, are far smaller than one in ten thousand. And yet we would be outraged to discover that an airline had knowingly allowed a plane to fly for a week with non-functioning emergency exits, oxygen masks, and lifejackets. So, even if it is true that your giving up factory-raised chicken has only a tiny chance of preventing suffering, given that the amount of suffering that would be prevented is in inverse proportion to your chance of preventing it, your continued consumption is not thereby excused.

But perhaps it is not even true that your giving up chicken has only a tiny chance of making any difference. Suppose again that the poultry industry only reduces production when a threshold of 10,000 fresh vegetarians is reached. Suppose also, as is almost certainly true, that vegetarianism is growing in popularity in the US (and elsewhere). Then, even if you are not the one, newly converted vegetarian, to reach the next threshold of 10,000, your conversion will reduce the time required before the next threshold is reached. The sooner the threshold is reached, the sooner production, and therefore animal suffering, is reduced. Your behavior, therefore, does make a difference. Furthermore, many people who become vegetarians influence others to become vegetarian, who in turn influence others, and so on. It appears, then, that the claim of causal impotence is mere wishful thinking, on the part of those meat lovers who are morally sensitive enough to realize that human gustatory pleasure does not justify inflicting extreme suffering on animals.

Perhaps there is a further difference between the treatment of Fred's puppies and the treatment of animals on factory farms. The suffering of the puppies is a necessary means to the production of gustatory pleasure, whereas the suffering of animals on factory farms is simply a by-product of the conditions dictated by economic considerations. Therefore, it might be argued, the suffering of the puppies is *intended as a means* to Fred's pleasure, whereas the suffering of factory raised animals is merely *foreseen* as a side-effect of a system that is a means to the gustatory pleasures of millions. The distinction between what is intended, either as a means or as an end in itself, and what is 'merely' foreseen is central to the Doctrine of Double Effect. Supporters of this doctrine claim that it is sometimes permissible to bring about an effect that is merely foreseen, even though the very same effect could not permissibly be brought about if intended. (Other conditions have to be met in order for the Doctrine of Double Effect to judge an action permissible, most notably that there be an outweighing good effect.) Fred acts impermissibly, according to this line of argument, because he intends the suffering of the puppies as a means to his pleasure. Most meat eaters, on the other hand, even if aware of the suffering of the animals, do not intend the suffering.

In response to this line of argument, I could remind the reader that Samuel Johnson said, or should have said, that the Doctrine of Double Effect is the last refuge of a scoundrel. I won't do that, however, since neither the doctrine itself, nor the alleged moral distinction between intending and foreseeing can justify the consumption of factory-raised meat. The Doctrine of Double Effect requires not merely that a bad effect be foreseen and not intended, but also that there be an outweighing good effect. In the case of the suffering of factory-raised animals, whatever good could plausibly be claimed to come out of the system clearly doesn't outweigh the bad. Furthermore, it would be easy to modify the story of Fred to render the puppies' suffering 'merely' foreseen. For example, suppose that the cocoamone is produced by a chemical reaction that can only occur when large quantities of drain-cleaner are forced down the throat of a conscious, unanaesthetized puppy. The consequent appalling suffering, while not itself a means to the production of cocoamone, is nonetheless an unavoidable side-effect of the means. In this variation of the story, Fred's behavior is no less abominable than in the original.

One last difference between the behavior of Fred and the behavior of the consumers of factory-raised meat is worth discussing, if only because it is so frequently cited in response to the arguments of this paper. Fred's behavior is abominable, according to this line of thinking, because it involves the suffering of *puppies*. The behavior of meat-eaters, on the other hand, 'merely' involves the suffering of chickens, pigs, cows, calves, sheep, and the like. Puppies (and probably dogs and cats in general) are morally different from the other animals. Puppies *count* (morally, that is), whereas the other animals don't, or at least not nearly as much.

So, what gives puppies a higher moral status than the animals we eat? Presumably there is some morally relevant property or properties possessed by puppies but not by farm animals. Perhaps puppies have a greater degree of rationality than farm animals, or a more finely developed moral sense, or at least a sense of loyalty and devotion. The problems with this kind of approach are obvious. It's highly unlikely that any property that has even an outside chance of being ethically relevant is both possessed by puppies and not possessed by any farm animals. For example, it's probably true that most puppies have a greater degree of rationality (whatever that means) than most chickens, but the comparison with pigs is far more dubious. Besides, if Fred were to inform the jury that he had taken pains to acquire particularly stupid, morally obtuse, disloyal and undevoted puppies, would they (or we) have declared his behavior to be morally acceptable? Clearly not.

I have been unable to discover any morally relevant differences between the behavior of Fred, the puppy torturer, and the behavior of the millions of people who purchase and consume factory-raised meat, at least those who do so in the knowledge that the animals live lives of suffering and deprivation. If morality demands that we not torture puppies merely to enhance our own eating pleasure, morality also demands that we not support factory farming by purchasing factory-raised meat. . . .

3. Humans' versus Animals' Ethical Status—The Rationality Gambit

For the purposes of this discussion, to claim that humans have a superior ethical status to animals is to claim that it is morally right to give the interests of humans greater weight than those of animals in deciding how to behave. Such claims will often be couched in terms of rights, such as the rights to life, liberty or respect, but nothing turns on this terminological matter. One may claim that it is generally wrong to kill humans, but not animals, because humans are rational, and animals are not. Or one may claim that the suffering of animals counts less than the suffering of humans (if at all), because humans are rational, and animals are not. . . .

What could ground the claim of superior moral status for humans? Just as the defender of a higher moral status for puppies than for farm animals needs to find some property or properties possessed by puppies but not by farm animals, so the defender of a higher moral status for humans need to find some property or properties possessed by humans but not by other animals. The traditional view, dating back at least to Aristotle, is that rationality is what separates humans, both morally and metaphysically, from other animals.

One of the most serious challenges to the traditional view involves a consideration of what philosophers refer to as 'marginal cases'. Whatever kind and level of rationality is selected as justifying the attribution of superior moral status to humans will either be lacking in some humans or present in some animals. To take one of the most commonly-suggested features, many humans are incapable of engaging in moral reflection. For some, this incapacity is temporary, as is the case with infants, or the temporarily cognitively disabled. Others who once had the capacity may have permanently lost it, as is the case with the severely senile or the irreversibly comatose. Still others never had and never will have the capacity, as is the case with the severely mentally disabled. If we base our claims for the moral superiority of humans over animals on the attribution of such capacities, won't we have to exclude many humans? Won't we then be forced to the claim that there is at least as much moral reason to use cognitively deficient humans in experiments and for food as to use animals? Perhaps we could exclude the only temporarily disabled, on the grounds of potentiality, though that move has its own problems. Nonetheless, the other two categories would be vulnerable to this objection.

I will consider two lines of response to the argument from marginal cases. The first denies that we have to attribute different moral status to marginal humans, but maintains that we are, nonetheless, justified in attributing different moral status to animals who are just as cognitively sophisticated as marginal humans, if not more so. The second admits that, strictly speaking, marginal humans are morally inferior to other humans, but proceeds to claim pragmatic reasons for treating them, at least usually, *as if* they had equal status.

As representatives of the first line of defense, I will consider arguments from three philosophers, Carl Cohen, Alan White, and David Schmidtz. First, Cohen:

> [the argument from marginal cases] fails; it mistakenly treats an essential feature of humanity as though it were a screen for sorting humans. The capacity for moral judgment that distinguishes humans from animals is

not a test to be administered to human beings one by one. Persons who are unable, because of some disability, to perform the full moral functions natural to human beings are certainly not for that reason ejected from the moral community. The issue is one of kind. . . .What humans retain when disabled, animals have never had.[1]

Alan White argues that animals don't have rights, on the grounds that they cannot intelligibly be spoken of in the full language of a right. By this he means that they cannot, for example, claim, demand, assert, insist on, secure, waive, or surrender a right. This is what he has to say in response to the argument from marginal cases:

> Nor does this, as some contend, exclude infants, children, the feeble-minded, the comatose, the dead, or generations yet unborn. Any of these may be for various reasons empirically unable to fulfill the full role of right-holder. But . . . they are logically possible subjects of rights to whom the full language of rights can significantly, however falsely, be used. It is a misfortune, not a tautology, that these persons cannot exercise or enjoy, claim, or waive, their rights or do their duty or fulfil their obligations.[2]

David Schmidtz defends the appeal to typical characteristics of species, such as mice, chimpanzees, and humans, in making decisions on the use of different species in experiments. He also considers the argument from marginal cases:

> Of course, some chimpanzees lack the characteristic features in virtue of which chimpanzees command respect as a species, just as some humans lack the characteristic features in virtue of which humans command respect as a species. It is equally obvious that some chimpanzees have cognitive capacities (for example) that are superior to the cognitive capacities of some humans. But whether every human being is superior to every chimpanzee is beside the point. The point is that we can, we do, and we should make decisions on the basis of our recognition that mice, chimpanzees, and humans are relevantly different *types*. We can have it both ways after all. Or so a speciesist could argue.[3]

---

1 Carl Cohen, "The Case for the Use of Animals in Biomedical Research", *The New England Journal of Medicine,* vol. 315, 1986.

2 Alan White, Rights, (OUP 1984). Reprinted in *Animal Rights and Human Obligations,* 2nd edition, Tom Regan and Peter Singer (eds.) (Prentice Hall, 1989), 120.

3 David Schmidtz, "Are All Species Equal?", *Journal of Applied Philosophy,* Vol. 15, no. 1 (1998), 61, my emphasis.

There is something deeply troublesome about the line of argument that runs through all three of these responses to the argument from marginal cases. A particular feature, or set of features is claimed to have so much moral significance that its presence or lack can make the difference to whether a piece of behavior is morally justified or morally outrageous. But then it is claimed that the presence or lack of the feature in any *particular* case is not important. The relevant question is whether the presence or lack of the feature is *normal*. Such an argument would seem perfectly preposterous in most other cases. Suppose, for example, that ten famous people are on trial in the afterlife for crimes against humanity. On the basis of conclusive evidence, five are found guilty and five are found not guilty. Four of the guilty are sentenced to an eternity of torment, and one is granted an eternity of bliss. Four of the innocent are granted an eternity of bliss, and one is sentenced to an eternity of torment. The one innocent who is sentenced to torment asks why he, and not the fifth guilty person, must go to hell. Saint Peter replies, "Isn't it obvious Mr. Ghandi? You are male. The other four men—Adolph Hitler, Joseph Stalin, George W. Bush, and Richard Nixon—are all guilty. Therefore the normal condition for a male defendant in this trial is guilt. The fact that you happen to be innocent is irrelevant. Likewise, of the five female defendants in this trial, only one was guilty. Therefore the normal condition for female defendants in this trial is innocence. That is why Margaret Thatcher gets to go to heaven instead of you."

As I said, such an argument is preposterous. Is the reply to the argument from marginal cases any better? Perhaps it will be claimed that a biological category such as a species is more 'natural', whatever that means, than a category like 'all the male (or female) defendants in this trial'. Even setting aside the not inconsiderable worries about the conventionality of biological categories, it is not at all clear why this distinction should be morally relevant. What if it turned out that there were statistically relevant differences in the mental abilities of men and women? Suppose that men were, on average, more skilled at manipulating numbers than women, and that women were, on average, more empathetic than men. Would such differences in what was 'normal' for men and women justify us in preferring an innumerate man to a female math genius for a job as an accountant, or an insensitive woman to an ultra-sympathetic man for a job as a counselor? I take it that the biological distinction between male and female is just as real as that between human and chimpanzee.

A second response to the argument from marginal cases is to concede that cognitively deficient humans really do have an inferior moral status to normal humans. Can we, then, use such humans as we do animals? I know of no-one who takes the further step of advocating the use of marginal humans for food . . . How can we advocate this second response while blocking the further step? Mary Anne Warren suggests that "there are powerful practical and emotional reasons for protecting non-rational human beings, reasons which are absent in the case of most non-human animals."[4] It would clearly outrage common human sensibilities, if we were to raise retarded children for food or medical experiments. Here is Steinbock in a similar vein:

> I doubt that anyone will be able to come up with a concrete and morally relevant difference that would justify, say, using a chimpanzee in an experiment rather than a human being with less capacity for reasoning, moral responsibility, etc. Should we then experiment on the severely retarded? Utilitarian considerations aside, we feel a special obligation to care for the handicapped members of our own species, who cannot survive in this world without such care. . . . In addition, when we consider the severely retarded, we think, 'That could be me'. It makes sense to think that one might have been born retarded, but not to think that one might have been born a monkey. . . . Here we are getting away from such things as 'morally relevant differences' and are talking about something much more difficult to articulate, namely, the role of feeling and sentiment in moral thinking.[5]

This line of response clearly won't satisfy those who think that marginal humans really do deserve equal moral consideration with other humans. It is also a very shaky basis on which to justify our current practices. What outrages human sensibilities is a very fragile thing. Human history is littered with examples of widespread acceptance of the systematic mistreatment of some groups who didn't generate any sympathetic response from others. That we do feel a kind of sympathy for retarded humans that we don't feel for dogs is, if true, a contingent matter. To see

---

4 Warren, op. cit. 483. Mary Anne Warren, "Difficulties with the Strong Animal Rights Position", *Between the Species* 2, no. 4, 1987. Reprinted in *Contemporary Moral Problems*, 5th edition, James E. White (ed.) (West. 1997), 482.

5 Steinbock, op. cit. 469–470. Bonnie Steinbock, "Speciesism and the Idea of Equality", *Philosophy* 53, no. 204 (April 1978). Reprinted in *Contemporary Moral Problems*, 5th edition, James E. White (ed.) (West, 1997) 467–468.

just how shaky a basis this is for protecting retarded humans, imagine that a new kind of birth defect (perhaps associated with beef from cows treated with bovine growth hormone) produces severe mental retardation, green skin, and a complete lack of emotional bond between parents and child. Furthermore, suppose that the mental retardation is of the same kind and severity as that caused by other birth defects that don't have the other two effects. It seems likely that denying moral status to such defective humans would not run the same risks of outraging human sensibilities as would the denial of moral status to other, less easily distinguished and more loved defective humans. Would these contingent empirical differences between our reactions to different sources of mental retardation justify us in ascribing different direct moral status to their subjects? The only difference between them is skin color and whether they are loved by others. Any theory that could ascribe moral relevance to differences such as these doesn't deserve to be taken seriously.

Finally, perhaps we could claim that the practice of giving greater weight to the interests of all humans than of animals is justified on evolutionary grounds. Perhaps such differential concern has survival value for the species. Something like this may well be true, but it is hard to see the moral relevance. We can hardly justify the privileging of human interests over animal interests on the grounds that such privileging serves human interests!

6. Agent and Patient—the Speciesist's Central Confusion

Although the argument from marginal cases certainly poses a formidable challenge to any proposed criterion of full moral standing that excludes animals, it doesn't, in my view, constitute the most serious flaw in such attempts to justify the status quo. The proposed criteria are all variations on the Aristotelian criterion of rationality. But what is the moral relevance of rationality? Why should we think that the possession of a certain level or kind of rationality renders the possessor's interests of greater moral significance than those of a merely sentient being? In Bentham's famous words "The question is not, Can they reason? nor Can they talk? But, Can they suffer?"[6]

What do defenders of the alleged superiority of human interests say in response to Bentham's challenge? Some, such as Carl Cohen, simply reiterate

---

6 Jeremy Bentham, *Introduction to the Principles of Morals and Legislation,* (Various) chapter 17.

the differences between humans and animals that they claim to carry moral significance. Animals are not members of moral communities, they don't engage in moral reflection, they can't be moved by moral reasons, *therefore* (?) their interests don't count as much as ours. Others, such as Steinbock and Warren, attempt to go further. Here is Warren on the subject:

> Why is rationality morally relevant? It does not make us "better" than other animals or more "perfect" . . . . But it is morally relevant insofar as it provides greater possibilities for cooperation and for the nonviolent resolution of problems.

Warren is certainly correct in claiming that a certain level and kind of rationality is morally relevant. Where she, and others who give similar arguments, go wrong is in specifying what the moral relevance amounts to. If a being is incapable of moral reasoning, at even the most basic level, if it is incapable of being moved by moral reasons, claims, or arguments, then it cannot be a moral agent. It cannot be subject to moral obligations, to moral praise or blame. Punishing a dog for doing something "wrong" is no more than an attempt to alter its future behavior.

All this is well and good, but what is the significance for the question of what weight to give to animal interests? That animals can't be moral *agents* doesn't seem to be relevant to their status as moral *patients*. Many, perhaps most, humans are both moral agents and patients. Most, perhaps all, animals are only moral patients. Why would the lack of moral agency give them diminished status as moral patients? Full status as a moral patient is not some kind of reward for moral agency. I have heard students complain in this regard that it is *unfair* that humans bear the burdens of moral responsibility, and don't get enhanced consideration of their interests in return. This is a very strange claim. Humans arc subject to moral obligations, because they are the kind of creatures who *can* be. What grounds moral agency is simply different from what grounds moral standing as a patient. It is no more unfair that humans and not animals are moral agents, than it is unfair that real animals and not stuffed toys are moral patients.

. . . It seems that any attempt to justify the claim that humans have a higher moral status than other animals by appealing to some version of rationality as the morally relevant difference between humans and animals will fail on at least two counts. It will fail to give an adequate answer to the argument from marginal cases, and, more importantly, it will fail to make

---

7 Warren, op. cit. 482.

the case that such a difference is morally relevant to the status of animals as moral patients as opposed to their status as moral agents.

I conclude that our intuitions that Fred's behavior is morally impermissible are accurate. Furthermore, given that the behavior of those who knowingly support factory farming is morally indistinguishable, it follows that their behavior is also morally impermissible.

Alastair Norcross: Puppies, Pigs and People: Eating Meat and Marginal Cases

1. Do you agree that Fred acts immorally in the case that Norcross describes? If so, what exactly is it about Fred's behavior that is morally objectionable? If not, why not?
2. Some might claim that eating meat from factory farms is relevantly different from Fred's behavior because individual consumers are powerless to change the factory-farming system, whereas Fred is fully in control of the puppies. How does Norcross respond to this claim?
3. Another disanalogy between Fred's behavior and that of most meat-eaters is that Fred *intends* to make the puppies suffer, while most consumers of meat don't intend to make any animals suffer. Does this disanalogy undermine Norcross's argument? Why or why not?
4. What is the "argument from marginal cases" and what is it supposed to show? What do you think is the strongest objection to the argument?
5. What is the difference between being a moral agent and being a moral patient? Why does Norcross think that nonhuman animals are moral patients? Do you agree with him?

27

Moral Standing, the Value of Lives, and Speciesism

R. G. Frey

Raymond Frey defends a view that he calls the unequal value thesis—the idea that human life is more valuable than animal life. Some philosophers have charged that this is a version of "speciesism," which is the view that being a member of the species *Homo sapiens* by itself makes human beings more important than other animals. One of the goals of Frey's article is to show that we can defend the unequal value thesis without relying on speciesist assumptions.

Frey denies that species membership is by itself a morally important trait. Being human is not what makes most us more valuable than any other kind of animal. Rather, our lives are valuable just in proportion to their quality: the higher the quality of life, the greater the value of that life. Frey tells us that the quality of life is itself a function of its capacity for enrichment. You and I have this capacity to a very high degree—we can make all sorts of complicated plans, take pleasure in a huge variety of activities, develop deep and complex relationships with others. When we compare the capacity for enriching our lives with that capacity as possessed, say, by a rabbit, it becomes clear that our capacity for an enriched life far outstrips the rabbit's. So our lives are moral valuable than a rabbit's (and any other animal we know of).

To reinforce the point that this is not a kind of speciesism, Frey invites us to compare the life of a normal adult human being with that

From *Between the Species*, http://digitalcommons.calpoly.edu/bts/

of an elderly patient fully in the grips of Alzheimer's disease. Surely, he says, the former life is more valuable than the latter. Late-stage Alzheimer's patients have far less capacity to enrich their lives than do you and I. Thus Frey judges that their lives are less valuable than ours. It is also the case, according to Frey, that the lives of some animals are *more* valuable than the lives of some humans, since some human beings have a lower quality of life than that of some animals.

Frey thinks that our moral duties to others depend in large part on the value of their lives. As a result, he thinks that, ordinarily, when we must choose between conducting experiments on animals or on humans, we are right to make animals our test subjects, since they usually possess lives of lesser value. But not always. So, morally speaking, we must sometimes conduct tests on humans and spare the animals.

....

I.

Those who concern themselves with the moral considerability of animals may well be tempted to suppose that their work is finished, once they successfully envelop animals within the moral community. Yet, to stop there is never *per se* to address the issue of the value of animal life and so never to engage the position that I, and others, hold on certain issues. Thus, I am a restricted vivisectionist; not because I think animals are outside the moral community but because of views I hold about the value of their lives. Again, I think it is permissible to use animal parts in human transplants, not because I think animals lack moral standing but because I think animal life is less valuable than human life.

I have written of views that I hold; the fact is, I think, that the vast majority of people share my view of the differing value of human and animal life. This view we might capture in the form of three propositions:

1. Animal life has some value;
2. Not all animal life has the same value;
3. Human life is more valuable than animal life.

Very few people today would seem to believe that animal life is without value and that, therefore, we need not trouble ourselves morally about taking it. Equally few people, however, would seem to believe that all animal life has the same value. Certainly, the lives of dogs, cats, and chimps are very widely held to be more valuable than the lives of mice, rats, and worms, and the legal protections we accord these different creatures, for example, reflect this fact. Finally, whatever value we take the lives of dogs and cats to have, most of us believe human life to be more valuable than animal life. We believe this, moreover, even as we oppose cruelty to animals and acknowledge value—in the case of some animals, considerable value—to their lives. I shall call this claim about the comparative value of human and animal life the unequal value thesis. A crucial question, obviously, is whether we who hold this thesis can defend it.

Many "animal rightists" themselves seem inclined to accept something like the unequal value thesis. With respect to the oft-cited raft example, in which one can save a man or a dog but not both, animal rightists often concede that, other things being equal, one ought to save the man. To be sure, this result only says something about our intuitions and about those *in extremis*; yet, what it is ordinarily taken to say about them—that we take human life to be more valuable than animal life—is not something we think in extreme circumstances only. Our intuitions about the greater value of human life seem apparent in and affect all our relations with animals, from the differences in the ways we regard, treat, and even bury humans and animals to the differences in the safeguards for their protection that we construct and the differences in penalties we exact for violation of those safeguards.

In a word, the unequal value thesis seems very much a part of the approach that most of us adopt towards animal issues. We oppose cruelty to animals as well as humans, but this does not lead us to suppose that the lives of humans and animals have the same value. Nor is there any entailment in the matter: one can perfectly consistently oppose cruelty to all sentient creatures without having to suppose that the lives of all such creatures are equally valuable.

We might note in passing that if this is right about our intuitions, then it is far from clear that it is the defender of the unequal value thesis who must assume the burden of proof in the present discussion. Our intuitions about pain and suffering are such that if a theorist today suggested that animal suffering did not count morally, then he would quickly find himself on the defensive. If I am right about our intuitions over the comparative value of human and animal life, why is the same not true in the case of the theorist who urges or assumes that these lives are of equal value? If, over suffering, our intuitions force the exclusion of the pains of animals to be defended, why, over the value of life, do they not force an *equal* value thesis to be defended?

Where pain and suffering are the central issue, most of us tend to think of the human and animal cases in the same way; thus, cruelty to a child and cruelty to a dog are wrong and wrong for the same reason. Pain is pain; it is an evil, and the evidence suggests that it is as much an evil for dogs as for humans. Furthermore, autonomy or agency (or the lack thereof) does not seem a relevant factor here, since the pains of non-autonomous creatures count as well as the pains of autonomous ones. Neither the child nor the dog is autonomous, at least in any sense that captures why autonomy is such an immensely important value; but the pains of both child and dog count and affect our judgments of rightness and wrongness with respect to what is done to them.

Where the value of life is the central issue, however, we do not tend to think of the human and animal cases alike. Here, we come down in favor of humans, as when we regularly experiment upon and kill animals in our laboratories for (typically) human benefit; and a main justification reflective people give for according humans such advantage invokes directly a difference in value between human and animal life. Autonomy or agency is now, moreover, of the utmost significance, since the exercise of autonomy by normal adult humans is one of the central ways they make possible further, important dimensions of value to their lives.

Arguably, even the extended justification of animal suffering in, say, medical research may make indirect appeal to the unequal value thesis. Though pain remains an evil, the nature and size of some benefit determine whether its infliction is justified in the particular cases. Nothing precludes this benefit from accruing to human beings, and when it does, we need an independent defence of the appeal to benefit in this kind of case. For the appeal is typically invoked in cases where those who suffer are those who benefit, as when we go to the dentist, and in the present instance human beings are the beneficiaries of animal suffering. Possibly the unequal value thesis can provide the requisite defence: what justifies the infliction of pain, if anything does, is the appeal to benefit; but what justifies use of the appeal in those cases where humans are the beneficiaries of animal suffering is, arguably, that human life is more valuable than animal life. Thus, while the unequal value thesis cannot alter the character of pain, which remains an evil, and cannot directly, independently of benefit, justify the infliction of pain, it can, the suggestion is, anchor a particular use of the appeal to benefit.

More broadly, I think a presumption, not in favor of, but against the use of animals in medical/scientific research would be desirable. Its intended effect would be to force researchers as a matter of routine to argue in depth a case for animal use. Such a presumption coheres with my earlier remarks. The unequal value thesis in no way compels its adherents to deny that animal lives have value; the destruction or impairment of such lives, therefore, needs to be argued for, which a presumption against use of animals would force researchers to do.

Clearly, a presumption against use is not the same thing as a bar; I allow, therefore, that researchers can make a case. That they must do so, that they must seek to justify the destruction or impairment of lives that have value, is the point.

II.

How might we defend the unequal value thesis? At least the beginnings of what I take to be the most promising option in this regard can be briefly sketched.

Pain is one thing, killing is another, and what makes killing wrong—a killing could be free of pain and suffering—seems to be the fact that it consists in the destruction of something of value. That is, killing and the value of life seem straightforwardly connected, since it is difficult to understand why taking a particular life would be wrong if it had no value. If few people consider animal life to be without value, equally few, I think, consider it to have the same value as normal (adult) human life. They need not be speciesists as a result: in my view, normal (adult) human life is of a much higher quality than animal life, not because of species, but because of richness; and the value of a life is a function of its quality.

Part of the richness of our lives involves activities that we have in common with animals but there are as well whole dimensions to our lives— love, marriage, educating children, jobs, hobbies, sporting events, cultural pursuits, intellectual development and striving, etc.—that greatly expand our range of absorbing endeavors and so significantly deepen the texture of our lives. An impoverished life for *us* need not be one in which food or sex or liberty is absent; it can equally well be a life in which these other dimensions have not taken root or have done so only minimally. When we look back over our lives and regret that we did not make more of them, we rarely have in mind only the kinds of activities that we share with animals; rather, we think much more in terms of precisely these other dimensions of our lives that equally go to make up a rich, full life.

The lives of normal (adult) humans betray a variety and richness that the lives of rabbits do not; certainly, we do not think of ourselves as constrained to live out our lives according to some (conception of a) life deemed appropriate to our species. Other conceptions of a life for ourselves are within our reach, and we can try to understand and appreciate them and to choose among them. Some of us are artists, others educators, still others mechanics; the richness of our lives is easily enhanced through developing and molding our talents so as to enable us to live out these conceptions of the good life. Importantly, also, we are not condemned to embrace in our lifetimes only a single conception of such a life; in the sense intended, the artist can choose to become an educator and the educator a mechanic. We can embrace at different times different conceptions of how we want to live.

Choosing among conceptions of the good life and trying to live out such a conception are not so intellectualized a set of tasks that only an elite few can manage them. Some reflection upon the life one wants to live is necessary, and some reflection is required in order to organize one's life to live out such a conception; but virtually all of us manage to engage in this degree of reflection. (One of the tragic aspects of Alzheimer's disease is how it undoes a person in just this regard, once it has reached advanced stages.) Even an uneducated man can see the choice between the army and professional boxing as one that requires him to sit down and ponder what he wants to do, whether he has the talents to do it, and what his other, perhaps conflicting desires come to in strength. Even an habitual street person, if free long enough from the influence of drink or drugs to be capable of addressing himself to the choice, can see the life the Salvation Army holds out before him as different in certain respects, some appealing, others perhaps not, from his present life. Choosing how one will live one's life can often be a matter of simply focussing upon these particulars and trying to gauge one's desires with respect to them.

Now, in the case of the rabbit the point is not that the activities which enrich an adult human's life are different from those which enrich its life; it is that the scope or potentiality for enrichment is truncated or severely diminished in the rabbit's case. The quality of a life is a function of its richness, which is a function of its scope or potentiality for enrichment; the scope or potentiality for enrichment in the rabbit's case never approaches that of the human. Nothing we have ever observed about rabbits, nothing we know of them, leads us to make judgments about the variety and richness of their life in anything even remotely comparable to the judgments we make in the human case. To assume as present in the rabbit's life dimensions that supply the full variety and richness of ours, only that these dimensions are hidden from us, provides no real answer, especially when the evidence we have about their lives runs in the other direction.

Autonomy is an important part of the human case. By exercising our autonomy we can mold our lives to fit a conception of the good life that we have decided upon for ourselves; we can then try to live out this conception, with all the sense of achievement, self-fulfillment, and satisfaction that this can bring. Some of us pursue athletic or cultural or intellectual endeavors; some of us are good with our hands and enjoy mechanical tasks and manual labor; and all of us see a job—be it the one we have or the one we should like to have—as an important part of a full life. (This is why unemployment affects more than just our incomes.) The emphasis is upon agency: we can *make* ourselves into repairmen, pianists, and accountants; by exercising our autonomy, we can *impose* upon our lives a conception of the good life that we have for the moment embraced. We can then try to live out this conception, with the consequent sense of fulfillment and achievement that this makes possible. Even failure can be part of the picture: a woman can try to make herself into an Olympic athlete and fail; but her efforts to develop and shape her talents and to take control of and to mold her life in the appropriate ways can enrich her life. Thus, by exercising our autonomy and trying to live out some conception of how we want to live, we make possible further, important dimensions of value to our lives.

We still share certain activities with rabbits, but no mere record of those activities would come anywhere near accounting for the richness of our lives. What is missing in the rabbit's case is the same scope or potentiality for enrichment; and lives of less richness have less value.

The kind of story that would have to be told to make us think that the rabbit's life *was* as rich as the life of a normal (adult) human is one that either postulates in the rabbit potentialities and abilities vastly beyond what we observe and take it to have, or lapses into a rigorous scepticism. By the latter, I mean that we should have to say either that we know nothing of the rabbit's life (and so can know nothing of that life's richness and quality) or that what we know can never be construed as adequate for grounding judgments about the rabbit's quality of life. But the real puzzle is how this recourse to scepticism is supposed to make us think that a rabbit's life is as varied and rich as a human's life. If I can know nothing of the rabbit's life, presumably because I do not live that life and so cannot experience it from the inside, then how do I know that the rabbit's life is as rich as a human's life? Plainly, if I cannot know this, I must for the argument's

sake assume it. But why should I do this? Nothing I observe and experience leads me to assume it; all the evidence I have about rabbits and
humans seems to run entirely in the opposite direction. So, why make this
assumption? Most especially, why assume animal lives are as rich as human
lives, when we do not even assume, or so I suggest below, that all *human*
lives have the same richness?

III.

Agency matters to the value of a life, and animals are not agents. Thus, we
require some argument to show that their lack of agency notwithstanding,
animals have lives of roughly equal richness and value to the lives of normal
(adult) humans. The view that they are members of the moral community
will not supply it, the demand is compatible with acknowledging that not
all life has the same value; and as we shall see, the argument from the value
of the lives of defective humans will not supply it. Any *assumption* that they
have lives of equal richness and value to ours seems to run up against, quite
apart from the evidence we take ourselves to have about the lives of animals,
the fact that, as we shall see, not all human lives have the same richness and
value.

Most importantly, it will not do to claim that the rabbit's life is as valuable as the normal (adult) human's life because it is the only life each has.
This claim does not as yet say that the rabbit's life has any particular value.
If the rabbit and man are dead, they have no life which they can carry on
living, at some quality or other; but this *per se* does not show that the lives
of the man and the rabbit have a particular value as such, let alone that
they have the same value. Put differently, both creatures must be alive in
order to have a quality of life, but nothing at all in this shows that they
have the same richness and quality of life and, therefore, value of life I am
not disputing that animals can have *a* quality of life and that their lives, as
a result, can have value; I am disputing that the richness, quality, and value
of their lives is that of normal (adult) humans.

IV.

Not all members of the moral community have lives of equal value. Human
life is more valuable than animal life. That is our intuition, and as I have
assumed, we must defend it. How we defend it is, however, a vitally

important affair. For I take the charge of speciesism—the attempt to justify either different treatment or the attribution of a different value of life by appeal to species membership—very seriously. In my view, if a defence of the unequal value thesis is open to that charge, then it is no defence at all.

As a result, one's options for grounding the unequal value thesis become limited; no ground will suffice that appeals, either in whole or in part, to species membership. Certainly, some ways of trying to differentiate the value of human from animal life in the past seem pretty clearly to be speciesist. But not all ways are; the important option set out above—one that construes the value of a life as a function of its quality, its quality as a function of its richness, and its richness as a function of its capacity of enrichment—does not use species membership to determine the value of lives. Indeed, it quite explicitly allows for the possibility that some animal life may be more valuable than some human life.

To see this, we have only to realize that the claim that not all members of the moral community have lives of equal value encompasses not only animals but also some humans. Some human lives have less value than others. An infant born without a brain, or any very severely handicapped infant, seems a case in point, as does an elderly person fully in the grip of Alzheimer's disease or some highly degenerative brain, nervous, or physi-ological disorder. In other words, I think we are compelled to admit that some human life is of a much lower quality and so value than normal (adult) human life. (This is true as well of infants generally, though read-ers may think in their unlike the cases of seriously defective infants and adults, some argument from potentiality may be adduced to place them in a separate category. The fact remains, however, that the lives of normal (adult) humans betray a variety and richness that the lives of animals, defective humans, and infants do not.)

Accordingly, we must understand the unequal value thesis to claim that normal (adult) human life is more valuable than animal life. If we justify this claim by appeal to the quality and richness of normal (adult) human life and if we at the same time acknowledge that some human life is of a much lower quality and value than normal (adult) human life, then it seems quite clear that we are not using species membership to determine the value of a life.

Moreover, because some human lives fall drastically below the quality of life of normal (adult) human life, we must face the prospect that the lives of some perfectly healthy animals have a higher quality and greater value than the lives of some humans. And we must face this prospect, with all the implications it may have for the use of these unfortunate humans by others, at least if we continue to justify the use of animals in medical/scientific research by appeal to the lower quality and value of their lives.

What justifies the medical/scientific use of perfectly healthy rabbits instead of humans with a low quality of life? If, for example, experiments on retinas are suggested, why use rabbits or chimps instead of defective humans with otherwise excellent retinas? 1 know of nothing that cedes human life of any quality, however low, greater value than animal life of any quality, however high. If, therefore, we are going to justify medical/scientific uses of animals by appeal to the value of their lives, we open up directly the possibility of our having to envisage die use of humans of a lower quality of life in preference to animals of a higher quality of life. It is important to bear in mind as well that other factors then come under consideration, such as (i) the nature and size of benefit to be achieved, (ii) the side-effects that any decision to use humans in preference to animals may evoke, (iii) the degree to which education and explanation can dissipate any such negative side-effects, and (iv) the projected reliability of animal results for the human case (as opposed to the projected reliability of human results for the human case). All these things may, in the particular case, work in favor of the use of humans.

The point, of course, is not that we *must* use humans; it is that we cannot invariably use animals in preference to humans, if appeal to the quality and value of lives is the ground we give for using animals. The only way we could justifiably do this is if we could cite something that always, no matter what, cedes human life greater value than animal life. I know of no such thing.

Always in the background, of course, are the benefits that medical/scientific research confers: if we desire to continue to obtain these benefits, are we prepared to pay the price of the use of defective humans? The answer, 1 think, must be positive, at least until the time comes when we no longer have to use either humans or animals for research purposes. Obviously, this deliberate use of some of the weakest members of our society is distasteful to contemplate and is not something, in the absence of substantial benefit, that we could condone; yet, we presently condone the use of perfectly healthy animals on an absolutely massive scale, and benefit is the justification we employ.

I remain a vivisectionist, therefore, because of the benefits medical/scientific research can bestow. Support for vivisection, however, exacts a cost: it forces us to envisage the use of defective humans in such research. Paradoxically, then, to the extent that one cannot bring oneself to envisage and consent to their use, to that extent, in my view, the case for anti-vivisectionism becomes stronger.

V.

The fact that not even all human life has the same value explains why some argument from marginal cases, one of the most common arguments in support of an equal value thesis, comes unstuck. Such an argument would only be possible if human life of a much lower quality were ceded equal value with normal (adult) human life. In that case, the same concession could be requested for animal life, and an argument from marginal or defective humans could get underway. On the account of the value of a life set out above, however, the initial concession is not made; it is not true that defective human life has the same quality and value as normal (adult) human life. Nor is this result unfamiliar to us today; it is widely employed in much theoretical and practical work in medical ethics.

This leaves the argument from marginal cases to try to force the admission of the equal value of human and animal life. Tom Regan has long relied upon this argument in a recent article Regan wonders what could be the basis for the view that human life is more valuable than animal life and moves at once to invoke the argument from marginal cases to dispel any such possibility:

> What could be the basis of our having more inherent value than animals? Their lack of reason, or autonomy, or intellect? Only if we are willing to make the same judgment in the case of humans who are similarly deficient. But it is not true that some humans—the retarded child, for example, or the mentally deranged—have less inherent value than you or I.[1]

Regan provides no argument for this claim (and, for that matter, no analysis of "inherent value"), but it seems at least to involve, if not to depend upon, our agreeing that human life of any quality, however low, has the same value as normal (adult) human life. I can see no reason whatever to accept this. Some human lives are so very deficient in quality that we

---

1 Tom Regan, "The Case for Animal Rights," in Peter Singer (ed.), *In Defence of Animals* (Oxford: Basil Blackwell, 1985), p. 23. This article mirrors some central claims of Regan's book of the same name.

would not wish those lives upon anyone, and there are few lengths to which we would not go in order to avoid such lives for ourselves and our loved ones. I can see little point in pretending that lives which we would do everything we could to avoid are of equal value to those normal (adult) human lives that we are presently living.

So far as I can see, the quality of some lives can plummet so disastrously that those lives can cease to have much value at all, can cease to be lives, that is, that are any longer worth living. I acknowledge the difficulty in determining in many cases when a life is no longer worth living; in other cases, however, such as an elderly person completely undone by Alzheimer's disease or an infant born with no or only half a brain, the matter seems far less problematic.

VI.

Is an involved defence of the unequal value thesis, however, really necessary? Is there not a much more direct and uncomplicated defence readily to hand? I have space for only a few words on several possibilities in this regard.

The defence of the unequal value thesis that I have begun to sketch, whether in its positive or negative aspect, does not make reference to religion; yet, it is true that certain religious beliefs seem to favor the thesis. The doctrine of the sanctity of life has normally been held with respect to human life alone; the belief in human dominion over the rest of creation has traditionally been held to set humans apart; and the belief that humans but not animals are possessed of an immortal soul seems plainly to allude to a further dimension of significance to human life. I am not myself religious, however, and I do not adopt a religious approach to questions about the value of lives. Any such approach would seem to tie one's defence of the unequal value thesis to the adequacy of one's theological views, something which a non-religious person can scarcely endorse. I seek a defence of the unequal value thesis, whatever the status of God's existence or the adequacy of this or that religion or religious doctrine. I do not prejudge the issue of whether a religious person can accept a quality-of-life defence of the sort I have favored; my point is simply that that defence does not rely upon theological premises.

It may be asked, however, why we need anything quite so sophisticated as a *defence* of the unequal value thesis at all. Why can we not just express a preference for our own kind and be done with the matter? After all, when a father gives a kidney to save his daughter's life, we perfectly well understand why he did not choose to give die kidney to a stranger *in preference to* his daughter. This "natural bias" we do not condemn and do not take to point to a moral defect in the father. Why, therefore, is not something similar possible in the case of our interaction with animals? Why, that is, can we not appeal to a natural bias in favor of members of our own species? There are a number of things that can be said in response, only several of which I shall notice here.

There is the problem, if one takes the charge of speciesism seriously, of how to articulate this bias in favor of members of our species in such a way as to avoid that charge. Then there is the problem of how to articulate this preference for our own kind in such a way as to exclude interpretations of "our own kind" that express preferences for one's own race, gender, or religion. Otherwise, one is going to let such preferences do considerable work in one's moral decision-making. I do not wish to foreclose all possibilities in these two cases, however; it may well be that a preference for our own kind *can* be articulated in a way that avoids these and some other problems.

Even so, I believe that there is another and deeper level of problem that this preference for our own kind encounters. On the one hand, we can understand the preference to express a bond we feel with members of our own species *over and above* the bond that we (or most of us) feel with ("higher") animals. Such a bond, if it exists, poses no direct problem, if its existence is being used to explain, for example, instances of behavior where we obviously exhibit sympathy for human beings. (We must be careful not to *under-value* the sympathy most people exhibit towards animals, especially domesticated ones.) On the other hand, we can understand this preference for our own kind to express the claim that we stand in a special moral relationship to members of our own species. This claim does pose a problem, since, if we systematically favor humans over animals on the basis of it, it does considerable moral work, work, obviously, that would not be done if the claim were rejected.

I cannot see that species membership is a ground for holding that we stand in a special moral relationship to our fellow humans. The father obviously stands in such a relationship to his daughter, and his decision to marry and to have children is how he comes to have or to stand in that relationship. But how, through merely being born, does one come to stand in a special moral relationship to humans generally? Typically, I can step in and out of special moral relationships; in the case of species membership, that is not true. In that case, so long as I live, nothing can change my relationship to others, so long as they live. If this were true, my morality would to an extent no longer express my view of myself at large in a world filled with other people but would be something foisted upon me simply through being born.

Since we do not choose our species membership, a special moral relationship I am supposed to stand in to humans generally would lie outside my control; whereas it is precisely the voluntary nature of such relationships that seems most central to their character. And it is precisely because of this voluntary nature, of, as it were, our ability to take on and shed such relationships, that these relationships can be read as expressing *my* view of myself at large in a world filled with other people.

We often do stand in special moral relationships to others; but mere species membership would have us stand in such a relationship to all others. There is something too sweeping about this, as if birth alone can give the rest of human creation a moral hold over me. In a real sense, such a view would sever me from my morality; for my morality would no longer consist in expressions of how I see myself interacting with others and how I choose to interact with them. My own choices and decisions have no effect upon species membership and so on a moral relationship that I am supposed to stand in to each and every living, human being. Such a view is at odds not only with how we typically understand special moral relationships but also with how we typically understand our relationship to our own morality.

VII.

It may well be tempting, I suppose, to try to develop another sense of "speciesism" and to hold that a position such as mine is speciesist in that sense. I have space here for only a few comments on one such sense.

If to be a *direct* speciesist is to discriminate among the value of lives solely on the basis of species membership, as it is, for example, for Peter Singer, then I am not, as I have tried to show, a direct speciesist. But am I not, it might be suggested, an *indirect* speciesist, in that, in order to determine the quality and value of a life, I use human-centred criteria as if they were appropriate for assessing the quality and value of all life? Thus, for instance, when

I emphasize cultural and artistic endeavors, when I emphasize autonomy and mental development and achievement, when I emphasize making choices, directing one's life, and selecting and living out conceptions of the good life, the effect is to widen the gulf between animals and humans by using human-centred criteria for assessing the quality and value of a life as if they were appropriate to appreciating the quality and value of animal life. And this will not do; for it amounts to trying to judge animals and animal lives by human standards. What one should do, presumably, is to judge the quality and value of animal life by criteria appropriate to each separate species of animals.

I stress again that the argument of this paper is not about whether rabbits have lives of value (I think that they do) but rather about whether they have lives of equal value to normal (adult) human life. It is unclear to me how the charge of indirect speciesism addresses this argument.

We must distinguish this charge of an indirect speciesism from the claim, noted earlier, that we can know nothing of animal lives and so nothing about their quality and value; indeed, the two claims may conflict. The point behind the speciesism charge is that I am not using criteria appropriate to a species of animal for assessing its quality of life, which presumably means that there *are* appropriate criteria available for selection. Knowledge of appropriate criteria seems to require that we know something of an animal's life, in order to make the judgment of appropriateness. Yet, the whole point behind the lack of knowledge claim is that we can know nothing of an animal's life, nothing of how it experiences the world, nothing, in essence, about how well or how badly its life is going. It would seem, therefore, as if the two views can conflict.

The crucial thing here about both claims, however, is this: both are advanced against my defence of the unequal value thesis and on behalf of the equality of value of human and animal life without it being in any wise clear how they show this equality.

The ignorance claim would seem to have it that, because we can know nothing of the animal case, we must assume that animal and human life have the same value. But why should we fall in with this assumption? The ignorance claim would have us start from the idea, presumably, that all life, irrespective of its level of development and complexity, has the same value; but why should be start from that particular idea? Surely there must be some reason for thinking all life whatever has the same value. It is this reason that needs to be stated and assessed.

The indirect speciesist claim would seem to have it that, were we only to select criteria for assessing the quality and value of life appropriate to animals' species, we must agree that animal and human life are of equal value. The temptation is to inquire after what these criteria might be in rabbits, but any such concern must be firmly understood in the light of the earlier discussion of the richness of our lives. What the unequal value thesis represents is our quest to gain some understanding of (i) the capacities of animals and humans, (ii) the differences among these various capacities, (iii) the complexity of lives, (iv) the role of agency in this complexity, and (v) the way agency enables humans to add further dimensions of value to their lives. The richness of our lives encompasses these multi-faceted aspects of our being and is a function of them. The point is not that a rabbit may not have a keener sense of smell than we do and may not derive intense, pleasurable sensations through that sense of smell; it is that we have to believe that something like this, augmented, perhaps, by other things we might say in the rabbit's case of like kind, suffices to make the rabbit's life as rich and as full as ours. If one thinks of our various capacities and of the different levels on which they operate, physical, mental, emotional, imaginative, then pointing out that rabbits can have as pleasurable sensations as we do in certain regards does not meet the point.

When we say of a woman that she has "tasted life to the full," we do not make a point about (or solely about) pleasurable sensations; we refer to the different dimensions of our being and to the woman's attempt to develop these in herself and to actualize them in the course of her daily life. And an important aspect in all this is what agency means to the woman: in the sense intended, she is not condemned to live the life that all of her ancestors have lived; she can mold and shape her life to "fit" her own conception of how she should live, thereby enabling her to add further dimensions of value to her life. It is this diversity and complexity in us that needs to be made good in the rabbit's case and that no mere catalogue of its pleasures through the sense of smell seems likely to accomplish.

Again, it is not that the rabbit cannot do things that we are unable to do and not that it has capacities which we lack; what has to be shown is how this sort of thing, given how rabbits behave and live out their days, so enriches their lives that the quality and value of them approach those of humans. And what *is* one going to say in the rabbits case that makes good the role agency plays in ours? The absence of agency from a human life is a terrible thing; it deeply impoverishes a life and forestalls completely one's making one's life into the life one wants to live. Yet, this must be the natural condition of rabbits. It is this gulf that agency creates, the gulf between living out the life appropriate to one's species and living out a life one has chosen for oneself and has molded and shaped accordingly, that is one of the things that it is difficult to understand what rabbits can do to overcome.

VIII.

In sum, I think the unequal value thesis is defensible and can be defended even as its adherent takes seriously the charge of speciesism. And it is the unequal value thesis that figures centrally in the justification of our use of animals in medical and scientific research. If as I have done here, we assume that the thesis must be defended, then the character of that defence, I think, requires that *if* we are to continue to use animals for research purposes, then we must begin to envisage the use of some humans for those same purposes. The cost of holding the unequal value thesis, and most of us, I suggest, do hold it, is to realize that, upon a quality-of-life defence of it, it encompasses the lives of some humans as well as animals. I cannot at the moment see that any other defence of it both meets the charge of speciesism and yet does indeed amount to a defence.

R.G. Frey: Moral Standing, the Value of Lives, and Speciesism

1. Explain Frey's unequal value thesis. What implications does it have for how we should treat nonhuman animals? What implications does it have for how we should treat other humans? Do you think any of these implications are problematic? Why or why not?
2. What, according to Frey, makes a life valuable? What reasons does he give in support of his account? Do you find the account plausible? Support your answer.
3. Explain the distinction between direct speciesism and indirect speciesism. Why might direct speciesist views be problematic? Why might indirect speciesist views be problematic? Does Frey's view qualify as one or the other? Why or why not?
4. According to Frey, what makes a being worthy of moral consideration? Which (if any) animals are members of the moral community? In

virtue of what are animals' lives more or less valuable than humans' lives? Do you agree with Frey's criteria? Why or why not?

5. Frey refers to himself as a "restricted vivisectionist." Explain what he means by this. Under what conditions does he think that animal experimentation is morally permissible? Under what conditions does he think that human experimentation is morally permissible? Do you think there is a relevant difference between the two that Frey has failed to appreciate? Explain your answer.

28

===== ❧ =====

The Ethics of Respect for Nature
Paul Taylor

....

Paul Taylor argues against the anthropocentric view that human interests, and the human perspective generally, are morally superior to all others. Instead, Taylor encourages us to take what he calls "an attitude of respect for nature," in which we regard all elements of nature as possessed of as much inherent worth as all others. He develops a "life-centered ethic" that assigns importance to the well-being of every living thing, regardless of whether it is rational, able to suffer, or even conscious. That something is alive, or is (like the biosphere or specific ecosystems) composed of living things, is enough to grant it moral importance.

Taylor proceeds to identify the four essential claims that make up a *biocentric* (i.e., life-centered) outlook on nature: (1) humans are members of the Earth's community of life; (2) the Earth's natural ecosystems are a complex web of interconnected environments; (3) each individual living thing has a good of its own; (4) the assertion of greater human merit or inherent worth is nothing but irrational bias. The remainder of the article is devoted to a discussion of each of these four elements. The last claim, (4), receives the most attention.

Human beings have long thought of themselves as more important than members of any other species. But what could justify this attitude? We have rationality and autonomy—they don't. But cheetahs have speed that we lack; birds can fly; eagles can see things we can't. Why think of our special traits as more important than theirs? Taylor

---

Paul Taylor, "The Ethics of Respect for Nature" from *Environmental Ethics*, 3 (1981): 197–201, 211–218.

says that there is no good answer to this question. From our perspective, we are likely to give more value to the features that we alone possess. But there is no neutral reason to assign our perspective any more importance than any other—to argue otherwise is already to assume the superiority of humanity. Taylor concludes by sketching some of the significant implications of taking up the life-centered ethic.

....

Human-Centered and Life-Centered Systems of Environmental Ethics

In this paper I show how the taking of a certain ultimate moral attitude toward nature, which I call "respect for nature," has a central place in the foundations of a life-centered system of environmental ethics. I hold that a set of moral norms (both standards of character and rules of conduct) governing human treatment of the natural world is a rationally grounded set if and only if, first, commitment to those norms is a practical entailment of adopting the attitude of respect for nature as an ultimate moral attitude, and second, the adopting of that attitude on the part of all rational agents can itself be justified. . . .

In designating the theory to be set forth as life-centered, I intend to contrast it with all anthropocentric views. According to the latter, human actions affecting the natural environment and its nonhuman inhabitants are right (or wrong) by either of two criteria: they have consequences which are favorable (or unfavorable) to human well-being, or they are consistent (or inconsistent) with the system of norms that protects and implements human rights. From this human-centered standpoint it is to humans and only to humans that all duties are ultimately owed. We may have responsibilities *with regard to* the natural ecosystems and biotic communities of our planet, but these responsibilities are in every case based on the contingent fact that our treatment of those ecosystems and communities of life can further the realization of human values and/or human rights. We have no obligation to promote or protect the good of nonhuman living things, independently of this contingent fact.

A life-centered system of environmental ethics is opposed to human-centered ones precisely on this point. From the perspective of a life-centered theory, we have prima facie moral obligations that are owed to wild plants and animals themselves as members of the Earth's biotic community. We are morally bound (other things being equal) to protect or promote their good for *their* sake. . . .

The Good of a Being and the Concept of Inherent Worth

What would justify acceptance of a life-centered system of ethical principles? In order to answer this it is first necessary to make clear the fundamental moral attitude that underlies and makes intelligible the commitment to live by such a system. It is then necessary to examine the considerations that would justify any rational agent's adopting that moral attitude.

Two concepts are essential to the taking of a moral attitude of the sort in question. . . . These concepts are, first, that of the good (well-being, welfare) of a living thing, and second, the idea of an entity possessing inherent worth. I examine each concept in turn.

(1) Every organism, species population, and community of life has a good of its own which moral agents can intentionally further or damage by their actions. To say that an entity has a good of its own is simply to say that, without reference to any *other* entity, it can be benefited or harmed. . . . We can think of the good of an individual nonhuman organism as consisting in the full development of its biological powers. Its good is realized to the extent that it is strong and healthy. . . .

The idea of a being having a good of its own, as I understand it, does not entail that the being must have interests or take an interest in what affects its life for better or for worse. We can act in a being's interest or contrary to its interest without its being interested in what we are doing to it in the sense of wanting or not wanting us to do it. It may, indeed, be wholly unaware that favorable and unfavorable events are taking place in its life. I take it that trees, for example, have no knowledge or desires or feelings. Yet it is undoubtedly the case that trees can be harmed or benefited by our actions. . . .

(2) The second concept essential to the moral attitude of respect for nature is the idea of inherent worth. We take that attitude toward wild living things (individuals, species populations, or whole biotic communities) when and only when we regard them as entities possessing inherent worth. Indeed, it is only because they are conceived in this way that moral agents can think of themselves as having validly binding duties, obligations, and responsibilities that are *owed* to them as their *due*. I am not at this juncture

arguing why they *should* be so regarded; I consider it at length below. But so regarding them is a presupposition of our taking the attitude of respect toward them and accordingly understanding ourselves as bearing certain moral relations to them. This can be shown as follows:

What does it mean to regard an entity that has a good of its own as possessing inherent worth? Two general principles are involved: the principle of moral consideration and the principle of intrinsic value.

According to the principle of moral consideration, wild living things are deserving of the concern and consideration of all moral agents simply in virtue of their being members of the Earth's community of life. From the moral point of view their good must be taken into account whenever it is affected for better or worse by the conduct of rational agents. This holds no matter what species the creature belongs to. The good of each is to be accorded some value and so acknowledged as having some weight in the deliberations of all rational agents. Of course, it may be necessary for such agents to act in ways contrary to the good of this or that particular organism or group of organisms in order to further the good of others, including the good of humans. But the principle of moral consideration prescribes that, with respect to each being an entity having its own good, every individual is deserving of consideration.

The principle of intrinsic value states that, regardless of what kind of entity it is in other respects, if it is a member of the Earth's community of life, the realization of its good is something *intrinsically* valuable. This means that its good is prima facie worthy of being preserved or promoted as an end in itself and for the sake of the entity whose good it is. Insofar as we regard any organism, species population, or life community as an entity having inherent worth, we believe that it must never be treated as if it were a mere object or thing whose entire value lies in being instrumental to the good of some other entity. The well-being of each is judged to have value in and of itself.

Combining these two principles, we can now define what it means for a living thing or group of living things to possess inherent worth. To say that it possesses inherent worth is to say that its good is deserving of the concern and consideration of all moral agents, and that the realization of its good has intrinsic value, to be pursued as an end in itself and for the sake of the entity whose good it is.

The duties owed to wild organisms, species populations, and communities of life in the Earth's natural ecosystems are grounded on their inherent worth. When rational, autonomous agents regard such entities as possessing inherent worth, they place intrinsic value on the realization of their good and so hold themselves responsible for performing actions that will have this effect and for refraining from actions having the contrary effect. . . .

The Biocentric Outlook on Nature

The biocentric outlook on nature has four main components. (1) Humans are thought of as members of the Earth's community of life, holding that membership on the same terms as apply to all the nonhuman members. (2) The Earth's natural ecosystems as a totality are seen as a complex web of interconnected elements, with the sound biological functioning of each being dependent on the sound biological functioning of the others. (This is the component referred to above as the great lesson that the science of ecology has taught us.) (3) Each individual organism is conceived of as a teleological center of life, pursuing its own good in its own way. (4) Whether we are concerned with standards of merit or with the concept of inherent worth, the claim that humans by their very nature are superior to other species is a groundless claim and, in the light of elements (1), (2), and (3) above, must be rejected as nothing more than an irrational bias in our own favor. . . .

The Denial of Human Superiority

This fourth component of the biocentric outlook on nature is the single most important idea in establishing the justifiability of the attitude of respect for nature. Its central role is due to the special relationship it bears to the first three components of the outlook. This relationship will be brought out after the concept of human superiority is examined and analyzed.

In what sense are humans alleged to be superior to other animals? We are different from them in having certain capacities that they lack. But why should these capacities be a mark of superiority? From what point of view are they judged to be signs of superiority and what sense of superiority is meant? After all, various nonhuman species have capacities that humans lack. There is the speed of a cheetah, the vision of an eagle, the agility of a monkey. Why should not these be taken as signs of *their* superiority over humans?

One answer that comes immediately to mind is that these capacities are not as *valuable* as the human capacities that are claimed to make us superior. Such uniquely human characteristics as rational thought, aesthetic creativity, autonomy and self-determination, and moral freedom, it might be held, have a higher value than the capacities found in other species. Yet we must ask: valuable to whom, and on what grounds?

The human characteristics mentioned are all valuable to humans. They are essential to the preservation and enrichment of our civilization and culture. Clearly it is from the human standpoint that they are being judged to be desirable and good. It is not difficult here to recognize a begging of the question. Humans are claiming human superiority from a strictly human point of view, that is, from a point of view in which the good of humans is taken as the standard of judgment. All we need to do is to look at the capacities of nonhuman animals (or plants, for that matter) from the standpoint of *their* good to find a contrary judgment of superiority. The speed of the cheetah, for example, is a sign of its superiority to humans when considered from the standpoint of the good of its species. If it were as slow a runner as a human, it would not be able to survive. And so for all the other abilities of nonhumans which further their good but which are lacking in humans. In each case the claim to human superiority would be rejected from a nonhuman standpoint.

When superiority assertions are interpreted in this way, they are based on judgments of *merit*. To judge the merits of a person or an organism one must apply grading or ranking standards to it. (As I show below, this distinguishes judgments of merit from judgments of inherent worth.) Empirical investigation then determines whether it has the "good-making properties" (merits) in virtue of which it fulfills the standards being applied. In the case of humans, merits may be either moral or nonmoral. We can judge one person to be better than (superior to) another from the moral point of view by applying certain standards to their character and conduct. Similarly, we can appeal to nonmoral criteria in judging someone to be an excellent piano player, a fair cook, a poor tennis player, and so on. Different social purposes and roles are implicit in the making of such judgments, providing the frame of reference for the choice of standards by which the nonmoral merits of people are determined. Ultimately such purposes and roles stem from a society's way of life as a whole. Now a society's way of life may be thought of as the cultural form given to the realization of human values. Whether moral or nonmoral standards are being applied, then, all judgments of people's merits finally depend on human values. All are made from an exclusively human standpoint.

The question that naturally arises at this juncture is: why should standards that are based on human values be assumed to be the only valid criteria of merit and hence the only true signs of superiority? This question is especially pressing when humans are being judged superior in merit to nonhumans. It is true that a human being may be a better mathematician than a monkey, but the monkey may be a better tree climber than a human being. If we humans value mathematics more than tree climbing, that is because our conception of civilized life makes the development of mathematical ability more desirable than the ability to climb trees. But is it not unreasonable to judge nonhumans by the values of human civilization, rather than by values connected with what it is for a member of *that* species to live a good life? If all living things have a good of their own, it at least makes sense to judge the merits of nonhumans by standards derived from *their* good. To use only standards based on human values is already to commit oneself to holding that humans are superior to nonhumans, which is the point in question.

A further logical flaw arises in connection with the widely held conviction that humans are *morally* superior beings because they possess, while others lack, the capacities of a moral agent (free will, accountability, deliberation, judgment, practical reason). This view rests on a conceptual confusion. As far as moral standards are concerned, only beings that have the capacities of a moral agent can properly be judged to be *either* moral (morally good) *or* immoral (morally deficient). Moral standards are simply not applicable to beings that lack such capacities. Animals and plants cannot therefore be said to be morally inferior in merit to humans. Since the only beings that can have moral merits *or be deficient in such merits* are moral agents, it is conceptually incoherent to judge humans as superior to nonhumans on the ground that humans have moral capacities while nonhumans don't.

Up to this point I have been interpreting the claim that humans are superior to other living things as a grading or ranking judgment regarding their comparative merits. There is, however, another way of understanding the idea of human superiority. According to this interpretation, humans are superior to nonhumans not as regards their merits but as regards their inherent worth. Thus the claim of human superiority is to be understood as asserting that all humans, simply in virtue of their humanity, have *a greater inherent worth* than other living things.

The inherent worth of an entity does not depend on its merits.[1] To consider something as possessing inherent worth, we have seen, is to place intrinsic value on the realization of its good. This is done regardless of whatever particular merits it might have or might lack, as judged by a set of grading or ranking standards. In human affairs, we are all familiar with the principle that one's worth as a person does not vary with one's merits or lack of merits. The same can hold true of animals and plants. To regard such entities as possessing inherent worth entails disregarding their merits and deficiencies, whether they are being judged from a human standpoint or from the standpoint of their own species.

The idea of one entity having more merit than another, and so being superior to it in merit, makes perfectly good sense. Merit is a grading or ranking concept, and judgments of comparative merit are based on the different degrees to which things satisfy a given standard. But what can it mean to talk about one thing being superior to another in inherent worth?. . .

The vast majority of people in modern democracies . . . do not maintain an egalitarian outlook when it comes to comparing human beings with other living things. Most people consider our own species to be superior to all other species and this superiority is understood to be a matter of inherent worth, not merit. There may exist thoroughly vicious and depraved humans who lack all merit. Yet because they are human they are thought to belong to a higher class of entities than any plant or animal. That one is born into the species *Homo sapiens* entitles one to have lordship over those who are one's inferiors, namely, those born into other species. The parallel with hereditary social classes is very close. Implicit in this view is a hierarchical conception of nature according to which an organism has a position of superiority or inferiority in the Earth's community of life simply on the basis of its genetic background. The "lower" orders of life are looked down upon and it is considered perfectly proper that they serve the interests of those belonging to the highest order, namely humans. The intrinsic value we place on the well-being of our fellow humans reflects our recognition of their rightful position as our equals. No such intrinsic value is to be placed on the good of other animals, unless we choose to do so out of fondness or affection for them. But their well-being imposes no

---

1 For this way of distinguishing between merit and inherent worth, I am indebted to Gregory Vlastos, "Justice and Equality," in R. Brandt, ed., *Social Justice* (Englewood Cliffs, N.J.: Prentice-Hall, 1962), pp. 31–72.

moral requirement on us. In this respect there is an absolute difference in moral status between ourselves and them.

This is the structure of concepts and beliefs that people are committed to insofar as they regard humans to be superior in inherent worth to all other species. I now wish to argue that this structure of concepts and beliefs is completely groundless. If we accept the first three components of the biocentric outlook and from that perspective look at the major philosophical traditions which have supported that structure, we find it to be at bottom nothing more than the expression of an irrational bias in our own favor. The philosophical traditions themselves rest on very questionable assumptions or else simply beg the question. I briefly consider three of the main traditions to substantiate the point. These are classical Greek humanism, Cartesian dualism, and the Judeo-Christian concept of the Great Chain of Being.

The inherent superiority of humans over other species was implicit in the Greek definition of man as a rational animal. Our animal nature was identified with "brute" desires that need the order and restraint of reason to rule them (just as reason is the special virtue of those who rule in the ideal state). Rationality was then seen to be the key to our superiority over animals. It enables us to live on a higher plane and endows us with a nobility and worth that other creatures lack. This familiar way of comparing humans with other species is deeply ingrained in our Western philosophical outlook. The point to consider here is that this view does not actually provide an argument *for* human superiority but rather makes explicit the framework of thought that is implicitly used by those who think of humans as inherently superior to nonhumans. The Greeks who held that humans, in virtue of their rational capacities, have a kind of worth greater than that of any nonrational being, never looked at rationality as but one capacity of living things among many others. But when we consider rationality from the standpoint of the first three elements of the ecological outlook, we see that its value lies in its importance for *human* life. Other creatures achieve their species-specific good without the need of rationality, although they often make use of capacities that humans lack. So the humanistic outlook of classical Greek thought does not give us a neutral (nonquestion-begging) ground on which to construct a scale of degrees of inherent worth possessed by different species of living things.

The second tradition, centering on the Cartesian dualism of soul and body, also fails to justify the claim to human superiority. That superiority is supposed to derive from the fact that we have souls while animals do not. Animals are mere automata and lack the divine element that makes us spiritual beings. I won't go into the now familiar criticisms of this two-substance view. I only add the point that, even if humans are composed of an immaterial, unextended soul and a material, extended body, this in itself is not a reason to deem them of greater worth than entities that are only bodies. Why is a soul substance a thing that adds value to its possessor? Unless some theological reasoning is offered here (which many, including myself, would find unacceptable on epistemological grounds), no logical connection is evident. An immaterial something which thinks is better than a material something which does not think only if thinking itself has value, either intrinsically or instrumentally. Now it is intrinsically valuable to humans alone, who value it as an end in itself, and it is instrumentally valuable to those who benefit from it, namely humans.

For animals that neither enjoy thinking for its own sake nor need it for living the kind of life for which they are best adapted, it has no value. Even if "thinking" is broadened to include all forms of consciousness, there are still many living things that can do without it and yet live what is for their species a good life. The anthropocentricity underlying the claim to human superiority runs throughout Cartesian dualism.

A third major source of the idea of human superiority is the Judeo-Christian concept of the Great Chain of Being. Humans are superior to animals and plants because their Creator has given them a higher place on the chain. It begins with God at the top, and then moves to the angels, who are lower than God but higher than humans, then to humans, positioned between the angels and the beasts (partaking of the nature of both), and then on down to the lower levels occupied by nonhuman animals, plants, and finally inanimate objects. Humans, being "made in God's image," are inherently superior to animals and plants by virtue of their being closer (in their essential nature) to God.

The metaphysical and epistemological difficulties with this conception of a hierarchy of entities are, in my mind, insuperable. Without entering into this matter here, I only point out that if we are unwilling to accept the metaphysics of traditional Judaism and Christianity, we are again left without good reasons for holding to the claim of inherent human superiority.

The foregoing considerations (and others like them) leave us with but one ground for the assertion that a human being, regardless of merit, is a higher kind of entity than any other living thing. This is the mere fact of the genetic makeup of the species *Homo sapiens*. But this is surely irrational and arbitrary. Why should the arrangement of genes of a certain type be a mark of superior value, especially when this fact about an organism is taken by itself, unrelated to any other aspect of its life? We might just as well refer to any other genetic makeup as a ground of superior value. Clearly we are confronted here with a wholly arbitrary claim that can only be explained as an irrational bias in our own favor.

That the claim is nothing more than a deep-seated prejudice is brought home to us when we look at our relation to other species in the light of the first three elements of the biocentric outlook. Those elements taken conjointly give us a certain overall view of the natural world and of the place of humans in it. When we take this view we come to understand other living things, their environmental conditions, and their ecological relationships in such a way as to awake in us a deep sense of our kinship with them as fellow members of the Earth's community of life. Humans and nonhumans alike are viewed together as integral parts of one unified whole in which all living things are functionally interrelated. Finally, when our awareness focuses on the individual lives of plants and animals, each is seen to share with us the characteristic of being a teleological center of life striving to realize its own good in its own unique way.

As this entire belief system becomes part of the conceptual framework through which we understand and perceive the world, we come to see ourselves as bearing a certain moral relation to nonhuman forms of life. Our ethical role in nature takes on a new significance. We begin to look at other species as we look at ourselves, seeing them as beings which have a good they are striving to realize just as we have a good we are striving to realize. We accordingly develop the disposition to view the world from the standpoint of their good as well as from the standpoint of our own good. Now if the groundlessness of the claim that humans are inherently superior to other species were brought clearly before our minds, we would not remain intellectually neutral toward that claim but would reject it as being fundamentally at variance with our total world outlook. In the absence of any good reasons for holding it, the assertion of human superiority would then appear simply as the expression of an irrational and self-serving prejudice that favors one particular species over several million others.

Rejecting the notion of human superiority entails its positive counterpart: the doctrine of species impartiality. One who accepts that doctrine regards all living things as possessing inherent worth—the *same* inherent worth, since no one species has been shown to be either "higher" or "lower" than any other. Now we saw earlier that, insofar as one thinks of a living thing as possessing inherent worth, one considers it to be the appropriate object of the attitude of respect and believes that attitude to be the only fitting or suitable one for all moral agents to take toward it.

Here, then, is the key to understanding how the attitude of respect is rooted in the biocentric outlook of nature. The basic connection is made through the denial of human superiority. Once we reject the claim that humans are superior either in merit or in worth to other living things, we are ready to adopt the attitude of respect. The denial of human superiority is itself the result of taking the perspective on nature built into the first three elements of the biocentric outlook.

Now the first three elements of the biocentric outlook, it seems clear, would be found acceptable to any rational and scientifically informed thinker who is fully "open" to the reality of the lives of nonhuman organisms. Without denying our distinctively human characteristics, such a thinker can acknowledge the fundamental respects in which we are members of the Earth's community of life and in which the biological conditions necessary for the realization of our human values are inextricably linked with the whole system of nature. In addition, the conception of individual living things as teleological centers of life simply articulates how a scientifically informed thinker comes to understand them as the result of increasingly careful and detailed observations. Thus, the biocentric outlook recommends itself as an acceptable system of concepts and beliefs to anyone who is clear-minded, unbiased, and factually enlightened, and who has a developed capacity of reality awareness with regard to the lives of individual organisms. This, I submit, is as good a reason for making the moral commitment involved in adopting the attitude of respect for nature as any theory of environmental ethics could possibly have.

Moral Rights and the Matter of Competing Claims

I have not asserted anywhere in the foregoing account that animals or plants have moral rights. This omission was deliberate. I do not think that the reference class of the concept, bearer of moral rights, should be extended to include nonhuman living things. My reasons for taking this position, however, go beyond the scope of this paper. I believe I have been able to accomplish many of the same ends which those who ascribe rights to animals or plants wish to accomplish. There is no reason, moreover, why plants and animals, including whole species populations and life communities, cannot be accorded *legal* rights under my theory. To grant them legal protection could be interpreted as giving them legal entitlement to be protected, and this, in fact, would be a means by which a society that subscribed to the ethics of respect for nature could give public recognition to their inherent worth.

There remains the problem of competing claims, even when wild plants and animals are not thought of as bearers of moral rights. If we accept the biocentric outlook and accordingly adopt the attitude of respect for nature as our ultimate moral attitude, how do we resolve conflicts that arise from our respect for persons in the domain of human ethics and our respect for nature in the domain of environmental ethics? This is a question that cannot adequately be dealt with here. My main purpose in this paper has been to try to establish a base point from which we can start working toward a solution to the problem. I have shown why we cannot just begin with an initial presumption in favor of the interests of our own species. It is after all within our power as moral beings to place limits on human population and technology with the deliberate intention of sharing the Earth's bounty with other species. That such sharing is an ideal difficult to realize even in an approximate way does not take away its claim to our deepest moral commitment.

Paul Taylor: The Ethics of Respect for Nature

1. In what sense is Taylor's view "life-centered"? How does his view differ from anthropocentric views?
2. What does it mean to say that an entity has "a good of its own"? Which entities does Taylor think have goods of their own? Do you agree with him on this?
3. What is the difference, according to Taylor, between merit and worth? Which does he think is important to determining whether an entity is morally considerable? Do you agree with him?
4. One reason people have given for thinking that humans are morally considerable while animals are not is that only humans are *rational*. How does Taylor respond to this line of argument? Do you find his response persuasive?
5. Taylor claims that the view that humans are morally superior to animals is "an irrational bias in our own favor." How does he argue for this claim? Is his argument a good one?

Ideals of Human Excellence and Preserving Natural Environments

Thomas Hill, Jr.

....

According to Thomas Hill, Jr., the standard moral theories have difficulty explaining what is wrong with the destruction of the environment. Utilitarianism runs into trouble, because it is possible that overall happiness is maximized when cutting down a virgin forest or bulldozing a field to make way for suburban homes. Kantian and rights-based moral theories have just as much trouble here, because it is very difficult to defend the idea that plants or ecosystems—incapable of reasoning, asserting claims, or even feeling anything—are possessed of rights. Contractarian theories are just as vulnerable on this score. If our basic duties are owed only to our fellow members of the social contract, then plants and ecosystems will again be left out in the cold.

These concerns lead Hill to consider an alternative way of understanding our ethical relations with the environment. Rather than focusing on the question of whether we have any duties directly toward the environment, Hill invites us to consider a virtue ethical approach, which places primary emphasis on the sort of person we should try to become. He argues that those who fail to treat the environment with respect are almost certainly going to be less than fully virtuous. They will fail to be admirable in a number of ways, and will exemplify a variety of vices. In particular, those who are indifferent to the value of nature

---

Thomas Hill, Jr., "Ideas of Human Excellence and Preserving Natural Environments" from *Environmental Ethics* 5 (1983), pp. 211–224.

will almost certainly be ignorant and self-important. They will lack proper humility, and will either fail to have a well-developed sense of beauty, or will be insufficiently grateful for the good things in life. Thus even if we can't defend the claim that nature has rights, or that we owe nature anything, there is still excellent reason to respect and preserve natural environments. For if we don't, we will fall short of plausible ideals of human excellence.

....

I

A wealthy eccentric bought a house in a neighborhood I know. The house was surrounded by a beautiful display of grass, plants, and flowers, and it was shaded by a huge old avocado tree. But the grass required cutting, the flowers needed tending, and the man wanted more sun. So he cut the whole lot down and covered the yard with asphalt. After all it was his property and he was not fond of plants.

It was a small operation, but it reminded me of the strip mining of large sections of the Appalachians. In both cases, of course, there were reasons for the destruction, and property rights could be cited as justification. But I could not help but wonder, "What sort of person would do a thing like that?"

Many Californians had a similar reaction when a recent governor defended the leveling of ancient redwood groves, reportedly saying, "If you have seen one redwood, you have seen them all."

Incidents like these arouse the indignation of ardent environmentalists and leave even apolitical observers with some degree of moral discomfort. The reasons for these reactions are mostly obvious. Uprooting the natural environment robs both present and future generations of much potential use and enjoyment. Animals too depend on the environment; and even if one does not value animals for their own sakes, their potential utility for us is incalculable. Plants are needed, of course, to replenish the atmosphere quite aside from their aesthetic value. These reasons for hesitating to destroy forests and gardens are not only the most obvious ones, but also the most persuasive for practical purposes. But, one wonders, is there nothing more behind our discomfort? Are we concerned solely about the potential use and enjoyment of the forests, etc., for ourselves, later generations, and perhaps animals? Is there not something else which disturbs us when we witness the destruction or even listen to those who would defend it in terms of cost/benefit analysis?

Imagine that in each of our examples those who would destroy the environment argue elaborately that, even considering future generations of human beings and animals, there are benefits in "replacing" the natural environment which outweigh the negative utilities which environmentalists cite. No doubt we could press the argument on the facts, trying to show that the destruction is shortsighted and that its defenders have underestimated its potential harm or ignored some pertinent rights or interests. But is this all we could say? Suppose we grant, for a moment, that the utility of destroying the redwoods, forests, and gardens is equal to their potential for use and enjoyment by nature lovers and animals. Suppose, further, that we even grant that the pertinent human rights and animal rights, if any, are evenly divided for and against destruction. Imagine that we also concede, for argument's sake, that the forests contain no potentially useful endangered species of animals and plants. Must we then conclude that there is no further cause for moral concern? Should we then feel morally indifferent when we see the natural environment uprooted?

II

Suppose we feel that the answer to these questions should be negative. Suppose, in other words, we feel that our moral discomfort when we confront the destroyers of nature is not fully explained by our belief that they have miscalculated the best use of natural resources or violated rights in exploiting them. Suppose, in particular, we sense that part of the problem is that the natural environment is being viewed exclusively as a natural resource. What could be the ground of such a feeling? That is, what is there in our system of normative principles and values that could account for our remaining moral dissatisfaction?

Some may be tempted to seek an explanation by appeal to the interests, or even the rights, of plants. After all, they may argue, we only gradually came to acknowledge the moral importance of all human beings, and it is even more recently that consciences have been aroused to give full weight to the welfare (and rights?) of animals. The next logical step, it may be argued, is to acknowledge a moral requirement to take into account the interests (and rights?) of plants. The problem with the strip miners, redwood cutters, and the like, on this view, is not just that they ignore the welfare and rights of people and animals: they also fail to give due weight to the survival and health of the plants themselves.

The temptation to make such a reply is understandable if one assumes that all moral questions are exclusively concerned with whether *acts* are right or wrong, and that this, in turn, is determined entirely by how the acts impinge on the rights and interests of those directly affected. On this assumption, if there is cause for moral concern, some right or interest has been neglected; and if the rights and interests of human beings and animals have already been taken into account, then there must be some other pertinent interests, for example, those of plants. A little reflection will show that the assumption is mistaken; but, in any case, the conclusion that plants have rights or morally relevant interests is surely untenable. We do speak of what is "good for" plants, and they can "thrive" and also be "killed." But this does not imply that they have "interests" in any morally relevant sense. Some people apparently believe that plants grow better if we talk to them, but the idea that the plants suffer and enjoy, desire and dislike, etc., is clearly outside the range of both common sense and scientific belief. The notion that the forests should be preserved to avoid *hurting* the trees or because they have a *right* to life is not part of a widely shared moral consciousness, and for good reason.

Another way of trying to explain our moral discomfort is to appeal to certain religious beliefs. If one believes that all living things were created by a God who cares for them and entrusted us with the use of plants and animals only for limited purposes, then one has a reason to avoid careless destruction of the forests, etc., quite aside from their future utility. Again, if one believes that a divine force is immanent in all nature, then too one might have reason to care for more than sentient things. But such arguments require strong and controversial premises, and, I suspect, they will always have a restricted audience.

Early in this century, due largely to the influence of G. E. Moore, another point of view developed which some may find promising.[1] Moore introduced, or at least made popular, the idea that certain states of affairs are intrinsically valuable—not just valued, but valuable, and not necessarily because of their effects on sentient beings. . . . The intrinsic goodness of something, he thought, was an objective, nonrelational property of the

---

1 G. E. Moore, *Principia Ethica* (Cambridge: Cambridge University Press. 1903); *Ethics* (London: H. Holt, 1912).

thing, like its texture or color, but not a property perceivable by sense perception or detectable by scientific instruments. In theory at least, a single tree thriving alone in a universe without sentient beings, and even without God, could be intrinsically valuable. . . . The survival of a forest might have worth beyond its worth *to* sentient beings.

Even if we try to . . . think in Moore's terms, it is far from obvious that everyone would agree that the existence of forests, etc., is intrinsically valuable. The test, says Moore, is what we would say when we imagine a universe with just the thing in question, without any effects or accompaniments, and then we ask, "Would its existence be better than its nonexistence?" Be careful. Moore would remind us, not to construe this question as, "Would you *prefer* the existence of that universe to its nonexistence?" The question is, "Would its existence have the objective, nonrelational property, intrinsic goodness?"

Now even among those who have no worries about whether this really makes sense, we might well get a diversity of answers. Those prone to destroy natural environments will doubtless give one answer, and nature lovers will likely give another. When an issue is as controversial as the one at hand, intuition is a poor arbiter.

The problem, then, is this. We want to understand what underlies our moral uneasiness at the destruction of the redwoods, forests, etc., even apart from the loss of these as resources for human beings and animals. But I find no adequate answer by pursuing the questions, "Are rights or interests of plants neglected?" "What is God's will on the matter?" and "What is the intrinsic value of the existence of a tree or forest?" My suggestion, which is in fact the main point of this paper, is that we look at the problem from a different perspective. That is, let us turn for a while from the effort to find reasons why certain *acts* destructive of natural environments are morally wrong to the ancient task of articulating our ideals of human excellence. Rather than argue directly with destroyers of the environment who say, "Show me why what I am doing is *immoral*," I want to ask, "What sort of person would want to do what they propose?" The point is not to skirt the issue with an *ad hominem*, but to raise a different moral question, for even if there is no convincing way to show that the destructive acts are wrong (independently of human and animal use and enjoyment), we may find that the willingness to indulge in them reflects the absence of human traits that we admire and regard as morally important.

This strategy of shifting questions may seem more promising if one reflects on certain analogous situations. Consider, for example, the Nazi who asks, in all seriousness, "Why is it wrong for me to make lampshades out of human skin—provided, of course, I did not myself kill the victims to get the skins?" We would react more with shock and disgust than with indignation, I suspect, because it is even more evident that the question reveals a defect in the questioner than that the proposed act is itself immoral. Sometimes we may not regard an act wrong at all though we see it as reflecting something objectionable about the person who does it. Imagine, for example, one who laughs spontaneously to himself when he reads a newspaper account of a plane crash that kills hundreds. Or, again, consider an obsequious grandson who, having waited for his grandmother's inheritance with mock devotion, then secretly spits on her grave when at last she dies. Spitting on the grave may have no adverse consequences and perhaps it violates no rights. The moral uneasiness which it arouses is explained more by our view of the agent than by any conviction that what he did was immoral. Had he hesitated and asked, "Why shouldn't I spit on her grave?" it seems more fitting to ask him to reflect on the sort of person he is than to try to offer reasons why he should refrain from spitting.

III

What sort of person, then, would cover his garden with asphalt, strip mine a wooded mountain, or level an irreplaceable redwood grove? Two sorts of answers, though initially appealing, must be ruled out. The first is that persons who would destroy the environment in these ways are either shortsighted, underestimating the harm they do, or else are too little concerned for the well-being of other people. Perhaps too they have insufficient regard for animal life. But these considerations have been set aside in order to refine the controversy. Another tempting response might be that we count it a moral virtue, or at least a human ideal, to love nature. Those who value the environment only for its utility must not really love nature and so in this way fall short of an ideal. But such an answer is hardly satisfying in the present context, for what is at issue is *why* we feel moral discomfort at the activities of those who admittedly value nature only for its utility. That it is ideal to care for nonsentient nature beyond its possible use is really just another way of expressing the general point which is under controversy.

What is needed is some way of showing that this ideal is connected with other virtues, or human excellences, not in question. To do so is difficult and my suggestions, accordingly, will be tentative and subject to qualification. The main idea is that, though indifference to nonsentient nature does not *necessarily* reflect the absence of virtues, it often signals the absence of certain traits which we want to encourage because they are, in most cases, a natural basis for the development of certain virtues. It is often thought, for example, that those who would destroy the natural environment must lack a proper appreciation of their place in the natural order, and so must either be ignorant or have too little humility. Though I would argue that this is not necessarily so, I suggest that, given certain plausible empirical assumptions, their attitude may well be rooted in ignorance, a narrow perspective, inability to see things as important apart from themselves and the limited groups they associate with, or reluctance to accept themselves as natural beings. Overcoming these deficiencies will not guarantee a proper moral humility, but for most of us it is probably an important psychological preliminary. Later I suggest, more briefly, that indifference to nonsentient nature typically reveals absence of either aesthetic sensibility or a disposition to cherish what has enriched one's life and that these, though not themselves moral virtues, are a natural basis for appreciation of the good in others and gratitude.

Consider first the suggestion that destroyers of the environment lack an appreciation of their place in the universe. Their attention, it seems, must be focused on parochial matters, on what is, relatively speaking, close in space and time. They seem not to understand that we are a speck on the cosmic scene, a brief stage in the evolutionary process, only one among millions of species on Earth, and an episode in the course of human history. Of course, they know that there are stars, fossils, insects, and ancient ruins; but do they have any idea of the complexity of the processes that led to the natural world as we find it? Are they aware how much the forces at work within their own bodies are like those which govern all living things and even how much they have in common with inanimate bodies? Admittedly scientific knowledge is limited and no one can master it all; but could one who had a broad and deep understanding of his place in nature really be indifferent to the destruction of the natural environment?

This first suggestion, however, may well provoke a protest from a sophisticated anti-environmentalist. "Perhaps *some* may be indifferent to nature from ignorance," the critic may object, "but I have studied astronomy, geology, biology, and biochemistry, and I still unashamedly regard the nonsentient environment as simply a resource for our use. It should not be wasted, of course, but what should be preserved is decidable by weighing long-term costs and benefits." "Besides," our critic may continue, "as philosophers you should know the old Humean formula, 'You cannot derive an *ought* from an *is*.' All the facts of biology, biochemistry, etc., do not entail that I ought to love nature or want to preserve it. What one understands is one thing; what one values is something else. Just as nature lovers are not necessarily scientists, those indifferent to nature are not necessarily ignorant."

Although the environmentalist may concede the critic's logical point, he may well argue that, as a matter of fact, increased understanding of nature tends to heighten people's concern for its preservation. If so, despite the objection, the suspicion that the destroyers of the environment lack deep understanding of nature is not, in most cases, unwarranted, but the argument need not rest here.

The environmentalist might amplify his original idea as follows: "When I said that the destroyers of nature do not appreciate their place in the universe, I was not speaking of intellectual understanding alone, for, after all, a person can *know* a catalog of facts without ever putting them together and seeing vividly the whole picture which they form. To see oneself as just one part of nature is to look at oneself and the world from a certain perspective which is quite different from being able to recite detailed information from the natural sciences. What the destroyers of nature lack is this perspective, not particular information."

Again our critic may object, though only after making some concessions: "All right," he may say, "*some* who are indifferent to nature may lack the cosmic perspective of which you speak, but again there is no *necessary* connection between this failing, if it is one, and any particular evaluative attitude toward nature. In fact, different people respond quite differently when they move to a wider perspective. When I try to picture myself vividly as a brief, transitory episode in the course of nature, I simply get depressed. Far from inspiring me with a love of nature, the exercise makes me sad and hostile. . . ." In sum, the critic may object, "Even if one should try to see oneself as one small transitory part of nature, doing so does not dictate any particular normative attitude. Some may come to love nature, but others are moved to live for the moment; some sink into sad resignation; others get depressed or angry. So indifference to nature is not necessarily a sign that a person fails to look at himself from the larger perspective."

The environmentalist might respond to this objection in several ways. He might, for example, argue that even though some people who see themselves as part of the natural order remain indifferent to nonsentient nature, this is not a common reaction. Typically, it may be argued, as we become more and more aware that we are parts of the larger whole we come to value the whole independently of its effect on ourselves. Thus, despite the possibilities the critic raises, indifference to nonsentient nature is still in most cases a sign that a person fails to see himself as part of the natural order.

If someone challenges the empirical assumption here, the environmentalist might develop the argument along a quite different line. The initial idea, he may remind us, was that those who would destroy the natural environment fail to *appreciate* their place in the natural order. "Appreciating one's place" is not simply an intellectual appreciation. It is also an attitude, reflecting what one values as well as what one knows. When we say, for example, that both the servile and the arrogant person fail to *appreciate* their place in a society of equals, we do not mean simply that they are ignorant of certain empirical facts, but rather that they have certain objectionable attitudes about their importance relative to other people. Similarly, to fail to appreciate one's place in nature is not merely to lack knowledge or breadth of perspective, but to take a certain attitude about what matters. A person who *understands* his place in nature but still views nonsentient nature merely as a resource takes the attitude that nothing is *important* but human beings and animals. Despite first appearances, he is not so much like the pre-Copernican astronomers who made the intellectual error of treating the Earth as the "center of the universe" when they made their calculations. He is more like the racist who, though well aware of other races, treats all races but his own as insignificant.

So construed, the argument appeals to the common idea that awareness of nature typically has, and should have, a humbling effect. The Alps, a storm at sea, the Grand Canyon, towering redwoods, and "the starry heavens above" move many a person to remark on the comparative insignificance of our daily concerns and even of our species, and this is generally taken to be a quite fitting response. What seems to be missing, then, in those who understand nature but remain unmoved is a proper humility.[2] Absence of proper humility is not the same as selfishness or egoism, for one can be devoted to self-interest while still viewing one's own pleasures and projects as trivial and unimportant. And one can have an exaggerated

---

2 By *"proper* humility" I mean that sort and degree of humility that is a morally admirable character trait. How precisely to define this is, of course, a controversial matter; but the point for present purposes is just to set aside obsequiousness, false modesty, underestimation of one's abilities, and the like.

view of one's own importance while grandly sacrificing for those one views as inferior. Nor is the lack of humility identical with belief that one has power and influence, for a person can be quite puffed up about himself while believing that the foolish world will never acknowledge him. The humility we miss seems not so much a belief about one's relative effectiveness and recognition as an attitude which measures the importance of things independently of their relation to oneself or to some narrow group with which one identifies. A paradigm of a person who lacks humility is the self-important emperor who grants status to his family because it is *his*, to his subordinates because *he* appointed them, and to his country because *he* chooses to glorify it. Less extreme but still lacking proper humility is the elitist who counts events significant solely in proportion to how they affect his class. The suspicion about those who would destroy the environment, then, is that what they count important is too narrowly confined insofar as it encompasses only what affects beings who, like us, are capable of feeling.

This idea that proper humility requires recognition of the importance of nonsentient nature is similar to the thought of those who charge meat eaters with "species-ism." In both cases it is felt that people too narrowly confine their concerns to the sorts of beings that are most like them. But, however intuitively appealing, the idea will surely arouse objections from our nonenvironmentalist critic. "Why," he will ask, "do you suppose that the sort of humility I *should* have requires me to acknowledge the importance of nonsentient nature aside from its utility? You cannot, by your own admission, argue that nonsentient nature *is* important, appealing to religious or intuitionist grounds. And simply to assert, without further argument, that an ideal humility requires us to view nonsentient nature as important for its own sake begs the question at issue. If proper humility is acknowledging the relative importance of things as one should, then to show that I must lack this you must first establish that one *should* acknowledge the importance of nonsentient nature."

Though some may wish to accept this challenge, there are other ways to pursue the connection between humility and response to nonsentient nature. For example, suppose we grant that proper humility requires only acknowledging a due status to sentient beings. We must admit, then, that it is logically possible for a person to be properly humble even though he viewed all nonsentient nature simply as a resource. But this logical possibility may be a psychological rarity. It may be that, given the sort of beings we are, we would never learn humility before persons without developing the general capacity to cherish, and regard important, many things for their own sakes. The major obstacle to humility before persons is self-importance, a tendency to measure the significance of everything by its relation to oneself and those with whom one identifies. The processes by which we overcome self-importance are doubtless many and complex, but it seems unlikely that they are exclusively concerned with how we relate to other people and animals. Learning humility requires learning to feel that something matters besides what will affect oneself and one's circle of associates. What leads a child to care about what happens to a lost hamster or a stray dog he will not see again is likely also to generate concern for a lost toy or a favorite tree where he used to live. Learning to value things for their own sake, and to count what affects them important aside from their utility, . . . is necessary to the development of humility and it seems likely to take place in experiences with nonsentient nature as well as with people and animals. If a person views all nonsentient nature merely as a resource, then it seems unlikely that he has developed the capacity needed to overcome self-importance.

IV

This last argument, unfortunately, has its limits. It presupposes an empirical connection between experiencing nature and overcoming self-importance, and this may be challenged. Even if experiencing nature promotes humility before others, there may be other ways people can develop such humility in a world of concrete, glass, and plastic. If not, perhaps all that is needed is limited experience of nature in one's early, developing years; mature adults, having overcome youthful self-importance, may live well enough in artificial surroundings. More importantly, the argument does not fully capture the spirit of the intuition that an ideal person stands humbly before nature. That idea is not simply that experiencing nature tends to foster proper humility before other people; it is, in part, that natural surroundings encourage and are appropriate to an ideal sense of oneself as part of the natural world. Standing alone in the forest, after months in the city, is not merely good as a means of curbing one's arrogance before others; it reinforces and fittingly expresses one's acceptance of oneself as a natural being.

Previously we considered only one aspect of proper humility, namely, a sense of one's relative importance with respect to other human beings. Another aspect, I think, is a kind of *self-acceptance*. This involves acknowledging, in more than a merely intellectual way, that we are the sort of creatures that we are. Whether one is self-accepting is not so much a matter of how one attributes *importance* comparatively to oneself, other people, animals, plants, and other things as it is a matter of understanding, facing squarely, and responding appropriately to who and what one is, e.g., one's powers and limits, one's affinities with other beings and differences from them, one's unalterable nature and one's freedom to change. Self-acceptance is not merely intellectual awareness, for one can be intellectually aware that one is growing old and will eventually die while nevertheless behaving in a thousand foolish ways that reflect a refusal to acknowledge these facts. On the other hand, self-acceptance is not passive resignation, for refusal to pursue what one truly wants within one's limits is a failure to accept the freedom and power one has. Particular behaviors, like dying one's gray hair and dressing like those twenty years younger, do not *necessarily* imply lack of self-acceptance, for there could be reasons for acting in these ways other than the wish to hide from oneself what one really is. One fails to accept oneself when the patterns of behavior and emotion are rooted in a desire to disown and deny features of oneself, to pretend to oneself that they are not there. This is not to say that a self-accepting person makes no value judgments about himself, that he likes all facts about himself, wants equally to develop and display them; he can, and should feel remorse for his past misdeeds and strive to change his current vices. The point is that he does not disown them, pretend that they do not exist or are facts about something other than himself. Such pretense is incompatible with proper humility because it is seeing oneself as better than one is.

Self-acceptance of this sort has long been considered a human excellence, under various names, but what has it to do with preserving nature? There is, I think, the following connection. As human beings we are part of nature, living, growing, declining, and dying by natural laws similar to those governing other living beings; despite our awesomely distinctive human powers, we share many of the needs, limits, and liabilities of animals and plants. These facts are neither good nor bad in themselves, aside from personal preference and varying conventional values. To say this is to utter a truism which few will deny, but to accept these facts, as facts about oneself, is not so easy—or so common. Much of what naturalists deplore about our increasingly artificial world reflects, and encourages, a denial of these facts, an unwillingness to avow them with equanimity. . . .

My suggestion is not merely that experiencing nature causally promotes such self-acceptance, but also that those who fully accept themselves as part of the natural world lack the common drive to disassociate themselves from nature by replacing natural environments with artificial ones. A storm in the wilds helps us to appreciate our animal vulnerability, but, equally important, the reluctance to experience it may *reflect* an unwillingness to accept this aspect of ourselves. The person who is too ready to destroy the ancient redwoods may lack humility, not so much in the sense that he exaggerates his importance relative to others, but rather in the sense that he tries to avoid seeing himself as one among many natural creatures.

V

My suggestion so far has been that, though indifference to nonsentient nature is not itself a moral vice, it is likely to reflect either ignorance, a self-importance, or a lack of self-acceptance which we must overcome to have proper humility. A similar idea might be developed connecting attitudes toward nonsentient nature with other human excellences. For example, one might argue that indifference to nature reveals a lack of either an aesthetic sense or some of the natural roots of gratitude.

When we see a hillside that has been gutted by strip miners or the garden replaced by asphalt, our first reaction is probably, "How ugly!" The scenes assault our aesthetic sensibilities. We suspect that no one with a keen sense of beauty could have left such a sight. Admittedly not everything in nature strikes us as beautiful, or even aesthetically interesting, and sometimes a natural scene is replaced with a more impressive architectural masterpiece. But this is not usually the situation in the problem cases which environmentalists are most concerned about. More often beauty is replaced with ugliness.

At this point our critic may well object that, even if he does lack a sense of beauty, this is no moral vice. His cost/benefit calculations take into account the pleasure others may derive from seeing the forests, etc., and so why should he be faulted?

Some might reply that, despite contrary philosophical traditions, aesthetics and morality are not so distinct as commonly supposed. Appreciation of beauty, they may argue, is a human excellence which morally ideal persons should try to develop. But, setting aside this controversial position, there still may be cause for moral concern about those who have no aesthetic response to nature. Even if aesthetic sensibility is not itself a moral virtue, many of the capacities of mind and heart which it presupposes may be ones which are also needed for an appreciation of other people. Consider, for example, curiosity, a mind open to novelty, the ability to look at things from unfamiliar perspectives, empathetic imagination, interest in details, variety, and order, and emotional freedom from the immediate and the practical. All these, and more, seem necessary to aesthetic sensibility, but they are also traits which a person needs to be fully sensitive to people of all sorts. The point is not that a moral person must be able to distinguish beautiful from ugly people; the point is rather that unresponsiveness to what is beautiful, awesome, dainty, dumpy, and otherwise aesthetically interesting in nature probably reflects a lack of the openness of mind and spirit necessary to appreciate the best in human beings.

The anti-environmentalist, however, may refuse to accept the charge that he lacks aesthetic sensibility. If he claims to appreciate seventeenth-century miniature portraits, but to abhor natural wildernesses, he will hardly be convincing. Tastes vary, but aesthetic sense is not *that* selective. He may, instead, insist that he *does* appreciate natural beauty. He spends his vacations, let us suppose, hiking in the Sierras, photographing wildflowers, and so on. He might press his argument as follows: "I enjoy natural beauty as much as anyone, but I fail to see what this has to do with preserving the environment independently of human enjoyment and use. Nonsentient nature is a resource, but one of its best uses is to give us pleasure. I take this into account when I calculate the costs and benefits of preserving a park, planting a garden, and so on. But the problem you raised explicitly set aside the desire to preserve nature as a means to enjoyment. I say, let us enjoy nature fully while we can, but if all sentient beings were to die tomorrow, we might as well blow up all plant life as well. A redwood grove that no one can use or enjoy is utterly worthless."

The attitude expressed here, I suspect, is not a common one, but it represents a philosophical challenge. The beginnings of a reply may be found in the following. When a person takes joy in something, it is a common (and perhaps natural) response to come to cherish it. To cherish something is not simply to be happy with it at the moment, but to care for it for its own sake. This is not to say that one necessarily sees it as having feelings and so wants it to feel good; nor does it imply that one judges the thing to have Moore's intrinsic value. One simply wants the thing to survive and (when appropriate) to thrive, and not simply for its utility. We see this attitude repeatedly regarding mementos. They are not simply valued as a means to remind us of happy occasions; they come to be valued for their own sake. Thus, if someone really took joy in the natural environment, but was prepared to blow it up as soon as sentient life ended, he would lack this common human tendency to cherish what enriches our lives. While this response is not itself a moral virtue, it may be a natural basis of the virtue we call "gratitude." People who have no tendency to cherish things that give them pleasure may be poorly disposed to respond gratefully to persons who are good to them. Again the connection is not one of logical necessity, but it may nevertheless be important. A nonreligious person unable to "thank" anyone for the beauties of nature may nevertheless feel "grateful" in a sense; and I suspect that the person who feels no such "gratitude" toward nature is unlikely to show proper gratitude toward people.

Suppose these conjectures prove to be true. One may wonder what is the point of considering them. Is it to disparage all those who view nature merely as a resource? To do so, it seems, would be unfair, for, even if this attitude typically stems from deficiencies which affect one's attitudes toward sentient beings, there may be exceptions and we have not shown that their view of nonsentient nature is itself blameworthy. But when we set aside questions of blame and inquire what sorts of human traits we want to encourage, our reflections become relevant in a more positive way. The point is not to insinuate that all anti-environmentalists are defective, but to see that those who value such traits as humility, gratitude, and sensitivity to others have reason to promote the love of nature.

Thomas Hill, Jr.: Ideals of Human Excellence and Preserving Natural Environments

1. Why does Hill think it is sometimes difficult to explain what is wrong with destroying the environment in terms of rights and welfare? What alternative framework does he propose for looking at the issue?
2. Hill presents several examples of acts which may not necessarily be immoral, but which would clearly reveal a defect in any person who performed them. Do you find his examples convincing? Is harming the environment relevantly similar to these actions?

3. Hill suggests that many environmentally destructive actions might be performed as a result of ignorance. How does he argue for this claim, and how might an "anti-environmentalist" respond?
4. What exactly is *humility*, and why does Hill claim that those who are unmoved by nature lack it? Do you agree with him?
5. What connection, if any, is there between self-acceptance and preserving nature? Can a person fully accept himself or herself while at the same time destroying natural environments?

30

———— ❧ ————

A Defense of Abortion

Judith Jarvis Thomson

﹟

....

In this article, Judith Thomson does what very few pro-choice advocates have been willing to do—namely, to grant, for the purposes of argument, that the fetus is as much a moral person as you or I. Still, she argues, being a person does not, by itself, entitle you to use someone else's resources, even if those resources are needed in order to preserve your life. Thus even if we grant that the fetus is a person, that is not enough to show that the fetus is entitled to the continued use of the mother's "resources" (her body). A pregnant woman has a right to bodily autonomy, and that right, in many cases, morally prevails over any rights possessed by a fetus.

Thomson uses a number of thought experiments to defend this claim. The most famous of these involves a world-class violinist. Suppose that you wake up one morning and find yourself connected to a transfusion machine that is providing life support for this musician. He surely has a right to life. But Thomson says that you would be within your rights to remove yourself from the apparatus—even knowing that, by doing this, he will die. The violinist, of course, is meant to be a stand-in for the fetus. According to Thomson, although it would be awfully nice of pregnant women to continue carrying their fetuses to term, they are not usually morally required to do so.

Thomson anticipates a variety of objections to this example, and provides further examples to support her view that women usually have a moral right to seek and obtain an abortion.

....

Most opposition to abortion relies on the premise that the fetus is a human being, a person, from the moment of conception. The premise is argued for, but, as I think, not well. Take, for example, the most common argument. We are asked to notice that the development of a human being from conception through birth into childhood is continuous; then it is said that to draw a line, to choose a point in this development and say "before this point the thing is not a person, after this point it is a person" is to make an arbitrary choice, a choice for which in the nature of things no good reason can be given. It is concluded that the fetus is, or anyway that we had better say it is, a person from the moment of conception. But this conclusion does not follow. Similar things might be said about the development of an acorn into an oak tree, and it does not follow that acorns are oak trees, or that we had better say they are. Arguments of this form are sometimes called "slippery slope arguments"—the phrase is perhaps self-explanatory—and it is dismaying that opponents of abortion rely on them so heavily and uncritically.

I am inclined to agree, however, that the prospects for "drawing a line" in the development of the fetus look dim. I am inclined to think also that we shall probably have to agree that the fetus has already become a human person well before birth. Indeed, it comes as a surprise when one first learns how early in its life it begins to acquire human characteristics. By the tenth week, for example, it already has a face, arms and legs, fingers and toes; it has internal organs, and brain activity is detectable. On the other hand, I think that the premise is false, that the fetus is not a person from the moment of conception. A newly fertilized ovum, a newly implanted clump of cells, is no more a person than an acorn is an oak tree. But I shall not discuss any of this. For it seems to me to be of great interest to ask what happens if, for the sake of argument, we allow the premise. How, precisely, are we supposed to get from there to the conclusion that abortion is morally impermissible? Opponents of abortion commonly spend most of their time establishing that the fetus is a person, and hardly any time explaining the step from there to the impermissibility of abortion. Perhaps they think the step too simple and obvious to require much comment. Or perhaps instead they are simply being economical in argument. Many of those who defend abortion rely on the premise that the fetus is not a person, but only a bit of tissue that will become a person at birth; and why pay out more arguments than you have to? Whatever the explanation, I suggest that the step they take is neither easy nor obvious, that it calls for closer examination than it is commonly given, and that when we do give it this closer examination we shall feel inclined to reject it.

I propose, then, that we grant that the fetus is a person from the moment of conception. How does the argument go from here? Something like this, I take it. Every person has a right to life. So the fetus has a right to life. No doubt the mother has a right to decide what shall happen in and to her body; everyone would grant that. But surely a person's right to life is stronger and more stringent than the mother's right to decide what happens in and to her body, and so outweighs it. So the fetus may not be killed; an abortion may not be performed.

It sounds plausible. But now let me ask you to imagine this. You wake up in the morning and find yourself back to back in bed with an unconscious violinist. A famous unconscious violinist. He has been found to have a fatal kidney ailment, and the Society of Music Lovers has canvassed all the available medical records and found that you alone have the right blood type to help. They have therefore kidnapped you, and last night the violinist's circulatory system was plugged into yours, so that your kidneys can be used to extract poisons from his blood as well as your own. The director of the hospital now tells you, "Look, we're sorry the Society of Music Lovers did this to you—we would never have permitted it if we had known. But still, they did it, and the violinist now is plugged into you. To unplug you would be to kill him. But never mind, it's only for nine months. By then he will have recovered from his ailment, and can safely be unplugged from you." Is it morally incumbent on you to accede to this situation? No doubt it would be very nice of you if you did, a great kindness. But do you *have* to accede to it? What if it were not nine months, but nine years? Or longer still? What if the director of the hospital says, "Tough luck, I agree, but you've now got to stay in bed, with the violinist plugged into you, for the rest of your life. Because remember this. All persons have a right to life, and violinists are persons. Granted you have a right to decide what happens in and to your body, but a person's right to life outweighs your right to decide what happens in and to your body. So you cannot ever be unplugged from him." I imagine you would regard this as outrageous, which suggests that something really is wrong with that plausible-sounding argument I mentioned a moment ago.

In this case, of course, you were kidnapped; you didn't volunteer for the operation that plugged the violinist into your kidneys. Can those who oppose abortion on the ground I mentioned make an exception for a pregnancy due to rape? Certainly. They can say that persons have a right to life only if they didn't come into existence because of rape; or they can say that all persons have a right to life, but that some have less of a right to life than others, in particular, that those who came into existence because of rape have less. But these statements have a rather unpleasant sound. Surely the question of whether you have a right to life at all, or how much of it you have, shouldn't turn on the question of whether or not you are the product of a rape. And in fact the people who oppose abortion on the ground I mentioned do not make this distinction, and hence do not make an exception in case of rape.

Nor do they make an exception for a case in which the mother has to spend the nine months of her pregnancy in bed. They would agree that would be a great pity, and hard on the mother; but all the same, all persons have a right to life, the fetus is a person, and so on. I suspect, in fact, that they would not make an exception for a case in which, miraculously enough, the pregnancy went on for nine years, or even the rest of the mother's life.

Some won't even make an exception for a case in which continuation of the pregnancy is likely to shorten the mother's life; they regard abortion as impermissible even to save the mother's life. Such cases are nowadays very rare, and many opponents of abortion do not accept this extreme view. All the same, it is a good place to begin: a number of points of interest come out in respect to it.

1. Let us call the view that abortion is impermissible even to save the mother's life "the extreme view." I want to suggest first that it does not issue from the argument I mentioned earlier without the addition of some fairly powerful premises. Suppose a woman has become pregnant, and now learns that she has a cardiac condition such that she will die if she carries the baby to term. What may be done for her? The fetus, being a person, has a right to life, but as the mother is a person too, so has she a right to life. Presumably they have an equal right to life. How is it supposed to come out that an abortion may not be performed? If mother and child have an equal right to life, shouldn't we perhaps flip a coin? Or should we add to the mother's right to life her right to decide what happens in and to her

body, which everybody seems to be ready to grant—the sum of her rights now outweighing the fetus' right to life?

The most familiar argument here is the following. We are told that performing the abortion would be directly killing[1] the child, whereas doing nothing would not be killing the mother, but only letting her die. Moreover, in killing the child, one would be killing an innocent person, for the child has committed no crime, and is not aiming at his mother's death. And then there are a variety of ways in which this might be continued. (1) But as directly killing an innocent person is always and absolutely impermissible, an abortion may not be performed. Or, (2) as directly killing an innocent person is murder, and murder is always and absolutely impermissible, an abortion may not be performed. Or, (3) as one's duty to refrain from directly killing an innocent person is more stringent than one's duty to keep a person from dying, an abortion may not be performed. Or, (4) if one's only options are directly killing an innocent person or letting a person die, one must prefer letting the person die, and thus an abortion may not be performed.

Some people seem to have thought that these are not further premises which must be added if the conclusion is to be reached, but that they follow from the very fact that an innocent person has a right to life. But this seems to me to be a mistake, and perhaps the simplest way to show this is to bring out that while we must certainly grant that innocent persons have a right to life, the theses in (1) through (4) are all false. Take (2), for example. If directly killing an innocent person is murder, and thus is impermissible, then the mother's directly killing the innocent person inside her is murder, and thus is impermissible. But it cannot seriously be thought to be murder if the mother performs an abortion on herself to save her life. It cannot seriously be said that she *must* refrain, that she *must* sit passively by and wait for her death. Let us look again at the case of you and the violinist. There you are, in bed with the violinist, and the director of the hospital says to you, "It's all most distressing, and I deeply sympathize, but you see this is putting an additional strain on your kidneys, and you'll be dead within the month. But you *have* to stay where you are all the same. Because unplugging you would be directly killing an innocent violinist, and that's murder, and that's impermissible." If anything in the world is true, it is that

---

1 The term "direct" in the arguments I refer to is a technical one. Roughly, what is meant by "direct killing" is either killing as an end in itself, or killing as a means to some end, for example, the end of saving someone else's life.

you do not commit murder, you do not do what is impermissible, if you reach around to your back and unplug yourself from that violinist to save your life.

The main focus of attention in writings on abortion has been on what a third party may or may not do in answer to a request from a woman for an abortion. This is in a way understandable. Things being as they are, there isn't much a woman can safely do to abort herself. So the question asked is what a third party may do, and what the mother may do, if it is mentioned at all, is deduced, almost as an afterthought, from what it is concluded that third parties may do. But it seems to me that to treat the matter in this way is to refuse to grant to the mother that very status of person which is so firmly insisted on for the fetus. For we cannot simply read off what a person may do from what a third party may do. Suppose you find yourself trapped in a tiny house with a growing child. I mean a very tiny house, and a rapidly growing child—you are already up against the wall of the house and in a few minutes you'll be crushed to death. The child on the other hand won't be crushed to death; if nothing is done to stop him from growing he'll be hurt, but in the end he'll simply burst open the house and walk out a free man. Now I could well understand it if a bystander were to say, "There's nothing we can do for you. We cannot choose between your life and his, we cannot be the ones to decide who is to live, we cannot intervene." But it cannot be concluded that you too can do nothing, that you cannot attack it to save your life. However innocent the child may be, you do not have to wait passively while it crushes you to death. Perhaps a pregnant woman is vaguely felt to have the status of house, to which we don't allow the right of self-defense. But if the woman houses the child, it should be remembered that she is a person who houses it.

I should perhaps stop to say explicitly that I am not claiming that people have a right to do anything whatever to save their lives. I think, rather, that there are drastic limits to the right of self-defense. If someone threatens you with death unless you torture someone else to death, I think you have not the right, even to save your life, to do so. But the case under consideration here is very different. In our case there are only two people involved, one whose life is threatened, and one who threatens it. Both are innocent: the one who is threatened is not threatened because of any fault, the one who threatens does not threaten because of any fault. For this reason we may feel that we bystanders cannot intervene. But the person threatened can.

In sum, a woman surely can defend her life against the threat to it posed by the unborn child, even if doing so involves its death. And this shows not merely that the theses in (1) through (4) are false; it shows also that the extreme view of abortion is false, and so we need not canvass any other possible ways of arriving at it from the argument I mentioned at the outset.

2. The extreme view could of course be weakened to say that while abortion is permissible to save the mother's life, it may not be performed by a third party, but only by the mother herself. But this cannot be right either. For what we have to keep in mind is that the mother and the unborn child are not like two tenants in a small house which has, by an unfortunate mistake, been rented to both: the mother *owns* the house. The fact that she does adds to the offensiveness of deducing that the mother can do nothing from the supposition that third parties can do nothing. But it does more than this: it casts a bright light on the supposition that third parties can do nothing. Certainly it lets us see that a third party who says "I cannot choose between you" is fooling himself if he thinks this is impartiality. If Jones has found and fastened on a certain coat, which he needs to keep him from freezing, but which Smith also needs to keep him from freezing, then it is not impartiality that says "I cannot choose between you" when Smith owns the coat. Women have said again and again "This body is *my* body!" and they have reason to feel angry, reason to feel that it has been like shouting into the wind. . . .

3. Where the mother's life is not at stake, the argument I mentioned at the outset seems to have a much stronger pull. "Everyone has a right to life, so the unborn person has a right to life." And isn't the child's right to life weightier than anything other than the mother's own right to life, which she might put forward as ground for an abortion?

This argument treats the right to life as if it were unproblematic. It is not, and this seems to me to be precisely the source of the mistake.

For we should now, at long last, ask what it comes to, to have a right to life. In some views having a right to life includes having a right to be given at least the bare minimum one needs for continued life. But suppose that what in fact *is* the bare minimum a man needs for continued life is something he has no right at all to be given? If I am sick unto death, and the only thing that will save my life is the touch of Henry Fonda's cool hand on my fevered brow, then all the same, I have no right to be given the touch of Henry Fonda's cool hand on my fevered brow. It would be frightfully nice of him to fly in from the West Coast to provide it. It would be less nice, though no doubt well meant, if my friends flew out to the West Coast and carried Henry Fonda back with them. But I have no right at all against anybody that he should do this for me. Or again, to return to the story I told earlier, the fact that for continued life that violinist needs the continued use of your kidneys does not establish that he has a right to be given the continued use of your kidneys. He certainly has no right against you that *you* should give him continued use of your kidneys. For nobody has any right to use your kidneys unless you give him such a right; and nobody has the right against you that you shall give him this right—if you do allow him to go on using your kidneys, this is a kindness on your part, and not something he can claim from you as his due. Nor has he any right against anybody else that *they* should give him continued use of your kidneys. Certainly he had no right against the Society of Music Lovers that they should plug him into you in the first place. And if you now start to unplug yourself, having learned that you will otherwise have to spend nine years in bed with him, there is nobody in the world who must try to prevent you, in order to see to it that he is given something he has a right to be given.

Some people are rather stricter about the right to life. In their view, it does not include the right to be given anything, but amounts to, and only to, the right not to be killed by anybody. But here a related difficulty arises. If everybody is to refrain from killing that violinist, then everybody must refrain from doing a great many different sorts of things. Everybody must refrain from slitting his throat, everybody must refrain from shooting him—and everybody must refrain from unplugging you from him. But does he have a right against everybody that they shall refrain from unplugging you from him? To refrain from doing this is to allow him to continue to use your kidneys. It could be argued that he has a right against us that *we* should allow him to continue to use your kidneys. That is, while he had no right against us that we should give him the use of your kidneys, it might be argued that he anyway has a right against us that we shall not now intervene and deprive him of the use of your kidneys. I shall come back to third-party interventions later. But certainly the violinist has no right against you that *you* shall allow him to continue to use your kidneys. As I said, if you do allow him to use them, it is a kindness on your part, and not something you owe him.

The difficulty I point to here is not peculiar to the right to life. It reappears in connection with all the other natural rights; and it is something which an adequate account of rights must deal with. For present purposes it is enough just to draw attention to it. But I would stress that I am not arguing that people do not have a right to life—quite to the contrary, it seems to me that the primary control we must place on the acceptability of an account of rights is that it should turn out in that account to be a truth that all persons have a right to life. I am arguing only that having a right to life does not guarantee having either a right to be given the use of or a right to be allowed continued use of another person's body—even if one needs it for life itself. So the right to life will not serve the opponents of abortion in the very simple and clear way in which they seem to have thought it would.

4. There is another way to bring out the difficulty. In the most ordinary sort of case, to deprive someone of what he has a right to is to treat him unjustly. Suppose a boy and his small brother are jointly given a box of chocolates for Christmas. If the older boy takes the box and refuses to give his brother any of the chocolates, he is unjust to him, for the brother has been given a right to half of them. But suppose that, having learned that otherwise it means nine years in bed with that violinist, you unplug yourself from him. You surely are not being unjust to him, for you gave him no right to use your kidneys, and no one else can have given him any such right. But we have to notice that in unplugging yourself, you are killing him; and violinists, like everybody else, have a right to life, and thus in the view we were considering just now, the right not to be killed. So here you do what he supposedly has a right you shall not do, but you do not act unjustly to him in doing it.

The emendation which may be made at this point is this: the right to life consists not in the right not to be killed, but rather in the right not to be killed unjustly. This runs a risk of circularity, but never mind: it would enable us to square the fact that the violinist has a right to life with the fact that you do not act unjustly toward him in unplugging yourself, thereby killing him. For if you do not kill him unjustly, you do not violate his right to life, and so it is no wonder you do him no injustice.

But if this emendation is accepted, the gap in the argument against abortion stares us plainly in the face: it is by no means enough to show that the fetus is a person, and to remind us that all persons have a right to life—we need to be shown also that killing the fetus violates its right to life, i.e., that abortion is unjust killing. And is it?

I suppose we may take it as a datum that in a case of pregnancy due to rape the mother has not given the unborn person a right to the use of her body for food and shelter. Indeed, in what pregnancy could it be supposed that the mother has given the unborn person such a right? It is not as if there were unborn persons drifting about the world, to whom a woman who wants a child says "I invite you in."

But it might be argued that there are other ways one can have acquired a right to the use of another person's body than by having been invited to use it by that person. Suppose a woman voluntarily indulges in intercourse, knowing of the chance it will issue in pregnancy, and then she does become pregnant; is she not in part responsible for the presence, in fact the very existence, of the unborn person inside her? No doubt she did not invite it in. But doesn't her partial responsibility for its being there itself give it a right to the use of her body? If so, then her aborting it would be more like the boy's taking away the chocolates, and less like your unplugging yourself from the violinist—doing so would be depriving it of what it does have a right to, and thus would be doing it an injustice.

And then, too, it might be asked whether or not she can kill it even to save her own life: If she voluntarily called it into existence, how can she now kill it, even in self-defense?

The first thing to be said about this is that it is something new. Opponents of abortion have been so concerned to make out the independence of the fetus, in order to establish that it has a right to life, just as its mother does, that they have tended to overlook the possible support they might gain from making out that the fetus is *dependent* on the mother, in order to establish that she has a special kind of responsibility for it, a responsibility that gives it rights against her which are not possessed by any independent person—such as an ailing violinist who is a stranger to her.

On the other hand, this argument would give the unborn person a right to its mother's body only if her pregnancy resulted from a voluntary act, undertaken in full knowledge of the chance a pregnancy might result from it. It would leave out entirely the unborn person whose existence is due to rape. Pending the availability of some further argument, then, we would be left with the conclusion that unborn persons whose existence is due to rape have no right to the use of their mothers' bodies, and thus that aborting them is not depriving them of anything they have a right to and hence is not unjust killing.

And we should also notice that it is not at all plain that this argument really does go even as far as it purports to. For there are cases and cases, and the details make a difference. If the room is stuffy, and I therefore open a window to air it, and a burglar climbs in, it would be absurd to say, "Ah, now he can stay, she's given him a right to the use of her house—for she is partially responsible for his presence there, having voluntarily done what

enabled him to get in, in full knowledge that there are such things as burglars, and that burglars burgle." It would be still more absurd to say this if I
had had bars installed outside my windows, precisely to prevent burglars
from getting in, and a burglar got in only because of a defect in the bars. It
remains equally absurd if we imagine it is not a burglar who climbs in, but
an innocent person who blunders or falls in. Again, suppose it were like
this: people-seeds drift about in the air like pollen, and if you open your
windows, one may drift in and take root in your carpets or upholstery. You
don't want children, so you fix up your windows with fine mesh screens, the
very best you can buy. As can happen, however, and on very, very rare occasions does happen, one of the screens is defective; and a seed drifts in and
takes root. Does the person-plant who now develops have a right to the use
of your house? Surely not—despite the fact that you voluntarily opened
your windows, you knowingly kept carpets and upholstered furniture, and
you knew that screens were sometimes defective. Someone may argue
that you are responsible for its rooting, that it does have a right to your
house, because after all you *could* have lived out your life with bare floors
and furniture, or with sealed windows and doors. But this won't do—for by
the same token anyone can avoid a pregnancy due to rape by having a hysterectomy, or anyway by never leaving home without a (reliable!) army.

It seems to me that the argument we are looking at can establish at
most that there are *some* cases in which the unborn person has a right to
the use of its mother's body, and therefore *some* cases in which abortion is
unjust killing. There is room for much discussion and argument as to precisely which, if any. But I think we should sidestep this issue and leave it
open, for at any rate the argument certainly does not establish that all
abortion is unjust killing.

5. There is room for yet another argument here, however. We surely
must all grant that there may be cases in which it would be morally indecent to detach a person from your body at the cost of his life. Suppose you
learn that what the violinist needs is not nine years of your life, but only
one hour: all you need do to save his life is to spend one hour in that bed
with him. Suppose also that letting him use your kidneys for that one hour
would not affect your health in the slightest. Admittedly you were kidnapped. Admittedly you did not give anyone permission to plug him into
you. Nevertheless it seems to me plain you *ought* to allow him to use your
kidneys for that hour—it would be indecent to refuse.

Again, suppose pregnancy lasted only an hour, and constituted no
threat to life or health. And suppose that a woman becomes pregnant as a

result of rape. Admittedly she did not voluntarily do anything to bring about the existence of a child. Admittedly she did nothing at all which would give the unborn person a right to the use of her body. All the same it might well be said, as in the newly emended violinist story, that she *ought* to allow it to remain for that hour—that it would be indecent in her to refuse. . . .

6. My argument will be found unsatisfactory on two counts by many of those who want to regard abortion as morally permissible. First, while I do argue that abortion is not impermissible, I do not argue that it is always permissible. There may well be cases in which carrying the child to term requires only Minimally Decent Samaritanism[2] of the mother, and this is a standard we must not fall below. I am inclined to think it a merit of my account precisely that it does *not* give a general yes or a general no. It allows for and supports our sense that, for example, a sick and desperately frightened fourteen-year-old schoolgirl, pregnant due to rape, may *of course* choose abortion, and that any law which rules this out is an insane law. And it also allows for and supports our sense that in other cases resort to abortion is even positively indecent. It would be indecent in the woman to request an abortion, and indecent in a doctor to perform it, if she is in her seventh month, and wants the abortion just to avoid the nuisance of postponing a trip abroad. The very fact that the arguments I have been drawing attention to treat all cases of abortion, or even all cases of abortion in which the mother's life is not at stake, as morally on a par ought to have made them suspect at the outset.

Secondly, while I am arguing for the permissibility of abortion in some cases, I am not arguing for the right to secure the death of the unborn child. It is easy to confuse these two things in that up to a certain point in the life of the fetus it is not able to survive outside the mother's body; hence removing it from her body guarantees its death. But they are importantly different. I have argued that you are not morally required to spend nine months in bed, sustaining the life of that violinist; but to say this is by no means to say that if, when you unplug yourself, there is a miracle and he survives, you then have a right to turn round and slit his throat. You may detach yourself even if this costs him his life; you have no right to be guaranteed his death, by some other means, if unplugging yourself does not kill him. There are some people who will feel dissatisfied by this feature of my argument. A woman may be utterly devastated by the thought of a

---

2 Meeting a standard of minimally decent treatment towards those in need.—Ed.

child, a bit of herself, put out for adoption and never seen or heard of again. She may therefore want not merely that the child be detached from her, but more, that it die. Some opponents of abortion are inclined to regard this as beneath contempt—thereby showing insensitivity to what is surely a powerful source of despair. All the same, I agree that the desire for the child's death is not one which anybody may gratify, should it turn out to be possible to detach the child alive.

At this place, however, it should be remembered that we have only been pretending throughout that the fetus is a human being from the moment of conception. A very early abortion is surely not the killing of a person, and so is not dealt with by anything I have said here.

Judith Jarvis Thomson: A Defense of Abortion

1. Thomson's first thought experiment is the case of the violinist. Do you agree that it would be permissible to unplug yourself from the violinist? What conclusions about abortion should we draw from this thought experiment?
2. What is the "extreme view"? What are Thomson's objections to the view? Do you find her objections compelling?
3. Thomson claims that the notion of a "right to life" cannot be interpreted as a right to "the bare minimum one needs for continued life." Why does she claim this? What, according to Thomson, does having a right to life amount to? Do you agree with her about this?
4. Why doesn't Thomson think that abortion always involves unjust killing? What does the justice of abortion depend on, according to Thomson?
5. Under what conditions (if any) do you think a woman grants a fetus the right to use her body?

31

Why Abortion Is Immoral

Don Marquis

In this article, Don Marquis argues, from entirely secular premises, to the conclusion that abortion is, in most circumstances, a form of murder. He does this by first trying to explain why it is immoral to kill people like you and me. After canvassing a few popular but mistaken options, he arrives at his answer. Such killing is immoral because it deprives us of a future of value.

Human fetuses—most of them, at least—also share this feature. And therefore it is ordinarily wrong to kill human fetuses. And so abortion is usually immoral. Marquis considers a variety of objections to his view, and concludes his article by trying to show how each of them can be met.

The view that abortion is, with rare exceptions, seriously immoral has received little support in the recent philosophical literature. No doubt most philosophers affiliated with secular institutions of higher education believe that the anti-abortion position is either a symptom of irrational religious dogma or a conclusion generated by seriously confused philosophical argument. The purpose of this essay is to undermine this general belief. This essay sets out an argument that purports to

Don Marquis, "Why Abortion Is Immoral" from *Journal of Philosophy* 86 (1989), pp. 183–202. Used by permission of Don Marquis and *The Journal of Philosophy*.

show, as well as any argument in ethics can show, that abortion is, except possibly in rare cases, seriously immoral, that it is in the same moral category as killing an innocent adult human being. . . .

I.

A sketch of standard anti-abortion and pro-choice arguments exhibits how those arguments possess certain symmetries that explain why partisans of those positions are so convinced of the correctness of their own positions, why they are not successful in convincing their opponents, and why, to others, this issue seems to be unresolvable. An analysis of the nature of this standoff suggests a strategy for surmounting it.

Consider the way a typical anti-abortionist argues. She will argue or assert that life is present from the moment of conception or that fetuses look like babies or that fetuses possess a characteristic such as a genetic code that is both necessary and sufficient for being human. Anti-abortionists seem to believe that (1) the truth of all of these claims is quite obvious, and (2) establishing any of these claims is sufficient to show that abortion is morally akin to murder.

A standard pro-choice strategy exhibits similarities. The pro-choicer will argue or assert that fetuses are not persons or that fetuses are not rational agents or that fetuses are not social beings. Pro-choicers seem to believe that (1) the truth of any of these claims is quite obvious, and (2) establishing any of these claims is sufficient to show that an abortion is not a wrongful killing.

In fact, both the pro-choice and the anti-abortion claims do seem to be true, although the "it looks like a baby" claim is more difficult to establish the earlier the pregnancy. We seem to have a standoff. How can it be resolved?

As everyone who has taken a bit of logic knows, if any of these arguments concerning abortion is a good argument, it requires not only some claim characterizing fetuses, but also some general moral principle that ties a characteristic of fetuses to having or not having the right to life or to some other moral characteristic that will generate the obligation or the lack of obligation not to end the life of a fetus. Accordingly, the arguments of the anti-abortionist and the pro-choicer need a bit of filling in to be regarded as adequate.

Note what each partisan will say. The anti-abortionist will claim that her position is supported by such generally accepted moral principles as

"It is always prima facie seriously wrong to take a human life" or "It is always prima facie seriously wrong to end the life of a baby." Since these are generally accepted moral principles, her position is certainly not obviously wrong. The pro-choicer will claim that her position is supported by such plausible moral principles as "Being a person is what gives an individual intrinsic moral worth" or "It is only seriously prima facie wrong to take the life of a member of the human community." Since these are generally accepted moral principles, the pro-choice position is certainly not obviously wrong. Unfortunately, we have again arrived at a standoff.

Now, how might one deal with this standoff? The standard approach is to try to show how the moral principles of one's opponent lose their plausibility under analysis. It is easy to see how this is possible. On the one hand, the anti-abortionist will defend a moral principle concerning the wrongness of killing which tends to be broad in scope in order that even fetuses at an early stage of pregnancy will fall under it. The problem with broad principles is that they often embrace too much. In this particular instance, the principle "It is always prima facie wrong to take a human life" seems to entail that it is wrong to end the existence of a living human cancer-cell culture, on the grounds that the culture is both living and human. Therefore, it seems that the anti-abortionist's favored principle is too broad.

On the other hand, the pro-choicer wants to find a moral principle concerning the wrongness of killing which tends to be narrow in scope in order that fetuses will *not* fall under it. The problem with narrow principles is that they often do *not* embrace enough. Hence, the needed principles such as "It is prima facie seriously wrong to kill only persons" or "It is prima facie wrong to kill only rational agents" do not explain why it is wrong to kill infants or young children or the severely retarded or even perhaps the severely mentally ill. Therefore, we seem again to have a standoff. The anti-abortionist charges, not unreasonably, that pro-choice principles concerning killing are too narrow to be acceptable; the pro-choicer charges, not unreasonably, that anti-abortionist principles concerning killing are too broad to be acceptable. . . .

All this suggests that a necessary condition of resolving the abortion controversy is a more theoretical account of the wrongness of killing. After all, if we merely believe, but do not understand, why killing adult human beings such as ourselves is wrong, how could we conceivably show that abortion is either immoral or permissible?

II.

In order to develop such an account, we can start from the following unproblematic assumption concerning our own case: it is wrong to kill *us*. Why is it wrong? Some answers can be easily eliminated. It might be said that what makes killing us wrong is that a killing brutalizes the one who kills. But the brutalization consists of being inured to the performance of an act that is hideously immoral; hence, the brutalization does not explain the immorality. It might be said that what makes killing us wrong is the great loss others would experience due to our absence. Although such hubris is understandable, such an explanation does not account for the wrongness of killing hermits, or those whose lives are relatively independent and whose friends find it easy to make new friends.

A more obvious answer is better. What primarily makes killing wrong is neither its effect on the murderer nor its effect on the victim's friends and relatives, but its effect on the victim. The loss of one's life is one of the greatest losses one can suffer. The loss of one's life deprives one of all the experiences, activities, projects, and enjoyments that would otherwise have constituted one's future. Therefore, killing someone is wrong, primarily because the killing inflicts (one of) the greatest possible losses on the victim. To describe this as the loss of life can be misleading, however. The change in my biological state does not by itself make killing me wrong. The effect of the loss of my biological life is the loss to me of all those activities, projects, experiences, and enjoyments which would otherwise have constituted my future personal life. These activities, projects, experiences, and enjoyments are either valuable for their own sakes or are means to something else that is valuable for its own sake. Some parts of my future are not valued by me now, but will come to be valued by me as I grow older and as my values and capacities change. When I am killed, I am deprived both of what I now value which would have been part of my future personal life, but also what I would come to value. Therefore, when I die, I am deprived of all of the value of my future. Inflicting this loss on me is ultimately what makes killing me wrong. This being the case, it would seem that what makes killing *any* adult human being prima facie seriously wrong is the loss of his or her future.[1]

---

1 I have been most influenced on this matter by Jonathan Glover, *Causing Death and Saving Lives* (New York: Penguin, 1977), ch. 3; and Robert Young, "What Is So Wrong with Killing People?" *Philosophy*, LIV, 210 (1979): 515–528.

How should this rudimentary theory of the wrongness of killing be evaluated? It cannot be faulted for deriving an 'ought' from an 'is', for it does not. The analysis assumes that killing me (or you, reader) is prima facie seriously wrong. The point of the analysis is to establish which natural property ultimately explains the wrongness of the killing, given that it is wrong. A natural property will ultimately explain the wrongness of killing, only if (1) the explanation fits with our intuitions about the matter and (2) there is no other natural property that provides the basis for a better explanation of the wrongness of killing. This analysis rests on the intuition that what makes killing a particular human or animal wrong is what it does to that particular human or animal. What makes killing wrong is some natural effect or other of the killing. Some would deny this. For instance, a divine-command theorist in ethics would deny it. Surely this denial is, however, one of those features of divine-command theory which renders it so implausible.

The claim that what makes killing wrong is the loss of the victim's future is directly supported by two considerations. In the first place, this theory explains why we regard killing as one of the worst of crimes. Killing is especially wrong, because it deprives the victim of more than perhaps any other crime. In the second place, people with AIDS or cancer who know they are dying believe, of course, that dying is a very bad thing for them. They believe that the loss of a future to them that they would otherwise have experienced is what makes their premature death a very bad thing for them. A better theory of the wrongness of killing would require a different natural property associated with killing which better fits with the attitudes of the dying. What could it be?

The view that what makes killing wrong is the loss to the victim of the value of the victim's future gains additional support when some of its implications are examined. In the first place, it is incompatible with the view that it is wrong to kill only beings who are biologically human. It is possible that there exists a different species from another planet whose members have a future like ours. Since having a future like that is what makes killing someone wrong, this theory entails that it would be wrong to kill members of such a species. Hence, this theory is opposed to the claim that only life that is biologically human has great moral worth, a claim which many anti-abortionists have seemed to adopt. This opposition, which this theory has in common with personhood theories, seems to be a merit of the theory.

In the second place, the claim that the loss of one's future is the wrong-making feature of one's being killed entails the possibility that the futures of some actual nonhuman mammals on our own planet are sufficiently like ours that it is seriously wrong to kill them also. Whether some animals do have the same right to life as human beings depends on adding to the account of the wrongness of killing some additional account of just what it is about my future or the futures of other adult human beings which makes it wrong to kill us. No such additional account will be offered in this essay. Undoubtedly, the provision of such an account would be a very difficult matter. Undoubtedly, any such account would be quite controversial. Hence, it surely should not reflect badly on this sketch of an elementary theory of the wrongness of killing that it is indeterminate with respect to some very difficult issues regarding animal rights.

In the third place, the claim that the loss of one's future is the wrong-making feature of one's being killed does not entail, as sanctity of human life theories do, that active euthanasia is wrong. Persons who are severely and incurably ill, who face a future of pain and despair, and who wish to die will not have suffered a loss if they are killed. It is, strictly speaking, the value of a human's future which makes killing wrong in this theory. This being so, killing does not necessarily wrong some persons who are sick and dying. Of course, there may be other reasons for a prohibition of active euthanasia, but that is another matter. Sanctity-of-human-life theories seem to hold that active euthanasia is seriously wrong even in an individual case where there seems to be good reason for it independently of public policy considerations. This consequence is most implausible, and it is a plus for the claim that the loss of a future of value is what makes killing wrong that it does not share this consequence.

In the fourth place, the account of the wrongness of killing defended in this essay does straightforwardly entail that it is prima facie seriously wrong to kill children and infants, for we do presume that they have futures of value. Since we do believe that it is wrong to kill defenseless little babies, it is important that a theory of the wrongness of killing easily account for this. Personhood theories of the wrongness of killing, on the other hand, cannot straightforwardly account for the wrongness of killing infants and young children. Hence, such theories must add special ad hoc accounts of the wrongness of killing the young. The plausibility of such ad hoc theories seems to be a function of how desperately one wants such theories to work. The claim that the primary wrong-making feature of a killing is the loss to the victim of the value of its future accounts for the wrongness of killing young children and infants directly; it makes the wrongness of such acts as obvious as we actually think it is. This is a further merit of this theory. Accordingly, it seems that this value of a future-like-ours theory of the wrongness of killing shares strengths of both sanctity-of-life and personhood accounts while avoiding weaknesses of both. In addition, it meshes with a central intuition concerning what makes killing wrong.

The claim that the primary wrong-making feature of a killing is the loss to the victim of the value of its future has obvious consequences for the ethics of abortion. The future of a standard fetus includes a set of experiences, projects, activities, and such which are identical with the futures of adult human beings and are identical with the futures of young children. Since the reason that is sufficient to explain why it is wrong to kill human beings after the time of birth is a reason that also applies to fetuses, it follows that abortion is prima facie seriously morally wrong.

This argument does not rely on the invalid inference that, since it is wrong to kill persons, it is wrong to kill potential persons also. The category that is morally central to this analysis is the category of having a valuable future like ours; it is not the category of personhood. The argument to the conclusion that abortion is prima facie seriously morally wrong proceeded independently of the notion of person or potential person or any equivalent. Someone may wish to start with this analysis in terms of the value of a human future, conclude that abortion is, except perhaps in rare circumstances, seriously morally wrong, infer that fetuses have the right to life, and then call fetuses "persons" as a result of their having the right to life. Clearly, in this case, the category of person is being used to state the *conclusion* of the analysis rather than to generate the *argument* of the analysis. . . .

Of course, this value of a future-like-ours argument, if sound, shows only that abortion is prima facie wrong, not that it is wrong in any and all circumstances. Since the loss of the future to a standard fetus, if killed, is, however, at least as great a loss as the loss of the future to a standard adult human being who is killed, abortion, like ordinary killing, could be justified only by the most compelling reasons. The loss of one's life is almost the greatest misfortune that can happen to one. Presumably abortion could be justified in some circumstances, only if the loss consequent on failing to abort would be at least as great. Accordingly, morally permissible abortions will be rare indeed unless, perhaps, they occur so early in pregnancy that a fetus is not yet definitely an individual. Hence, this argument should be taken as showing that abortion is presumptively very seriously wrong, where the presumption is very strong—as strong as the presumption that killing another adult human being is wrong.

III.

How complete an account of the wrongness of killing does the value of a future-like-ours account have to be in order that the wrongness of abortion is a consequence? This account does not have to be an account of the necessary conditions for the wrongness of killing. Some persons in nursing homes may lack valuable human futures, yet it may be wrong to kill them for other reasons. Furthermore, this account does not obviously have to be the sole reason killing is wrong where the victim did have a valuable future. This analysis claims only that, for any killing where the victim did have a valuable future like ours, having that future by itself is sufficient to create the strong presumption that the killing is seriously wrong.

One way to overturn the value of a future-like-ours argument would be to find some account of the wrongness of killing which is at least as intelligible and which has different implications for the ethics of abortion. . . .

One move of this sort is based upon the claim that a necessary condition of one's future being valuable is that one values it. Value implies a valuer. Given this one might argue that, since fetuses cannot value their futures, their futures are not valuable to them. Hence, it does not seriously wrong them deliberately to end their lives.

This move fails, however, because of some ambiguities. Let us assume that something cannot be of value unless it is valued by someone. This does not entail that my life is of no value unless it is valued by me. I may think, in a period of despair, that my future is of no worth whatsoever, but I may be wrong because others rightly see value—even great value—in it. Furthermore, my future can be valuable to me even if I do not value it. This is the case when a young person attempts suicide, but is rescued and goes on to significant human achievements. Such young people's futures are ultimately valuable to them, even though such futures do not seem to be valuable to them at the moment of attempted suicide. A fetus's future can be valuable to it in the same way. Accordingly, this attempt to limit the anti-abortion argument fails.

Another similar attempt to reject the anti-abortion position is based on Tooley's claim that an entity cannot possess the right to life unless it has the capacity to desire its continued existence. It follows that, since fetuses lack the conceptual capacity to desire to continue to live, they lack the right to life. Accordingly, Tooley concludes that abortion cannot be seriously prima facie wrong.[2] . . .

One might attempt to defend Tooley's basic claim on the grounds that, because a fetus cannot apprehend continued life as a benefit, its continued life cannot be a benefit or cannot be something it has a right to or cannot be something that is in its interest. This might be defended in terms of the general proposition that, if an individual is literally incapable of caring about or taking an interest in some X, then one does not have a right to X or X is not a benefit or X is not something that is in one's interest.

Each member of this family of claims seems to be open to objections. As John C. Stevens[3] has pointed out, one may have a right to be treated with a certain medical procedure (because of a health insurance policy one has purchased), even though one cannot conceive of the nature of the procedure. And, as Tooley himself has pointed out, persons who have been indoctrinated, or drugged, or rendered temporarily unconscious may be literally incapable of caring about or taking an interest in something that is in their interest or is something to which they have a right, or is something that benefits them. Hence, the Tooley claim that would restrict the scope of the value of a future-like-ours argument is undermined by counterexamples. . . .[4]

IV.

In this essay, it has been argued that the correct ethic of the wrongness of killing can be extended to fetal life and used to show that there is a strong presumption that any abortion is morally impermissible. If the ethic of killing adopted here entails, however, that contraception is also seriously immoral, then there would appear to be a difficulty with the analysis of this essay.

But this analysis does not entail that contraception is wrong. Of course, contraception prevents the actualization of a possible future of value. Hence, it follows from the claim that futures of value should be maximized that contraception is prima facie immoral. This obligation to

---

2 Michael Tooley, *Abortion and Infanticide* (NY: Oxford University Press, 1984), pp. 46–47.

3 "Must the Bearer of a Right Have the Concept of That to Which He Has a Right?" *Ethics*, xcv, 1 (1984): 68–74.

4 See Tooley again in *Abortion and Infanticide*, pp. 47–49.

maximize does not exist, however; furthermore, nothing in the ethics of killing in this paper entails that it does. The ethics of killing in this essay would entail that contraception is wrong only if something were denied a human future of value by contraception. Nothing at all is denied such a future by contraception, however.

Candidates for a subject of harm by contraception fall into four categories: (1) some sperm or other, (2) some ovum or other, (3) a sperm and an ovum separately, and (4) a sperm and an ovum together. Assigning the harm to some sperm is utterly arbitrary, for no reason can be given for making a sperm the subject of harm rather than an ovum. Assigning the harm to some ovum is utterly arbitrary, for no reason can be given for making an ovum the subject of harm rather than a sperm. One might attempt to avoid these problems by insisting that contraception deprives both the sperm and the ovum separately of a valuable future like ours. On this alternative, too many futures are lost. Contraception was supposed to be wrong, because it deprived us of one future of value, not two. One might attempt to avoid this problem by holding that contraception deprives the combination of sperm and ovum of a valuable future like ours. But here the definite article misleads. At the time of contraception, there are hundreds of millions of sperm, one (released) ovum and millions of possible combinations of all of these. There is no actual combination at all. Is the subject of the loss to be a merely possible combination? Which one? This alternative does not yield an actual subject of harm either. Accordingly, the immorality of contraception is not entailed by the loss of a future-like-ours argument simply because there is no nonarbitrarily identifiable subject of the loss in the case of contraception.

Don Marquis: Why Abortion Is Immoral

1. Marquis begins by criticizing some common arguments on both sides of the abortion issue. Do his criticisms succeed in refuting the common arguments? Why or why not?
2. What, according to Marquis, is wrong with killing adult humans? Is his theory the best account of what is wrong with such killing?
3. Marquis claims that abortion is wrong for the same reason that killing adult humans is wrong. Are there any differences between the two that would justify abortion?
4. One might object to Marquis's claim that fetuses have a valuable future by pointing out that fetuses do not have the cognitive capacities to value

anything. How does Marquis respond to this objection? Do you find his response convincing?

5. Marquis admits that his theory would be problematic if it led to the view that contraception is seriously morally wrong. How does he argue that his theory does not do this? Do you think he succeeds?

==== ❧ ====

32

Abortion and the Doctrine of Double Effect

Philippa Foot

....

In this article, Philippa Foot (1920–2010) introduces and discusses the merits of the ethical principle known as the doctrine of double effect. The doctrine states that, under certain conditions, it is permitted to cause harm if the harm is merely foreseen, rather than directly intended. Foot offers a variety of fascinating cases to explore the difference between foresight and intention. Many of these cases have become classic examples within moral philosophy, none more so than the Trolley Problem.

The Trolley Problem has generated many variations, but the central case is simple. There is a runaway trolley; you can either allow it to continue on its way, or switch it to a spur. Why would you do either? Well, there are five people on the track ahead, and only one on the spur. All six are innocent. Intuitively, it seems at least permissible, and many think it required, to pull the lever that will send the trolley to the spur. From this example, you might infer that whenever we have to choose between saving a greater and a lesser number of innocent lives, we ought to save the greater number. But, as Foot shows, such a claim is deeply problematic.

In its most general formulation, the challenge is to explain precisely why it is only sometimes, and not always, morally acceptable to minimize harm. The doctrine of double effect has been introduced to

Philippa Foot, "The Problem of Abortion and the Doctrine of the Double Effect" from *Oxford Review* 5 (1967), pp. 5–15. Reprinted by permission of the Principal and Fellows of Somerville College Oxford.

do the needed explaining, but Foot finds the doctrine flawed. She concludes with a presentation of her own solution, and an application of it to the issue of abortion.

....

One of the reasons why most of us feel puzzled about the problem of abortion is that we want, and do not want, to allow to the unborn child the rights that belong to adults and children. When we think of a baby about to be born it seems absurd to think that the next few minutes or even hours could make so radical a difference to its status; yet as we go back in the life of the foetus we are more and more reluctant to say that this is a human being and must be treated as such. No doubt this is the deepest source of our dilemma, but it is not the only one. For we are also confused about the general question of what we may and may not do where the interests of human beings conflict. We have strong intuitions about certain cases; saying, for instance, that it is all right to raise the level of education in our country, though statistics allow us to predict that a rise in the suicide rate will follow, while it is not all right to kill the feeble-minded to aid cancer research. It is not easy, however, to see the principles involved, and one way of throwing light on the abortion issue will be by setting up parallels involving adults or children once born. So we will be able to isolate the "equal rights" issue, and should be able to make some advance.

I shall not, of course, discuss all the principles that may be used in deciding what to do where the interests or rights of human beings conflict. What I want to do is to look at one particular theory, known as the "doctrine of the double effect" which is invoked by Catholics in support of their views on abortion but supposed by them to apply elsewhere. As used in the abortion argument this doctrine has often seemed to non-Catholics to be a piece of complete sophistry. . . . And yet this principle has seemed to some non-Catholics as well as to Catholics to stand as the only defence against decisions on other issues that are quite unacceptable. It will help us in our difficulty about abortion if this conflict can be resolved.

The doctrine of the double effect is based on a distinction between what a man foresees as a result of his voluntary action and what, in the strict sense, he intends. He intends in the strictest sense both those things that he aims at as ends and those that he aims at as means to his ends. The latter may be regretted in themselves but nevertheless desired for the sake of the end, as we may intend to keep dangerous lunatics confined for the sake of our safety. By contrast a man is said not strictly, or directly, to intend the foreseen consequences of his voluntary actions where these are neither the end at which he is aiming nor the means to this end. Whether the word "intention" should be applied in both cases is not of course what matters: Bentham spoke of "oblique intention," contrasting it with the "direct intention" of ends and means, and we may as well follow his terminology. Everyone must recognize that some such distinction can be made, though it may be made in a number of different ways, and it is the distinction that is crucial to the doctrine of the double effect. The words "double effect" refer to the two effects that an action may produce: the one aimed at, and the one foreseen but in no way desired. By "the doctrine of the double effect" I mean the thesis that it is sometimes permissible to bring about by oblique intention what one may not directly intend. Thus the distinction is held to be relevant to moral decision in certain difficult cases. It is said for instance that the operation of hysterectomy involves the death of the foetus as the foreseen but not strictly or directly intended consequence of the surgeon's act, while other operations kill the child and count as the direct intention of taking an innocent life, a distinction that has evoked particularly bitter reactions on the part of non-Catholics. If you are permitted to bring about the death of the child, what does it matter how it is done? The doctrine of the double effect is also used to show why in another case, where a woman in labour will die unless a craniotomy operation is performed, the intervention is not to be condoned. There, it is said, we may not operate, but must let the mother die. We foresee her death but do not directly intend it, whereas to crush the skull of the child would count as direct intention of its death.

This last application of the doctrine has been queried by Professor Hart on the ground that the child's death is not strictly a means to saving the mother's life and should logically be treated as an unwanted but foreseen consequence by those who make use of the distinction between direct and oblique intention. To interpret the doctrine in this way is perfectly reasonable given the language that has been used; it would, however, make nonsense of it from the beginning. A certain event may be desired under one of its descriptions, unwanted under another, but we cannot treat these as two different events, one of which is aimed at and the other not. And even if it be argued that there are here two different events—the crushing of the child's skull and its death—the two are obviously much too close for an application of the doctrine of the double effect. To see how odd it would be to apply the principle like this we may consider the story, well known to philosophers, of the fat man stuck in the mouth of the cave. A party of potholers have imprudently allowed the fat man to lead them as they make their way out of the cave, and he gets stuck, trapping the others behind him. Obviously the right thing to do is to sit down and wait until the fat man grows thin; but philosophers have arranged that flood waters should be rising within the cave. Luckily (luckily?) the trapped party have with them a stick of dynamite with which they can blast the fat man out of the mouth of the cave. Either they use the dynamite or they drown. In one version the fat man, whose head is *in* the cave, will drown with them; in the other he will be rescued in due course. Problem: may they use the dynamite or not? Later we will find parallels to this example. Here it is introduced for light relief and because it will serve to show how ridiculous one version of the doctrine of the double effect would be. For suppose that the trapped explorers were to argue that the death of the fat man might be taken as a merely foreseen consequence of the act of blowing him up. ("We didn't want to kill him ... only to blow him into small pieces" or even " ... only to blast him out of the mouth of the cave.") I believe that those who use the doctrine of the double effect would rightly reject such a suggestion, though they will, of course, have considerable difficulty in explaining where the line is to be drawn. What is to be the criterion of "closeness" if we say that anything very close to what we are literally aiming at counts as if part of our aim?

Let us leave this difficulty aside and return to the arguments for and against the doctrine, supposing it to be formulated in the way considered most effective by its supporters, and ourselves bypassing the trouble by taking what must on any reasonable definition be clear cases of "direct" or "oblique" intention.

The first point that should be made clear, in fairness to the theory, is that no one is suggesting that it does not matter what you bring about as long as you merely foresee and do not strictly intend the evil that follows. We might think, for instance, of the (actual) case of wicked merchants selling, for cooking, oil they knew to be poisonous and thereby killing a number of innocent people, comparing and contrasting it with that of some unemployed gravediggers, desperate for custom, who got hold of this same oil and sold it (or perhaps *they* secretly gave it away) in order to create orders for graves. They strictly (directly) intend the deaths they cause, while the merchants could say that it was not part of their *plan* that anyone should die. In morality, as in law, the merchants, like the gravediggers, would be considered as murderers; nor are the supporters of the doctrine of the double effect bound to say that there is the least difference between them in respect of moral turpitude. What they are committed to is the thesis that *sometimes* it makes a difference to the permissibility of an action involving harm to others that this harm, although foreseen, is not part of the agent's direct intention. An end such as earning one's living is clearly not such as to justify *either* the direct or oblique intention of the death of innocent people, but in certain cases one is justified in bringing about knowingly what one could not directly intend.

It is now time to say why this doctrine should be taken seriously in spite of the fact that it sounds rather odd, that there are difficulties about the distinction on which it depends, and that it seemed to yield one sophistical conclusion when applied to the problem of abortion. The reason for its appeal is that its opponents have often *seemed* to be committed to quite indefensible views. Thus the controversy has raged around examples such as the following. Suppose that a judge or magistrate is faced with rioters demanding that a culprit be found for a certain crime and threatening otherwise to take their own bloody revenge on a particular section of the community. The real culprit being unknown, the judge sees himself as able to prevent the bloodshed only by framing some innocent person and having him executed. Beside this example is placed another in which a pilot whose aeroplane is about to crash is deciding whether to steer from a more to a less inhabited area. To make the parallel as close as possible it may rather be supposed that he is the driver of a runaway tram which he can only steer from one narrow track on to another; five men are working on one track and one man on the other; anyone on the track he enters is bound to be killed. In the case of the riots the mob have five hostages, so that in both the exchange is supposed to be one man's life for the lives of five. The question is why we should say, without hesitation, that the driver should steer for the less occupied track, while most of us would be appalled at the idea that the innocent man could be framed. It may be suggested that the special feature of the latter case is that it involves the corruption of justice, and this is, of course, very important indeed. But if we remove that special feature, supposing that some private individual is to kill an innocent person and pass him off as the criminal, we still find ourselves horrified by the idea. The doctrine of the double effect offers us a way out of the difficulty, insisting that it is one thing to steer towards someone foreseeing that you will kill him and another to aim at his death as part of your plan.

Moreover there is one very important element of good in what is here insisted. In real life it would hardly ever be certain that the man on the narrow track would be killed. Perhaps he might find a foothold on the side of the tunnel and cling on as the vehicle hurtled by. The driver of the tram does not then leap off and brain him with a crowbar. The judge, however, needs the death of the innocent man for his (good) purposes. If the victim proves hard to hang he must see to it that he dies another way. To choose to execute him is to choose that this evil *shall come about,* and this must therefore count as a *certainty* in weighing up the good and evil involved. The distinction between direct and oblique intention is crucial here, and is of great importance in an uncertain world. Nevertheless this is no way to defend the doctrine of the double effect. For the question is whether the difference between aiming at something and obliquely intending it is *in itself* relevant to moral decisions; not whether it is important when correlated with a difference of certainty in the balance of good and evil. Moreover we are particularly interested in the application of the doctrine of the double effect to the question of abortion, and no one can deny that in medicine there are sometimes certainties so complete that it would be a mere quibble to speak of the "probable outcome" of this course of action or that. It is not, therefore, with a merely philosophical interest that we should put aside the uncertainty and scrutinize the examples to test the doctrine of the double effect. Why can we not argue from the case of the steering driver to that of the judge?

Another pair of examples poses a similar problem. We are about to give to a patient who needs it to save his life a massive dose of a certain drug in short supply. There arrive, however, five other patients each of whom could be saved by one-fifth of that dose. We say with regret that we cannot spare our whole supply of the drug for a single patient, just as we should say that we could not spare the whole resources of a ward for one dangerously ill individual when ambulances arrive bringing in the victims of a multiple crash. We feel bound to let one man die rather than many if that is our only choice. Why then do we not feel justified in killing people in the interests of cancer research or to obtain, let us say, spare parts for grafting on to those who need them? We can suppose, similarly, that several dangerously ill people can be saved only if we kill a certain individual and make a serum from his dead body. (These examples are not over fanciful considering present controversies about prolonging the life of mortally ill patients whose eyes or kidneys are to be used for others.) Why cannot we argue from the case of the scarce drug to that of the body needed for medical purposes? Once again the doctrine of the double effect comes up with an explanation. In one kind of case but not the other we aim at the death of the innocent man.

A further argument suggests that if the doctrine of the double effect is rejected this has the consequence of putting us hopelessly in the power of bad men. Suppose for example that some tyrant should threaten to torture five men if we ourselves would not torture one. Would it be our duty to do so, supposing we believed him, because this would be no different from choosing to rescue five men from his torturers rather than one? If so anyone who wants us to do something we think wrong has only to threaten that otherwise he himself will do something we think worse. A mad murderer, known to keep his promises, could thus make it our duty to kill some innocent citizen to prevent him from killing two. From this conclusion we are again rescued by the doctrine of the double effect. If we refuse, we foresee that the greater number will be killed but we do not intend it: it is he who intends (that is strictly or directly intends) the death of innocent persons; we do not.

At one time I thought that these arguments in favour of the doctrine of the double effect were conclusive, but I now believe that the conflict should be solved in another way. The clue that we should follow is that the strength of the doctrine seems to lie in the distinction it makes between what we do (equated with direct intention) and what we allow (thought of as obliquely intended). Indeed it is interesting that the disputants tend to argue about whether we are to be held responsible for what we allow as we are for what we do. Yet it is not obvious that this is what they should be discussing, since the distinction between what one does and what one allows to happen is not the same as that between direct and oblique intention. To see this one has only to consider that it is possible *deliberately* to allow something to happen, aiming at it either for its own sake or as part of one's plan for obtaining something else. So one person might want another person dead, and deliberately allow him to die. And again one may be said to do things that one does not aim at, as the steering driver would kill the man on the track. Moreover there is a large class of things said to be brought about rather than either done or allowed, and either kind of intention is possible. So it is possible to *bring about* a man's death by getting him to go to sea in a leaky boat, and the intention of his death may be either direct or oblique.

Whatever it may, or may not, have to do with the doctrine of the double effect, the idea of *allowing* is worth looking into in this context. I shall leave aside the special case of giving permission, which involves the idea of authority, and consider the two main divisions into which cases of allowing seem to fall. There is firstly the allowing which is forbearing to prevent. For this we need a sequence thought of as somehow already in train, and something that the agent could do to intervene. (The agent must be able to intervene, but does not do so.) So, for instance, he could warn someone, but *allows* him to walk into a trap. He could feed an animal but *allows* it to die for lack of food. He could stop a leaking tap but *allows* the water to go on flowing. This is the case of allowing with which we shall be concerned, but the other should be mentioned. It is the kind of allowing which is roughly equivalent to *enabling*, the root idea being the removal of some obstacle which is, as it were, holding back a train of events. So someone may remove a plug and *allow* water to flow; open a door and *allow* an animal to get out; or give someone money and *allow* him to get back on his feet.

The first kind of allowing requires an omission, but there is no other general correlation between omission and allowing, commission and bringing about or doing. An actor who fails to turn up for a performance will generally spoil it rather than allow it to be spoiled. I mentioned the distinction between omission and commission only to not set it aside.

Thinking of the first kind of allowing (forbearing to prevent), we should ask whether there is any difference, from the moral point of view, between what one does or causes and what one merely allows. It seems clear that on occasions one is just as bad as the other, as is recognized in both morality and law. A man may murder his child or his aged relatives, by allowing them to die of starvation as well as by giving poison; he may also be convicted of murder on either account. In another case we would, however, make a distinction. Most of us allow people to die of starvation in India and Africa, and there is surely something wrong with us that we do; it would be nonsense, however, to pretend that it is only in law that we make a distinction between allowing people in the underdeveloped countries to die of starvation and sending them poisoned food. There is worked into our moral system a distinction between what we owe people in the form of aid and what we owe them in the way of noninterference. Salmond, in his *Jurisprudence*, expressed as follows the distinction between the two.

> A positive right corresponds to a positive duty, and is a right that he on whom the duty lies shall do some positive act on behalf of the person entitled. A negative right corresponds to a negative duty, and is a right

that the person bound shall refrain from some act which would operate to the prejudice of the person entitled. The former is a right to be
positively benefited; the latter is merely a right not to be harmed.[1]

As a general account of rights and duties this is defective, since not all are
so closely connected with benefit and harm. Nevertheless for our purposes it
will do well. Let us speak of negative duties when thinking of the obligation
to refrain from such things as killing or robbing, and of the positive duty, e.g.,
to look after children or aged parents. It will be useful, however, to extend the
notion of positive duty beyond the range of things that are strictly called
duties, bringing acts of charity under this heading. These are owed only in a
rather loose sense, and some acts of charity could hardly be said to be owed
at all, so I am not following ordinary usage at this point.

Let us now see whether the distinction of negative and positive duties
explains why we see differently the action of the steering driver and that of
the judge, of the doctors who withhold the scarce drug and those who
obtain a body for medical purposes, of those who choose to rescue the five
men rather than one man from torture and those who are ready to torture
the one man themselves in order to save five. In each case we have a conflict of duties, but what kind of duties are they? Are we, in each case,
weighing positive duties against positive, negative against negative, or one
against the other? Is the duty to refrain from injury, or rather to bring aid?

The steering driver faces a conflict of negative duties, since it is his
duty to avoid injuring five men and also his duty to avoid injuring one. In
the circumstances he is not able to avoid both, and it seems clear that he
should do the least injury he can. The judge, however, is weighing the duty
of not inflicting injury against the duty of bringing aid. He wants to rescue
the innocent people threatened with death but can do so only by inflicting
injury himself. Since one does not *in general* have the same duty to help
people as to refrain from injuring them, it is not possible to argue to a
conclusion about what he should do from the steering driver case. It is
interesting that, even where the strictest duty of positive aid exists, this still
does not weigh as if a negative duty were involved. It is not, for instance,
permissible to commit a murder to bring one's starving children food. If
the choice is between inflicting injury on one or many there seems only
one rational course of action; if the choice is between aid to some at the
cost of injury to others, and refusing to inflict the injury to bring the aid,

---

1 J. Salmond, *Jurisprudence*, 11th edition, p. 283.

the whole matter is open to dispute. So it is not inconsistent of us to think that the driver must steer for the road on which only one man stands while the judge (or his equivalent) may not kill the innocent person in order to stop the riots. Let us now consider the second pair of examples, which concern the scarce drug on the one hand and on the other the body needed to save lives. Once again we find a difference based on the distinction between the duty to avoid injury and the duty to provide aid. Where one man needs a massive dose of the drug and we withhold it from him in order to save five men, we are weighing aid against aid. But if we consider killing a man in order to use his body to save others, we are thinking of doing him injury to bring others aid. In an interesting variant of the model, we may suppose that instead of killing someone we deliberately let him die. (Perhaps he is a beggar to whom we are thinking of giving food, but then we say "No, they need bodies for medical research.") Here it does seem relevant that in allowing him to die we are aiming at his death, but presumably we are inclined to see this as a violation of negative rather than positive duty. If this is right, we see why we are unable in either case to argue to a conclusion from the case of the scarce drug.

In the examples involving the torturing of one man or five men, the principle seems to be the same as for the last pair. If we are bringing aid (rescuing people about to be tortured by the tyrant), we must obviously rescue the larger rather than the smaller group. It does not follow, however, that we would be justified in inflicting the injury, or getting a third person to do so, in order to save the five. We may therefore refuse to be forced into acting by the threats of bad men. To refrain from inflicting injury ourselves is a stricter duty than to prevent other people from inflicting injury, which is not to say that the other is not a very strict duty indeed.

So far the conclusions are the same as those at which we might arrive following the doctrine of the double effect, but in others they will be different, and the advantage seems to be on the side of the alternative. Suppose, for instance, that there are five patients in a hospital whose lives could be saved by the manufacture of a certain gas, but that this inevitably releases lethal fumes into the room of another patient whom for some reason we are unable to move. His death, being of no use to us, is clearly a side effect, and not directly intended. Why then is the case different from that of the scarce drug, if the point about that is that we foresaw but did not strictly intend the death of the single patient? Yet it surely is different. The relatives of the gassed patient would presumably be successful if they sued the hospital and the whole story came out. We may find it particularly revolting that someone should be *used* as in the case where he is killed or allowed to die in the interest of medical research, and the fact of *using* may even determine what we would decide to do in some cases, but the principle seems unimportant compared with our reluctance to bring such injury for the sake of giving aid.

My conclusion is that the distinction between direct and oblique intention plays only a quite subsidiary role in determining what we say in these cases, while the distinction between avoiding injury and bringing aid is very important indeed. I have not, of course, argued that there are no other principles. For instance it clearly makes a difference whether our positive duty is a strict duty or rather an act of charity: feeding our own children or feeding those in far away countries. It may also make a difference whether the person about to suffer is one thought of as uninvolved in the threatened disaster, and whether it is his presence that constitutes the threat to the others. In many cases we find it very hard to know what to say, and I have not been arguing for any general conclusion such as that we may never, whatever the balance of good and evil, bring injury to one for the sake of aid to others, even when this injury amounts to death. I have only tried to show that even if we reject the doctrine of the double effect we are not forced to the conclusion that the size of the evil must always be our guide.

Let us now return to the problem of abortion, carrying out our plan of finding parallels involving adults or children rather than the unborn. We must say something about the different cases in which abortion might be considered on medical grounds.

First of all there is the situation in which nothing that can be done will save the life of child and mother, but where the life of the mother can be saved by killing the child. This is parallel to the case of the fat man in the mouth of the cave who is bound to be drowned with the others if nothing is done. Given the certainty of the outcome, as it was postulated, there is no serious conflict of interests here, since the fat man will perish in either case, and it is reasonable that the action that will save someone should be done. It is a great objection to those who argue that the direct intention of the death of an innocent person is never justifiable that the edict will apply even in this case. The Catholic doctrine on abortion must here conflict with that of most reasonable men. Moreover we would be justified in performing the operation whatever the method used, and it is neither a necessary nor a good justification of the special case of hysterectomy that the child's death is not directly intended, being rather a foreseen consequence of what is done. What difference could it make as to how the death is brought about?

Secondly we have the case in which it is possible to perform an operation which will save the mother and kill the child or kill the mother and save the child. This is parallel to the famous case of the shipwrecked mariners who believed that they must throw someone overboard if their boat was not to founder in a storm, and to the other famous case of the two sailors, Dudley and Stephens, who killed and ate the cabin boy when adrift on the sea without food. Here again there is no conflict of interests so far as the decision to act is concerned; only in deciding whom to save. Once again it would be reasonable to act, though one would respect someone who held back from the appalling action either because he preferred to perish rather than do such a thing or because he held on past the limits of reasonable hope. In real life the certainties postulated by philosophers hardly ever exist, and Dudley and Stephens were rescued not long after their ghastly meal. Nevertheless if the certainty were absolute, as it might be in the abortion case, it would seem better to save one than none. Probably we should decide in favour of the mother when weighing her life against that of the unborn child, but it is interesting that, a few years later, we might easily decide it the other way.

The worst dilemma comes in the third kind of example where to save the mother we must kill the child, say by crushing its skull, while if nothing is done the mother will perish but the child can be safely delivered after her death. Here the doctrine of the double effect has been invoked to show that we may not intervene, since the child's death would be directly intended while the mother's would not. On a strict parallel with cases not involving the unborn we might find the conclusion correct though the reason given was wrong. Suppose, for instance, that in later life the presence of a child was certain to bring death to the mother. We would surely not think ourselves justified in ridding her of it by a process that involved its death. For in general we do not think that we can kill one innocent person to rescue another, quite apart from the special care that we feel is due to children once they have prudently got themselves born. What we would be prepared to do when a great many people were involved is another matter, and this is probably the key to one quite common view of abortion on the part of those who take quite seriously the rights of the unborn child. They probably feel that if *enough* people are involved one must be sacrificed, and they think of the mother's life against the unborn child's life as if it were many against one. But of course many people do not view it like this at all, having no inclination to accord to the foetus or unborn child anything like ordinary human status in the matter of rights. I have not been arguing for or against these points of view but only trying to discern some of the currents that are pulling us back and forth. The levity of the examples is not meant to offend.

Philippa Foot: Abortion and the Doctrine of Double Effect

1. What is the doctrine of double effect? Why does Foot think that the doctrine should be taken seriously?
2. What kinds of cases is the doctrine of double effect supposed to explain? Do you think the doctrine offers the correct moral verdict in these cases?
3. According to Foot, some have suggested that rejecting the doctrine of double effect would have "the consequence of putting us hopelessly in the power of bad men." What reason is there to believe this? Do you find the claim plausible?
4. What alternative to the doctrine of double effect does Foot offer? Does her theory succeed in explaining the cases that the doctrine of double effect was supposed to explain?
5. What advantages does Foot believe her theory has over the doctrine of double effect? Which theory do you think is better?
6. What conclusions does Foot draw about the morality of abortion? What other considerations, besides those Foot discusses, are relevant to the question of when (if ever) abortion is morally permissible?

33

=== ❧ ===

Justifying Legal Punishment
Igor Primoratz

....

In this excerpt from his book *Justifying Legal Punishment* (1989), Igor Primoratz defends the retributivist idea that a punishment is justified only if it gives a criminal his just deserts. But what do criminals deserve? Primoratz argues for the following principle: criminals deserve to be deprived of the same value that they deprived their victims of. Primoratz regards all human beings as possessed of lives of equal moral worth, and also believes that nothing is as valuable as human life. So murderers deserve to die. Since justice is a matter of giving people what they deserve, it follows that justice demands that murderers be executed.

Primoratz considers the most popular arguments of the opposing camp, and finds problems for each of them. Opponents claim that capital punishment violates a murderer's right to life; that killing murderers is contradictory; that capital punishment is disproportionally harsh; that the innocent are inevitably going to be executed; and that systematic discrimination undermines any chance at moral legitimacy. Primoratz carefully considers each objection and offers his replies. In the end, he thinks that justice requires the death penalty, that justice is the supreme legal virtue, and that none of the objections is strong enough to undermine the case for capital punishment. Therefore the state ought to execute convicted murderers.

....

... According to the retributive theory, consequences of punishment, however important from the practical point of view, are irrelevant when it comes to its justification; *the* moral consideration is its justice. Punishment is morally justified insofar as it is meted out as retribution for the offense committed. When someone has committed an offense, he deserves to be punished: it is just, and consequently justified, that he be punished. The offense is the sole ground of the state's right and duty to punish. It is also the measure of legitimate punishment: the two ought to be proportionate. So the issue of capital punishment within the retributive approach comes down to the question, Is this punishment ever proportionate retribution for the offense committed, and thus deserved, just, and justified?

The classic representatives of retributivism believed that it was, and that it was the only proportionate and hence appropriate punishment, if the offense was *murder*—that is, criminal homicide perpetrated voluntarily and intentionally or in wanton disregard of human life. In other cases, the demand for proportionality between offense and punishment can be satisfied by fines or prison terms; the crime of murder, however, is an exception in this respect, and calls for the literal interpretation of the *lex talionis*. The uniqueness of this crime has to do with the uniqueness of the value which has been deliberately or recklessly destroyed. We come across this idea as early as the original formulation of the retributive view—the biblical teaching on punishment: "You shall accept no ransom for the life of a murderer who is guilty of death; but he shall be put to death."[1] The rationale of this command—one that clearly distinguishes the biblical conception of the criminal law from contemporaneous criminal law systems in the Middle East—is that man was not only created *by* God, like every other creature, but also, alone among all the creatures, *in the image of God*:

> That man was made in the image of God ... is expressive of the peculiar and supreme worth of man. Of all creatures, Genesis 1 relates, he alone possesses this attribute, bringing him into closer relation to God than all the rest and conferring upon him the highest value. ... This view of the uniqueness and supremacy of human life ... places life beyond the reach of other values. The idea that life may be measured in terms of money or other property ... is excluded. Compensation of any kind is ruled out. The guilt of the murderer is infinite because the

---

1 Numbers 35.31 (R.S.V.).

murdered life is invaluable; the kinsmen of the slain man are not competent to say when he has been paid for. An absolute wrong has been committed, a sin against God which is not subject to human discussion. . . . Because human life is invaluable, to take it entails the death penalty.[2]

This view that the value of human life is not commensurable with other values, and that consequently there is only one truly equivalent punishment for murder, namely death, does not necessarily presuppose a theistic outlook. It can be claimed that, simply because we have to be alive if we are to experience and realize any other value at all, there is nothing equivalent to the murderous destruction of a human life except the destruction of the life of the murderer. Any other retribution, no matter how severe, would still be less than what is proportionate, deserved, and just. As long as the murderer is alive, no matter how bad the conditions of his life may be, there are always at least *some* values he can experience and realize. This provides a plausible interpretation of what the classical representatives of retributivism as a philosophical theory of punishment, such as Kant and Hegel, had to say on the subject.[3]

It seems to me that this is essentially correct. With respect to the larger question of the justification of punishment in general, it is the retributive theory that gives the right answer. Accordingly, capital punishment ought to be retained where it obtains, and reintroduced in those jurisdictions that have abolished it, although we have no reason to believe that, as a means of deterrence, it is any better than a very long prison term. It ought to be retained, or reintroduced, for one simple reason: that justice be done in cases of murder, that murderers be punished according to their deserts.

There are a number of arguments that have been advanced against this rationale of capital punishment. . . .

---

2 M. Greenberg, "Some Postulates of Biblical Criminal Law," in J. Goldin (ed.), *The Jewish Expression* (New York: Bantam, 1970), pp. 25–26. (Post-biblical Jewish law evolved toward the virtual abolition of the death penalty, but that is of no concern here.)

3 "There is no *parallel* between death and even the most miserable life, so that there is no equality of crime and retribution [in the case of murder] unless the perpetrator is judicially put to death" (I. Kant, "The Metaphysics of Morals," *Kant's Political Writings*, ed. H. Reiss, trans. H. B. Nisbet [Cambridge: Cambridge University Press, 1970], p. 156). "Since life is the full compass of a man's existence, the punishment [for murder] cannot simply consist in a 'value', for none is great enough, but can consist only in taking away a second life" (G. W. F. Hegel, *Philosophy of Right*, trans. T. M. Knox [Oxford: Oxford University Press, 1965], p. 247).

[One] abolitionist argument . . . simply says that capital punishment is illegitimate because it violates the right to life, which is a fundamental, absolute, sacred right belonging to each and every human being, and therefore ought to be respected even in a murderer.

If any rights are fundamental, the right to life is certainly one of them; but to claim that it is absolute, inviolable under any circumstances and for any reason, is a different matter. If an abolitionist wants to argue his case by asserting an absolute right to life, she will also have to deny moral legitimacy to taking human life in war, revolution, and self-defense. This kind of pacifism is a consistent but farfetched and hence implausible position.

I do not believe that the right to life (nor, for that matter, any other right) is absolute. I have no general theory of rights to fall back upon here; instead, let me pose a question. Would we take seriously the claim to an absolute, sacred, inviolable right to life—coming from the mouth of a *confessed murderer*? I submit that we would not, for the obvious reason that it is being put forward by the person who confessedly denied another human being this very right. But if the murderer cannot plausibly claim such a right for himself, neither can *anyone else* do that in his behalf. This suggests that there is an element of reciprocity in our general rights, such as the right to life or property. I can convincingly claim these rights only so long as I acknowledge and respect the same rights of others. If I violate the rights of others, I thereby lose the same rights. If I am a murderer, I have no *right* to live.

Some opponents of capital punishment claim that a criminal law system which includes this punishment is contradictory, in that it prohibits murder and at the same time provides for its perpetration: "It is one and the same legal regulation which prohibits the individual from murdering, while allowing the state to murder. . . . This is obviously a terrible irony, an abnormal and immoral logic, against which everything in us revolts."[4]

This seems to be one of the more popular arguments against the death penalty, but it is not a good one. If it were valid, it would prove too much. Exactly the same might be claimed of other kinds of punishment: of prison terms, that they are "contradictory" to the legal protection of liberty; of fines, that they are "contradictory" to the legal protection of property. Fortunately enough, it is not valid, for it begs the question at issue. In order to be able to talk of the state as "murdering" the person it executes, and to claim that there is "an abnormal and immoral logic" at work here, which

---

4 S. V. Vulović, *Problem smrtne kazne* (Belgrade: Geca Kon, 1925), pp. 23–24.

thrives on a "contradiction," one has to use the word "murder" in the very same sense—that is, in the usual sense, which implies the idea of the *wrongful* taking the life of another—both when speaking of what the murderer has done to the victim and of what the state is doing to him by way of punishment. But this is precisely the question at issue: whether capital punishment *is* "murder," whether it is wrongful or morally justified and right.

The next two arguments attack the retributive rationale of capital punishment by questioning the claim that it is only this punishment that satisfies the demand for proportion between offense and punishment in the case of murder. The first points out that any two human lives are different in many important respects, such as age, health, physical and mental capability, so that it does not make much sense to consider them equally valuable. What if the murdered person was very old, practically at the very end of her natural life, while the murderer is young, with most of his life still ahead of him, for instance? Or if the victim was gravely and incurably ill, and thus doomed to live her life in suffering and hopelessness, without being able to experience almost anything that makes a human life worth living, while the murderer is in every respect capable of experiencing and enjoying things life has to offer? Or the other way round? Would not the death penalty in such cases amount either to taking a more valuable life as a punishment for destroying a less valuable one, or *vice versa?* Would it not be either too much, or too little, and in both cases disproportionate, and thus unjust and wrong, from the standpoint of the retributive theory itself?

Any plausibility this argument might appear to have is the result of a conflation of differences between, and value of, human lives. No doubt, any two human lives are *different* in innumerable ways, but this does not entail that they are not *equally valuable*. I have no worked-out general theory of equality to refer to here, but I do not think that one is necessary in order to do away with this argument. The modern humanistic and democratic tradition in ethical, social, and political thought is based on the idea that all human beings are equal. This finds its legal expression in the principle of equality of people under the law. If we are not willing to give up this principle, we have to stick to the assumption that, all differences notwithstanding, any two human lives, *qua* human lives, are equally valuable. If, on the other hand, we allow that, on the basis of such criteria as age, health, or mental or physical ability, it can be claimed that the life of one person is more or less valuable than the life of another, and we admit such claims in the sphere of law, including criminal law, we shall thereby give up the principle of equality of people under the law. In all consistency, we shall not be able to demand that property, physical and personal integrity, and all other rights and interests of individuals be given equal consideration in courts of law either—that is, we shall have to accept systematic discrimination between individuals on the basis of the same criteria across the whole field. I do not think anyone would seriously contemplate an overhaul of the whole legal system along these lines.

The second argument having to do with the issue of proportionality between murder and capital punishment draws our attention to the fact that the law normally provides for a certain period of time to elapse between the passing of a death sentence and its execution. It is a period of several weeks or months; in some cases it extends to years. This period is bound to be one of constant mental anguish for the condemned. And thus, all things considered, what is inflicted on him is disproportionately hard and hence unjust. It would be proportionate and just only in the case of "a criminal who had warned his victim of the date at which he would inflict a horrible death on him and who, from that moment onward, had confined him at his mercy for months."[5]

The first thing to note about this argument is that it does not support a full-fledged abolitionist stand; if it were valid, it would not show that capital punishment is *never* proportionate and just, but only that it is *very rarely* so. Consequently, the conclusion would not be that it ought to be abolished outright, but only that it ought to be restricted to those cases that would satisfy the condition cited above. Such cases do happen, although, to be sure, not very often; the murder of Aldo Moro, for instance, was of this kind. But this is not the main point. The main point is that the argument actually does not hit at capital punishment itself, although it is presented with that aim in view. It hits at something else: a particular way of carrying out this punishment, which is widely adopted in our time. Some hundred years ago and more, in the Wild West, they frequently hanged the man convicted to die almost immediately after pronouncing the sentence. I am not arguing here that we should follow this example today; I mention this piece of historical fact only in order to show that the interval between sentencing someone to death and carrying out the sentence is not a *part* of capital punishment itself. However unpalatable we might find those Wild West hangings, whatever objections we might want

---

5 A. Camus, "Reflections on the Guillotine," *Resistance, Rebellion and Death*, trans. J. O'Brien (London: Hamish Hamilton, 1961), p. 143.

to voice against the speed with which they followed the sentencing, surely we shall not deny them the *description* of "executions." So the implication of the argument is not that we ought to do away with capital punishment altogether, nor that we ought to restrict it to those cases of murder where the murderer had warned the victim weeks or months in advance of what he was going to do to her, but that we ought to reexamine the procedure of carrying out this kind of punishment. We ought to weigh the reasons for having this interval between the sentencing and executing, against the moral and human significance of the repercussions such an interval inevitably carries with it.

These reasons, in part, have to do with the possibility of miscarriages of justice and the need to rectify them. Thus we come to the argument against capital punishment which, historically, has been the most effective of all: many advances of the abolitionist movement have been connected with discoveries of cases of judicial errors. Judges and jurors are only human, and consequently some of their beliefs and decisions are bound to be mistaken. Some of their mistakes can be corrected upon discovery; but precisely those with most disastrous repercussions—those which result in innocent people being executed—can never be rectified. In all other cases of mistaken sentencing we can revoke the punishment, either completely or in part, or at least extend compensation. In addition, by exonerating the accused we give moral satisfaction. None of this is possible after an innocent person has been executed; capital punishment is essentially different from all other penalties by being completely irrevocable and irreparable. Therefore, it ought to be abolished.

A part of my reply to this argument goes along the same lines as what I had to say on the previous one. It is not so far-reaching as abolitionists assume; for it would be quite implausible, even fanciful, to claim that there have *never* been cases of murder which left no room whatever for reasonable doubt as to the guilt and full responsibility of the accused. Such cases may not be more frequent than those others, but they do happen. Why not retain the death penalty at least for them?

Actually, this argument, just as the preceding one, does not speak out against capital punishment itself, but against the existing procedures for trying capital cases. Miscarriages of justice result in innocent people being sentenced to death and executed, even in the criminal-law systems in which greatest care is taken to ensure that it never comes to that. But this does not stem from the intrinsic nature of the institution of capital punishment; it results from deficiencies, limitations, and imperfections of the criminal law procedures in which this punishment is meted out. Errors of justice do not demonstrate the need to do away with capital punishment; they simply make it incumbent on us to do everything possible to improve even further procedures of meting it out.

To be sure, this conclusion will not find favor with a diehard abolitionist. "I shall ask for the abolition of Capital Punishment until I have the infallibility of human judgement demonstrated to me," that is, as long as there is even the slightest possibility that innocent people may be executed because of judicial errors, Lafayette said in his day.[6] Many an opponent of this kind of punishment will say the same today. The demand to do away with capital punishment altogether, so as to eliminate even the smallest chance of that ever happening—the chance which, admittedly, would remain even after everything humanly possible has been done to perfect the procedure, although then it would be very slight indeed—is actually a demand to give a privileged position to murderers as against all other offenders, big and small. For if we acted on this demand, we would bring about a situation in which proportionate penalties would be meted out for all offenses, *except* for murder. Murderers would not be receiving the only punishment truly proportionate to their crimes, the punishment of death, but some other, lighter, and thus disproportionate penalty. All other offenders would be punished according to their deserts; only murderers would be receiving less than *they* deserve. In all other cases justice would be done in full; only in cases of the gravest of offenses, the crime of murder, justice would not be carried out in full measure. It is a great and tragic miscarriage of justice when an innocent person is mistakenly sentenced to death and executed, but systematically giving murderers advantage over all other offenders would also be a grave injustice. Is the fact that, as long as capital punishment is retained, there is a possibility that over a number of years, or even decades, an injustice of the first kind may be committed, unintentionally and unconsciously, reason enough to abolish it altogether, and thus end up with a system of punishments in which injustices of the second kind are perpetrated daily, consciously, and inevitably?

There is still another abolitionist argument that actually does not hit out against capital punishment itself, but against something else. Figures are sometimes quoted which show that this punishment is much more often meted out to the uneducated and poor than to the educated, rich,

---

6 Quoted in E. R. Calvert, *Capital Punishment in the Twentieth Century* (London: G. P. Putnam's Sons, 1927), p. 132.

and influential people; in the United States, much more often to blacks than to whites. These figures are adduced as a proof of the inherent injustice of this kind of punishment. On account of them, it is claimed that capital punishment is not a way of doing justice by meting out deserved punishment to murderers, but rather a means of social discrimination and perpetuation of social injustice.

I shall not question these findings, which are quite convincing, and anyway, there is no need to do that in order to defend the institution of capital punishment. For there seems to be a certain amount of discrimination and injustice not only in sentencing people to death and executing them, but also in meting out other penalties. The social structure of the death rows in American prisons, for instance, does not seem to be basically different from the general social structure of American penitentiaries. If this argument were valid, it would call not only for abolition of the penalty of death, but for doing away with other penalties as well. But it is not valid; as Burton Leiser has pointed out,

> ... this is not an argument, either against the death penalty or against any other form of punishment. It is an argument against the unjust and inequitable distribution of penalties. If the trials of wealthy men are less likely to result in convictions than those of poor men, then something must be done to reform the procedure in criminal courts. If those who have money and standing in the community are less likely to be charged with serious offenses than their less affluent fellow citizens, then there should be a major overhaul of the entire system of criminal justice.... But the maldistribution of penalties is no argument against any particular form of penalty.[7]

Igor Primoratz: Justifying Legal Punishment

1. Retributivists such as Primoratz hold that the punishment of a crime ought to be proportional to the offense. Do you find such a view plausible? Are there any other morally relevant considerations when considering how someone should be punished?

2. Primoratz argues that the only punishment proportional to the offense of murder is the death penalty. What reasons does he give for thinking this? Do you think he is correct?

---

7 B. M. Leiser, *Liberty, Justice and Morals: Contemporary Value Conflicts* (New York: Macmillan, 1973), p. 225.

3. Some argue that capital punishment violates the right to life. Primoratz responds that the right to life is not "absolute." What does he mean by this, and how does he argue for it? Do you agree with him?

4. How does Primoratz respond to the objection that the death penalty is hypocritical because it involves killing people for the offense of killing other people? Do you find his response convincing?

5. Many people object to the death penalty on the grounds that it sometimes results in innocent people being executed, and is often applied in a discriminatory way. Why doesn't Primoratz think these concerns justify abolishing the death penalty? Do you agree?

34

An Eye for an Eye?

Stephen Nathanson

In this excerpt from his book *An Eye for an Eye?* (1987), Stephen Nathanson argues against the classic retributivist principle of punishment: *lex talionis*. This principle tells us to treat criminals just as they treated their victims—an eye for an eye, a tooth for a tooth. Nathanson finds two major problems for *lex talionis*. First, it advises us to commit highly immoral actions—raping a rapist, for instance, or torturing a torturer. Second, it is impossible to apply in many cases of deserved punishment—for instance, the principle offers no advice about what to do with drunk drivers, air polluters, embezzlers, or spies.

Retributivists might replace *lex talionis* with a principle of proportional punishment, according to which increasingly bad crimes must be met with increasingly harsher punishment. This proposal is plausible, says Nathanson, but it offers no justification for the death penalty. All it tells us is that the worst crimes ought to be met with the harshest punishments. But it says nothing about how harsh those punishments should be.

Nathanson concludes by discussing the symbolism of abolishing the death penalty, and claims that we express a respect for each person's inalienable rights by refraining from depriving a murderer of his life.

"An Eye for an Eye?" from *An Eye for an Eye?* by Steven Nathanson (1987). Reprinted with permission of Rowman & Littlefield.

S uppose we . . . try to determine what people deserve from a strictly moral point of view. How shall we proceed?

The most usual suggestion is that we look at a person's actions because what someone deserves would appear to depend on what he or she does. A person's actions, it seems, provide not only a basis for a moral appraisal of the person but also a guide to how he should be treated. According to the *lex talionis* or principle of "an eye for an eye," we ought to treat people as they have treated others. What people deserve as recipients of rewards or punishments is determined by what they do as agents.

This is a powerful and attractive view, one that appears to be backed not only by moral common sense but also by tradition and philosophical thought. The most famous statement of philosophical support for this view comes from Immanuel Kant, who linked it directly with an argument for the death penalty. Discussing the problem of punishment, Kant writes,

> What kind and what degree of punishment does legal justice adopt as its principle and standard? None other than the principle of equality . . . the principle of not treating one side more favorably than the other. Accordingly, any undeserved evil that you inflict on someone else among the people is one that you do to yourself. If you vilify, you vilify yourself; if you steal from him, you steal from yourself; if you kill him, you kill yourself. Only the law of retribution *(jus talionis)* can determine exactly the kind and degree of punishment.[1]

Kant's view is attractive for a number of reasons. First, it accords with our belief that what a person deserves is related to what he does. Second, it appeals to a moral standard and does not seem to rely on any particular legal or political institutions. Third, it seems to provide a measure of appropriate punishment that can be used as a guide to creating laws and instituting punishments. It tells us that the punishment is to be identical with the crime. Whatever the criminal did to the victim is to be done in turn to the criminal.

In spite of the attractions of Kant's view, it is deeply flawed. When we see why, it will be clear that the whole "eye for an eye" perspective must be rejected.

---

1 Kant, *Metaphysical Elements of Justice*, translated by John Ladd (Indianapolis: Bobbs-Merrill, 1965), p. 101.

Problems with the Equal Punishment Principle

... [Kant's view] does not provide an adequate criterion for determining appropriate levels of punishment.

... We can see this, first, by noting that for certain crimes, Kant's view recommends punishments that are not morally acceptable. Applied strictly, it would require that we rape rapists, torture torturers, and burn arsonists whose acts have led to deaths. In general, where a particular crime involves barbaric and inhuman treatment, Kant's principle tells us to act barbarically and inhumanly in return. So, in some cases, the principle generates unacceptable answers to the question of what constitutes appropriate punishment.

This is not its only defect. In many other cases, the principle tells us nothing at all about how to punish. While Kant thought it obvious how to apply his principle in the case of murder, his principle cannot serve as a general rule because it does not tell us how to punish many crimes. Using the Kantian version or the more common "eye for an eye" standard, what would we decide to do to embezzlers, spies, drunken drivers, airline hijackers, drug users, prostitutes, air polluters, or persons who practice medicine without a license? If one reflects on this question, it becomes clear that there is simply no answer to it. We could not in fact design a system of punishment simply on the basis of the "eye for an eye" principle.

In order to justify using the "eye for an eye" principle to answer our question about murder and the death penalty, we would first have to show that it worked for a whole range of cases, giving acceptable answers to questions about amounts of punishment. Then, having established it as a satisfactory general principle, we could apply it to the case of murder. It turns out, however, that when we try to apply the principle generally, we find that it either gives wrong answers or no answers at all. Indeed, I suspect that the principle of "an eye for an eye" is no longer even a principle. Instead, it is simply a metaphorical disguise for expressing belief in the death penalty. People who cite it do not take it seriously. They do not believe in a kidnapping for a kidnapping, a theft for a theft, and so on. Perhaps "an eye for an eye" once was a genuine principle, but now it is merely a slogan. Therefore, it gives us no guidance in deciding whether murderers deserve to die.

In reply to these objections, one might defend the principle by saying that it does not require that punishments be strictly identical with crimes. Rather, it requires only that a punishment produce an amount of suffering in the criminal which is equal to the amount suffered by the victim. Thus, we don't have to hijack airplanes belonging to airline hijackers, spy on spies, etc. We simply have to reproduce in them the harm done to others.

Unfortunately, this reply really does not solve the problem. It provides no answer to the first objection, since it would still require us to behave barbarically in our treatment of those who are guilty of barbaric crimes. Even if we do not reproduce their actions exactly, any action which caused equal suffering would itself be barbaric. Second, in trying to produce equal amounts of suffering, we run into many problems. Just how much suffering is produced by an airline hijacker or a spy? And how do we apply this principle to prostitutes or drug users, who may not produce any suffering at all? We have rough ideas about how serious various crimes are, but this may not correlate with any clear sense of just how much harm is done.

Furthermore, the same problem arises in determining how much suffering a particular punishment would produce for a particular criminal. People vary in their tolerance of pain and in the amount of unhappiness that a fine or a jail sentence would cause them. Recluses will be less disturbed by banishment than extroverts. Nature lovers will suffer more in prison than people who are indifferent to natural beauty. A literal application of the principle would require that we tailor punishments to individual sensitivities, yet this is at best impractical. To a large extent, the legal system must work with standardized and rather crude estimates of the negative impact that punishments have on people.

The move from calling for a punishment that is identical to the crime to favoring one that is equal in the harm done is no help to us or to the defense of the principle. "An eye for an eye" tells us neither what people deserve nor how we should treat them when they have done wrong.

Proportional Retributivism

The view we have been considering can be called "equality retributivism," since it proposes that we repay criminals with punishments equal to their crimes. In the light of problems like those I have cited, some people have proposed a variation on this view, calling not for equal punishments but rather for punishments which are *proportional* to the crime. In defending such a view as a guide for setting criminal punishments, Andrew von Hirsch writes:

If one asks how severely a wrongdoer deserves to be punished, a familiar principle comes to mind: Severity of punishment should be commensurate with the seriousness of the wrong. Only grave wrongs merit severe penalties; minor misdeeds deserve lenient punishments. Disproportionate penalties are undeserved—severe sanctions for minor wrongs or vice versa. This principle has variously been called a principle of "proportionality" or "just deserts"; we prefer to call it commensurate deserts.[2]

Like Kant, von Hirsch makes the punishment which a person deserves depend on that person's actions, but he departs from Kant in substituting proportionality for equality as the criterion for setting the amount of punishment.

In implementing a punishment system based on the proportionality view, one would first make a list of crimes, ranking them in order of seriousness. At one end would be quite trivial offenses like parking meter violations, while very serious crimes such as murder would occupy the other. In between, other crimes would be ranked according to their relative gravity. Then a corresponding scale of punishments would be constructed, and the two would be correlated. Punishments would be proportionate to crimes so long as we could say that the more serious the crime was, the higher on the punishment scale was the punishment administered.

This system does not have the defects of equality retributivism. It does not require that we treat those guilty of barbaric crimes barbarically. This is because we can set the upper limit of the punishment scale so as to exclude truly barbaric punishments. Second, unlike the equality principle, the proportionality view is genuinely general, providing a way of handling all crimes. Finally, it does justice to our ordinary belief that certain punishments are unjust because they are too severe or too lenient for the crime committed.

The proportionality principle does, I think, play a legitimate role in our thinking about punishments. Nonetheless, it is no help to death penalty advocates, because it does not require that murderers be executed. All

---

2 *Doing Justice* (New York: Hill & Wang, 1976), p. 66; reprinted in *Sentencing*, edited by H. Gross and A. von Hirsch (Oxford University Press, 1981), p. 243. For a more recent discussion and further defense by von Hirsch, see his *Past or Future Crimes* (New Brunswick, N.J.: Rutgers University Press, 1985).

that it requires is that if murder is the most serious crime, then murder should be punished by the most severe punishment on the scale. The principle does not tell us what this punishment should be, however, and it is quite compatible with the view that the most severe punishment should be a long prison term.

This failure of the theory to provide a basis for supporting the death penalty reveals an important gap in proportional retributivism. It shows that while the theory is general in scope, it does not yield any *specific* recommendations regarding punishment. It tells us, for example, that armed robbery should be punished more severely than embezzling and less severely than murder, but it does not tell us how much to punish any of these. This weakness is, in effect, conceded by von Hirsch, who admits that if we want to implement the "commensurate deserts" principle, we must supplement it with information about what level of punishment is needed to deter crimes.[3] In a later discussion of how to "anchor" the punishment system, he deals with this problem in more depth, but the factors he cites as relevant to making specific judgments (such as available prison space) have nothing to do with what people deserve. He also seems to suggest that a range of punishments may be appropriate for a particular crime. This runs counter to the death penalty supporter's sense that death alone is appropriate for some murderers.[4]

Neither of these retributive views, then, provides support for the death penalty. The equality principle fails because it is not in general true that the appropriate punishment for a crime is to do to the criminal what he has done to others. In some cases this is immoral, while in others it is impossible. The proportionality principle may be correct, but by itself it cannot determine specific punishments for specific crimes. Because of its flexibility and open-endedness, it is compatible with a great range of different punishments for murder.[5] . . .

---

3 Von Hirsch, *Doing Justice*, pp. 93–94. My criticisms of proportional retributivism are not novel. For helpful discussions of the view, see Hugo Bedau, "Concessions to Retribution in Punishment," in *Justice and Punishment*, edited by J. Cederblom and W. Blizek (Cambridge, Mass.: Ballinger, 1977), and M. Golding, *Philosophy of Law* (Englewood Cliffs, N.J.: Prentice Hall, 1975), pp. 98–99.

4 See von Hirsch, *Past or Future Crimes*, ch. 8.

5 For more positive assessments of these theories, see Jeffrey Reiman, "Justice, Civilization, and the Death Penalty," *Philosophy and Public Affairs* 14 (1985): 115–48; and Michael Davis, "How to Make the Punishment Fit the Crime," *Ethics* 93 (1983).

The Symbolism of Abolishing the Death Penalty

What is the symbolic message that we would convey by deciding to renounce the death penalty and to abolish its use?

I think that there are two primary messages. The first is the most frequently emphasized and is usually expressed in terms of the sanctity of human life, although I think we could better express it in terms of respect for human dignity. One way we express our respect for the dignity of human beings is by abstaining from depriving them of their lives, even if they have done terrible deeds. In defense of human well-being, we may punish people for their crimes, but we ought not to deprive them of everything, which is what the death penalty does.

If we take the life of a criminal, we convey the idea that by his deeds he has made himself worthless and totally without human value. I do not believe that we are in a position to affirm that of anyone. We may hate such a person and feel the deepest anger against him, but when he no longer poses a threat to anyone, we ought not to take his life.

But, one might ask, hasn't the murderer forfeited whatever rights he might have had to our respect? Hasn't he, by his deeds, given up any rights that he had to decent treatment? Aren't we morally free to kill him if we wish?

These questions express important doubts about the obligation to accord any respect to those who have acted so deplorably, but I do not think that they prove that any such forfeiture has occurred. Certainly, when people murder or commit other crimes, they do forfeit some of the rights that are possessed by the law-abiding. They lose a certain right to be left alone. It becomes permissible to bring them to trial and, if they are convicted, to impose an appropriate—even a dreadful—punishment on them.

Nonetheless, they do not forfeit all their rights. It does not follow from the vileness of their actions that we can do anything whatsoever to them. This is part of the moral meaning of the constitutional ban on cruel and unusual punishments. No matter how terrible a person's deeds, we may not punish him in a cruel and unusual way. We may not torture him, for example. His right not to be tortured has not been forfeited. Why do these limits hold? Because this person remains a human being, and we think that there is something in him that we must continue to respect in spite of his terrible acts.

One way of seeing why those who murder still deserve some consideration and respect is by reflecting again on the idea of what it is to *deserve* something. In most contexts, we think that what people deserve depends on what they have done, intended, or tried to do. It depends on features that are qualities of individuals. The best person for the job deserves to be hired. The person who worked especially hard deserves our gratitude. We can call the concept that applies in these cases *personal* desert.

There is another kind of desert, however, that belongs to people by virtue of their humanity itself and does not depend on their individual efforts or achievements. I will call this impersonal kind of desert *human* desert. We appeal to this concept when we think that everyone deserves a certain level of treatment no matter what their individual qualities are. When the signers of the Declaration of Independence affirmed that people had inalienable rights to "life, liberty, and the pursuit of happiness," they were appealing to such an idea. These rights do not have to be earned by people. They are possessed "naturally," and everyone is bound to respect them.

According to the view that I am defending, people do not lose all of their rights when they commit terrible crimes. They still deserve some level of decent treatment simply because they remain living, functioning human beings. This level of moral desert need not be earned, and it cannot be forfeited. This view may sound controversial, but in fact everyone who believes that cruel and unusual punishment should be forbidden implicitly agrees with it. That is, they agree that even after someone has committed a terrible crime, we do not have the right to do anything whatsoever to him.

What I am suggesting is that by renouncing the use of death as a punishment, we express and reaffirm our belief in the inalienable, unforfeitable core of human dignity.

Why is this a worthwhile message to convey? It is worth conveying because this belief is both important and precarious. Throughout history, people have found innumerable reasons to degrade the humanity of one another. They have found qualities in others that they hated or feared, and even when they were not threatened by these people, they have sought to harm them, deprive them of their liberty, or take their lives from them. They have often felt that they had good reasons to do these things, and they have invoked divine commands, racial purity, and state security to support their deeds.

These actions and attitudes are not relics of the past. They remain an awful feature of the contemporary world. By renouncing the death penalty, we show our determination to accord at least minimal respect even to those whom we believe to be personally vile or morally vicious. This is, perhaps, why we speak of the *sanctity* of human life rather than its value or worth. That which is sacred remains, in some sense, untouchable, and its value is not dependent on its worth or usefulness to us. Kant expressed this ideal of respect in the famous second version of the Categorical Imperative: "So act as to treat humanity, whether in thine own person or in that of any other, in every case as an end withal, never as a means only." . . .

When the state has a murderer in its power and could execute him but does not, this conveys the idea that even though this person has done wrong and even though we may be angry, outraged, and indignant with him, we will nonetheless control ourselves in a way that he did not. We will not kill him, even though we could do so and even though we are angry and indignant. We will exercise restraint, sanctioning killing only when it serves a protective function.

Why should we do this? Partly out of a respect for human dignity. But also because we want the state to set an example of proper behavior. We do not want to encourage people to resort to violence to settle conflicts when there are other ways available. We want to avoid the cycle of violence that can come from retaliation and counter-retaliation. Violence is a contagion that arouses hatred and anger, and if unchecked, it simply leads to still more violence. The state can convey the message that the contagion must be stopped, and the most effective principle for stopping it is the idea that only defensive violence is justifiable. Since the death penalty is not an instance of defensive violence, it ought to be renounced.

We show our respect for life best by restraining ourselves and allowing murderers to live, rather than by following a policy of a life for a life. Respect for life and restraint of violence are aspects of the same ideal. The renunciation of the death penalty would symbolize our support of that ideal.

Stephen Nathanson: An Eye for an Eye?

1. Nathanson rejects the principle of *lex talionis*, according to which we ought to treat criminals as they have treated others. What reasons does he give for rejecting this principle? Do you find his reasons convincing?
2. Nathanson considers the following modification of the principle of *lex talionis*: "a punishment should produce an amount of suffering in the criminal which is equal to the amount suffered by the victim." Do you

think this is a plausible principle? What objections does Nathanson offer to the principle?

3. What is the principle of proportional retributivism? Why doesn't Nathanson think that this principle supports the death penalty? Do you agree with him?

4. What symbolic message does Nathanson think that abolishing the death penalty would convey? Is this a good reason to abolish the death penalty?

5. Are the any reasons for supporting the death penalty that Nathanson does not consider? If so, are these reasons ever strong enough to justify sentencing someone to death?

35

Letter from Birmingham City Jail
Martin Luther King, Jr.

Martin Luther King, Jr. (1929–1968) was the most prominent leader of the U.S. civil rights movement. During one of the many times that he was imprisoned for his activities, he penned this letter to his fellow clergymen, offering his justifications for the policy of nonviolent civil disobedience that he championed. He argues that such a policy does not unreasonably precipitate violence, does not lead to anarchy, is not objectionably extremist, and does not exhibit disrespect for the law. Further, this policy will minimize harm in the long run and is supported by considerations of natural law.

This reading is not your typical sober, linear philosophical essay, but rather as much an impassioned and eloquent plea as it is a sustained argument. King here appeals to the hearts and minds of his readership, in an effort to justify the peaceful efforts of the social movement he so ably led prior to his assassination.

16 April 1963

My Dear Fellow Clergymen:

While confined here in the Birmingham city jail, I came across your recent statement calling my present activities "unwise and untimely." Seldom do I pause to answer criticism of my work and ideas. If I sought to answer all the criticisms that cross my desk, my secretaries would have little time for anything other than such correspondence in the course of the day, and I would have no time for constructive work. But since I feel that you are men of genuine good will and that your criticisms are sincerely set forth, I want to try to answer your statement in what I hope will be patient and reasonable terms. . . .

You deplore the demonstrations taking place in Birmingham. But your statement, I am sorry to say, fails to express a similar concern for the conditions that brought about the demonstrations. I am sure that none of you would want to rest content with the superficial kind of social analysis that deals merely with effects and does not grapple with underlying causes. It is unfortunate that demonstrations are taking place in Birmingham, but it is even more unfortunate that the city's white power structure left the Negro community with no alternative.

In any nonviolent campaign there are four basic steps: collection of the facts to determine whether injustices exist; negotiation; self purification; and direct action. We have gone through all these steps in Birmingham. There can be no gainsaying the fact that racial injustice engulfs this community. Birmingham is probably the most thoroughly segregated city in the United States. Its ugly record of brutality is widely known. Negroes have experienced grossly unjust treatment in the courts. There have been more unsolved bombings of Negro homes and churches in Birmingham than in any other city in the nation. These are the hard, brutal facts of the case. On the basis of these conditions, Negro leaders sought to negotiate with the city fathers. But the latter consistently refused to engage in good faith negotiation. . . .

You may well ask: "Why direct action? Why sit-ins, marches and so forth? Isn't negotiation a better path?" You are quite right in calling for negotiation. Indeed, this is the very purpose of direct action. Nonviolent direct action seeks to create such a crisis and foster such a tension that a community which has constantly refused to negotiate is forced to confront the issue. It seeks so to dramatize the issue that it can no longer be ignored. My citing the creation of tension as part of the work of the nonviolent resister may sound rather shocking. But I must confess that I am not afraid of the word "tension." I have earnestly opposed violent tension, but there is a type of constructive, nonviolent tension which is necessary for growth. Just as Socrates felt that it was necessary to create a tension in the mind so that individuals could rise from the bondage of myths and half truths to the unfettered realm of creative analysis and objective appraisal, so must we see the need for nonviolent gadflies to create the kind of tension in society that will help men rise from the dark depths of prejudice and racism to the majestic heights of understanding and brotherhood. The purpose of our direct action program is to create a situation so crisis-packed that it will inevitably open the door to negotiation. I therefore concur with you in your call for negotiation. Too long has our beloved Southland been bogged down in a tragic effort to live in monologue rather than dialogue. . . .

We know through painful experience that freedom is never voluntarily given by the oppressor; it must be demanded by the oppressed. Frankly, I have yet to engage in a direct action campaign that was "well timed" in the view of those who have not suffered unduly from the disease of segregation. For years now I have heard the word "Wait!" It rings in the ear of every Negro with piercing familiarity. This "Wait" has almost always meant "Never." We must come to see, with one of our distinguished jurists, that "justice too long delayed is justice denied."

We have waited for more than 340 years for our constitutional and God-given rights. The nations of Asia and Africa are moving with jetlike speed toward gaining political independence, but we still creep at horse-and-buggy pace toward gaining a cup of coffee at a lunch counter. Perhaps it is easy for those who have never felt the stinging darts of segregation to say, "Wait." But when you have seen vicious mobs lynch your mothers and fathers at will and drown your sisters and brothers at whim; when you have seen hate-filled policemen curse, kick and even kill your black brothers and sisters; when you see the vast majority of your twenty million Negro brothers smothering in an airtight cage of poverty in the midst of an affluent society; when you suddenly find your tongue twisted and your speech stammering as you seek to explain to your six-year-old daughter why she can't go to the public amusement park that has just been advertised on television, and see tears welling up in her eyes when she is told that Funtown is closed to colored children, and see ominous clouds of inferiority beginning to form in her little mental sky, and see her beginning to distort her personality by developing an unconscious bitterness toward white people; when you have to concoct an answer for a five-year-old son who is asking: "Daddy, why do white people treat colored people so mean?"; when you take a cross-county drive and find it necessary to sleep night after night in the uncomfortable corners of your automobile because no motel will accept you; when you are humiliated day in and day out by nagging signs reading "white" and "colored"; when your first name becomes "nigger," your middle name becomes "boy" (however old you are) and your last name becomes "John," and your wife and mother are never given the respected title "Mrs."; when you are harried by day and haunted by night by the fact that you are a Negro, living constantly at tiptoe stance, never quite knowing what to expect next, and are plagued with inner fears and outer resentments; when you are forever fighting a degenerating sense of "nobodiness"—then you will understand why we find it difficult to wait. There comes a time when the cup of endurance runs over, and men are no longer willing to be plunged into the abyss of despair. I hope, sirs, you can understand our legitimate and unavoidable impatience.

You express a great deal of anxiety over our willingness to break laws. This is certainly a legitimate concern. Since we so diligently urge people to obey the Supreme Court's decision of 1954 outlawing segregation in the public schools, at first glance it may seem rather paradoxical for us consciously to break laws. One may well ask: "How can you advocate breaking some laws and obeying others?" The answer lies in the fact that there are two types of laws: just and unjust. I would be the first to advocate obeying just laws. One has not only a legal but a moral responsibility to obey just laws. Conversely, one has a moral responsibility to disobey unjust laws. I would agree with St. Augustine that "an unjust law is no law at all."

Now, what is the difference between the two? How does one determine whether a law is just or unjust? A just law is a man-made code that squares with the moral law or the law of God. An unjust law is a code that is out of harmony with the moral law. To put it in the terms of St. Thomas Aquinas: An unjust law is a human law that is not rooted in eternal law and natural law. Any law that uplifts human personality is just. Any law that degrades human personality is unjust. All segregation statutes are unjust because segregation distorts the soul and damages the personality. It gives the segregator a false sense of superiority and the segregated a false sense of inferiority. Segregation, to use the terminology of the Jewish philosopher Martin Buber, substitutes an "I-it" relationship for an "I-thou" relationship and ends up relegating persons to the status of things. Hence segregation is not only politically, economically and sociologically unsound, it is morally wrong and sinful. Paul Tillich has said that sin is separation. Is not segregation an existential expression of man's tragic separation, his awful estrangement, his terrible sinfulness? Thus it is that I can urge men to obey the 1954 decision of the Supreme Court, for it is morally right; and I can urge them to disobey segregation ordinances, for they are morally wrong.

Let us consider a more concrete example of just and unjust laws. An unjust law is a code that a numerical or power majority group compels a minority group to obey but does not make binding on itself. This is difference made legal. By the same token, a just law is a code that a majority compels a minority to follow and that it is willing to follow itself. This is sameness made legal.

Let me give another explanation. A law is unjust if it is inflicted on a minority that, as a result of being denied the right to vote, had no part in enacting or devising the law. Who can say that the legislature of Alabama which set up that state's segregation laws was democratically elected? Throughout Alabama all sorts of devious methods are used to prevent Negroes from becoming registered voters, and there are some counties in which, even though Negroes constitute a majority of the population, not a single Negro is registered. Can any law enacted under such circumstances be considered democratically structured?

Sometimes a law is just on its face and unjust in its application. For instance, I have been arrested on a charge of parading without a permit. Now, there is nothing wrong in having an ordinance which requires a permit for a parade. But such an ordinance becomes unjust when it is used to maintain segregation and to deny citizens the First Amendment privilege of peaceful assembly and protest.

I hope you are able to see the distinction I am trying to point out. In no sense do I advocate evading or defying the law, as would the rabid segregationist. That would lead to anarchy. One who breaks an unjust law must do so openly, lovingly, and with a willingness to accept the penalty. I submit that an individual who breaks a law that conscience tells him is unjust, and who willingly accepts the penalty of imprisonment in order to arouse the conscience of the community over its injustice, is in reality expressing the highest respect for law.

Of course, there is nothing new about this kind of civil disobedience. It was evidenced sublimely in the refusal of Shadrach, Meshach and Abednego to obey the laws of Nebuchadnezzar, on the ground that a higher moral law was at stake. It was practiced superbly by the early Christians, who were willing to face hungry lions and the excruciating pain of chopping blocks rather than submit to certain unjust laws of the Roman Empire. To a degree, academic freedom is a reality today because Socrates practiced civil disobedience. In our own nation, the Boston Tea Party represented a massive act of civil disobedience.

We should never forget that everything Adolf Hitler did in Germany was "legal" and everything the Hungarian freedom fighters did in Hungary was "illegal." It was "illegal" to aid and comfort a Jew in Hitler's Germany. Even so, I am sure that, had I lived in Germany at the time, I would have aided and comforted my Jewish brothers. If today I lived in a Communist country where certain principles dear to the Christian faith are suppressed, I would openly advocate disobeying that country's antireligious laws.

I must make two honest confessions to you, my Christian and Jewish brothers. First, I must confess that over the past few years I have been gravely disappointed with the white moderate. I have almost reached the regrettable conclusion that the Negro's great stumbling block in his stride toward freedom is not the White Citizen's Counciler or the Ku Klux Klanner, but the white moderate, who is more devoted to "order" than to justice; who prefers a negative peace which is the absence of tension to a positive peace which is the presence of justice; who constantly says: "I agree with you in the goal you seek, but I cannot agree with your methods of direct action"; who paternalistically believes he can set the timetable for another man's freedom; who lives by a mythical concept of time and who constantly advises the Negro to wait for a "more convenient season." Shallow understanding from people of good will is more frustrating than absolute misunderstanding from people of ill will. Lukewarm acceptance is much more bewildering than outright rejection.

I had hoped that the white moderate would understand that law and order exist for the purpose of establishing justice and that when they fail in this purpose they become the dangerously structured dams that block the flow of social progress. I had hoped that the white moderate would understand that the present tension in the South is a necessary phase of the transition from an obnoxious negative peace, in which the Negro passively accepted his unjust plight, to a substantive and positive peace, in which all men will respect the dignity and worth of human personality. Actually, we who engage in nonviolent direct action are not the creators of tension. We merely bring to the surface the hidden tension that is already alive.

We bring it out in the open, where it can be seen and dealt with. Like a boil that can never be cured so long as it is covered up but must be opened with all its ugliness to the natural medicines of air and light, injustice must be exposed, with all the tension its exposure creates, to the light of human conscience and the air of national opinion before it can be cured.

In your statement you assert that our actions, even though peaceful, must be condemned because they precipitate violence. But is this a logical assertion? Isn't this like condemning a robbed man because his possession of money precipitated the evil act of robbery? Isn't this like condemning Socrates because his unswerving commitment to truth and his philosophical inquiries precipitated the act by the misguided populace in which they made him drink hemlock? Isn't this like condemning Jesus because his unique God-consciousness and never-ceasing devotion to God's will precipitated the evil act of crucifixion? We must come to see that, as the federal courts have consistently affirmed, it is wrong to urge an individual to cease his efforts to gain his basic constitutional rights because the quest may precipitate violence. Society must protect the robbed and punish the robber.

I had also hoped that the white moderate would reject the myth concerning time in relation to the struggle for freedom. I have just received a letter from a white brother in Texas. He writes: "All Christians know that the colored people will receive equal rights eventually, but it is possible that you are in too great a religious hurry. It has taken Christianity almost two thousand years to accomplish what it has. The teachings of Christ take time to come to earth." Such an attitude stems from a tragic misconception of time, from the strangely irrational notion that there is something in the very flow of time that will inevitably cure all ills. Actually, time itself is neutral; it can be used either destructively or constructively. More and more I feel that the people of ill will have used time much more effectively than have the people of good will. We will have to repent in this generation not merely for the hateful words and actions of the bad people but for the appalling silence of the good people. Human progress never rolls in on wheels of inevitability; it comes through the tireless efforts of men willing to be coworkers with God, and without this hard work, time itself becomes an ally of the forces of social stagnation. We must use time creatively, in the knowledge that the time is always ripe to do right. Now is the time to make real the promise of democracy and transform our pending national elegy into a creative psalm of brotherhood. Now is the time to lift our national policy from the quicksand of racial injustice to the solid rock of human dignity.

You speak of our activity in Birmingham as extreme. At first I was rather disappointed that fellow clergymen would see my nonviolent efforts as those of an extremist. I began thinking about the fact that I stand in the middle of two opposing forces in the Negro community. One is a force of complacency, made up in part of Negroes who, as a result of long years of oppression, are so drained of self-respect and a sense of "somebodiness" that they have adjusted to segregation; and in part of a few middle-class Negroes who, because of a degree of academic and economic security and because in some ways they profit by segregation, have become insensitive to the problems of the masses. The other force is one of bitterness and hatred, and it comes perilously close to advocating violence. It is expressed in the various black nationalist groups that are springing up across the nation, the largest and best known being Elijah Muhammad's Muslim movement. Nourished by the Negro's frustration over the continued existence of racial discrimination, this movement is made up of people who have lost faith in America, who have absolutely repudiated Christianity, and who have concluded that the white man is an incorrigible "devil."

I have tried to stand between these two forces, saying that we need emulate neither the "do-nothingism" of the complacent nor the hatred and despair of the black nationalist. For there is the more excellent way of love and nonviolent protest. I am grateful to God that, through the influence of the Negro church, the way of nonviolence became an integral part of our struggle. If this philosophy had not emerged, by now many streets of the South would, I am convinced, be flowing with blood. And I am further convinced that if our white brothers dismiss as "rabble rousers" and "outside agitators" those of us who employ nonviolent direct action, and if they refuse to support our nonviolent efforts, millions of Negroes will, out of frustration and despair, seek solace and security in black nationalist ideologies—a development that would inevitably lead to a frightening racial nightmare.

Oppressed people cannot remain oppressed forever. The yearning for freedom eventually manifests itself, and that is what has happened to the American Negro. Something within has reminded him of his birthright of freedom, and something without has reminded him that it can be gained. Consciously or unconsciously, he has been caught up by the Zeitgeist, and with his black brothers of Africa and his brown and yellow brothers of Asia, South America and the Caribbean, the United States Negro is moving with a sense of great urgency toward the promised land of racial justice. Recognizing this vital urge that has engulfed the Negro community, one should readily understand why public demonstrations are taking place. The Negro has many pent-up resentments and latent frustrations, and he must release them. So let him march; let him have his prayer pilgrimages to the city hall; understand why he must have sit-ins and freedom rides. If his repressed emotions are not released in nonviolent ways, they will seek expression through violence; this is not a threat but a fact of history. So I have not said to my people: "Get rid of your discontent." Rather, I have tried to say that this normal and healthy discontent can be channeled into the creative outlet of nonviolent direct action. And now this approach is being dismissed as extremist.

But though I was initially disappointed at being categorized as an extremist, as I continued to think about the matter I gradually gained a measure of satisfaction from the label. Was not Jesus an extremist for love: "Love your enemies, bless them that curse you, do good to them that hate you, and pray for them which despitefully use you, and persecute you." Was not Amos an extremist for justice: "Let justice roll down like waters and righteousness like an ever-flowing stream." Was not Paul an extremist for the Christian gospel: "I bear in my body the marks of the Lord Jesus." Was not Martin Luther an extremist: "Here I stand; I cannot do otherwise, so help me God." And John Bunyan: "I will stay in jail to the end of my days before I make a butchery of my conscience." And Abraham Lincoln: "This nation cannot survive half slave and half free." And Thomas Jefferson: We hold these truths to be self-evident, that all men are created equal. . ." So the question is not whether we will be extremists, but what kind of extremists we will be. Will we be extremists for hate or for love? Will we be extremists for the preservation of injustice or for the extension of justice? In that dramatic scene on Calvary's hill three men were crucified. We must never forget that all three were crucified for the same crime— the crime of extremism. Two were extremists for immorality, and thus fell below their environment. The other, Jesus Christ, was an extremist for love, truth and goodness, and thereby rose above his environment. Perhaps the South, the nation and the world are in dire need of creative extremists. . . .

Before closing I feel impelled to mention one other point in your statement that has troubled me profoundly. You warmly commended the Birmingham police force for keeping "order" and "preventing violence." I doubt that you would have so warmly commended the police force if you had seen its dogs sinking their teeth into unarmed, nonviolent Negroes. I doubt that you would so quickly commend the policemen if you were to observe their ugly and inhumane treatment of Negroes here in the city jail; if you were to watch them push and curse old Negro women and young Negro girls; if you were to see them slap and kick old Negro men and young boys; if you were to observe them, as they did on two occasions, refuse to give us food because we wanted to sing our grace together. I cannot join you in your praise of the Birmingham police department.

It is true that the police have exercised a degree of discipline in handling the demonstrators. In this sense they have conducted themselves rather "nonviolently" in public. But for what purpose? To preserve the evil system of segregation. Over the past few years I have consistently preached that nonviolence demands that the means we use must be as pure as the ends we seek. I have tried to make clear that it is wrong to use immoral means to attain moral ends. But now I must affirm that it is just as wrong, or perhaps even more so, to use moral means to preserve immoral ends. Perhaps Mr. Connor and his policemen have been rather nonviolent in public, as was Chief Pritchett in Albany, Georgia, but they have used the moral means of nonviolence to maintain the immoral end of racial injustice. As T. S. Eliot has said: "The last temptation is the greatest treason: To do the right deed for the wrong reason."

I wish you had commended the Negro sit-inners and demonstrators of Birmingham for their sublime courage, their willingness to suffer and their amazing discipline in the midst of great provocation. One day the South will recognize its real heroes. They will be the James Merediths, with the noble sense of purpose that enables them to face jeering and hostile mobs, and with the agonizing loneliness that characterizes the life of the pioneer. They will be old, oppressed, battered Negro women, symbolized in a seventy-two-year-old woman in Montgomery, Alabama, who rose up with a sense of dignity and with her people decided not to ride segregated buses, and who responded with ungrammatical profundity to one who inquired about her weariness: "My feets is tired, but my soul is at rest." They will be the young high school and college students, the young ministers of the gospel and a host of their elders, courageously and nonviolently sitting in at lunch counters and willingly going to jail for conscience' sake. One day the South will know that when these disinherited children of God sat down at lunch counters, they were in reality standing up for what is best in the American dream and for the most sacred values in our Judaeo-Christian heritage, thereby bringing our nation back to those great wells of democracy which were dug deep by the founding fathers in their formulation of the Constitution and the Declaration of Independence.

Never before have I written so long a letter. I'm afraid it is much too long to take your precious time. I can assure you that it would have been much shorter if I had been writing from a comfortable desk, but what else can one do when he is alone in a narrow jail cell, other than write long letters, think long thoughts and pray long prayers?

If I have said anything in this letter that overstates the truth and indicates an unreasonable impatience, I beg you to forgive me. If I have said anything that understates the truth and indicates my having a patience that allows me to settle for anything less than brotherhood, I beg God to forgive me.

I hope this letter finds you strong in the faith. I also hope that circumstances will soon make it possible for me to meet each of you, not as an integrationist or a civil-rights leader but as a fellow clergyman and a Christian brother. Let us all hope that the dark clouds of racial prejudice will soon pass away and the deep fog of misunderstanding will be lifted from our fear-drenched communities, and in some not too distant tomorrow the radiant stars of love and brotherhood will shine over our great nation with all their scintillating beauty.

Yours for the cause of Peace and Brotherhood,
Martin Luther King, Jr.

Martin Luther King, Jr.: Letter from Birmingham City Jail

1. Do you agree with King that it is sometimes morally permissible to break the law? Why or why not?
2. How does King think that we can distinguish just laws from unjust laws? Do you agree with him about this?
3. King claims that the "white moderate" is nearly as big a stumbling block to the pursuit of civil rights as the overt racist. What objections does King have to the white moderate?
4. How does King respond to the charge that he is an extremist? Do you agree with his claim that "the nation and the world are in dire need of creative extremists"?
5. King condemns violent forms of resistance, claiming that "it is wrong to use immoral means to attain moral ends." Do you agree with him on this? Are there times when the ends justify distasteful means?

36

America's Unjust Drug War

Michael Huemer

Michael Huemer argues that the recreational use of drugs, including cocaine and heroin, ought to be legal, and that the long-standing U.S. policy of criminalizing their possession and sale is morally unjustified. He presents, and then seeks to rebut, what he regards as the two most prominent arguments for their criminalization.

The first argument is that drugs are very harmful to those who use them, and the prevention of such harm justifies the state in criminalizing drug use. The second is that drug use reliably causes harm to third parties, and since the state's mission is to prevent such harm, the state is again justified in outlawing drug use. Huemer agrees that there are some cases in which drug use does threaten others (such as when one drives while under the influence), and agrees that such activity ought to be prohibited. But, he argues, this represents a small minority of cases—in all other situations, drug use ought to be legally permitted.

Huemer then turns from criticizing prohibitionist arguments, and offers a positive argument for decriminalization. This argument claims that we have a natural moral right—i.e., one that exists independently of its recognition by society—to use our bodies as we please, so long as we do not violate the rights of others in doing so. Unusual exceptions aside, we do not violate another's rights when we use drugs. Therefore

Michael Huemer, "America's Unjust Drug War" from *The New Prohibition*, ed. Bill Masters (Accurate Press, 2004), pp. 133–144. Reprinted with the permission of Michael Huemer.

we have a moral right to use drugs. Huemer thinks that the government thus violates our moral rights when it prohibits most drug use.

....

Should the recreational use of drugs such as marijuana, cocaine, heroin, and LSD, be prohibited by law? *Prohibitionists* answer yes. They usually argue that drug use is extremely harmful both to drug users and to society in general, and possibly even immoral, and they believe that these facts provide sufficient reasons for prohibition. *Legalizers* answer no. They usually give one or more of three arguments: First, some argue that drug use is not as harmful as prohibitionists believe, and even that it is sometimes beneficial. Second, some argue that drug prohibition "does not work," in other words, it is not very successful in preventing drug use and/ or has a number of very bad consequences. Lastly, some argue that drug prohibition is unjust or violates rights.

I won't attempt to discuss all these arguments here. Instead, I will focus on what seem to me the three most prominent arguments in the drug legalization debate: first, the argument that drugs should be outlawed because of the harm they cause to drug users; second, the argument that they should be outlawed because they harm people other than the user; and third, the argument that drugs should be legalized because drug prohibition violates rights. I shall focus on the moral/philosophical issues that these arguments raise, rather than medical or sociological issues. I shall show that the two arguments for prohibition fail, while the third argument, for legalization, succeeds.

I. Drugs and Harm to Users

The first major argument for prohibition holds that drugs should be prohibited because drug use is extremely harmful to the users themselves, and prohibition decreases the rate of drug abuse. This argument assumes that the proper function of government includes preventing people from harming themselves. Thus, the argument is something like this:

1. Drug use is very harmful to users.
2. The government should prohibit people from doing things that harm themselves.
3. Therefore, the government should prohibit drug use.

Obviously, the second premise is essential to the argument; if I believed that drug use was very harmful, but I did *not* think that the government should prohibit people from harming themselves, then I would not take this as a reason for prohibiting drug use. But premise (2), if taken without qualification, is extremely implausible. Consider some examples of things people do that are harmful (or entail a risk of harm) to themselves: smoking tobacco, drinking alcohol, eating too much, riding motorcycles, having unprotected or promiscuous sex, maintaining relationships with inconsiderate or abusive boyfriends and girlfriends, maxing out their credit cards, working in dead-end jobs, dropping out of college, moving to New Jersey, and being rude to their bosses. Should the government prohibit all of these things?[1] Most of us would agree that the government should not prohibit *any* of these things, let alone all of them. And this is not merely for logistical or practical reasons; rather, we think that controlling those activities is not the business of government.

Perhaps the prohibitionist will argue, not that the government should prohibit *all* activities that are harmful to oneself, but that it should prohibit activities that harm oneself in a certain way, or to a certain degree, or that also have some other characteristic. It would then be up to the prohibitionist to explain how the self-inflicted harm of drug use differs from the self-inflicted harms of the other activities mentioned above. Let us consider three possibilities.

(1) One suggestion would be that drug use also harms people other than the user; we will discuss this harm to others in section II. If, as I will contend, neither the harm to drug users nor the harm to others justifies prohibition, then there will be little plausibility in the suggestion that the combination of harms justifies prohibition. Of course, one could hold that a certain threshold level of total harm must be reached before prohibition of an activity is justified, and that the combination of the harm of drugs to users and their harm to others passes that threshold even though neither kind of harm does so by itself. But if, as I will contend, the "harm to users" and "harm to others" arguments both fail because it is not the government's business to apply criminal sanctions to prevent the kinds of harms in question, *then* the combination of the two harms will not make a convincing case for prohibition.

---

1 Douglas Husak (*Legalize This! The Case for Decriminalizing Drugs*, London: Verso, 2002, pages 7, 101–103) makes this sort of argument. I have added my own examples of harmful activities to his list.

(2) A second suggestion is that drug use is generally *more* harmful than the other activities listed above. But there seems to be no reason to believe this. As one (admittedly limited) measure of harmfulness, consider the mortality statistics. In the year 2000, illicit drug use directly or indirectly caused an estimated 17,000 deaths in the United States.[2] By contrast, tobacco caused an estimated 435,000 deaths.[3] Of course, more people use tobacco than use illegal drugs,[4] so let us divide by the number of users: tobacco kills 4.5 people per 1000 at-risk persons per year; illegal drugs kill 0.66 people per 1000 at-risk persons per year.[5] Yet almost no one favors outlawing tobacco and putting smokers in prison. On a similar note, obesity caused an estimated 112,000 deaths in the same year (due to increased incidence of heart disease, strokes, and so on), or 1.8 per 1000

2 Ali Mokdad, James Marks, Donna Stroup, and Julie Gerberding, "Actual Causes of Death in the United States, 2000," *Journal of the American Medical Association* 291, no. 10, 2004: 1238–45, p. 1242. The statistic includes estimated contributions of drug use to such causes of death as suicide, homicide, motor vehicle accidents, and HIV infection.

3 Mokdad et al., p. 1239; the statistic includes estimated effects of secondhand smoke. The Centers for Disease Control provides an estimate of 440,000 ("Annual Smoking-Attributable Mortality, Years of Potential Life Lost, and Economic Costs—United States, 1995–1999," *Morbidity and Mortality Weekly Report* 51, 2002: 300–303, http://www.cdc.gov/mmwr/PDF/wk/mm5114.pdf, page 300).

4 James Inciardi ("Against Legalization of Drugs" in Arnold Trebach and James Inciardi, *Legalize It? Debating American Drug Policy*, Washington, D.C.: American University Press, 1993, pp. 161, 165) makes this point, accusing drug legalizers of "sophism." He does not go on to calculate the number of deaths per user, however.

5 I include both current and former smokers among "at risk persons." The calculation for tobacco is based on Mokdad et al.'s report (p. 1239) that 22.2% of the adult population were smokers and 24.4% were former smokers in 2000, and the U.S. Census Bureau's estimate of an adult population of 209 million in the year 2000 ("Table 2: Annual Estimates of the Population by Sex and Selected Age Groups for the United States: April 1, 2000 to July 1, 2007 [NC-EST2007-02]," release date May 1, 2008, http://www.census.gov/popest/national/asrh/NC-EST2007/NC-EST2007-02.xls). The calculation for illicit drugs is based on the report of the Office of National Drug Control Policy (hereafter, ONDCP) that, in the year 2000, 11% of persons aged 12 and older had used illegal drugs in the previous year ("Drug Use Trends," October 2002, http://www.whitehousedrugpolicy.gov/publications/factsht/druguse/), and the U.S. Census Bureau's report of a population of about 233 million Americans aged 12 and over in 2000 ("Table 1: Annual Estimates of the Population by Sex and Five-Year Age Groups for the United States: April 1, 2000 to July 1, 2007 [NC-EST2007-01]," release date May 1, 2008, http://www.census.gov/popest/national/asrh/NC-EST2007/NC-EST2007-02.xls). Interpolation was applied to the Census Bureau's "10 to 14" age category to estimate the number of persons aged 12 to 14. In the case of drugs, if "at risk persons" are considered to include only those who admit to having used illegal drugs in the past month, then the death rate is 1.2 per 1000 at-risk persons.

at-risk persons.[6] Health professionals have warned about the pandemic of obesity, but no one has yet called for imprisoning obese people.

There are less tangible harms of drug use—harms to one's general quality of life. These are difficult to quantify. But compare the magnitude of the harm to one's quality of life that one can bring about by, say, dropping out of high school, working in a dead-end job for several years, or marrying a jerk—these things can cause extreme and lasting detriment to one's well-being. And yet no one proposes jailing those who drop out, work in bad jobs, or make poor marriage decisions. The idea of doing so would seem ridiculous, clearly beyond the state's prerogatives.

(3) Another suggestion is that drug use harms users *in a different way* than the other listed activities. What sorts of harms do drugs cause? First, illicit drugs may worsen users' health and, in some cases, entail a risk of death. But many other activities—including the consumption of alcohol, tobacco, and fatty foods; sex; and (on a broad construal of "health") automobiles—entail health risks, and yet almost no one believes those activities should be criminalized.

Second, drugs may damage users' relationships with others—particularly family, friends, and lovers—and prevent one from developing more satisfying personal relationships.[7] Being rude to others can also have this effect, yet no one believes you should be put in jail for being rude. Moreover, it is very implausible to suppose that people should be subject to criminal sanctions for ruining their personal relationships. I have no general theory of what sort of things people should be punished for, but consider the following example: suppose that I decide to break up with my girlfriend, stop calling my family, and push away all my friends. I do this for no good reason—I just feel like it. This would damage my personal relationships as much as anything could. Should the police now arrest me and put me in jail? If not, then why should they arrest me for doing something that only has a *chance* of indirectly bringing about a

---

6 Based on 112,000 premature deaths caused by obesity in 2000 (Katherine Flegal, Barry Graubard, David Williamson, and Mitchell Gail, "Excess Deaths Associated With Underweight, Overweight, and Obesity," *Journal of the American Medical Association* 293, no. 15, 2005: 1861–7), a 30.5% obesity rate among U.S. adults in 2000 (Allison Hedley, Cynthia Ogden, Clifford Johnson, Margaret Carroll, Lester Curtin, and Katherine Flegal, "Prevalence of Overweight and Obesity Among U.S. Children, Adolescents, and Adults, 1999–2002," *Journal of the American Medical Association* 291, no. 23, 2004: 2847–2850) and a U.S. adult population of 209 million in 2000 (U.S. Census Bureau, "Table 2," *op. cit.*).

7 Inciardi, pp. 167, 172.

similar result? The following seems like a reasonable political principle: If it would be wrong (because not part of the government's legitimate functions) to punish people for *directly bringing about* some result, then it would also be wrong to punish people for doing some other action on the grounds that the action has a *chance* of bringing about that result indirectly. If the state may not prohibit me from *directly cutting off* my relationships with others, then the fact that my drug use *might have the result* of damaging those relationships does not provide a good reason to prohibit me from using drugs.

Third, drugs may harm users' financial lives, costing them money, causing them to lose their jobs or not find jobs, and preventing them from getting promotions. The same principle applies here: if it would be an abuse of government power to prohibit me from directly bringing about those sorts of negative financial consequences, then surely the fact that drug use might indirectly bring them about is not a good reason to prohibit drug use. Suppose that I decide to quit my job and throw all my money out the window, for no reason. Should the police arrest me and put me in prison?

Fourth and finally, drugs may damage users' moral character, as James Q. Wilson believes:

> [I]f we believe—as I do—that dependency on certain mind-altering drugs *is* a moral issue and that their illegality rests in part on their immorality, then legalizing them undercuts, if it does not eliminate altogether, the moral message. That message is at the root of the distinction between nicotine and cocaine. Both are highly addictive; both have harmful physical effects. But we treat the two drugs differently not simply because nicotine is so widely used as to be beyond the reach of effective prohibition, but because its use does not destroy the user's essential humanity. Tobacco shortens one's life, cocaine debases it. Nicotine alters one's habits, cocaine alters one's soul. The heavy use of crack, unlike the heavy use of tobacco, corrodes those natural sentiments of sympathy and duty that constitute our human nature and make possible our social life.[8]

In this passage, Wilson claims that the use of cocaine (a) is immoral, (b) destroys one's humanity, (c) alters one's soul, and (d) corrodes one's sense of sympathy and duty. One problem with Wilson's argument is the

---

8   James Q. Wilson, "Against the Legalization of Drugs," *Commentary* 89, 1990: 21–8, p. 26.

lack of evidence supporting claims (a)–(d). Before we put people in prison for corrupting their souls, we should require some objective evidence that their souls are in fact being corrupted. Before we put people in prison for being immoral, we should require some argument showing that their actions are in fact immoral. Perhaps Wilson's charges of immorality and corruption all come down to the charge that drug users lose their sense of sympathy and duty—that is, claims (a)–(c) all rest upon claim (d). It is plausible that *heavy* drug users experience a decreased sense of sympathy with others and a decreased sense of duty and responsibility. Does this provide a good reason to prohibit drug use?

Again, it seems that one should not prohibit an activity on the grounds that it may indirectly cause some result, unless it would be appropriate to prohibit the direct bringing about of that result. Would it be appropriate, and within the legitimate functions of the state, to punish people for being unsympathetic and undutiful, or for behaving in an unsympathetic and undutiful way? Suppose that Howard—though not a drug user—doesn't sympathize with others. When people try to tell Howard their problems, he just tells them to quit whining. Friends and coworkers who ask Howard for favors are rudely rebuffed. Furthermore—though he does not harm others in ways that would be against our current laws—Howard has a poor sense of duty. He doesn't bother to show up for work on time, nor does he take any pride in his work; he doesn't donate to charity; he doesn't try to improve his community. All around, Howard is an ignoble and unpleasant individual. Should he be put in jail?

If not, then why should someone be put in jail merely for doing something that would have a *chance* of causing them to become like Howard? If it would be an abuse of governmental power to punish people for being jerks, then the fact that drug use may cause one to become a jerk is not a good reason to prohibit drug use.

II. Drugs and Harm to Others

Some argue that drug use must be outlawed because drug use harms the user's family, friends, and coworkers, and/or society in general. A report produced by the Office of National Drug Control Policy states:

> Democracies can flourish only when their citizens value their freedom and embrace personal responsibility. Drug use erodes the individual's capacity to pursue both ideals. It diminishes the individual's capacity to operate effectively in many of life's spheres—as a student, a parent, a

spouse, an employee—even as a coworker or fellow motorist. And, while some claim it represents an expression of individual autonomy, drug use is in fact inimical to personal freedom, producing a reduced capacity to participate in the life of the community and the promise of America.[9]

At least one of these alleged harms—dangerous driving—*is* clearly the business of the state. For this reason, I entirely agree that people should be prohibited from driving while under the influence of drugs. But what about the rest of the alleged harms?

Return to our hypothetical citizen Howard. Imagine that Howard—again, for reasons having nothing to do with drugs—does not value freedom, nor does he embrace personal responsibility. It is unclear exactly what this means, but, for good measure, let us suppose that Howard embraces a totalitarian political ideology and denies the existence of free will. He constantly blames other people for his problems and tries to avoid making decisions. Howard is a college student with a part-time job. However, he is a terrible student and worker. He hardly ever studies and frequently misses assignments, as a result of which he gets poor grades. As mentioned earlier, Howard comes to work late and takes no pride in his work. Though he does nothing against our current laws, he is an inattentive and inconsiderate spouse and parent. Nor does he make any effort to participate in the life of his community, or the promise of America. He would rather lie around the house, watching television and cursing the rest of the world for his problems. In short, Howard does all the bad things to his family, friends, coworkers, and society that the ONDCP says *may* result from drug use. And most of this is voluntary.

Should Congress pass laws against what Howard is doing? Should the police then arrest him, and the district attorney prosecute him, for being a loser?

Once again, it seems absurd to suppose that we would arrest and jail someone for behaving in these ways, undesirable as they may be. Since drug use only has a *chance* of causing one to behave in each of these ways, it is even more absurd to suppose that we should arrest and jail people for drug use on the grounds that drug use has these potential effects.

---

9 NDCP, *National Drug Control Strategy 2002*, Washington, D.C.: Government Printing Office, http://www.whitehousedrugpolicy.gov/publications/policy/03ndcs/, pp. 1–2.

III. The Injustice of Drug Prohibition

Philosopher Douglas Husak has characterized drug prohibition as the greatest injustice perpetrated in the United States since slavery.[10] This is no hyperbole. If the drug laws are unjust, then America has over half a million people unjustly imprisoned.[11]

Why think the drug laws are *unjust*? Husak's argument invokes a principle with which few could disagree: it is unjust for the state to punish people without having a good reason for doing so.[12] We have seen the failure of the most common proposed rationales for drug prohibition. If nothing better is forthcoming, then we must conclude that prohibitionists have no rational justification for punishing drug users. We have deprived hundreds of thousands of people of basic liberties and subjected them to severe hardship conditions, for no good reason.

This is bad enough. But I want to say something stronger: it is not merely that we are punishing people for no good reason. We are punishing people for exercising their natural rights. Individuals have a right to use drugs. This right is neither absolute nor exceptionless; suppose, for example, that there existed a drug which, once ingested, caused a significant proportion of users, without any further free choices on their part, to attack other people without provocation. I would think that stopping the use of this drug would be the business of the government. But no existing drug satisfies this description. Indeed, though I cannot take time to delve into the matter here, I think it is clear that the drug *laws* cause far more crime than drugs themselves do.

The idea of a right to use drugs derives from the idea that individuals own their own bodies. That is, a person has the right to exercise control

---

10 Husak, *Legalize This!*, p. 2.

11 In 2006, there were approximately 553,000 people in American prisons and jails whose most serious offense was a drug offense. This included 93,751 federal inmates (U.S. Department of Justice, "Prisoners in 2006," December 2007, http://www.ojp.usdoj.gov/bjs/pub/pdf/p06 .pdf, p. 9). State prisons held another 269,596 drug inmates, based on the 2006 state prison population of 1,377,815 ("Prisoners in 2006," p. 2) and the 2004 rate of 19.57% of state prisoners held on drug charges ("Prisoners in 2006," p. 24). Local jails held another 189,204 drug inmates, based on the 2006 local jail population of 766,010 ("Prisoners in 2006," p. 3) and the 2002 rate of 24.7% of local inmates held on drug charges (U.S. Department of Justice, "Profile of Jail Inmates 2002," published July 2004, revised October 12, 2004, http://www.ojp.usdoj.gov/bjs/ pub/pdf/pji02.pdf, p. 1). In all cases, I have used the latest statistics available as of this writing.

12 Husak, *Legalize This!*, p. 15. See his chapter 2 for an extended discussion of various proposed rationales for drug prohibition, including many issues that I lack space to discuss here.

over his own body—including the right to decide how it should be used, and to exclude others from using it—in a manner similar to the way one may exercise control over one's (other) property. This statement is somewhat vague; nevertheless, we can see the general idea embodied in common sense morality. Indeed, it seems that if there is *anything* one would have rights to, it would be one's own body. This explains why we think others may not physically attack you or kidnap you. It explains why we do not accept the use of unwilling human subjects for medical experiments, even if the experiments are beneficial to society—the rest of society may not decide to use your body for its own purposes without your permission. It explains why some believe that women have a right to an abortion—and why some others do not. The former believe that a woman has the right to do what she wants with her own body; the latter believe that the fetus is a distinct person, and a woman does not have the right to harm *its* body. Virtually no one disputes that, *if* a fetus is merely a part of the woman's body, *then* a woman has a right to choose whether to have an abortion; just as virtually no one disputes that, *if* a fetus is a distinct person, then a woman lacks the right to destroy it. Almost no one disputes that persons have rights over their own bodies but not over others' bodies.

The right to control one's body cannot be interpreted as implying a right to use one's body in *every* conceivable way, any more than we have the right to use our property in every conceivable way. Most importantly, we may not use our bodies to harm others in certain ways, just as we may not use our property to harm others. But drug use seems to be a paradigm case of a legitimate exercise of the right to control one's own body. Drug consumption takes place in and immediately around the user's own body; the salient effects occur *inside* the user's body. If we consider drug use merely as altering the user's own body and mind, it is hard to see how anyone who believes in rights at all could deny that it is protected by a right, for: (a) it is hard to see how anyone who believes in rights could deny that individuals have rights over their own bodies and minds, and (b) it is hard to see how anyone who believes in such rights could deny that drug use, considered merely as altering the user's body and mind, is an example of the exercise of one's rights over one's own body and mind.

Consider two ways a prohibitionist might object to this argument. First, a prohibitionist might argue that drug use does not *merely* alter the user's own body and mind, but also harms the user's family, friends, co-workers, and society. I responded to this sort of argument in section II. Not just *any* way in which an action might be said to "harm" other people makes the action worthy of criminal sanctions. Here we need not try to state a general criterion for what sorts of harms make an action worthy of criminalization; it is enough to note that there are some kinds of "harms" that virtually no one would take to warrant criminal sanctions, and that these include the "harms" I cause to others by being a poor student, an incompetent worker, or an apathetic citizen.[13] That said, I agree with the prohibitionists at least this far: no one should be permitted to drive or operate heavy machinery while under the influence of drugs that impair their ability to do those things; nor should pregnant mothers be permitted to ingest drugs, if it can be proven that those drugs cause substantial risks to their babies (I leave open the question of what the threshold level of risk should be, as well as the empirical questions concerning the actual level of risk created by illegal drugs). But, in the great majority of cases, drug use does not harm anyone in any *relevant* ways—that is, ways that we normally take to merit criminal penalties—and should not be outlawed.

Second, a prohibitionist might argue that drug use fails to qualify as an exercise of the user's rights over his own body, because the individual is not truly acting freely in deciding to use drugs. Perhaps individuals only use drugs because they have fallen prey to some sort of psychological compulsion, because drugs exercise a siren-like allure that distorts users' perceptions, because users don't realize how bad drugs are, or something of that sort. The exact form of this objection doesn't matter; in any case, the prohibitionist faces a dilemma. If users do not freely choose to use drugs, then it is unjust to *punish* them for using drugs. For if users do not choose freely, then they are not morally responsible for their decision, and it is unjust to punish a person for something he is not responsible for. But if users *do* choose freely in deciding to use drugs, then this choice is an exercise of their rights over their own bodies.

I have tried to think of the best arguments prohibitionists could give, but in fact prohibitionists have remained puzzlingly silent on this issue. When a country goes to war, it tends to focus on how to win, sparing little thought for the rights of the victims in the enemy country. Similarly, one effect of America's declaring "war" on drug users seems to have been that prohibitionists have given almost no thought to the rights of drug users. Most either ignore the issue or mention it briefly only to dismiss it without

---

13 Husak (*Drugs and Rights*, Cambridge University Press, 1992, pp. 166–168), similarly, argues that no one has a *right* that I be a good neighbor, proficient student, and so on, and that only harms that violate rights can justify criminal sanctions.

argument.[14] In an effort to discredit legalizers, the Office of National Drug Control Policy produced the following caricature—

> The easy cynicism that has grown up around the drug issue is no accident. Sowing it has been the deliberate aim of a decades-long campaign by proponents of legalization, critics whose mantra is "nothing works," and whose central insight appears to be that they can avoid having to propose the unmentionable—a world where drugs are ubiquitous and where use and addiction would skyrocket—if they can hide behind the bland management critique that drug control efforts are "unworkable."[15]

apparently denying the existence of the central issues I have discussed in this essay. It seems reasonable to assume that an account of the state's right to forcibly interfere with individuals' decisions regarding their own bodies is not forthcoming from these prohibitionists.

IV. Conclusion

Undoubtedly, the drug war has been disastrous in many ways that others can more ably describe—in terms of its effects on crime, on police corruption, and on other civil liberties, to name a few. But more than that, the drug war is morally outrageous in its very conception. If we are to call ours a free society, we cannot deploy force to deprive people of their liberty and property for whimsical reasons. The exercise of such coercion requires a powerful and clearly-stated rationale. Most of the reasons that have been proposed in the case of drug prohibition would be considered feeble if advanced in other contexts. Few would take seriously the suggestion that people should be imprisoned for harming their own health, being poor students, or failing to share in the American dream. It is still less credible that we should imprison people for an activity that only *may* lead to those consequences. Yet these and other, similarly weak arguments form the core of prohibition's defense.

Prohibitionists are likewise unable to answer the argument that individuals have a right to use drugs. Any such answer would have to deny

---

14 See Inciardi for an instance of ignoring and Daniel Lungren ("Legalization Would Be a Mistake" in Timothy Lynch, ed., *After Prohibition*, Washington, D.C.: Cato Institute, 2000, page 180) for an instance of unargued dismissal. Wilson (p. 24) addresses the issue, if at all, only by arguing that drug use makes users worse parents, spouses, employers, and co-workers. This fails to refute the contention that individuals have a right to use drugs.

15 ONDCP, *National Drug Control Strategy 2002*, p. 3.

either that persons have rights of control over their own bodies, or that consuming drugs constituted an exercise of those rights. We have seen that the sort of harms drug use allegedly causes to society do not make a case against its being an exercise of the user's rights over his own body. And the claim that drug users can't control their behavior or don't know what they are doing renders it even more mysterious why one would believe drug users deserve to be punished for what they are doing.

I will close by responding to a query posed by prohibition-advocate James Inciardi:

> The government of the United States is not going to legalize drugs any-time soon, if ever, and certainly not in this [the 20th] century. So why spend so much time, expense, and intellectual and emotional effort on a quixotic undertaking? . . . [W]e should know by now that neither politicians nor the polity respond positively to abrupt and drastic strategy alterations.[16]

The United States presently has 553,000 people unjustly imprisoned. Inciardi may—tragically—be correct that our government has no intention of stopping its flagrant violations of the rights of its people any time soon. Nevertheless, it remains the duty of citizens and of political and social theorists to identify the injustice, and not to tacitly assent to it. Imagine a slavery advocate, decades before the Civil War, arguing that abolitionists were wasting their breath and should move on to more productive activities, such as arguing for incremental changes in the way slaves are treated, since the southern states had no intention of ending slavery any time soon. The institution of slavery is a black mark on our nation's history, but our history would be even more shameful if no one at the time had spoken against the injustice.

Is this comparison overdrawn? I don't think so. The harm of being unjustly imprisoned is qualitatively comparable (though it usually ends sooner) to the harm of being enslaved. The increasingly popular scapegoating and stereotyping of drug users and sellers on the part of our nation's leaders is comparable to racial prejudices of previous generations. Yet very few seem willing to speak on behalf of drug users. Perhaps the unwillingness of those in public life to defend drug users' rights stems from the negative image we have of drug users and the fear of being associated with them. Yet these attitudes remain baffling. I have used illegal drugs myself.

---

16 Inciardi, p. 205.

I know of many decent and successful individuals who have used illegal drugs. Nearly half of all Americans over the age of 11 have used illegal drugs—including at least two United States Presidents, one Vice-President, one Speaker of the House, and one Supreme Court Justice.[17] But now leave aside the absurdity of recommending criminal sanctions for all these people. My point is this: if we are convinced of the injustice of drug prohibition, then—even if our protests should fall on deaf ears—we can not remain silent in the face of such a large-scale injustice in our own country. And, fortunately, radical social reforms *have* occurred, more than once in our history, in response to moral arguments.

Michael Huemer: America's Unjust Drug War

1. Huemer admits that using drugs can be harmful to the user, but points out that alcohol, tobacco, unhealthy food, and unsafe sex can also be harmful. Is there any morally relevant difference between the harms caused by drugs and the harms caused by these other activities?

2. Huemer invokes the following principle: "if it would be wrong to punish people for *directly bringing about* some result, then it would also be wrong to punish people for doing some other action on the grounds that the action has a *chance* of bringing about that result indirectly." Do you find this principle plausible? Why or why not?

3. Consider Huemer's case involving Howard. Should Howard be punished for acting the way he does? If not, does it follow that we should not punish drug users?

4. Do individuals have a right to use drugs? What is Huemer's argument for thinking that they do? Do you find it convincing?

5. Suppose that we accept Huemer's contention that we ought to legalize recreational drug use. Does it follow that all of those currently in prison for drug-related offenses have been unjustly imprisoned?

---

17 In 2006, 45% of Americans aged 12 and over reported having used at least one illegal drug (U.S. Department of Health and Human Services, "National Survey on Drug Use and Health," 2006, Table 1.1B, http://www.oas.samhsa.gov/NSDUH/2k6NSDUH/tabs/Sect1peTabs1to46. htm). Bill Clinton, Al Gore, Newt Gingrich and Clarence Thomas have all acknowledged past drug use (reported by David Phinney, "Dodging the Drug Question," ABC News, August 19, 1999, http://abcnews.go.com/sections/politics/DailyNews/prez_questions990819.html). George W. Bush has refused to state whether he has ever used illegal drugs. Barack Obama has admitted to cocaine and marijuana use (*Dreams from My Father*, New York: Random House, 2004, p. 93).

37

===== ❧ =====

The Case against Perfection
Michael Sandel

....

Michael Sandel argues against genetic enhancement and engineering by asking us to focus on what he calls "the gifted character of human powers and achievements." By this he means that our talents and our abilities are not entirely a product of our efforts. And this, he argues, is a very good thing. That much of what is important in a life is effectively outside of our control should encourage in us a degree of humility about our accomplishments. Genetic enhancement and engineering are an effort to control the key elements of our appearance, fitness, and personality in a way that supports pride and arrogance rather than humility. Further, we expand our human sympathies and sense of social solidarity if we recognize that the problems and difficulties confronted by others are not always of their own making.

Sandel draws a parallel between genetic engineering and the kind of "hyperparenting" in which parents obsessively attend to every detail of their children's lives. In both cases, a quest for perfection "represents the anxious excess of mastery and dominion that misses the sense of life as a gift." Recognizing a child's limitations and vulnerabilities not only helps a parent to develop important moral virtues such as compassion, sympathy, and empathy, but also provides an opportunity to appreciate the frailty and imperfections that come in every life.

Another worry about genetic engineering is that it is really no different from the eugenics programs of old. Those state-run programs

Originally appeared in *The Atlantic Monthly*, April 2004. For a longer version of this essay, see Michael J. Sandel, *The Case Against Perfection: Ethics in the Age of Genetic Engineering* (Harvard University Press, 2007).

forcibly sterilized or compelled abortions of members of unpopular minority groups in the name of creating a finer "race" of human beings. Although the state coercion at the heart of such programs is certainly morally troubling, Sandel argues that the impulse to genetically engineer a more perfect next generation is still morally problematic, even if we imagine that such engineering is done without any coercion at all.

. . . .

. . . It is commonly said that genetic enhancements undermine our humanity by threatening our capacity to act freely, to succeed by our own efforts, and to consider ourselves responsible—worthy of praise or blame—for the things we do and for the way we are. It is one thing to hit seventy home runs as the result of disciplined training and effort, and something else, something less, to hit them with the help of steroids or genetically enhanced muscles. Of course, the roles of effort and enhancement will be a matter of degree. But as the role of enhancement increases, our admiration for the achievement fades—or, rather, our admiration for the achievement shifts from the player to his pharmacist. This suggests that our moral response to enhancement is a response to the diminished agency of the person whose achievement is enhanced.

Though there is much to be said for this argument, I do not think the main problem with enhancement and genetic engineering is that they undermine effort and erode human agency. The deeper danger is that they represent a kind of hyperagency—a Promethean aspiration to remake nature, including human nature, to serve our purposes and satisfy our desires. The problem is not the drift to mechanism but the drive to mastery. And what the drive to mastery misses and may even destroy is an appreciation of the gifted character of human powers and achievements.

To acknowledge the giftedness of life is to recognize that our talents and powers are not wholly our own doing, despite the effort we expend to develop and to exercise them. It is also to recognize that not everything in the world is open to whatever use we may desire or devise. Appreciating the gifted quality of life constrains the Promethean project and conduces to a certain humility. It is in part a religious sensibility. But its resonance reaches beyond religion.

It is difficult to account for what we admire about human activity and achievement without drawing upon some version of this idea. Consider two types of athletic achievement. We appreciate players like Pete Rose, who are not blessed with great natural gifts but who manage, through striving, grit, and determination, to excel in their sport. But we also admire players like Joe DiMaggio, who display natural gifts with grace and effortlessness. Now, suppose we learned that both players took performance-enhancing drugs. Whose turn to drugs would we find more deeply disillusioning? Which aspect of the athletic ideal—effort or gift—would be more deeply offended?

Some might say effort: the problem with drugs is that they provide a shortcut, a way to win without striving. But striving is not the point of sports; excellence is. And excellence consists at least partly in the display of natural talents and gifts that are no doing of the athlete who possesses them. This is an uncomfortable fact for democratic societies. We want to believe that success, in sports and in life, is something we earn, not something we inherit. Natural gifts, and the admiration they inspire, embarrass the meritocratic faith; they cast doubt on the conviction that praise and rewards flow from effort alone. In the face of this embarrassment we inflate the moral significance of striving, and depreciate giftedness. This distortion can be seen, for example, in network-television coverage of the Olympics, which focuses less on the feats the athletes perform than on heartrending stories of the hardships they have overcome and the struggles they have waged to triumph over an injury or a difficult upbringing or political turmoil in their native land.

But effort isn't everything. No one believes that a mediocre basketball player who works and trains even harder than Michael Jordan deserves greater acclaim or a bigger contract. The real problem with genetically altered athletes is that they corrupt athletic competition as a human activity that honors the cultivation and display of natural talents. From this standpoint, enhancement can be seen as the ultimate expression of the ethic of effort and willfulness—a kind of high-tech striving. The ethic of willfulness and the biotechnological powers it now enlists are arrayed against the claims of giftedness.

The ethic of giftedness, under siege in sports, persists in the practice of parenting. But here, too, bioengineering and genetic enhancement threaten to dislodge it. To appreciate children as gifts is to accept them as they come, not as objects of our design or products of our will or instruments of our ambition. Parental love is not contingent on the talents and attributes a child happens to have. We choose our friends and spouses at least partly on the basis of qualities we find attractive. But we do not choose our children. Their qualities are unpredictable, and even the most conscientious parents cannot be held wholly responsible for the kind of children they have. That is why parenthood, more than other human relationships, teaches what the theologian William F. May calls an "openness to the unbidden."

May's resonant phrase helps us see that the deepest moral objection to enhancement lies less in the perfection it seeks than in the human disposition it expresses and promotes. The problem is not that parents usurp the autonomy of a child they design. The problem lies in the hubris of the designing parents, in their drive to master the mystery of birth. Even if this disposition did not make parents tyrants to their children, it would disfigure the relation between parent and child, and deprive the parent of the humility and enlarged human sympathies that an openness to the unbidden can cultivate.

To appreciate children as gifts or blessings is not, of course, to be passive in the face of illness or disease. Medical intervention to cure or prevent illness or restore the injured to health does not desecrate nature but honors it. Healing sickness or injury does not override a child's natural capacities but permits them to flourish.

Nor does the sense of life as a gift mean that parents must shrink from shaping and directing the development of their child. Just as athletes and artists have an obligation to cultivate their talents, so parents have an obligation to cultivate their children, to help them discover and develop their talents and gifts. As May points out, parents give their children two kinds of love: accepting love and transforming love. Accepting love affirms the being of the child, whereas transforming love seeks the well-being of the child. Each aspect corrects the excesses of the other, he writes: "Attachment becomes too quietistic if it slackens into mere acceptance of the child as he is." Parents have a duty to promote their children's excellence.

These days, however, overly ambitious parents are prone to get carried away with transforming love—promoting and demanding all manner of accomplishments from their children, seeking perfection. "Parents find it difficult to maintain an equilibrium between the two sides of love," May observes. "Accepting love, without transforming love, slides into indulgence and finally neglect. Transforming love, without accepting love, badgers and finally rejects." May finds in these competing impulses a parallel with modern science: it, too, engages us in beholding the given world, studying and savoring it, and also in molding the world, transforming and perfecting it.

The mandate to mold our children, to cultivate and improve them, complicates the case against enhancement. We usually admire parents who seek the best for their children, who spare no effort to help them achieve happiness and success. Some parents confer advantages on their children by enrolling them in expensive schools, hiring private tutors, sending them to tennis camp, providing them with piano lessons, ballet lessons, swimming lessons, SAT-prep courses, and so on. If it is permissible and even admirable for parents to help their children in these ways, why isn't it equally admirable for parents to use whatever genetic technologies may emerge (provided they are safe) to enhance their children's intelligence, musical ability, or athletic prowess?

The defenders of enhancement are right to this extent: improving children through genetic engineering is similar in spirit to the heavily managed, high-pressure child-rearing that is now common. But this similarity does not vindicate genetic enhancement. On the contrary, it highlights a problem with the trend toward hyperparenting. One conspicuous example of this trend is sports-crazed parents bent on making champions of their children. Another is the frenzied drive of overbearing parents to mold and manage their children's academic careers.

As the pressure for performance increases, so does the need to help distractible children concentrate on the task at hand. This may be why diagnoses of attention deficit and hyperactivity disorder have increased so sharply. Lawrence Diller, a pediatrician and the author of *Running on Ritalin*, estimates that five to six percent of American children under eighteen (a total of four to five million kids) are currently prescribed Ritalin, Adderall, and other stimulants, the treatment of choice for ADHD. (Stimulants counteract hyperactivity by making it easier to focus and sustain attention.) The number of Ritalin prescriptions for children and adolescents has tripled over the past decade, but not all users suffer from attention disorders or hyperactivity. High school and college students have learned that prescription stimulants improve concentration for those with normal attention spans, and some buy or borrow their classmates' drugs to enhance their performance on the SAT or other exams. Since stimulants work for both medical and nonmedical purposes, they raise the same moral questions posed by other technologies of enhancement.

However those questions are resolved, the debate reveals the cultural distance we have traveled since the debate over marijuana, LSD, and other drugs a generation ago. Unlike the drugs of the 1960s and 1970s, Ritalin and Adderall are not for checking out but for buckling down, not for beholding the world and taking it in but for molding the world and fitting in. We used to speak of nonmedical drug use as "recreational." That term no longer applies. The steroids and stimulants that figure in the enhancement debate are not a source of recreation but a bid for compliance—a way of answering a competitive society's demand to improve our performance and perfect our nature. This demand for performance and perfection animates the impulse to rail against the given. It is the deepest source of the moral trouble with enhancement.

Some see a clear line between genetic enhancement and other ways that people seek improvement in their children and themselves. Genetic manipulation seems somehow worse—more intrusive, more sinister— than other ways of enhancing performance and seeking success. But morally speaking, the difference is less significant than it seems. Bioengineering gives us reason to question the low-tech, high-pressure child-rearing practices we commonly accept. The hyperparenting familiar in our time represents an anxious excess of mastery and dominion that misses the sense of life as a gift. This draws it disturbingly close to eugenics.

The shadow of eugenics hangs over today's debates about genetic engineering and enhancement. Critics of genetic engineering argue that human cloning, enhancement, and the quest for designer children are nothing more than "privatized" or "free-market" eugenics. Defenders of enhancement reply that genetic choices freely made are not really eugenic—at least not in the pejorative sense. To remove the coercion, they argue, is to remove the very thing that makes eugenic policies repugnant.

Sorting out the lesson of eugenics is another way of wrestling with the ethics of enhancement. The Nazis gave eugenics a bad name. But what, precisely, was wrong with it? Was the old eugenics objectionable only insofar as it was coercive? Or is there something inherently wrong with the resolve to deliberately design our progeny's traits?

James Watson, the biologist who, with Francis Crick, discovered the structure of DNA, sees nothing wrong with genetic engineering and enhancement, provided they are freely chosen rather than state-imposed. And yet Watson's language contains more than a whiff of the old eugenic sensibility. "If you really are stupid, I would call that a disease," he recently told *The Times* of London. "The lower 10 percent who really have difficulty, even in elementary school, what's the cause of it? A lot of people would like to say, 'Well, poverty, things like that.' It probably isn't. So I'd like to get rid of that, to help the lower 10 percent." A few years ago Watson stirred controversy by saying that if a gene for homosexuality were discovered, a woman should be free to abort a fetus that carried it. When his remark provoked an uproar, he replied that he was not singling out gays but asserting a principle: women should be free to abort fetuses for any reason of genetic preference—for example, if the child would be dyslexic, or lacking musical talent, or too short to play basketball.

Watson's scenarios are clearly objectionable to those for whom all abortion is an unspeakable crime. But for those who do not subscribe to the pro-life position, these scenarios raise a hard question: If it is morally troubling to contemplate abortion to avoid a gay child or a dyslexic one, doesn't this suggest that something is wrong with acting on any eugenic preference, even when no state coercion is involved?

Consider the market in eggs and sperm. The advent of artificial insemination allows prospective parents to shop for gametes with the genetic traits they desire in their offspring. It is a less predictable way to design children than cloning or pre-implantation genetic screening, but it offers a good example of a procreative practice in which the old eugenics meets the new consumerism. A few years ago some Ivy League newspapers ran an ad seeking an egg from a woman who was at least five feet ten inches tall and athletic, had no major family medical problems, and had a combined SAT score of 1400 or above. The ad offered $50,000 for an egg from a donor with these traits. More recently a Web site was launched claiming to auction eggs from fashion models whose photos appeared on the site, at starting bids of $15,000 to $150,000.

On what grounds, if any, is the egg market morally objectionable? Since no one is forced to buy or sell, it cannot be wrong for reasons of coercion. Some might worry that hefty prices would exploit poor women by presenting them with an offer they couldn't refuse. But the designer eggs that fetch the highest prices are likely to be sought from the privileged, not the poor. If the market for premium eggs gives us moral qualms, this, too, shows that concerns about eugenics are not put to rest by freedom of choice.

A tale of two sperm banks helps explain why. The Repository for Germinal Choice, one of America's first sperm banks, was not a commercial enterprise. It was opened in 1980 by Robert Graham, a philanthropist dedicated to improving the world's "germ plasm" and counteracting the rise of "retrograde humans." His plan was to collect the sperm of Nobel Prize-winning scientists and make it available to women of high intelligence, in hopes of breeding supersmart babies. But Graham had trouble persuading Nobel laureates to donate their sperm for his bizarre scheme, and so settled for sperm from young scientists of high promise. His sperm bank closed in 1999.

In contrast, California Cryobank, one of the world's leading sperm banks, is a for-profit company with no overt eugenic mission. Cappy Rothman, M.D., a co-founder of the firm, has nothing but disdain for Graham's eugenics, although the standards Cryobank imposes on the sperm it recruits are exacting. Cryobank has offices in Cambridge, Massachusetts, between Harvard and MIT, and in Palo Alto, California, near Stanford. It advertises for donors in campus newspapers (compensation up to $900 a month), and accepts less than five percent of the men who apply. Cryobank's marketing materials play up the prestigious source of its sperm. Its catalogue provides detailed information about the physical characteristics of each donor, along with his ethnic origin and college major. For an extra fee prospective customers can buy the results of a test that assesses the donor's temperament and character type. Rothman reports that Cryobank's ideal sperm donor is six feet tall, with brown eyes, blond hair, and dimples, and has a college degree—not because the company wants to propagate those traits, but because those are the traits his customers want: "If our customers wanted high school dropouts, we would give them high school dropouts."

Not everyone objects to marketing sperm. But anyone who is troubled by the eugenic aspect of the Nobel Prize sperm bank should be equally troubled by Cryobank, consumer-driven though it be. What, after all, is the moral difference between designing children according to an explicit eugenic purpose and designing children according to the dictates of the market? Whether the aim is to improve humanity's "germ plasm" or to cater to consumer preferences, both practices are eugenic insofar as both make children into products of deliberate design.

A number of political philosophers call for a new "liberal eugenics." They argue that a moral distinction can be drawn between the old eugenic policies and genetic enhancements that do not restrict the autonomy of the child. "While old-fashioned authoritarian eugenicists sought to produce citizens out of a single centrally designed mould," writes Nicholas Agar, "the distinguishing mark of the new liberal eugenics is state neutrality." Government may not tell parents what sort of children to design, and parents may engineer in their children only those traits that improve their capacities without biasing their choice of life plans. A recent text on genetics and justice, written by the bioethicists Allen Buchanan, Dan W. Brock, Norman Daniels, and Daniel Wikler, offers a similar view. The "bad reputation of eugenics," they write, is due to practices that "might be avoidable in a future eugenic program." The problem with the old eugenics was that its burdens fell disproportionately on the weak and the poor, who were unjustly sterilized and segregated. But provided that the benefits and burdens of genetic improvement are fairly distributed, these bioethicists argue, eugenic measures are unobjectionable and may even be morally required.

The libertarian philosopher Robert Nozick proposed a "genetic supermarket" that would enable parents to order children by design without imposing a single design on the society as a whole: "This supermarket system has the great virtue that it involves no centralized decision fixing the future human type(s)."

Even the leading philosopher of American liberalism, John Rawls, in his classic *A Theory of Justice* (1971), offered a brief endorsement of noncoercive eugenics. Even in a society that agrees to share the benefits and burdens of the genetic lottery, it is "in the interest of each to have greater natural assets," Rawls wrote. "This enables him to pursue a preferred plan of life." The parties to the social contract "want to insure for their descendants the best genetic endowment (assuming their own to be fixed)." Eugenic policies are therefore not only permissible but required as a matter of justice. "Thus over time a society is to take steps at least to preserve the general level of natural abilities and to prevent the diffusion of serious defects."

But removing the coercion does not vindicate eugenics. The problem with eugenics and genetic engineering is that they represent the one-sided triumph of willfulness over giftedness, of dominion over reverence, of molding over beholding. Why, we may wonder, should we worry about this triumph? Why not shake off our unease about genetic enhancement as so much superstition? What would be lost if biotechnology dissolved our sense of giftedness?

From a religious standpoint the answer is clear: To believe that our talents and powers are wholly our own doing is to misunderstand our place in creation, to confuse our role with God's. Religion is not the only source of reasons to care about giftedness, however. The moral stakes can also be described in secular terms. If bioengineering made the myth of the "self-made man" come true, it would be difficult to view our talents as gifts for which we are indebted, rather than as achievements for which we are responsible. This would transform three key features of our moral landscape: humility, responsibility, and solidarity.

In a social world that prizes mastery and control, parenthood is a school for humility. That we care deeply about our children and yet cannot choose the kind we want teaches parents to be open to the unbidden. Such openness is a disposition worth affirming, not only within families but in the wider world as well. It invites us to abide the unexpected, to live with dissonance, to rein in the impulse to control. A *Gattaca*-like world in which parents became accustomed to specifying the sex and genetic traits of their children would be a world inhospitable to the unbidden, a gated community writ large. The awareness that our talents and abilities are not wholly our own doing restrains our tendency toward hubris.

Though some maintain that genetic enhancement erodes human agency by overriding effort, the real problem is the explosion, not the erosion, of responsibility. As humility gives way, responsibility expands to daunting proportions. We attribute less to chance and more to choice. Parents become responsible for choosing, or failing to choose, the right traits for their children. Athletes become responsible for acquiring, or failing to acquire, the talents that will help their teams win.

One of the blessings of seeing ourselves as creatures of nature, God, or fortune is that we are not wholly responsible for the way we are. The more we become masters of our genetic endowments, the greater the burden we bear for the talents we have and the way we perform. Today when a basketball player misses a rebound, his coach can blame him for being out of position. Tomorrow the coach may blame him for being too short. Even now the use of performance-enhancing drugs in professional sports is subtly transforming the expectations players have for one another; on some teams players who take the field free from amphetamines or other stimulants are criticized for "playing naked."

The more alive we are to the chanced nature of our lot, the more reason we have to share our fate with others. Consider insurance. Since people do not know whether or when various ills will befall them, they pool their risk by buying health insurance and life insurance. As life plays itself out, the healthy wind up subsidizing the unhealthy, and those who live to a ripe old age wind up subsidizing the families of those who die before their time. Even without a sense of mutual obligation, people pool their risks and resources and share one another's fate.

But insurance markets mimic solidarity only insofar as people do not know or control their own risk factors. Suppose genetic testing advanced to the point where it could reliably predict each person's medical future and life expectancy. Those confident of good health and long life would opt out of the pool, causing other people's premiums to skyrocket. The solidarity of insurance would disappear as those with good genes fled the actuarial company of those with bad ones.

The fear that insurance companies would use genetic data to assess risks and set premiums recently led the Senate to vote to prohibit genetic discrimination in health insurance. But the bigger danger, admittedly more speculative, is that genetic enhancement, if routinely practiced, would make it harder to foster the moral sentiments that social solidarity requires.

Why, after all, do the successful owe anything to the least-advantaged members of society? The best answer to this question leans heavily on the notion of giftedness. The natural talents that enable the successful to flourish are not their own doing but, rather, their good fortune—a result of the genetic lottery. If our genetic endowments are gifts, rather than achievements for which we can claim credit, it is a mistake and a conceit to assume that we are entitled to the full measure of the bounty they reap in a market economy. We therefore have an obligation to share this bounty with those who, through no fault of their own, lack comparable gifts.

A lively sense of the contingency of our gifts—a consciousness that none of us is wholly responsible for his or her success—saves a meritocratic society from sliding into the smug assumption that the rich are rich because they are more deserving than the poor. Without this, the successful would become even more likely than they are now to view themselves as self-made and self-sufficient, and hence wholly responsible for their success. Those at the bottom of society would be viewed not as disadvantaged, and thus worthy of a measure of compensation, but as simply unfit, and thus worthy of eugenic repair. The meritocracy, less chastened by chance, would become harder, less forgiving. As perfect genetic knowledge would end the simulacrum of solidarity in insurance markets, so perfect genetic control would erode the actual solidarity that arises when men and women reflect on the contingency of their talents and fortunes.

Thirty-five years ago Robert L. Sinsheimer, a molecular biologist at the California Institute of Technology, glimpsed the shape of things to come. In an article titled "The Prospect of Designed Genetic Change" he argued that freedom of choice would vindicate the new genetics, and set it apart from the discredited eugenics of old.

> To implement the older eugenics. . . . would have required a massive social programme carried out over many generations. Such

a programme could not have been initiated without the consent and co-operation of a major fraction of the population, and would have been continuously subject to social control. In contrast, the new eugenics could, at least in principle, be implemented on a quite individual basis, in one generation, and subject to no existing restrictions.

According to Sinsheimer, the new eugenics would be voluntary rather than coerced, and also more humane. Rather than segregating and eliminating the unfit, it would improve them. "The old eugenics would have required a continual selection for breeding of the fit, and a culling of the unfit," he wrote. "The new eugenics would permit in principle the conversion of all the unfit to the highest genetic level."

Sinsheimer's paean to genetic engineering caught the heady, Promethean self-image of the age. He wrote hopefully of rescuing "the losers in that chromosomal lottery that so firmly channels our human destinies," including not only those born with genetic defects but also "the 50,000,000 'normal' Americans with an IQ of less than 90." But he also saw that something bigger than improving on nature's "mindless, age-old throw of dice" was at stake. Implicit in technologies of genetic intervention was a more exalted place for human beings in the cosmos. "As we enlarge man's freedom, we diminish his constraints and that which he must accept as given," he wrote. Copernicus and Darwin had "demoted man from his bright glory at the focal point of the universe," but the new biology would restore his central role. In the mirror of our genetic knowledge we would see ourselves as more than a link in the chain of evolution: "We can be the agent of transition to a whole new pitch of evolution. This is a cosmic event."

There is something appealing, even intoxicating, about a vision of human freedom unfettered by the given. It may even be the case that the allure of that vision played a part in summoning the genomic age into being. It is often assumed that the powers of enhancement we now possess arose as an inadvertent by-product of biomedical progress—the genetic revolution came, so to speak, to cure disease, and stayed to tempt us with the prospect of enhancing our performance, designing our children, and perfecting our nature. That may have the story backwards. It is more plausible to view genetic engineering as the ultimate expression of our resolve to see ourselves astride the world, the masters of our nature. But that promise of mastery is flawed. It threatens to banish our appreciation of life as a gift, and to leave us with nothing to affirm or behold outside our own will.

Michael J. Sandel: The Case against Perfectionism

1. Explain the difference between "accepting love" and "transforming love." To illustrate, give an example of each. Why does Sandel think both are important and how does he think they should be balanced? According to Sandel, what implications does this have for how parents should treat their children? Do you agree? Why or why not?

2. Explain how "liberal eugenics" differs from "old-fashioned authoritarian eugenics." Under what conditions do the proponents of "liberal eugenics" think that genetic engineering is morally permissible? Do you think that these conditions could ever be met? If they could be met, do you agree that in such circumstances genetic engineering would be morally permissible? Why or why not?

3. What does Sandel think the point of sports is? Explain the distinction between talent and striving, and how each contributes to our assessments of athletes and athletic performances. How do these considerations mirror those relevant to the moral permissibility of human enhancement? What lesson does Sandel draw from his consideration of athletics?

4. Sandel thinks that the practice of bioengineering will "[dissolve] our sense of giftedness," which in turn will "transform three key features of our moral landscape." Identify these three features and explain how Sandel thinks bioengineering would transform them. Do you agree with his assessment? Do you think the likely effects of bioengineering are a good reason to reject it? Defend your answer.

5. What does Sandel mean by "the ethic of giftedness"? What obligations does it impose upon us? What kind of obligations do we have that conflict with giftedness? According to Sandel, what implications does the ethic of giftedness have for the moral permissibility of human enhancement? Do you agree with this assessment? Why or why not?

38
===== ❧ =====

Genetic Interventions and the Ethics of Enhancement of Human Beings

Julian Savulescu

....

Julian Savulescu offers three arguments in defense of the genetic enhancement of human beings.

First, suppose that parents could greatly improve their child's intelligence by altering the child's diet. They are lazy and fail to do this. We would condemn the parents for their laziness. Things are no different when it comes to genetic enhancements. If parents have the opportunity to greatly benefit their children, but deliberately or negligently fail to do so, then they have acted wrongly. It doesn't matter whether the benefit is conferred by enhanced diet or by introducing genetic changes.

Second, consistency requires that we treat "environmental" and biological enhancements in the same way. We train our children to be cooperative, intelligent, and well behaved. Such parental "interventions" alter a child's brain structure in irreversible but highly beneficial ways. This is exactly what many genetic interventions do. Instilling useful and enjoyable traits in one's child is morally required. Genetic enhancement helps parents to meet this requirement.

Third, if we accept the treatment and prevention of disease as an important goal, then we should accept genetic interventions. Diseases

Julian Savulescu, "Genetic Interventions and the Ethics of Enhancement of Human Beings" from *The Oxford Handbook of Bioethics* (Oxford University Press, 2007), Bonnie Steinbock (ed.), pp. 516–535.

undermine health, which in turn undermines a person's well-being and quality of life. Failure to prevent diseases by the use of genetic intervention is just as bad as failure to prevent them by the use of available drugs or surgeries.

Savulescu then replies to various objections that have been leveled against genetic enhancement. (1) Such practices amount to "playing God." Reply: we rightly make life-or-death decisions all the time, and many are permissible. (2) Genetic interventions will have discriminatory results. Reply: many people are born with serious biological handicaps, and genetic intervention can level the playing field and thus erase much existing disparity between those who were favored in the "natural lottery" and those who weren't. (3) Genetic engineering will lead to a single model of a desired child, and a sterile world where the surprise and mystery of life would disappear. Reply: manipulating genes will never erase differences among people and will still leave huge elements of our lives subject to chance. (4) Genetic enhancement is contrary to human nature. Reply: our nature as human beings is to be rational, and that requires us to use our reason to determine how best to improve our lives. Genetic engineering will do just that. (5) Genetic enhancement is self-defeating; its goal of making some people superior—more beautiful, intelligent, hard-working than others—will fail if everyone is genetically enhanced. Reply: critics have mistaken the goal of such enhancement: it is not to create or reinforce social divisions, but rather to improve people's lives.

....

Should we use science and medical technology not just to prevent or treat disease, but to intervene at the most basic biological levels to improve biology and enhance people's lives? By 'enhance', I mean help them to live a longer and/or better life than normal. There are various ways in which we can enhance people but I want to focus on biological enhancement, especially genetic enhancement.

The Ethics of Enhancement

I will now give three arguments in favour of enhancement and then consider several objections.

First Argument for Enhancement: Choosing Not to Enhance Is Wrong

Consider the case of the Neglectful Parents. The Neglectful Parents give birth to a child with a special condition. The child has a stunning intellect but requires a simple, readily available, cheap dietary supplement to sustain his intellect. But they neglect the diet of this child and this results in a child with a stunning intellect becoming normal. This is clearly wrong.

But now consider the case of the Lazy Parents. They have a child who has a normal intellect but if they introduced the same dietary supplement, the child's intellect would rise to the same level as the child of the Neglectful Parent. They can't be bothered with improving the child's diet so the child remains with a normal intellect. Failure to institute dietary supplementation means a normal child fails to achieve a stunning intellect. The inaction of the Lazy Parents is as wrong as the inaction of the Neglectful Parents. It has exactly the same consequence: a child exists who could have had a stunning intellect but is instead normal.

Some argue that it is not wrong to fail to bring about the best state of affairs. This may or may not be the case. But in these kinds of case, when there are no other relevant moral considerations, the failure to introduce a diet that sustains a more desirable state is as wrong as the failure to introduce a diet that brings about a more desirable state. The costs of inaction are the same, as are the parental obligations.

If we substitute 'biological intervention' for 'diet', we see that in order not to wrong our children, we should enhance them. Unless there is something special and optimal about our children's physical, psychological, or cognitive abilities, or something different about other biological interventions, it would be wrong not to enhance them.

Second Argument: Consistency

Some will object that, while we do have an obligation to institute better diets, biological interventions like genetic interventions are different from dietary supplementation. I will argue that there is no difference between these interventions.

In general, we accept environmental interventions to improve our children. Education, diet, and training are all used to make our children better people and increase their opportunities in life. We train children to be well behaved, cooperative, and intelligent. Indeed, researchers are looking at ways to make the environment more stimulating for young children to maximize their intellectual development. But in the study of the rat model of Huntington's Chorea, the stimulating environment acted to change the brain structure of the rats. The drug Prozac acted in just the same way. These environmental manipulations do not act mysteriously. They alter our biology.

The most striking example of this is a study of rats that were extensively mothered and rats that were not mothered. The mothered rats showed genetic changes (changes in the methylation of the DNA) that were passed on to the next generation. . . . More generally, environmental manipulations can profoundly affect biology. Maternal care and stress have been associated with abnormal brain (hippocampal) development, involving altered nerve growth factors and cognitive, psychological, and immune deficits later in life.

Some argue that genetic manipulations are different because they are irreversible. But environmental interventions can equally be irreversible. Child neglect or abuse can scar a person for life. It may be impossible to unlearn the skill of playing the piano or riding a bike, once learnt. One may be wobbly, but one is a novice only once. Just as the example of mothering of rats shows that environmental interventions can cause biological changes that are passed onto the next generation, so too can environmental interventions be irreversible, or very difficult to reverse, within one generation.

Why should we allow environmental manipulations that alter our biology but not direct biological manipulations? What is the moral difference between producing a smarter child by immersing that child in a stimulating environment, giving the child a drug, or directly altering the child's brain or genes?

One example of a drug that alters brain chemistry is Prozac, which is a serotonin reuptake inhibitor. Early in life it acts as a nerve growth factor, but it may also alter the brain early in life to make it more prone to stress and anxiety later in life by altering receptor development. . . . Drugs like Prozac and maternal deprivation may have the same biological effects.

If the outcome is the same, why treat biological manipulation differently from environmental manipulation? Not only may a favourable environment improve a child's biology and increase a child's opportunities, so too may direct biological interventions. Couples should maximize the genetic opportunity of their children to lead a good life and a productive, cooperative social existence. There is no relevant moral difference between environmental and genetic intervention.

Third Argument: No Difference from Treating Disease

If we accept the treatment and prevention of disease, we should accept enhancement. The goodness of health is what drives a moral obligation to treat or prevent disease. But health is not what ultimately matters—health enables us to live well; disease prevents us from doing what we want and what is good. Health is instrumentally valuable—valuable as a resource that allows us to do what really matters, that is, lead a good life.

What constitutes a good life is a deep philosophical question. According to hedonistic theories, what is good is having pleasant experiences and being happy. According to desire fulfilment theories, and economics, what matters is having our preferences satisfied. According to objective theories, certain activities are good for people: developing deep personal relationships, developing talents, understanding oneself and the world, gaining knowledge, being a part of a family, and so on. We need not decide on which of these theories is correct in order to understand what is bad about ill health. Disease is important because it causes pain, is not what we want, and stops us engaging in those activities that give meaning to life. Sometimes people trade health for well-being: mountain climbers take on risk to achieve, smokers sometimes believe that the pleasures outweigh the risks of smoking, and so on. Life is about managing risk to health and life to promote well-being.

Beneficence—the moral obligation to benefit people—provides a strong reason to enhance people in so far as the biological enhancement increases their chance of having a better life. But can biological enhancements increase people's opportunities for well-being? There are reasons to believe that they might.

Many of our biological and psychological characteristics profoundly affect how well our lives go. In the 1960s Walter Mischel conducted impulse control experiments in which 4-year-old children were left in a room with one marshmallow, after being told that if they did not eat the marshmallow, they could later have two. Some children would eat it as soon as the researcher left; others would use a variety of strategies to help control their behaviour and ignore the temptation of the single marshmallow. A decade later they reinterviewed the children and found that those who were better at delaying gratification had more friends, better academic performance, and more motivation to succeed. Whether the child had grabbed for the marshmallow had a much stronger bearing on their SAT scores than did their IQ (Mischel *et al.* 1988).

Impulse control has also been linked to socio-economic control and avoiding conflict with the law. The problems of a hot and uncontrollable temper can be profound.

Shyness too can greatly restrict a life. I remember one newspaper story about a woman who blushed violet every time she went into a social situation. This led her to a hermitic, miserable existence. She eventually had the autonomic nerves to her face surgically cut. This revolutionized her life and had a greater effect on her well-being than the treatment of many diseases.

Buchanan and colleagues have discussed the value of 'all purpose goods' (Buchanan et al. 2000). These are traits that are valuable regardless of the kind of life a person chooses to live. They give us greater all-round capacities to live a vast array of lives. Examples include intelligence, memory, self-discipline, patience, empathy, a sense of humour, optimism, and just having a sunny temperament. All of these characteristics—sometimes described as virtues—may have some biological and psychological basis capable of manipulation using technology.

Technology might even be used to improve our *moral character*. We certainly seek through good instruction and example, discipline, and other methods to make better children. It may be possible to alter biology to make people predisposed to be more moral by promoting empathy, imagination, sympathy, fairness, honesty, etc.

In so far as these characteristics have some genetic basis, genetic manipulation could benefit us. There is reason to believe that complex virtues like fair-mindedness may have a biological basis. In one famous experiment a monkey was trained to perform a task and rewarded with either a grape or a piece of cucumber. He preferred the grape. On one occasion he performed the task successfully and was given a piece of cucumber. He watched as another monkey who had not performed the task was given a grape and he became very angry. This shows that even monkeys have a sense of fairness and desert—or at least self-interest!

At the other end, there are characteristics that we believe do not make for a good and happy life. One Dutch family illustrates the extreme end of the spectrum. For over thirty years this family recognized that there were a disproportionate number of male family members who exhibited aggressive and criminal behaviour (Morell 1993). This was characterized by aggressive outbursts resulting in arson, attempted rape, and exhibitionism. When a family tree was constructed, the pattern of inheritance was clearly X-linked recessive. This means, roughly, that women can carry the gene without being affected; 50 per cent of men at risk of inheriting the gene get the gene and are affected by the disease.

Genetic analysis suggested that the likely defective gene was a part of the X chromosome known as the monoamine oxidase region. This region codes for two enzymes that assist in the breakdown of neurotransmitters. Neurotransmitters are substances that play a key role in the conduction of nerve impulses in our brain. Enzymes like the monoamine oxidases are required to degrade the neurotransmitters after they have performed their desired task. It was suggested that the monoamine oxidase activity might be disturbed in the affected individuals. Urine analysis showed a higher than normal amount of neurotransmitters being excreted in the urine of affected males (Morell 1993). These results were consistent with a reduction in the functioning of one of the enzymes (monoamine oxidase A).

How can such a mutation result in violent and antisocial behaviour? A deficiency of the enzyme results in a build-up of neurotransmitters. These abnormal levels of neurotransmitters result in excessive, and even violent, reactions to stress. This hypothesis was further supported by the finding that genetically modified mice that lack this enzyme are more aggressive.

This family is an extreme example of how genes can influence behaviour: it is the only family in which this mutation has been isolated. Most genetic contributions to behaviour will be weaker predispositions, but there may be some association between genes and behaviour that results in criminal and other antisocial behaviour.

How could information such as this be used? Some criminals have attempted a 'genetic defence' in the United States, stating that their genes caused them to commit the crime, but this has never succeeded. However, it is clear that couples should be allowed to test to select offspring who do not have the mutation that predisposes them to act in this way, and if interventions were available, it might be rational to correct it since children without the mutation have a better chance of a good life.

'Genes, Not Men, May Hold the Key to Female Pleasure' ran the title of one recent newspaper article (*The Age* 2005), which reported the results of a large study of female identical twins in Britain and Australia. It found that 'genes accounted for 31 per cent of the chance of having an orgasm during intercourse and 51 per cent during masturbation'. It concluded that the 'ability to gain sexual satisfaction is largely inherited' and went on to speculate that 'The genes involved could be linked to physical differences in sex organs and hormone levels or factors such as mood and anxiety.'

Our biology profoundly affects how our lives go. If we can increase sexual satisfaction by modifying biology, we should. Indeed, vast numbers of men attempt to do this already through the use of Viagra.

Summary: The Case for Enhancement

What matters is human well-being, not just treatment and prevention of disease. Our biology affects our opportunities to live well. The biological route to improvement is no different from the environmental. Biological manipulation to increase opportunity is ethical. If we have an obligation to treat and prevent disease, we have an obligation to try to manipulate these characteristics to give an individual the best opportunity of the best life.

How Do We Decide?

If we are to enhance certain qualities, how should we decide which to choose? Eugenics was the movement early in the last century that aimed to use selective breeding to prevent degeneration of the gene pool by weeding out criminals, those with mental illness, and the poor, on the false belief that these conditions were simple genetic disorders. The eugenics movement had its inglorious peak when the Nazis moved beyond sterilization to extermination of the genetically unfit.

What was objectionable about the eugenics movement, besides its shoddy scientific basis, was that it involved the imposition of a state vision for a healthy population and aimed to achieve this through coercion. The movement was aimed not at what was good for individuals, but rather at what benefited society. Modern eugenics in the form of testing for disorders, such as Down syndrome, occurs very commonly but is acceptable because it is voluntary, gives couples a choice of what kind of child to have, and enables them to have a child with the greatest opportunity for a good life.

There are four possible ways in which our genes and biology will be decided:

1. nature or God;
2. 'experts' (philosophers, bioethicists, psychologists, scientists);
3. 'authorities' (government, doctors);
4. people themselves: liberty and autonomy.

It is a basic principle of liberal states like the United Kingdom that the state be 'neutral' to different conceptions of the good life. This means that we allow individuals to lead the life that they believe is best for themselves, implying respect for their personal autonomy or capacity for self-rule. The sole ground for interference is when that individual choice may harm others. Advice, persuasion, information, dialogue are permissible. But coercion and infringement of liberty are impermissible.

There are limits to what a liberal state should provide:

1. safety: the intervention should be reasonably safe;
2. harm to others: the intervention (like some manipulation that increases uncontrollable aggressiveness) should not result in harm. Such harm should not be direct or indirect, for example, by causing some unfair competitive advantage;
3. distributive justice: the interventions should be distributed according to principles of justice.

The situation is more complex with young children, embryos, and fetuses, who are incompetent. These human beings are not autonomous and cannot make choices themselves about whether a putative enhancement is a benefit or a harm. If a proposed intervention can be delayed until that human reaches maturity and can decide for himself or herself, then the intervention should be delayed. However, many genetic interventions will have to be performed very early in life if they are to have an effect. Decisions about such interventions should be left to parents, according to a principle of procreative liberty and autonomy. This states that parents have the freedom to choose when to have children, how many children to have, and arguably what kind of children to have.

Just as parents have wide scope to decide on the conditions of the upbringing of their children, including schooling and religious education, they should have similar freedom over their children's genes. Procreative autonomy or liberty should be extended to enhancement for two reasons. First, reproduction: bearing and raising children is a very private matter. Parents must bear much of the burden of having children, and they have a legitimate stake in the nature of the child they must invest so much of their lives raising.

But there is a second reason. John Stuart Mill argued that when our actions only affect ourselves, we should be free to construct and act on our own conception of what is the best life for us. Mill was not a libertarian. He did not believe that such freedom is valuable solely for its own sake.

He believed that freedom is important in order for people to discover for themselves what kind of life is best for themselves. It is only through 'experiments in living' that people discover what works for them and others come to see the richness and variety of lives that can be good. Mill strongly praised 'originality' and variety in choice as being essential to discovering which lives are best for human beings.

Importantly, Mill believed that some lives are worse than others. Famously, he said that it is better to be Socrates dissatisfied than a fool satisfied. He distinguished between 'higher pleasures' of 'feelings and imagination' and 'lower pleasures' of 'mere sensation' (Mill 1910: 7). He criticized 'ape-like imitation', subjugation of oneself to custom and fashion, indifference to individuality, and lack of originality (1910: 119–20, 123). Nonetheless, he was the champion of people's right to live their lives as they choose.

I have said that it is important to give the freest scope possible to uncustomary things, in order that it may appear in time which of these are fit to be converted into customs. But independence of action, and disregard of custom, are not solely deserving of encouragement for the chance they afford that better modes of action, and customs more worthy of general adoption, may be struck out; nor is it only persons of decided mental superiority who have a just claim to carry on their lives in their own way. There is no reason that all human existence should be constructed on some one or small number of patterns. If a person possesses any tolerable amount of common sense and experience, his own mode of laying out his existence is the best, not because it is the best in itself, but because it is his own mode (Mill 1910:125).

I believe that reproduction should be about having children with the best prospects. But to discover what are the best prospects, we must give individual couples the freedom to act on their own value judgement of what constitutes a life with good prospects. 'Experiments in reproduction' are as important as 'experiments in living' (as long as they don't harm the children who are produced). For this reason, procreative freedom is important.

There is one important limit to procreative autonomy that is different from the limits to personal autonomy. The limits to procreative autonomy should be:

1. safety;
2. harm to others;

3. distributive justice;
4. *such that the parent's choices are based on a plausible conception of well-being and a better life for the child;*
5. *consistent with development of autonomy in the child and a reasonable range of future life plans.*

These last two limits are important. It makes for a higher standard of 'proof' that an intervention will be an enhancement because the parents are making choices for their child, not themselves. The critical question to ask in considering whether to alter some gene related to complex behaviour is: Would the change be better for the individual? Is it better for the individual to have a tendency to be lazy or hardworking, monogamous or polygamous? These questions are difficult to answer. While we might let adults choose to be monogamous or polygamous, we would not let parents decide on their child's predispositions unless we were reasonably clear that some trait was better for the child.

There will be cases where some intervention is plausibly in a child's interests: increased empathy with other people, better capacity to understand oneself and the world around, or improved memory. One quality is especially associated with socio-economic success and staying out of prison: impulse control. If it were possible to correct poor impulse control, we should correct it. Whether we should remove impulsiveness altogether is another question.

Joel Feinberg has described a child's right to an open future (Feinberg 1980). An open future is one in which a child has a reasonable range of possible lives to choose from and an opportunity to choose what kind of person to be; that is, to develop autonomy. Some critics of enhancement have argued that genetic interventions are inconsistent with a child's right to an open future (Davis 1997). Far from restricting a child's future, however, some biological interventions may increase the possible futures or at least their quality. It is hard to see how improved memory or empathy would restrict a child's future. Many worthwhile possibilities would be open. But it is true that parental choice should not restrict the development of autonomy or reasonable range of possible futures open to a child. In general, fewer enhancements will be permitted in children than in adults. Some interventions, however, may still be clearly enhancements for our children, and so just like vaccinations or other preventative health care.

Objections

Playing God or Against Nature

This objection has various forms. Some people in society believe that children are a gift, of God or of nature, and that we should not interfere in human nature. Most people implicitly reject this view: we screen embryos and fetuses for diseases, even mild correctable diseases. We interfere in nature or God's will when we vaccinate, provide pain relief to women in labour (despite objections of some earlier Christians that these practices thwarted God's will), and treat cancer. No one would object to the treatment of disability in a child if it were possible. Why, then, not treat the embryo with genetic therapy if that intervention is safe? This is no more thwarting God's will than giving antibiotics.

Another variant of this objection is that we are arrogant if we assume we could have sufficient knowledge to meddle with human nature. Some people object that we cannot know the complexity of the human system, which is like an unknowable magnificent symphony. To attempt to enhance one characteristic may have other unknown, unforeseen effects elsewhere in the system. We should not play God since, unlike God, we are not omnipotent or omniscient. We should be humble and recognize the limitations of our knowledge.

A related objection is that genes are pleiotropic—which means they have different effects in different environments. The gene or genes that predispose to manic depression may also be responsible for heightened creativity and productivity.

One response to both of these objections is to limit intervention, until our knowledge grows, to selecting between different embryos, and not intervening to enhance particular embryos or people. Since we would be choosing between complete systems on the basis of their type, we would not be interfering with the internal machinery. In this way, selection is less risky than enhancement.

But such a precaution could also be misplaced when considering biological interventions. When benefits are on offer, such objections remind us to refrain from hubris and over-confidence. We must do adequate research before intervening. And because the benefits may be fewer than when we treat or prevent disease, we may require the standards of safety to be higher than for medical interventions. But we must weigh the risks against the benefits. If confidence is justifiably high, and benefits outweigh harms, we should enhance.

Once technology affords us the power to enhance our own and our children's lives, to fail to do so would be to be responsible for the consequences. To fail to treat our children's diseases is to wrong them. To fail to prevent them from getting depression is to wrong them. To fail to improve their physical, musical, psychological, and other capacities is to wrong them, just as it would be to harm them if we gave them a toxic substance that stunted or reduced these capacities.

Another variant of the 'Playing God' objection is that there is a special value in the balance and diversity that natural variation affords, and enhancement will reduce this. But in so far as we are products of evolution, we are merely random chance variations of genetic traits selected for our capacity to survive long enough to reproduce. There is no design to evolution. Evolution selects genes, according to environment, that confer the greatest chance of survival and reproduction. Evolution would select a tribe that was highly fertile but suffered great pain the whole of their lives over another tribe that was less fertile but suffered less pain. Medicine has changed evolution: we can now select individuals who experience less pain and disease. The next stage of human evolution will be rational evolution, according to which we select children who not only have the greatest chance of surviving, reproducing, and being free of disease, but who have the greatest opportunities to have the best lives in their likely environment. Evolution was indifferent to how well our lives went; we are not. We want to retire, play golf, read, and watch our grandchildren have children.

'Enhancement' is a misnomer. It suggests luxury. But enhancement is no luxury. In so far as it promotes well-being, it is the very essence of what is necessary for a good human life. There is no moral reason to preserve some traits—such as uncontrollable aggressiveness, a sociopathic personality, or extreme deviousness. Tell the victim of rape and murder that we must preserve diversity and the natural balance.

Genetic Discrimination

Some people fear the creation of a two-tier society of the enhanced and the unenhanced, where the inferior, unenhanced are discriminated against and disadvantaged all through life.

We must remember that nature allots advantage and disadvantage with no gesture to fairness. Some are born horribly disadvantaged, destined to die after short and miserable lives. Some suffer great genetic disadvantage while others are born gifted, physically, musically, or intellectually.

There is no secret that there are 'gifted' children naturally. Allowing choice to change our biology will, if anything, be more egalitarian, allowing the ungifted to approach the gifted. There is nothing fair about the natural lottery: allowing enhancement may be fairer.

But more importantly, how well the lives of those who are disadvantaged go depends not on whether enhancement is permitted, but on the social institutions we have in place to protect the least well off and provide everyone with a fair chance. People have disease and disability: egalitarian social institutions and laws against discrimination are designed to make sure everyone, regardless of natural inequality, has a decent chance of a decent life. This would be no different if enhancement were permitted. There is no necessary connection between enhancement and discrimination, just as there is; no necessary connection between curing disability and discrimination against people with disability.

The Perfect Child, Sterility, and Loss of the Mystery of Life

If we engineered perfect children, this objection goes, the world would be a sterile, monotonous place where everyone was the same, and the mystery and surprise of life would be gone.

It is impossible to create perfect children. We can only attempt to create children with better opportunities of a better life. There will necessarily be difference. Even in the case of screening for disability, like Down syndrome, 10 per cent of people choose not to abort a pregnancy known to be affected by Down syndrome. People value different things. There will never be complete convergence. Moreover, there will remain massive challenges for individuals to meet in their personal relationships and in the hurdles our unpredictable environment presents. There will remain much mystery and challenge—we will just be better able to deal with these. We will still have to work to achieve, but our achievements may have greater value.

Against Human Nature

One of the major objections to enhancement is that it is against human nature. Common alternative phrasings are that enhancement is tampering with our nature or an affront to human dignity. I believe that what separates us from other animals is our rationality, our capacity to make normative judgements and act on the basis of reasons. When we make decisions to improve our lives by biological and other manipulations, we express our rationality and express what is fundamentally important about our nature. And if those manipulations improve our capacity to make rational and normative judgements, they further improve what is fundamentally human. Far from being against the human spirit, such improvements express the human spirit. To be human is to be better.

Enhancements Are Self-Defeating

Another familiar objection to enhancement is that enhancements will have self-defeating or other adverse social effects. A typical example is increase in height. If height is socially desired, then everyone will try to enhance the height of their children at great cost to themselves and the environment (as taller people consume more resources), with no advantage in the end since there will be no relative gain.

If a purported manipulation does not improve well-being or opportunity, there is no argument in favour of it. In this case, the manipulation is not an enhancement. In other cases, such as enhancement of intelligence, the enhancement of one individual may increase that individual's opportunities only at the expense of another. So-called positional goods are goods only in a relative sense.

But many enhancements will have both positional and non-positional qualities. Intelligence is good not just because it allows an individual to be more competitive for complex jobs, but because it allows an individual to process information more rapidly in her own life, and to develop greater understanding of herself and others. These non-positional effects should not be ignored. Moreover, even in the case of so-called purely positional goods, such as height, there may be important non-positional values. It is better to be taller if you are a basketball player, but being tall is a disadvantage in balance sports such as gymnastics, skiing, and surfing.

Nonetheless, if there are significant social consequences of enhancement, this is of course a valid objection. But it is not particular to enhancement: there is an old question about how far individuals in society can pursue their own self-interest at a cost to others. It applies to education, health care, and virtually all areas of life.

Not all enhancements will be ethical. The critical issue is that the intervention is expected to bring about more benefits than harms to the individual. It must be safe and there must be a reasonable expectation of improvement. Some of the other features of ethical enhancements are summarized below.

What Is an Ethical Enhancement?

An ethical enhancement:

1. is in the person's interests;
2. is reasonably safe;
3. increases the opportunity to have the best life;
4. promotes or does not unreasonably restrict the range of possible lives open to that person;
5. does not unreasonably harm others directly through excessive costs in making it freely available;
6. does not place that individual at an unfair competitive advantage with respect to others, e.g. mind-reading;
7. is such that the person retains significant control or responsibility for her achievements and self that cannot be wholly or directly attributed to the enhancement;
8. does not unreasonably reinforce or increase unjust inequality and discrimination—economic inequality, racism.

What Is an Ethical Enhancement for a Child or Incompetent Human Being?

Such an ethical enhancement is all the above, but in addition:

1. the intervention cannot be delayed until the child can make its own decision;
2. the intervention is plausibly in the child's interests;
3. the intervention is compatible with the development of autonomy.

Conclusion

Enhancement is already occurring. In sport, human erythropoietin boosts red blood cells. Steroids and growth hormone improve muscle strength. Many people seek cognitive enhancement through nicotine, Ritalin, Modavigil, or caffeine. Prozac, recreational drugs, and alcohol all enhance mood. Viagra is used to improve sexual performance.

And of course mobile phones and aeroplanes are examples of external enhancing technologies. In the future, genetic technology, nanotechnology, and artificial intelligence may profoundly affect our capacities.

Will the future be better or just disease-free? We need to shift our frame of reference from health to life enhancement. What matters is how we live. Technology can now improve that. We have two options:

1. Intervention:
   - treating disease;
   - preventing disease;
   - supra-prevention of disease—preventing disease in a radically unprecedented way;
   - protection of well-being;
   - enhancement of well-being.
2. No intervention, and to remain in a state of nature—no treatment or prevention of disease, no technological enhancement.

I believe that to be human is to be better. Or, at least, to strive to be better. We should be here for a *good* time, not just a *long* time. Enhancement, far from being merely permissible, is something we should aspire to achieve.

References

Buchanan, A., Brock, D., Daniels, N., and Wikler, D. (2000), *From Chance to Choice* (Cambridge: Cambridge University Press).

Davis, D. (1997) 'Genetic Dilemmas and the Child's Right to an Open Future', *Hastings Center Report,* 27/2 (Mar.–Apr.), 7–15.

Feinberg, J. (1980), 'The Child's Right to an Open Future', in W. Aiken and H. LaFollette (eds.), *Whose Child? Parental Rights, Parental Authority and State Power* (Totowa, NJ: Rowman and Litdefield), 124–53.

Mill, J. S. (1910), *On Liberty* (London: J. M. Dent).

Mischel, W., Shoda, Y., and Peake, P. K. (1988), 'The Nature of Adolescent Competencies Predicted by Preschool Delay of Gratification', *Journal of Personality and Social Psychology,* 54/4:687–96.

Morell, V. (1993), 'Evidence Found for a Possible "Aggression Gene"', *Science,* 260: 1722–3.

Julian Savulescu: Genetic Interventions and the Ethics of Enhancement of Human Beings

1. What limits does Savulescu place on procreative autonomy over and above the limits placed on personal autonomy? Why does he think these limits are important? Do you think these limits are enough to protect the rights of children? Explain and defend your answer.

2. Explain Savulescu's consistency argument. What do you think the most powerful objection to this argument is? How do you think Savulescu would respond? Do you think this objection is ultimately successful? Why or why not?

3. Explain why eugenics might pose a problem for Savulescu's view. According to Savulescu, who should decide when and how to enhance certain qualities? Do you think his account is enough to neutralize the eugenics worry? Defend your response.

4. Savulescu considers a number of objections to his account. Reconstruct one of the objections as a valid argument. Then, explain how Savulescu responds to this argument by saying which premise he rejects and why. Do you think his response is successful? Why or why not?

5. Savulescu defends genetic enhancement by arguing that it is analogous to treating disease. Explain this argument. Then discuss the potential differences between treating disease and genetic enhancement. Is Savulescu right to say that there is *morally relevant* difference between the two? Defend your response.

6. Explain the principle of procreative liberty and autonomy. Then, explain the two reasons Savulescu cites for applying this principle to human enhancement. Do you think that this is enough to show that parents should have some freedom in determining their children's genes? Why or why not?

AFFIRMATIVE ACTION

39

━━ ❧ ━━

The Case against Affirmative Action
Louis P. Pojman

....

Louis Pojman argues that strong affirmative action (AA) policies are never morally justified. He makes his case by seeking to undermine pro-AA arguments and then offering some criticisms of AA programs.

Of the familiar arguments in favor of AA, Pojman highlights the following. First, we all need good role models, and AA will ensure that women and minorities, who are the primary beneficiaries of these policies, will have this need fulfilled. Second, women and African-Americans have been the victims of terrible historical injustices, and this justifies AA as a form of compensation for these harms. Third, today's white males, while obviously not participating in (say) the enslavement of Africans and African-Americans, nevertheless enjoy a variety of undeserved benefits as a result of this legacy of oppression, and AA can serve as a form of leveling the playing field. Fourth, diversity in the workforce, business world, and college campuses is important in its own right and serves a variety of important social goals, and AA is an effective way to ensure diversity in these areas. Finally, the existing social and economic inequalities between men and women, and between whites and minorities, must be the result not of any inherent inferiority on the part of women and minorities, but rather of unequal opportunities and discrimination. AA will enhance opportunities for these traditionally disadvantaged groups and thus reduce a legacy of discrimination.

Pojman finds fault with each of these arguments. He then introduces two arguments of his own to show why AA is immoral. First, Pojman claims that AA is itself a form of unjust discrimination against young white males. As he sees it, all discrimination against innocent people is immoral, no matter its target. Second, Pojman thinks that social and economic benefits ought to be distributed according to merit, rather than to skin color, sex, or gender. But AA violates this principle of merit and is therefore unjustified.

. . . .

In this essay I set forth . . . arguments against Strong Affirmative Action, which I define as preferential treatment, discriminating in favor of members of under-represented groups, which have been treated unjustly in the past, against innocent people. I distinguish this from Weak Affirmative Action, which simply seeks to promote equal opportunity to the goods and offices of a society. I do not argue against this policy. I argue against Strong Affirmative Action, attempting to show that two wrongs don't make a right. This form of Affirmative Action, as it is applied against White males, is both racist and sexist….It is the policy that is currently being promoted under the name of Affirmative Action, so I will use that term or "AA" for short throughout this essay to stand for this version of affirmative action. I will not argue for or against the principle of Weak Affirmative Action. Indeed, I think it has some moral weight. Strong Affirmative Action has none, or so I will argue. . . .

I. A Critique of Arguments for Affirmative Action

1. The Need for Role Models

This argument is straightforward. We all have need of role models, and it helps to know that others like us can be successful. We learn and are encouraged to strive for excellence by emulating our heroes and "our kind of people" who have succeeded.

In the first place, it's not clear that role models of one's own racial or sexual type are necessary (let alone sufficient) for success. One of my heroes was Gandhi, an Indian Hindu; another was my grade school science teacher, Miss DeVoe, and another Martin Luther King, behind whom I marched in Civil Rights demonstrations. More important than having role models of one's "own type" is having genuinely good people, of whatever race or gender, to emulate. Our common humanity should be a sufficient basis for us to see the possibility of success in people of virtue and merit.

To yield to the demand, however tempting it may be to do so, for "role-models-just-like-us" is to treat people like means not ends. It is to elevate morally irrelevant particularity over relevant traits, such as ability and integrity. We don't need people exactly like us to find inspiration. As Steve Allen once quipped, "If I had to follow a role model exactly, I would have become a nun."

Furthermore, even if it is of some help to people with low self-esteem to gain encouragement from seeing others of their particular kind in successful positions, it is doubtful whether this need is a sufficient reason to justify preferential hiring or reverse discrimination. What good is a role model who is inferior to other professors or physicians or business personnel? The best way to create role models is not to promote people because of race or gender but because they are the best qualified for the job. It is the violation of this fact that is largely responsible for the widespread whisper in the medical field (at least in New York) "Never go to a Black physician under 40" (referring to the fact that AA has affected the medical system during the past twenty years). Fight the feeling how I will, I cannot help wondering on seeing a Black or woman in a position of honor, "Is she in this position because she merits it or because of Affirmative Action?" Where Affirmative Action is the policy, the "figment of pigment" creates a stigma of undeservedness, whether or not it is deserved.

Finally, entertain this thought experiment. Suppose we discovered that tall handsome white males somehow made the best role models for the most people, especially poor people. Suppose even large numbers of minority people somehow found inspiration in their sight. Would we be justified in hiring tall handsome white males over better qualified short Hispanic women, who were deemed less role-model worthy?

2. The Compensation Argument

The argument goes like this: blacks have been wronged and severely harmed by whites. Therefore white society should compensate blacks for the injury caused them. Reverse discrimination in terms of preferential hiring, contracts, and scholarships is a fitting way to compensate for the past wrongs.

This argument actually involves a distorted notion of compensation. Normally, we think of compensation as owed by a specific person A to another person B whom A has wronged in a specific way C. For example, if I have stolen your car and used it for a period of time to make business profits that would have gone to you, it is not enough that I return your car. I must pay you an amount reflecting your loss and my ability to pay. If I have only made $5,000 and only have $10,000 in assets, it would not be possible for you to collect $20,000 in damages—even though that is the amount of loss you have incurred.

Sometimes compensation is extended to groups of people who have been unjustly harmed by the greater society. For example, the United States government has compensated the Japanese-Americans who were interred during the Second World War, and the West German government has paid reparations to the survivors of Nazi concentration camps. But here a specific people have been identified who were wronged in an identifiable way by the government of the nation in question.

On the face of it, demands by blacks for compensation does not fit the usual pattern. Perhaps Southern states with Jim Crow laws could be accused of unjustly harming blacks, but it is hard to see that the United States government was involved in doing so. Much of the harm done to blacks was the result of private discrimination, not state action. So the Germany/US analogy doesn't hold. Furthermore, it is not clear that all blacks were harmed in the same way or whether some were unjustly harmed or harmed more than poor whites and others (e.g. short people). Finally, even if identifiable blacks were harmed by identifiable social practices, it is not clear that most forms of Affirmative Action are appropriate to restore the situation. The usual practice of a financial payment seems more appropriate than giving a high level job to someone unqualified or only minimally qualified, who, speculatively, might have been better qualified had he not been subject to racial discrimination. If John is the star tailback of our college team with a promising professional future, and I accidentally (but culpably) drive my pick-up truck over his legs, and so cripple him, John may be due compensation, but he is not due the tailback spot on the football team.

Still, there may be something intuitively compelling about compensating members of an oppressed group who are minimally qualified. Suppose that the Hatfields and the McCoys are enemy clans and some youths from the Hatfields go over and steal diamonds and gold from the McCoys, distributing it within the Hatfield economy. Even though we do not know which Hatfield youths did the stealing, we would want to restore the wealth, as far as possible, to the McCoys. One way might be to tax the Hatfields, but another might be to give preferential treatment in terms of scholarships and training programs and hiring to the McCoys.

This is perhaps the strongest argument for Affirmative Action, and it may well justify some weaker versions of AA, but it is doubtful whether it is sufficient to justify strong versions with quotas and goals and time tables in skilled positions. There are at least two reasons for this. First, we have no way of knowing how many people of any given group would have achieved some given level of competence had the world been different. This is especially relevant if my objections to the Equal Results Argument (#5 below) are correct. Secondly, the normal criterion of competence is a strong prima facie consideration when the most important positions are at stake. There are three reasons for this: (1) treating people according to their merits respects them as persons, as ends in themselves, rather than as means to social ends (if we believe that individuals possess a dignity which deserves to be respected, then we ought to treat that individual on the basis of his or her merits, not as a mere instrument for social policy); (2) society has given people expectations that if they attain certain levels of excellence they will be awarded appropriately and (3) filling the most important positions with the best qualified is the best way to insure efficiency in job-related areas and in society in general. These reasons are not absolutes. They can be overridden. But there is a strong presumption in their favor so that a burden of proof rests with those who would override them.

At this point we get into the problem of whether innocent non-blacks should have to pay a penalty in terms of preferential hiring of blacks. We turn to that argument.

3. The Argument for Compensation from Those Who Innocently Benefitted from Past Injustice

Young White males as innocent beneficiaries of unjust discrimination against blacks and women have no grounds for complaint when society seeks to level the tilted field. They may be innocent of oppressing blacks, other minorities, and women, but they have unjustly benefitted from that oppression or discrimination. So it is perfectly proper that less qualified women and blacks be hired before them.

The operative principle is: He who knowingly and willingly benefits from a wrong must help pay for the wrong. Judith Jarvis Thomson puts it this way. "Many [white males] have been direct beneficiaries of policies which have down-graded blacks and women . . . and even those who did not directly benefit . . . had, at any rate, the advantage in the competition which comes of the confidence in one's full membership [in the community], and of one's right being recognized as a matter of course."[1] That is, white males obtain advantages in self-respect and self-confidence deriving from a racist/sexist system which denies these to blacks and women.

Here is my response to this argument: As I noted in the previous section, compensation is normally individual and specific. If A harms B regarding x, B has a right to compensation from A in regards to x. If A steals B's car and wrecks it, A has an obligation to compensate B for the stolen car, but A's son has no obligation to compensate B. Furthermore, if A dies or disappears, B has no moral right to claim that society compensate him for the stolen car—though if he has insurance, he can make such a claim to the insurance company. Sometimes a wrong cannot be compensated, and we just have to make the best of an imperfect world.

Suppose my parents, divining that I would grow up to have an unsurpassable desire to be a basketball player, bought an expensive growth hormone for me. Unfortunately, a neighbor stole it and gave it to little Michael, who gained the extra 13 inches—my 13 inches—and shot up to an enviable 6 feet 6 inches. Michael, better known as Michael Jordan, would have been a runt like me but for his luck. As it is he profited from the injustice, and excelled in basketball, as I would have done had I had my proper dose.

Do I have a right to the millions of dollars that Jordan made as a professional basketball player—the unjustly innocent beneficiary of my growth hormone? I have a right to something from the neighbor who stole the hormone, and it might be kind of Jordan to give me free tickets to the Bull's basketball games, and perhaps I should be remembered in his will. As far as I can see, however, he does not owe me anything, either legally or morally.

Suppose further that Michael Jordan and I are in high school together and we are both qualified to play basketball, only he is far better than I. Do I deserve to start in his position because I would have been as good as he is had someone not cheated me as a child? Again, I think not. But if being the lucky beneficiary of wrong-doing does not entail that Jordan (or the coach) owes me anything in regards to basketball, why should it be a reason to engage in preferential hiring in academic positions or highly coveted jobs? If minimal qualifications are not adequate to override

---

1 Judith Jarvis Thomson, "Preferential Hiring" in Marshall Cohen, Thomas Nagel and Thomas Scanlon eds, *Equality and Preferential Treatment* (Princeton: Princeton University Press, 1977).

excellence in basketball, even when the minimality is a consequence of wrongdoing, why should they be adequate in other areas?

4. The Diversity Argument

It is important that we learn to live in a pluralistic world, learning to get along with those of other races and cultures, so we should have fully integrated schools and employment situations. We live in a shrinking world and need to appreciate each other's culture and specific way of looking at life. Diversity is an important symbol and educative device. . . . Thus preferential treatment is warranted to perform this role in society.

Once again, there is some truth in these concerns. Diversity of ideas challenges us to scrutinize our own values and beliefs, and diverse customs have aesthetic and moral value, helping us to appreciate the novelty and beauty in life. Diversity may expand our moral horizons. But, again, while we can admit the value of diversity, it hardly seems adequate to override the moral requirement to treat each person with equal respect. Diversity for diversity's sake is moral promiscuity, since it obfuscates rational distinctions, undermines treating individuals as ends, treating them, instead as mere means (to the goals of social engineering), and, furthermore, unless those hired are highly qualified, the diversity factor threatens to become a fetish. At least at the higher levels of business and the professions, competence far outweighs considerations of diversity. I do not care whether the group of surgeons operating on me reflect racial or gender balance, but I do care that they are highly qualified. Neither do most football or basketball fans care whether their team reflects ethnic and gender diversity, but whether they are the best combination of players available. And likewise with airplane pilots, military leaders, business executives, and, may I say it, teachers and university professors. One need not be a white male to teach, let alone, appreciate Shakespeare, nor need one be Black to teach, let alone appreciate, Alice Walker's *Color Purple*.

There may be times when diversity may seem to be "crucial" to the well-being of a diverse community, such as a diverse police force. Suppose that White policemen overreact to young Black males and the latter group distrust White policemen. Hiring more less qualified Black policemen, who would relate better to these youth, may have overall utilitarian value. But such a move, while we might make it as a lesser evil, could have serious consequences in allowing the demographic prejudices to dictate social policy. A better strategy would be to hire the best police, that is, those who can perform in disciplined, intelligent manner, regardless of their race. A White policeman must be able to arrest a Black burglar, even as a Black policeman must be able to arrest a White rapist. The quality of the policeman or woman, not their race or gender, is what counts.

On the other hand, if the Black policeman, though lacking formal skills of the White policeman, really is able to do a better job in the Black community, this might constitute a case of merit, not Affirmative Action. This is similar to the legitimacy of hiring Chinese men to act as undercover agents in Chinatown.

5. The Equal Results Argument

Some philosophers and social scientists hold that human nature is roughly identical, so that on a fair playing field the same proportion from every race and ethnic group and both genders would attain to the highest positions in every area of endeavor. It would follow that any inequality of results itself is evidence for inequality of opportunity.

History is important when considering governmental rules . . . because low scores by blacks can be traced in large measure to the legacy of slavery and racism: segregation, poor schooling, exclusion from trade unions, malnutrition, and poverty have all played their roles. Unless one assumes that blacks are naturally less able to pass the test, the conclusion must be that the results are themselves socially and legally constructed, not a mere given for which law and society can claim no responsibility.

The conclusion seems to be that genuine equality eventually requires equal results. Obviously blacks have been treated unequally throughout US history, and just as obviously the economic and psychological effects of that inequality linger to this day, showing up in lower income and poorer performance in school and on tests than whites achieve. Since we have no reason to believe that differences in performance can be explained by factors other than history, equal results are a good benchmark by which to measure progress made toward genuine equality. . . .

However, [proponents of Stong AA] fail even to consider studies that suggest that there are innate differences between races, sexes, and groups. If there are genetic differences in intelligence and temperament within families, why should we not expect such differences between racial groups and the two genders? Why should the evidence for this be completely discounted?

[Their] reasoning is as follows: Since we don't know for certain whether groups proportionately differ in talent, we should presume that they are equal in every respect. So we should presume that if we were living in a just society, there would be roughly proportionate representation in every field (e.g., equal representation of doctors, lawyers, professors, carpenters, air-plane pilots, basketball players, and criminals). Hence, it is only fair—productive of justice—to aim at proportionate representation in these fields.

But the logic is flawed. Under a situation of ignorance we should not presume equality or inequality of representation—but conclude that we don't know what the results would be in a just society. Ignorance doesn't favor equal group representation any more than it favors unequal group representation. It is neutral between them.

Consider this analogy. Suppose that you were the owner of a National Basketball Association team. Suppose that I and other frustrated White basketball players bring a class-action suit against you and all the other owners, claiming that you have subtly and systematically discriminated against White and Asian basketball players who make up less than 20% of the NBA players. When you respond to our charges that you and your owners are just responding to individual merit, we respond that the discrimination is a function of deep prejudice against White athletes, especially basketball players, who are discouraged in every way from competing on fair terms with Blacks who dominate the NBA. You would probably wish that the matter of unequal results was not brought up in the first place, but once it has been, would you not be in your rights to defend yourself by producing evidence, showing that average physiological differences exist between Blacks and Whites and Asians, so that we should not presume unjust discrimination?

Similarly, the proponents of the doctrine of equal results open the door to a debate over average ability in ethnic, racial and gender groups. The proponent of equal or fair opportunity would just as soon downplay this feature in favor of judging people as individuals by their merit (hard though that may be). But if the proponent of AA insists on the Equal Results Thesis, we are obliged to examine the Equal Abilities Thesis, on which it is based—the thesis that various ethnic and gender groups all have the same distribution of talent on the relevant characteristic. With regard to cognitive skills we must consult the best evidence we have on average group differences. We need to compare average IQ scores, SAT scores, standard personality testing, success in academic and professional areas and the like. If the evidence shows that group differences are nonexistent, the AA proponent may win, but if the evidence turns out to be against the Equal Abilities Thesis, the AA proponent loses.

Consider for a start that the average white and Asian scores 195 points higher on the SAT tests and that on virtually all IQ tests for the past seven or eight decades the average Black IQ is 85 as opposed to the average White and Asian IQ at over 100, or that males and females differ significantly on cognitive ability tests. Females outperform males in reading comprehension, perceptual speed, and associative memory (ratios of 1.4 to 2.2), but males typically outnumbering females among high scoring individuals in mathematics, science and social science (by a ratio of 7.0 in the top 1% of overall mathematics distribution).[2] The results of average GRE, LSAT, MCAT scores show similar patterns or significant average racial difference. The Black scholar Glenn Loury notes, "In 1990 black high school seniors from families with annual incomes of $70,000 or more scored an average of 855 on the SAT, compared with average scores of 855 and 879 respectively for Asian-American and white seniors whose families had incomes between $10,000 and 20,000 per year."[3] Note, we are speaking about statistical averages. There are brilliant and retarded people in each group.

When such statistics are discussed many people feel uncomfortable and want to drop the subject. Perhaps these statistics are misleading, but then we need to look carefully at the total evidence. The proponent of equal opportunity would urges us to get beyond racial and gender criteria in assignment of offices and opportunities and treat each person, not as an average white or Black or female or male, but as a person judge on his or her own merits.

Furthermore, on the logic of [Strong AA proponent Albert] Mosley and company, we should take aggressive AA against Asians and Jews since they are over-represented in science, technology, and medicine, and we should presume that Asians and Jews are no more talented than average. So that each group receives its fair share, we should ensure that 12% of the philosophers in the United States are Black, reduce the percentage of Jews from an estimated 15% to 2%—firing about 1,300 Jewish philosophers. The fact that Asians are producing 50% of Ph.D.s in science and math in this country and blacks less than 1% clearly shows, on this reasoning, that we are providing special secret advantages to Asians. By this logic, we should reduce the quota of Blacks in the NBA to 12%.

---

2 Larry Hedges and Amy Nowell, "Sex Differences in Mental Test Scores, Variability, and Numbers of High-Scoring Individuals," *Science* vol. 269 (July 1995), pp. 41–45.

3 Glenn Loury, "Getting Involved: An Appeal for Greater Community Participation in the Public Schools," *Washington Post Education Review* (August 6, 1995).

But why does society have to enter into this results game in the first place? Why do we have to decide whether all difference is environmental or genetic? Perhaps we should simply admit that we lack sufficient evidence to pronounce on these issues with any certainty—but if so, should we not be more modest in insisting on equal results?

We have considered [five] arguments for Affirmative Action and have found no compelling case for Strong AA and only one plausible argument (a version of the compensation argument) for Weak AA. We must now turn to the arguments against Affirmative Action to see whether they fare any better.

II. Arguments against Affirmative Action

Affirmative Action Requires Discrimination against a Different Group

Weak Affirmative Action weakly discriminates against new minorities, mostly innocent young white males, and Strong Affirmative Action strongly discriminates against these new minorities. As I argued in I. 4, this discrimination is unwarranted, since, even if some compensation to blacks were indicated, it would be unfair to make innocent white males bear the whole brunt of the payments.

Recently I had this experience. I knew a brilliant philosopher, with outstanding publications in first level journals, who was having difficulty getting a tenure-track position. For the first time in my life I offered to make a phone call on his behalf to a university to which he had applied. When I got the Chair of the Search Committee, he offered that the committee was under instructions from the Administration to hire a woman or a Black. They had one of each on their short-list, so they weren't even considering the applications of White males. At my urging he retrieved my friend's file, and said, "This fellow looks far superior to the two candidates we're interviewing, but there's nothing I can do about it." Cases like this come to my attention regularly. In fact, it is poor white youth who become the new pariahs on the job market. The children of the wealthy have no trouble getting into the best private grammar schools and, on the basis of superior early education, into the best universities, graduate schools, managerial and professional positions. Affirmative Action simply shifts injustice, setting Blacks, Hispanics, Native Americans, Asians and women against young white males, especially ethnic and poor white males.

It makes no more sense to discriminate in favor of a rich Black or female who had the opportunity of the best family and education available against a poor White, than it does to discriminate in favor of White males against Blacks or women. It does little to rectify the goal of providing equal opportunity to all. . . .

Respect for persons entails that we treat each person as an end in him or herself, not simply as a means to be used for social purposes. What is wrong about discrimination against Blacks is that it fails to treat Black people as individuals, judging them instead by their skin color not their merit. What is wrong about discrimination against women is that it fails to treat them as individuals, judging them by their gender, not their merit. What is equally wrong about Affirmative Action is that it fails to treat White males with dignity as individuals, judging them by both their race and gender, instead of their merit. Strong Affirmative Action is both racist and sexist.

An Argument from the Principle of Merit

Traditionally, we have believed that the highest positions in society should be awarded to those who are best qualified. The Koran states that "A ruler who appoints any man to an office, when there is in his dominion another man better qualified for it, sins against God and against the State." Rewarding excellence both seems just to the individuals in the competition and makes for efficiency. Note that one of the most successful acts of racial integration, the Brooklyn Dodger's recruitment of Jackie Robinson in the late 40s, was done in just this way, according to merit. If Robinson had been brought into the major league as a mediocre player or had batted .200 he would have been scorned and sent back to the minors where he belonged.

As I mentioned earlier, merit is not an absolute value, but there are strong prima facie reasons for awarding positions on its basis, and it should enjoy a weighty presumption in our social practices.

In a celebrated article Ronald Dworkin says that "Bakke had no case" because society did not owe Bakke anything. That may be, but then why does it owe anyone anything? Dworkin puts the matter in Utility terms, but if that is the case, society may owe Bakke a place at the University of California/Davis, for it seems a reasonable rule-utilitarian principle that achievement should be rewarded in society. We generally want the best to have the best positions, the best qualified candidate to win the political office, the most brilliant and competent scientist to be chosen for the most challenging research project, the best qualified pilots to become commercial pilots, only the best soldiers to become generals. Only when little is at stake do we weaken the standards and content ourselves with sufficiency (rather than excellence)—there are plenty of jobs where "sufficiency" rather than excellence is required. Perhaps we have even come to feel that medicine or law or university professorships are so routine that they can be performed by minimally qualified people—in which case AA has a place.

Note! No one is calling for quotas or proportional representation of underutilized groups in the National Basketball Association where blacks make up 80% of the players. But, surely, if merit and merit alone reigns in sports, should it not be valued at least as much in education and industry?

The case for meritocracy has two pillars. One pillar is a deontological argument which holds that we ought to treat people as ends and not merely means. By giving people what they deserve as individuals, rather than as members of groups, we show respect for their inherent worth. If you and I take a test, and you get 95% of the answers correct and I only get 50% correct, it would be unfair to you to give both of us the same grade, say an A, and even more unfair to give me a higher grade A+ than your B+. Although I have heard cases where teachers have been instructed to "race norm" in grading (giving Blacks and Hispanics higher grades for the same numerical scores), most proponents of Affirmative Action stop short of advocating such a practice. But, I would ask them, what's really the difference between taking the overall average of a White and a Black and "race norming" it? If teachers shouldn't do it, why should administrators?

The second pillar for meritocracy is utilitarian. In the end, we will be better off by honoring excellence. We want the best leaders, teachers, policemen, physicians, generals, lawyers, and airplane pilots that we can possibly produce in society. So our program should be to promote equal opportunity, as much as is feasible in a free market economy, and reward people according to their individual merit.

Conclusion

Let me sum up my discussion. The goal of the Civil Rights movement and of moral people everywhere has been justice for all, including equal opportunity. The question is: how best to get there. Civil Rights legislation removed the legal barriers, opening the way towards equal opportunity, but it did not tackle the deeper causes that produce differential results. Weak Affirmative Action aims at encouraging minorities in striving for the highest positions without unduly jeopardizing the rights of majorities. The problem of Weak Affirmative Action is that it easily slides into Strong Affirmative Action where quotas, "goals and time-tables," "equal results"—in a word, reverse discrimination—prevails and is forced onto groups, thus promoting mediocrity, inefficiency, and resentment. Furthermore, Affirmative Action aims at the higher levels of society—universities and skilled jobs—but if we want to improve our society, the best way to do it is to concentrate on families, children, early education, and the like, so all are prepared to avail themselves of opportunity. Affirmative Action, on the one hand, is too much, too soon and on the other hand, too little, too late.

Louis P. Pojman: The Case against Affirmative Action

1. Explain Pojman's distinction between "Strong Affirmative Action" and "Weak Affirmative Action." Then, explain one of the two arguments *against* Affirmative Action. Do you think this argument applies equally well to Strong and Weak Affirmative action? Explain and defend your response.

2. In your own words, explain the *compensation argument* in favor of Affirmative Action. Under what conditions do you think compensation is owed? Why does Pojman think that Strong Affirmative Action cannot be justified on the grounds that it compensates for past injustices? Do you agree with his assessment? Why or why not?

3. Explain Pojman's example involving Michael Jordan and the expensive growth hormone. What lesson does Pojman draw from this example? How does it apply to the moral permissibility of Strong Affirmative Action? Do you think the example shows what Pojman intends it to show? Explain and defend your answer.

4. In your own words, explain the *equal results argument*. Why might someone find such an argument plausible? How does Pojman respond to this argument? Do you find his response satisfying? Why or why not?

5. Reconstruct Pojman's argument for the conclusion that Strong Affirmative Action is just as wrong as discrimination against minorities. Do you think Pojman has captured all of the wrong-making features of racial discrimination? Do you think Strong Affirmative Action is genuinely analogous to racial discrimination? Explain and defend your response.

6. What are the two pillars of the case for meritocracy? Explain how each supports Pojman's position against Strong Affirmative Action. Do you think that when it comes to important positions we should always select the candidate who is best qualified? Do you think that there are any other considerations might be important? Explain and defend your response.

Affirmative Action: Bad Arguments and Some Good Ones

Daniel M. Hausman

....

In this paper, Daniel Hausman sets himself two goals. First, he wants to reveal the flaws of some popular arguments for and against policies of preferential hiring and admissions (PHA). Second, he offers an argument in favor of PHA that he believes is successful in showing that the practice can be justified.

Many people favor or oppose PHA on the basis of their view of its results. But, as Hausman notes, the actual results of PHA programs are difficult to determine and are highly disputed. Hausman does not take a stand, for instance, on whether PHA has actually improved or damaged the self-esteem of minorities, reduced or increased prejudice, etc. The evidence, he thinks, is inconclusive. But we can still assess the merits of arguments for and against PHA even in the absence of such evidence.

One classic argument opposing PHA claims that it is "racism in reverse." Hausman rejects this line of reasoning, pointing out that PHA is not grounded in assumptions of racial inferiority or racial hatred, and that it is not designed to oppress, humiliate, and exclude. Hausman also rejects arguments against PHA that assume that it is morally wrong in hiring or admissions to take into account anything other than the applicant's qualifications.

On the other side, defenders of PHA often rely on arguments from rectification or reparation to make their case. Many defenders think that harms should be rectified (remedied); racist acts are harmful; so they must be rectified, and PHA will do a good job of that. Hausman agrees that harms should be remedied, but by those who have actually done the harm. The harms of slavery, for instance, can no longer be rectified by those who perpetrated them, so this is a poor basis on which to justify PHA.

Arguments from reparations fare no better. Reparations are compensation owed by the government for wrongs that it has done or permitted. Hausman agrees that the U.S. and state governments were indeed responsible for many racist harms. But he offers a variety of reasons for thinking that PHA is not a good way of correcting for those harms.

Hausman concludes with an argument in favor of PHA. Ensuring equality of opportunity is a fundamental government responsibility. Hausman argues that PHA will help to advance this important goal. PHA won't by itself solve all of the problems that our long legacy of racism has created. But it will to some degree level a playing field that unjustly favors white males.

. . . .

Affirmative action has many aspects. Some, such as requiring that job openings be advertised so that minorities can learn of them, are not controversial. Other aspects, such as preferential hiring and admissions (PHA), with which this essay is concerned, are hotly disputed. PHA takes minority status to increase an applicant's chance of getting a job or getting admitted to a university. Though the policy favors applicants with minority status, it does not imply that minority status should determine hiring or admission all by itself. (Nobody is proposing hiring blind bus drivers because they are minorities.) The idea is to favor otherwise qualified applicants who belong to disadvantaged groups. Because the pool of qualified minority applicants is often small, the direct benefits of PHA are also rather small. To limit the discussion, I shall focus in this essay largely on preferential hiring and admissions of African Americans, because they have a special history of slavery and oppression——even though the greatest beneficiaries of PHA have in fact been women.

There are many arguments defending preferential hiring and admissions and many criticizing it. Many of these arguments depend crucially on facts about the consequences. So, for example, critics have argued that PHA harms those it intends to benefit by undermining their self-confidence or by putting them in positions beyond their abilities in which they are bound to fail. Critics have also argued that those favored by PHA are often incompetent, and PHA thus undermines the credentials of beneficiaries, incites racism, and diminishes economic efficiency. Defenders argue that PHA has changed the American population's conception of what minorities and women can aspire to and that PHA has lessened racial disparities. These arguments would be powerful if their factual premises were true. But it is hard to know what the effects of PHA have been, and there is little evidence supporting any of these claims about the consequences of PHA. Heartwarming tales of successes of recipients of PHA and horror stories of harms and abuses are not serious evidence.[1]

The most prominent arguments do not rely on controversial factual premises. Critics argue that PHA is racism in reverse: discrimination is wrong, regardless of whether it is directed against or for African Americans. Defenders argue that PHA helps to rectify past injustices committed against African Americans. These are the arguments one most often hears. But they are not good arguments. Defenders and critics should stop making them.

"Racism in Reverse"

If it was morally impermissible to exclude African Americans from universities and jobs on the basis of their race, how can it be morally permissible to exclude whites on the basis of their race? Lisa Newton, a philosopher at Fairfield University, enunciates this criticism as follows: "The quota system, as employed by the University of California's medical school at Davis or any similar institution, is unjust, for all the same reasons that the discrimination it attempts to reverse is unjust."[2] Louis Pojman writes in this volume that PHA is a racist policy.

Let us formulate this argument precisely. The word "discrimination" causes confusion, because it has both a neutral and a negative sense. In the neutral sense, discrimination is simply drawing distinctions, which may be a good or a bad thing to do. An admissions office does nothing wrong

---

1 There have been serious investigations of the effects, which I cannot summarize here. In my view, the results have been inconclusive.
2 *National Forum* 58.1 (Winter 1978), pp. 22–23.

when it discriminates (in this sense) among candidates on the basis of factors such as test scores and high school grade averages. In the negative sense, discrimination consists in drawing distinctions unjustly. In the neutral sense, PHA obviously involves discriminates among candidates. Does it also discriminate in the negative sense—that is, unjustly? To avoid confusing the two meanings, it is best to avoid the word "discrimination" altogether, and ask instead whether the distinctions PHA draws among candidates are unjust.

Why might it be unjust to allow an applicant's race to influence hiring or admissions? Perhaps injustice lies simply in allowing race to influence choices. But it not always wrong to take race into account. A director making a movie of the life of Martin Luther King commits no injustice in refusing to consider white actors for the lead role. Refusing to hire a white short-order cook is, on the other hand, harder to justify. What's the difference? The answer seems to be that race is relevant to playing Martin Luther King, while it is not relevant to frying eggs.

One way to capture the racism in reverse argument is as follows:

1. It is wrong in hiring or admissions to take into account anything other than the applicant's qualifications.
2. PHA takes the applicant's race into account.
3. Race is almost always not a qualification.
4. Thus, PHA is almost always wrong.

I hope the reader agrees that this is a good way to formulate the racism in reverse argument, because I am trying to get at the truth rather than to win points in a political debate by misrepresenting the critic's position.

Crucial to this argument is the notion of a "qualification." A qualification is any fact about an applicant that is relevant to how successfully the applicant can promote the legitimate goals of the organization to which the applicant is applying. For example, high school class rank and ACT scores are qualifications, because they are correlated with academic performance in college. Running the 100-meter dash in under ten seconds is also a qualification for admission if the success of its athletic teams is among the legitimate goals of a university. For universities without sports teams, like those in Europe, it is not a qualification. The race of applicants would be relevant to a university devoted to white racial supremacy, but the promotion of racial supremacy is not a legitimate goal. Since, as the Martin Luther King movie example illustrates, race is sometimes a qualification, this argument does not conclude that PHA is always wrong, just that it is almost always wrong. On the view that this argument makes precise, what was wrong with the exclusion and special hurdles faced by African Americans during the Jim Crow era was that their prospects were not determined exclusively by their qualifications.

The argument formulated above is a valid argument. The conclusion follows logically from the premises. To assert all three of the premises and at the same time deny the conclusion is to contradict oneself. Constructing valid arguments can be very helpful. If those whom you are trying to persuade grant the premises, then, on pain of contradiction, they must accept the conclusion. Alternatively, if those you are attempting to persuade reject the conclusion, then they must reject at least one of the premises.

Let us examine whether the argument is also sound—that is, whether as well as being valid, all its premises are true. Premise 2 is obviously true: preferential hiring and admission of African Americans takes race into account. Premise 3 in contrast is debatable, because diversity among students and employees arguably serves legitimate goals of universities and some firms. Among the objectives of universities is to train business and political leaders who can interact with and understand people from many different backgrounds. Diversity within the student body serves this purpose.

More can be said about premise 3 and the importance of diversity, but let us focus on premise 1, which says that hiring and admissions should depend exclusively on qualifications. Premise 1 may seem plausible. It apparently explains why the racist exclusion of African Americans from schools, unions, and many professions was wrong: those exclusions were not based on qualifications. But premise 1 is false, and it does not correctly identify what was wrong with racist exclusions of African Americans. Consider three examples of hiring or admissions that depend on more than just qualifications:

- Case 1: Veterans are given preferences on civil service examinations and in college admissions.
- Case 2: An owner of a small grocery store hires his teenage daughter (rather than a more responsible teenager) to deliver groceries after school because he wants to keep an eye on her.
- Case 3: My father, who owned his own small company, often hired ex-convicts rather than applicants without criminal records because he thought that people who had served their time deserved a second chance. He did not hire ex-convicts because he had any illusions that they would be better workers.

Are the hiring or admissions policies in these three examples wrong? Before answering, it is important to set aside unrelated reasons why the conduct may be wrong. Suppose, for example, that instead of owning his own company, my father was the personnel officer in a corporation, and he was instructed to hire the most qualified employees. If he then hired less qualified ex-cons because of his concern about their plight, he would be failing in his duties to the company that pays his salary. His actions would be wrong, because they violated company policy, whether or not it is permissible to take factors other than qualifications into account. If instead he had instructions to give preferences to ex-cons and refused to follow them, he would be equally at fault. Second, if the grocery store owner were to put out a sign saying "Help wanted. I shall hire whoever is most qualified," and he then hired his daughter even though he knew there were more qualified applicants, he would be acting wrongly. The wrong consists in deceiving the applicants, not in taking into account his personal relationship to his daughter.

There is no defensible general principle that requires hiring and admissions to depend only on qualifications. It is not automatically wrong to take into account a veteran's past service to the nation when providing education or hiring, even when having patrolled the streets of Baghdad or losing a limb is not a qualification. I'm proud of my father's hiring, even though it was not based only on qualifications. If PHA is wrong, it is not because it takes into account factors other than qualifications.

If it is sometimes acceptable to take factors other than qualifications into account, does that mean that it was okay to exclude blacks from universities, from unions, from neighborhoods, swimming pools, even bathrooms? Of course not! Those policies were despicable, but what explains those wrongs is not that they took factors other than qualifications into account. Consider segregated bathrooms, which are of no economic importance and superficially appear to treat the races equally. (I was with my father almost sixty years ago, when he was thrown out of a "whites only" bathroom in Florida.) What's wrong with having separate bathrooms for different races? Is it only that the bathrooms for whites were nicer? If the bathrooms had been equally nice and the restrictions had been symmetrical, with whites not allowed into the "colored only" bathrooms as blacks were not allowed into the "whites only" bathroom, how could the policy be unjust or harmful to blacks?

Social context is crucial. In a racist black nation where there was a widespread view that contact with whites was defiling, segregated bathrooms would be a racist insult to whites. In the U.S., segregated bathrooms, hotels, train cars, and so forth were a humiliating insult to blacks, not to whites. In 1941, when Marian Anderson, the great African-American contralto, gave a concert at Lawrence University, she could not spend the night in Appleton, Wisconsin, where I used to live. In the 1940s, Appleton did not allow African Americans to reside within city limits. Fortunately, Anderson could stay in a hotel in a nearby town. The inconvenience was not enormous, but the insult was. Think about how it feels to be treated as if you were "unclean"— as if mere contact was defiling.

As these examples suggest, the mistreatment of African Americans that constituted Jim Crow consisted in their systematic denigration by white society, which resulted in their poverty, oppression, and exclusion. It relied on intimidation, beatings, humiliation, and murder. It was deeply wrong because of how it treated African Americans, not because it picked its victims by their race. If those mistreated were chosen not because of their skin color but via lottery and then marked as inferior, perhaps with a tattoo on their foreheads, the mistreatment would be no less repugnant and unjust.

In contrast, preferential hiring and admissions policies—whatever their virtues or vices—are not grounded in hatred of whites. PHA does not denigrate or oppress whites, or exclude them from the mainstream of American life. The admissions offices at universities are not full of white-hating racists out to keep whites from soiling their universities. Lisa Newton is wrong: PHA is not unjust "for all the same reasons that the discrimination it attempts to reverse is unjust." If PHA is unjust, it is not for any of the reasons that racial discrimination against blacks is unjust.

The failure of this common criticism of preferential hiring and admissions does not mean that PHA is fair or advisable. There may be other and better criticisms. But there is no moral prohibition on taking factors other than qualification into account in hiring and admissions, and in any case race is sometimes a qualification. PHA is not reverse racism.

Rectification, Reparations, and PHA

The main argument in defense of PHA fares no better. It maintains that PHA is a good way of rectifying past injustices perpetrated against African Americans. Rectification is a familiar idea. If my neighbor, Henry, were to steal my bicycle, justice would require that Henry give it back to me and compensate me for the inconvenience. When rights have been violated, justice requires that, as far as possible, the injustice be "rectified"—that the world be restored to how it would have been if there had been no injustice. African Americans have over the past centuries been the victims of incalculable injustices. They were enslaved, kidnapped, beaten, raped, tortured, and murdered and, after the Civil War brought slavery to an end, African Americans suffered more than a century of lynching, peonage, and relegation to the status of second-class citizens. Though racism persists, things are obviously better now. But these past injustices have not been rectified. Accordingly, many argue that PHA is justified as a form of rectification.

One might state the core of their argument as follows:

1. Those who commit injustices owe their victims damages.
2. Massive injustices have been perpetrated against African Americans.
3. Thus, those who committed these injustices owe damages to their African-American victims.

If intended to justify PHA, this argument has three problems. First, to rectify past injustice, one needs to identify the perpetrators of injustices and the victims of injustices and to determine the magnitude of the damages the perpetrators should pay to the victims. With respect to slavery, both perpetrators and victims are long dead. Descendants of victims of crimes may have claims to particular goods stolen from parents or grandparents, but their claims are limited. Children are not responsible for their parents' and grandparents' crimes, and members of a race are not responsible for injustices committed by other members of their race. How could PHA constitute the compensation that perpetrators of past injustices owe to their victims?

Second, rectification of an injustice is designed to restore people and their circumstances to that condition that would have obtained if no injustice had been done. Rectification in this sense for the wrongs of slavery is impossible. There is no way to know how the world would have been if there had been no slavery. Life in this country would have been utterly different. Few of our parents or more distant ancestors would have met, and consequently only a small portion of contemporary Americans would have existed in a hypothetical world without slavery. How can we possibly envision how things would have been under circumstances so different that they do not even contain the same people?

Third, identifying those who should pay compensation and those to whom compensation is owed would lead to a divisive inquiry into the virtues and vices of our ancestors, when they came to the United States, whether they conserved or squandered ill-gotten gains, and so forth. This is not a road that those who hope to improve race relations should want to follow.

Although widely misunderstood, invoking reparations rather than rectification solves the problem of identifying the responsible party. Reparations are a form of compensation provided by the government (and hence ultimately taxpayers) to acknowledge and partly to rectify past injustices perpetrated or permitted by the government. For example, the U.S. government provided $20,000 in reparations to Japanese-Americans who were interned during World War II, or to their immediate descendants. The funds were raised through taxation of all Americans, including Japanese-Americans. There was no distinction between those people who may have profited from the internment and the great majority who did not benefit from it, because reparations are a civic responsibility for a civic wrong, rather than a personal responsibility for personal wrongs. Because government at all levels perpetrated injustices toward African Americans and acquiesced in many other injustices that could and should have been prevented, it bears a great responsibility for past injustices toward African Americans.

Conceptualizing PHA as the paying of reparations rather than as rectifying individual injustices should thus in principle avoid divisive inquiries into the vices of our ancestors. But public discussion tramples subtle distinctions, and, unfortunately, proponents and critics misunderstand reparations and turn discussion of the issue into acrimonious finger pointing concerning the intergenerational transmission of personal guilt. A few years ago David Horowitz placed advertisements criticizing reparations in a number of college newspapers. These advertisements led to violent protests by those concerned about the disadvantages that African Americans must deal with. Among Horowitz's ten reasons to oppose reparations were: (1) we cannot identify the descendants of the perpetrators of the crimes of slavery; (2) few Americans owned slaves, and (3) most Americans have no clear connection to slavery. Since reparations are a civic responsibility for the wrongs government caused or permitted, these claims are irrelevant, but neither Horowitz nor most of his readers appear to have understood that. Supporters of reparations are just as confused. For example, in an op-ed piece in the *New York Times* (April 23, 2010), Henry Lewis Gates takes the most vexing problem of reparations to be "how to parcel out blame to those directly involved in the capture and sale of human beings for immense economic gain," and he believes that historical research now makes it possible "to publicly attribute responsibility and culpability where they truly belong, to white people and black people."

Even if reparations did not cause such confusions, other problems with rectification apply equally to reparations. How much should be paid? To whom should reparations be paid? Though there are powerful reasons to diminish the huge racial disparities that divide our nation, those policies should not be regarded as reparations. The risks of misunderstanding, the problems in identifying the recipients, and the problems in determining how much should be paid are reasons not to invoke reparations to justify policies that diminish racial disparities.

Furthermore, even if reparations could be ascertained without provoking confused racial animosity, preferential hiring and admissions policies are not a defensible way of paying reparations. PHA does not focus on those who have been most harmed by past injustices, and it does not distribute the costs of paying reparations in a justifiable way. It unfairly imposes the cost of reparations—a civic responsibility—entirely on nonminority college applicants and job seekers, who bear no more responsibility for past injustices than anyone else. These costs, like the benefits PHA provide, are generally small, but it is still unjust both to make one group in society pay all the costs and arbitrarily to benefit just one group. If PHA were only one of a set of programs whose costs were distributed throughout the population, this objection would not be cogent. But apart from PHA, public policy does little to address racial disparities.

I am not arguing that Americans should forget past injustices. Without understanding the past, how could we understand the present and know what to do about it? Moreover, the fact that the problems of the present arose through past injustices creates a special obligation to address them. But it is impossible to undo the past or rectify old and large-scale injustices. We have no idea what would constitute rectification, and could not carry it out if we did. Although we need to look to the past for understanding, our moral concern should focus on the future. How can we free it of racism and of the disparities that racism has caused?

Preferential Admissions and Equal Opportunity

The other major arguments that do not depend on factual knowledge of details of the consequences of PHA invoke the value of equal opportunity. Critics maintain that equal opportunity condemns PHA. Defenders maintain that PHA promotes equal opportunity. Obviously, both cannot be right.

Consider an analogy. Suppose that in the local elementary school there are two first-grade and two second-grade classes. One of the first-grade teachers is excellent, and one is terrible. One of the second-grade teachers is also excellent, and one is terrible. The socioeconomic status of the families in this community is uniform, and the children have had similar preschool experiences. The school board assigns students to first-grade teachers by lottery on the grounds that the fairest policy gives every student an equal chance at a good first-grade experience.

There is disagreement, however, about how to assign children to the second-grade teachers. Some school board members argue that every child should have one good and one bad teacher. Those children who had the good first-grade teacher should get the bad second-grade teacher and vice versa. These board members say, "If every child has both a good teacher and a bad teacher, then the children's schooling and overall future opportunities will be as close to equal as we can make them." Other school board members argue for a second lottery. They say, "Why should students be punished for having had a good teacher in first grade? Equal opportunity demands that every child should have an equal chance of having a good second-grade teacher."

This analogy is helpful in several regards. First, it explains why it can appear that PHA both promotes and impedes equal opportunity. If one is thinking narrowly about the chance of getting a good second-grade teacher, then a second lottery equalizes opportunity, just as (if there were no racism) the absence of PHA would equalize the chances of being hired or admitted of otherwise equally qualified applicants of different races. On the other hand, if one is concerned with opportunities over a lifetime, insuring that every child has one good teacher and one bad one promotes equality of opportunity, just as PHA does (on the assumption that the opportunities and resources available previously to black applicants have, on average, been worse than those available to white applicants). Those concerned with equal opportunity should be concerned with lifetime opportunities, not opportunities to acquire one or another immediate benefit or burden. Because of past inequalities and continued racism, PHA lessens inequalities in opportunity.

The school analogy also makes clear that PHA does not punish white applicants, just as assigning children who had the good first-grade teacher to the bad second-grade teacher does not punish them. These kids have done nothing wrong. Indeed, it may be that nobody has done anything wrong. The policy of making sure that each student has one good and one bad teacher is not a way of rectifying in second grade an injustice done in first grade, because no injustice has been done. The justification for the second-grade teacher assignments is to provide children with similar overall opportunities, not to restore children to where they would have been if they had not previously been treated unjustly. In the case of PHA, unlike the elementary school analogy, some of the past inequalities in opportunity have been the result of injustices, but the point is to diminish inequality rather than to rectify injustice.

It is important to distinguish between compensation as rectifying injustice and compensation as equalizing opportunity. The former does not justify PHA, because, as I argued earlier, it is unfair to impose the costs of reparations or rectification on white applicants, since reparations are a social responsibility, and rectification is the responsibility of individual wrongdoers. By contrast, equalizing opportunity can justify PHA, because it is not unjust to diminish the chances of applicants whose prospects have on average been inflated by previous inequalities. The relevant question for a rejected white applicant is not "With my qualifications, would I have been admitted or hired if there were no PHA policy?" Nor is it "With my qualifications, would I have been admitted or hired if I were black?" The relevant question is "If the qualifications of all the applicants (including me) had not been skewed by past inequalities in opportunity and if there were no continuing racism, would I have been admitted or hired?"

Given previous inequalities and continuing discrimination, PHA brings us on average closer to equal opportunity.[3] Like the children who had the good first-grade teacher, white applicants on average have had previous advantages. PHA diminishes these inequalities and counteracts some of the continued racist discrimination in hiring.

This argument assumes that the opportunities for black applicants have been in fact on average worse than the opportunities for white applicants. But there can be no serious doubt about its truth. According to the Pew Research Center, the median wealth of African Americans in 2009

---

3 For example, in one study mailed applications with common African-American names were only half as likely to get callbacks as applications with names that are not associated with African Americans. See "Are Emily and Greg More Employable than Lakisha and Jamal? A Field Experiment on Labor Market Discrimination" by Marianne Bertrand and Sendhil Mullainathan (2004) (http://www.economics.harvard.edu/faculty/mullainathan/files/emilygreg.pdf).

was one-twentieth that of whites. There is no plausible explanation of inequalities in outcomes that are this enormous other than unequal opportunities, and such large inequalities in outcomes obviously translate into inequalities in opportunity. A far higher percentage of black children live in poverty and in single-parent homes. On average the parents of African-American children are likely to have had less education, and the schools African-American children attend typically have worse facilities, lower-paid teachers, and larger class sizes. Some black applicants are highly privileged and many white applicants have grown up in dire circumstances, but on average, black applicants have had to cope with greater poverty, more difficult environments, and worse schooling. Their opportunities have been on average considerably worse, and they face the additional burden of continued discrimination.[4] PHA does a little to lessen these inequalities in opportunity. Valuing equal opportunity (not equal results) is a reason to support it, not to oppose it.

Conclusions

This essay has focused on the most popular arguments concerning PHA. Their popularity does not reflect well on the subtlety of public discourse, because they are not good arguments. PHA is not racism is reverse. It is not racist. It does not aim to denigrate, exclude, oppress, or punish whites. The main argument in defense of PHA is just as weak. PHA is not justified as a form of rectification or of reparations. Reparations and rectification are impractical, racially divisive, and incapable of justifying a policy that imposes costs arbitrarily on only one segment of the population.

As we have seen, there are good arguments to be made in defense of PHA as promoting diversity and equal opportunity, but it could turn out that other consequences of PHA are so harmful that there is good reason to abandon the policies. If we knew the effects of PHA on racial animosity, on the self-conception and status of the minorities it aims to benefit, and on the extent to which they and others are successful, we would be in a better position to reach a definite conclusion concerning whether PHA is beneficial. But we do not know its effects well enough.

One other consideration should be mentioned. Preferential hiring and admissions policies are more or less the only social policies in the

---

4 This conclusion does not rest on the silly view that all differences in outcomes among members of different social groups result from differences in opportunities.

United States that acknowledge the special handicaps disadvantaged minorities face and, in a small way, concretely aim to lessen them. Disadvantaged minorities would inevitably see the abandonment of PHA, without putting something substantial in its place, as white America turns its back on a disgracefully unjust situation. The deck is stacked, and white America gets to shuffle the cards. Will it do anything about the poor hands that minorities have been dealt?

Daniel M. Hausman: Affirmative Action: Bad Arguments and Some Good Ones

1. Why isn't it racist for schools to offer preferential admissions to Blacks and Hispanics? What's the difference between not admitting someone because they are Black or Hispanic and not admitting someone because they are White?
2. If what was wrong with slavery and "Jim Crow" laws was not their racial basis, then what was wrong with them?
3. Suppose that the United States Government were to pay reparations to the descendants of slaves. Why should people who are not descended from slave holders (such as recent immigrants) have to pay taxes to support paying these reparations?
4. What is the point of the parable of the two first-grade and two second-grade classes? Is it a good analogy to the circumstances in which preferential hiring or admissions might be called for?
5. What other arguments can you think of supporting or criticizing preferential hiring and admissions? Can you provide logically valid formulations of these arguments?